DATABASE MANAGEMENT

George Diehr
University of Washington

Scott, Foresman and Company
Glenview, Illinois   London

Library of Congress Cataloging-in-Publication Data
Diehr, George.
  Database Management.

  Bibliography: p.
  Includes index.
  1. Database management.   2. Database design.   I. Title
QA76.9.D3D52   1989   005.74   89–4286
ISBN 0–673–18820–5

1   2   3   4   5   6   KPF   93   92   91   90   89   88

Table of Contents

Preface and Acknowledgements, 11

PART I. INTRODUCTION

1 An Overview of the Database Approach, 2

Definition of a Database Management System (DBMS), 3

The Guaranteed Student Loan (GSL) System Model Database, 4

Resources of a Database System, 6
- *Data, 6 • Hardware, 11 • Software, 11 • People (Users), 02*
- *Data Dictionary, 13*

Objectives and Advantages of a Database Approach, 13
- *Centralization of Control and Enforcement of Standards, 14*
- *Less Data Redundancy, 15 • Greater Consistency and Integrity of Data, 15*
- *Fewer Problems Correlating Data, 15 • Data Sharing, 16*
- *Easier Access and Use of Data, 16 • Easier Data Security, 16*

Data Independence, 16
- *Types of Data Independence, 16 • Benefits of Data Independence, 18*

Overview of Database Design, 19

Questions, 19

References, 20

2 The Internal Level: Physical File Structure, 21

Data Hierarchy, 22
- *Storage Device Characteristics, 25*

File Organization, 27
- *Sequential File Organization, 27*

Indexed Files, 28
- *Indexed Sequential File Organization, 28 • B-tree-based File Structures, 30*
- *Secondary B+tree Indexes, 35*

Hashed File Organization, 37
- *Hash Function, 37 • Impact of Blocking and Load Factor, 38*
- *Overflow Handling, 41 • Hashed File Processing, 41*
- *Reorganization Requirements, 42 • Hashed Indexes, 43*
- *Extendible Hashed File, 43 • Hashed File Summary, 43*

Summary and Comparison of File Organizations, 44

File Organizations Using Linked Lists, 46
- *Linked List Structure, 46 • Applications and Functions of Linked Lists, 46*
- *Record Retrieval and Physical Organization of a Linked List, 47*

• *Adding and Deleting Records, 48* • *Other Characteristics and Features of Linked Lists, 50* • *Linked Lists vs. Indexes, 51*

Conclusion, 52

Questions and Problems, 52

References, 55

3   Data Levels and DBMS System Architecture, 57

The Three Levels of Database Architecture, 57
• *Reality, 58* • *Conceptual (or Logical) Level, 60* • *Internal Level, 60*
• *External Level, 60*

DBMS Languages and Operation, 60
• *The Data Sublanguage (DSL): DDL and DML, 60*
• *DBMS Operation and Data Realms, 62*

The Three Data Models, 62
• *Relational Model, 62* • *Hierarchical Model, 65* • *Network Model, 67*
• *Commercial DBMSs, 69*

Other DBMS Software Components, 69
• *Data Communications, 69* • *Utilities, 70* • *Applications Tools, 70*

Questions, 71

References, 72

PART II.   THE RELATIONAL MODEL AND RELATIONAL DBMSs

4   The Relational Model and Relational Algebra, 75

Relational Structure: Example and Overview, 75
• *Domains, 77* • *Relations, 79* • *Integrity Rules, 84*

Relational Algebra, 85
• *Introduction, 85* • *Relational Algebra: Definition, 85*
• *Database Updates, 95*

Definition of a Relational System, 96

Commercial Relational Products, 97

Questions and Problems, 98

References, 102

5   An SQL-based System: ORACLE, 103

Introduction and Overview of SQL-based Systems, 103

Data Definition Language, 104
• *Defining a Relation, 105*

Data Retrievals, 107
• *The SQL SELECT Statement, Simple Form, 107* • *Single Relation Queries, 109* • *Queries Using Joins, 117* • *Queries with EXISTS and NOT EXISTS, 123* • *Using GROUP BY and Aggregate Functions, 126*
• *Specifying a Restriction by GROUP: The HAVING operator, 129*
• *UNION Operator, 130*

Updates, 130
> • *Single-Row Update, Addition, Deletion, 130* • *Multiple-Record Updates, 132* • *Assigning Results to a Relation: Multiple-Row Insertion, 133*

Concluding Comments, 135

Appendix: ORACLE SQL Functions and Manipulating Date Data Types, 135
> • *Arithmetic Functions, 135* • *Character String Functions, 136* • *Date Arithmetic, 137*

APPENDIX: Editing SQL Statements, 137

Questions and Problems, 139

References, 143

6 Additional Features and Characteristics of ORACLE, 145

Views, 145
> • *Defining Views, 145* • *Objectives and Benefits of Views, 156*

Report Writer, 157

System Catalog, 162
> • *Contents and Organization of the Catalog, 162*

Miscellaneous SQL/UFI Features: Help, Convenience, Data Transfer, 163
> • *Convenience Features, 164*

Embedded SQL, 165
> • *Single Row Manipulations, 166* • *Multiple-Row Manipulations, 170*

Physical Structure of SQL Databases, 173

Compiling Queries, 176
> • *The Optimizer, 178*

Questions and Problems, 180

References, 182

7 Other Relational Systems and Capabilities, 183

Important Features and Characteristics of DB2 and SQL/DS, 183

INGRES, 184
> • *Introduction, 184* • *The QUEL Data Definition Language, 184* • *The QUEL Data Manipulation Language, 185* • *QUEL vs. SQL, 187* • *INGRES System Architecture, 187* • *Conclusion, 188*

QBE, 188
> • *QBE Summary, 191*

RDBMS Products, 192

Questions and Problems, 192

References, 193

8 R:BASE: A Personal Computer Relational DBMS, 195

Introduction to R:BASE, 195
> • *R:BASE Modules, 196* • *Database Structure, 197*

Defining an R:BASE Database, 199

• *Using Definition EXPRESS, 199* • *Definition Using Command Mode, 199* • *Naming the Database, 200* • *Database Definition using CREATE TABLE, 202* • *Displaying the Defined Database, 202*

Loading Data, 203

Data Manipulation, 205

• *SELECT Command, 205* • *"Statistics" Commands, 209*

Additional Relational Operations, 212

• *Project Command, 213* • *Natural Join: The INTERSECT Command, 214* • *Self-join Using INTERSECT and RENAME, 216* • *SUBTRACT Command, 218* • *UNION Command, 219* • *Eliminating Unneeded Tables, 221*

Exiting R:BASE, 221

Views, 221

Updating, 223

Conclusion, 223

Questions and Problems, 224

References, 227

PART III. NONRELATIONAL SYSTEMS

9 CODASYL Network Systems, 231

Introduction to the Network Model, 231

• *History of the CODASYL Standard, 232* • *DBMS Operation, 233*

Overview of Network Database Structure and Manipulation, 234

• *Network DBMS Architecture, 236*

Network Database Structure, 236

• *Records and Data Items, 236* • *Sets, 237*

CODASYL (Schema) Data Definition Language, 245

• *Schema Overview, 245* • *Record Definition, 247* • *Set Definition, 249* • *Schema Summary, 254*

Data Manipulation, 254

• *Currency, 255* • *FIND and GET, 256* • *MODIFY, STORE, ERASE, 259* • *CONNECT, DISCONNECT, RECONNECT, 260* • *DML Summary, 261*

Subschema, 262

Extensions: OnLine Query and IDMS/R, 263

• *OnLine Query, 263* • *Logical Record Facility, 263* • *Automatic System Facility, 264*

Conclusion, 265

Questions and Problems, 266

References, 270

10 A Hierarchical System: IMS, 271

Introduction to Hierarchical Systems and IMS, 271

The Hierarchical Data Model, 272

Data Definition Language, 275
• *Example Database Definition, 275*

External Logical Database Definition, 277
• *External View on a Single PDB, 277* • *External Views over Multiple Physical Databases, 279*

Data Manipulation, 281
• *IMS Retrieval Examples, 284* • *IMS Update Examples, 285*

Physical Structure, 285
• *Access Method, 285* • *Additional IMS Physical Storage Features and Options, 289*

Summary, 291

Questions and Problems, 292

References, 295

PART IV. DATABASE DESIGN AND ADMINISTRATION

11 The Database Design Process and Logical Data Modeling, 299

Overview of the Database Design Process, 299

Planning a Database, 300
• *Importance of Database Planning, 300* • *Organizational Environment, 301* • *Strategic, Tactical, and Operational Level Needs, 302* • *Database Planning Process, 304* • *Summary of Database* • *Planning, 308*

Introduction to Entity-Relationship Modeling and Constructs, 308
• *Basic ERM Constructs: Entities, Attributes, and Relationships, 308* • *Additional ERM Features and Extensions, 310* • *Degree of Relationship, 310* • *Identifing Entities and Attributes, 313* • *Defining Relationships, 315* • *Transformations to Relations, 315*

Summary of E-ERM, 317

Questions and Problems, 318

References, 321

12 Normalization, 323

Introduction, 323
• *What Are Normal Forms?, 323*

Functional Dependence, 324

Second, Third, and Boyce/Codd Normal Forms, 326
• *Second Normal Form, 326* • *Third and Boyce-Codd Normal Forms, 328* • *BCNF vs. 3NF, 329* • *Examples, 331*

Multivalued Dependencies and Fourth Normal Form, 332

Nonloss and Independent Decompositions, 334

• *Fifth Normal Form, 336*
Conclusion, 337
Questions and Problems, 338
References, 341

13 Database Implementation and Physical Design, 343
Mapping to a Relational DBMS, 343
Physical Design for Relational DBMS, 344
  • *Vertical Partitioning, 344* • *Horizontal Partitioning, 347* • *Prejoins, 348*
  • *Other "Denormalization", 349* • *File Structure and Selecting Attributes
  to Index, 350* • *Clustering Indexes, 351* • *Selecting Additional Indexes, 354*
Relational Database Design Summary, 356
Mapping to a Network DBMS, 358
  • *Mapping Relations to a Network Model, 358*
Physical Design of Network Databases, 361
  • *Partitioning, 361* • *Prejoins, 362* • *Physical File Structure: Primary Access
  Path, 362* • *Physical Representation of Owner-Member Relations, 362*
  • *Defining System Sets, 366*
Network Database Design Summary, 367
Mapping Relations to a Hierarchical DBMS: IMS, 369
IMS Logical Database Design, 369
Physical Design of the IMS Database, 371
  • *Access Methods, 371* • *Order of Dependent Segments, 374* • *Secondary
  Indexes, 374* • *Database Partitioning: Secondary Data Set Groups, 375*
Hierarchical Database Design Summary, 375
Questions and Problems, 377
References, 381

14 Database Administration and the Database Environment, 383
Database Administration, 383
  • *Introduction, 383* • *The Roles of Data Administrator and Database
  Administrator, 383* • *Interaction with Management, Users, and
  System Personnel, 384*
Data Dictionary/Directory, 385
  • *Objectives of the Data Dictionary/Directory System, 385* • *Functions, 385*
Database Security, 386
  • *Introduction: Security vs. Integrity, 386* • *Security Problems and
  Threats, 386* • *Methods of Security Control, 387*
Database Integrity, 388
Database Recovery, 388
  • *Transaction Concept, 388* • *Types of Failure, 389*
Concurrency Control, 390
  • *Example Problem: Lost Updates, 390* • *Approaches to Concurrency
  Control: Locking, 390* • *Deadlock and Deadlock Protection, 390*

Questions, 391
References, 391

PART V.   DATABASE ISSUES AND FUTURE DEVELOPMENT

15   Database Issues and Future Development, 395

Introduction, 395
Current Relational DBMS Directions and Issues, 396
  • *Application Tools, 396*
Distributed DBMSs, 401
  • *Problems of Distributed Database Systems, 402*
  • *Distributed DBMS Summary, 405*
DBMS and Artificial Intelligence, 406
Extensions to the Relational Model and Alternative Data Models, 407
Hardware Technology Impact on Database, 408
  • *Database Computers, 408* • *Optical Storage Devices, 409*
Summary, 410
Questions, 411
References, 411

Index, 413

Preface

Audience

This book is intended for information systems majors whose job objective is to be a programmer or a systems analyst. Many of these students will take positions in finance, accounting, and marketing, but will become involved in the development of decision-support systems(usually on micros). They will use mainframe DBMSs to access data for transfer to a PC, where it will be stored in a DBMS. Over time, some readers will eventually hold positions as database administrators, corporate information resource managers, and information systems managers. The student is not someone who will develop a DBMS.

Objectives

The objective of the text is to provide skills that are immediately useful as well as concepts and theories that will be of value over at least a five- to ten-year period. Skills for immediate use include logical-database design and writing queries in common high-level database languages such as SQL. Concepts and theories of longer-term value will include relational algebra, normalization theory, distributed database design, and physical database design.

Emphasis

The relational model has evolved as the prevalent one, and the text emphasizes the entity-based approach to thinking about data with some discussion on the new directions such as object oriented data models and the semantic data model. Chapters on hierarchical and network models are included for complete coverage.

Organization

The text is organized into five parts, with fifteen chapters. Part One, "Introduction, contains three chapters. Chapter One, "An Overview of the Database Approach," describes the concepts of databases and database management systems and the advantages of the so-called database approach. Chapter Two, "The Internal Level: Physical File Structures," is a summary of various file structures typically implemented in DBMSs. Wile an understanding of file structures is not strictly necessary in order to use a DBMS and to perform logical design, it is essential for physical design and relevant to logical design. Chapter Three, "Data Levels and Database System Architecture," introduces the concepts of data levels and how a DBMS implements the levels and gives an overview and examples of how DBMS data manipulations language works.

Part Two, "The Relational Model and Relational DBMSs," contains the beef of the book. Five chapters focus on relational databases. Chapter Four, "The Relational Model and Relational Algebra," provides the theoretical basis for relational DBMSs. Chapters Five and Six, "An SQL-based System: ORACLE," and "Additional Features and Characteristics of ORACLE," provide comprehensive coverage of this system. Chapter Seven, "Other Relational Systems and Capabilities," gives an overview of the essential features of several relational DBMSs, and emphasizes the differences that distinguish these systems from ORACLE. Chapter Eight, "R:BASE: A Personal Computer Relational DBMS, is an optional chapter and gives enough depth to actually use the system.

Part Three, "Nonrelational Systems," has two chapters, 9 and 10, and they provide an introduction and overview of two important alternative data models/DBMS types. Chapter Nine, "CODASYL Network Systems," covers IDMS. Chapter Ten, "A Hierarchical System: IMS."

Part Four, "Database Design and Administration," contains four chapters. There are many approaches to database design. There are no set standard guidelines for the overall database design process. Thus, while our audience should be exposed to the concepts, methods, and theories of database design, the coverage in this secction is less extensive and intensive than the coverage of database useage. Chapter Eleven, "The Database Design Process and Logical Data Modeling," begins with a discussion of the overall design process, then turns to issues of determining the data needs of the firms and concludes the design of conceptual files. Chapter Twelve, "Normalization," can stand by itself, although it is part of Logical Data Modeling, it has been given a separate chapter because of the amount of material. Chapter Thirteen, "Database Implementation and Physical Design," covers relational, network, and hierarchical models. Chapter Fourteen, "Database Administration and the Database Environment," is a collection of several topics. It introduces the database administration process and describes some of the tools (such as a data dictionary) used in database administration. Concurrency control and recovery are covered in the second part of the chapter.

Part Five, "Database Issues and Future Development," has a single chapter presenting a number of topics and issues of current concern and speculations on future directions in database systems.

Illustrative Relational Models

Relational systems are rapidly being improved. Data processing departments are implementing relational databases for both transaction processing and decision support. While the text is not dependent on a specific system, there are two DBMSs that were selected for illustrative purposes. The first choice for a specific relational system is the SQL-based system ORACLE. ORACLE implements SQL in essentially the same from as IBM's DBMSs. Thus, someone who learns ORACLE, for example, also "knows" INGRES, DB2, and SQL/DS as well as other systems. The second system selected is the microcomputer system R:BASE. R:BASE was selected over dBASE as the illustrative model for a microcomputer database because it more faithfully implements the relational model.

Guaranteed Student Loan Database

Throughout the text, an example database, Guaranteed Student Loan (GSL) database is used. It is a subset of the database used by the U.S. Department of Education to manage this student loan program. It includes student, loan, and bank relations in its simplest form. It is sometimes extended to include schools, attendance, and payment relations.

Disk Available

A data disk containing ASCII files is available from the publisher for use in conjunction with the database problems in the text. The disk contains three separate databases. The first is the Graduate Student Loan system with students, loans, payments, and banks. This database contains 50 to 100 records per file. The second is Western Regional Rentals, the database of an organization that manages apartment houses. The third is an order-entry database, with customers, orders, line-items, and parts (inventory).

Major Features

In introducing and explaining DBMSs, this book:

- Emphasizes relational models and relational DBMSs.
- Explains SQL
- Uses two relational systems for illustration: ORACLE and R:BASE
- Is designed for the information systems major
- Provides immediately usable skills for database programming
- Provides basic skills for database design
- Uses one case example throughout, the Graduate Student Loan database, (GSL)
- Provides an instructor's guide

The instructor's guide is available to instructors and contains suggested course outlines, suggested lectures, and answers to end-of-chapter questions and database problems.

Acknowledgments

It is no small task to write a textbook on any subject, much less the challenging field of database. Years of teaching and research and of truly understanding the subject matter are central to any well-crafted textbook. The implementation of this knowledge requires a number of writers, reviewers, and editors. To that end I would like to thank Ken Knecht and Neil Scott who, in the final hours, contributed Chapters 14 and 15; writer Carlton Adams; and Grace LaTorra who edited my edits and revised my work. Final thank-yous go to editors Susan Nelle of BMR and Roger Holloway of Scott, Foresman.

Reviewers

Thanks are due to the many reviewers who provided positive feedback and encouragement: David C. Whitney, San Francisco State University; William Korn, University of Wisconsin at Eau Claire; William R. Cornette, Southwest Missouri State University; Neil E. Swanson, Southwest Missouri State University; David Rine, George Mason University; Robert S. Fritz, American River College; and Richard G. Ramirez, Arizona State University.

P A R T   I

Introduction

1 *An Overview of the Database Approach*

This chapter describes the concepts of databases and database management systems (DBMSs) and the advantages of the so-called database approach. The resources of a database system (data, software, hardware, people, and metadata) are outlined. Our discussion emphasizes that data is a critical corporate resource that must be made easily available, have high quality, be easy to understand, and be protected. The database approach, along with the primary tool for working with it, the DBMS, is shown to be the key to the efficient and effective management of data.

The advantages of a database approach are described and contrasted with the traditional applications-oriented approach. Many of these advantages are explained by describing the problems associated with an applications-based approach.

Data independence is shown to be an important concept of the database approach. The degree of data independence is a measure of the sophistication of a DBMS. The greater its data independence, the lower the labor costs associated with developing a database and, more critically, the lower the maintenance costs.

There are some disadvantages to a database approach. In general, setting up and operating a database system is expensive. These costs are incurred in several areas: the necessary DBMS software is usually expensive to purchase; planning and implementing a database require more effort than traditional approaches; costly data conversions may be required while the database is being set up; operating costs are often higher because DBMS software places heavy demands on hardware (more internal and external memory and faster central processing unit (CPU) are required for a given level of performance). But we conclude that in almost all environments the advantages significantly outweigh the disadvantages.

Definition of a Database Management System (DBMS)

An organization's database is the collection of data that the organization requires to record its operations and to support decision making. We are particularly interested here in data that is maintained on computer media (as opposed to data that might be stored as hardcopy or microfilm). A database management system (DBMS) is a software system for managing a computer database. The DBMS provides for the description of the database (its contents and their forms), data access, entry, update, and data security and integrity.

Formally speaking, the database stores raw facts, or *data*, as opposed to *information*. The database stores facts about the things (people, objects, etc.) and events (sales, payments, hours worked, grades received, etc.) relevant to the organization. This data may be in the form of text, numbers, audio, graphics, or visual images. The emphasis here will be on databases that represent facts as text or numbers, since these are the major, and usually only, data domains of most current DBMSs. However, a few systems exist, and others are being researched, that extend the database to a wider domain of data types.

Information is data that has been transformed so that it has value for decision making. Whether a collection of symbols is data or information usually depends on the user. For example, to the CEO of my bank, my current checking account balance is probably just data (unless my balance becomes extremely negative). To an operational manager (typically called a vice-president in a bank) my account balance will be information, especially if it is negative and a check is written against it. On the other hand, aggregate statistics on all account balances would be information to the CEO, but probably not to the operational manager. A database usually stores low-level detailed data. Some of this data may represent information (to some users), but much of it will require manipulation or processing before it becomes valuable. The DBMS both provides for the management of detailed data and facilitates the conversion of data to information.

Data is generated by all parts of an organization: management, accounting, inventory, production, marketing, and personnel. There are also many sources of information that are external to an organization. Primary sources of external data are competitors, industry summaries, and various government agencies. The DBMS provides the following capabilities to manage this proliferation of data:

- Define and modify the structure of the database
- Adds data to the database
- Retrieve data
- Update data
- Delete data

The Guaranteed Student Loan (GSL) System Model Database

Figure 1–1 shows a small subset of a database to support the operation of the federal government's Guaranteed Student Loan (GSL) program. Data is maintained on students who apply for and receive loans, lending institutions that participate in the program by making loans and receiving government subsidies, and the loans themselves. Thus, there are three major files in this database: STUDENT, BANK, and LOAN. The data on students includes a unique student number (SID), name, age, level in college, and location represented by a ZIP code. (Note that we are using only a tiny subset of the data that would be included in a full database.) Information on banks includes the bank identifier (BID), location as represented by ZIP code, and type (that is, full-service bank, savings and loan, credit union, or mutual savings bank). Loan-specific data includes a loan identifier (LID), date the loan was taken out, number of years, interest rate, and amount. Data about a loan includes two items that relate it to a student and a bank: the SID relates a loan to a specific student who received the loan in the STUDENT file; and the BID relates the loan to the bank in the BANK file that provided the loan.

The data is used to support activities of GSL administration such as loan application and approval, monitoring of loan status (payments on schedule, late, or worse), pursuit and collection of default loans, and payment subsidies to lending institutions (since loan interest rates are below market rates, the federal government subsidizes lenders). In addition, reports are generated from the database for congressional committees to assist them in decisions regarding legislation and funding for the GSL program.

STUDENT Table

SID	NAME	SLEVEL	AGE	SZIP
9735	ALLEN	1	21	98101
4494	ALTER	2	19	98112
8767	CABEEN	5	24	98118
2368	JONES	4	23	98155
6793	SANDS	1	17	98101
3749	WATSON	5	29	98168

BANK Table

BID	BZIP	TYPE
FIDELITY	98101	MSB
SEAFIRST	98101	BANK
PEOPLES	98109	BANK
CAPITAL	98033	SL
HOME	98031	SL

LOAN Table

LID	LDATE	YEARS	INT_RATE	AMOUNT	SID	BID
27	15-SEP-85	5	8.5	1200	9735	HOME
78	21-JUN-86	5	7.75	1000	9735	PEOPLES
87	07-SEP-83	5	7.0	2000	9735	SEAFIRST
92	12-JAN-85	6	7.5	2100	4494	FIDELITY
99	15-JAN-86	6	9.0	2200	4494	FIDELITY
170	30-APR-83	6	6.5	1900	8767	PEOPLES
490	07-MAY-84	6	6.0	2500	3749	PEOPLES
493	24-JUN-85	7	7.5	3000	3749	PEOPLES

Fig 1-1   The Guaranteed Student Loan (GSL) System Model Database

Files of the type shown in Figure 1–1 are frequently referred to as *tables* because of the way they are organized into rows and columns. The rows of the tables represent the records contained in the file. The columns of the tables represent the data items within the records. The terms *row* and *record* are frequently used interchangeably, as are the terms *column*, *data item*, *attribute* and (occasionally) *field*.

Figure 1–2 illustrates typical DBMS operations of retrieval (SELECT), the addition of a record (INSERT), the modification of a record (UPDATE), and the removal of a record (DELETE) on these files. The operations shown in these examples use a database language called *Structured Query Language*, commonly known as SQL. SQL was developed at IBM's San Jose Research Labs for the System R DBMS. It was later adopted as the DBMS language for several products including DB2 and SQL/DS. Numerous other vendors also use SQL in database products that run on hardware systems ranging from microcomputers to the large mainframes. There is an American National Standards Institute (ANSI) specification for SQL. Later chapters will cover SQL in some detail.

Operation:	**Explanations:**
Selecting data from a file:	Display the name age, and level of all rows from the STUDENT table where SZIP = 98101

```
SELECT NAME, AGE, SLEVEL
FROM STUDENT
WHERE SZIP =98101;
```

Result: (displayed on screen or printed)

```
----    ---    ------
NAME    AGE    SLEVEL
----    ---    ------
ALLEN    21        1
SANDS    17        1
```

Inserting new data:

Adds a row with SID = 5238 Name = BROWN, level = 3, age = 22 and SZIP = 98149

```
INSERT INTO STUDENT
VALUES(5238,'BROWN',3,22,98149);
```

Updating existing data:

Changes the value of INT_RATE to 8.0 for the loan with LID = 92

```
UPDATE LOAN
SET INT_RATE = 8.0
WHERE LID = 92;
```

Deleting existing data:

Explanation: Removes the row from loan with LID = 27

```
DELETE FROM LOAN
WHERE LID = 27;
```

Fig 1-2   Retrieving, Inserting, Updating, and Deleting Data from Files in GSL Database

Resources of a Database System

Data

The data gathered by an organization is used by many different people, often in quite different ways. We see in Figure 1–3 that data and decisions are part of a cyclic process. Data provides the information to make decisions, decisions lead to actions, actions create more facts, and facts lead to more data.

Collecting and managing the data needed for decisions can cost organizations a great deal of money. One of the objectives of the database approach is to protect that investment by improving the efficiency of the processes involved in collecting, managing, and using data. Significant benefits can be realized from the proper management of data.

Before we look at how data is managed, we focus for a moment on how facts are represented in a database. First, the primary unit about which data is represented is termed an *entity*.

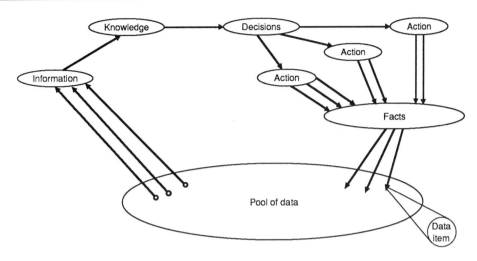

Fig 1-3   The Data-Decision Cycle

An entity is an object that may be real (a person, a product, etc.), or abstract (a loan, an employment history, etc.). An entity is something about which facts are known: it has *properties*. A student is an example of an entity, in this case a person with the following properties:

    Name = JONES
    Student Identity Number = 2368
    Level = 4
    Age = 23
    Zip code = 98155

The properties of an entity are called *attributes*. A collection of entities with similar attributes is called an *entity class* or an *entity type*. For example, the other students (ALLEN, ALTER, CABEEN, SANDS, and WATSON), are also entities with the same properties. They are all members of the same entity class: STUDENT. Notice that while they have the same attributes, they do not all have the same *values* for those attributes. (If there is possible confusion as to whether we are talking about individual entities or groups of entities, we will refer to an individual occurrence of an entity as an *entity instance*.) Data management consists of managing entity instances, entity classes, and the relationships that exist between them. Figure 1–4 shows these for the GSL database example.

Attributes are also known as *data items* or *fields*. The value of an attribute is represented by a number or character string. The association of an attribute value with a specific entity instance represents a fact; for example, the fact that a specific person is 23 years old is data. However, an isolated value is not a fact. By itself, the number 23 is nothing more than a number, but in the context of a particular data item (AGE) and a specific individual, it is data.

Each entity class will have a set of one or more attributes that uniquely identify each individual entity instance. For example, an entity class, such as employee, often uses a person's social security number as a unique attribute. In the GSL database example, the unique attribute of STUDENT is the Student Identification Number (SID). Such identifying attributes are called *primary keys*. In some cases more than one attribute may be required

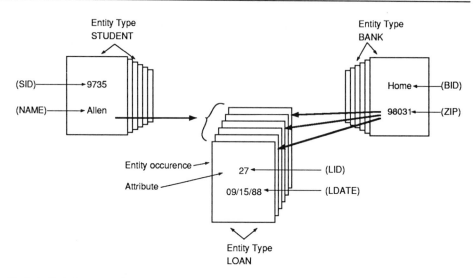

Fig 1-4   Entity Instances, Entity Types, and Relationships

to form a primary key. For example, in an airline database, a flight number cannot be used as a primary key for specifying a particular flight since the same flight may occur every day. However, combining the flight number with the date of the flight produces a unique primary key.

Finally, data management also manages relationships. In the GSL database there is a relationship between Students and Loans: a student receives a loan. There is also a relationship between Bank and Loan: a loan is "owned" by a single bank. In Figure 1–4, the relationships are represented by lines connecting entities.

Data as a Corporate Resource

The effective operation of any organization relies on the collection and management of four major resources: people, capital, material, and information. Each of these incurs a cost to the organization and has particular value to the organization. Information has a special significance because it has a direct bearing on the effective and efficient use of all the other resources.

Different users require different data. In the GSL database, certain users will need information about banks, students, and loans. Other users will need information only about students and loans. In the past it was common for each section of an organization to create its own collection of data and to develop software for extracting the information it needed. This approach leads to needless duplication of stored data within the organization and often results in the presence of different or conflicting versions of the same data. An alternative is to centralize planning and control over data to avoid unnecessary duplication in both data acquisition and storage. Then, automated methods are provided to allow individuals to view the data relevant to their needs. This concept is the basis of the corporate database: a unified repository for all of the data required by an organization and an efficient method for allowing each member of the organization to access and use the particular information he or she needs.

The physical arrangements for storing the data vary from one organization to another. In some, a single large database holds all data, with users interacting from remote terminals. In others, the data is physically stored in several databases that may be linked to one another by a data network. The approach used by any particular organization depends on factors such as size of the organization, the number of geographical locations and the distances between them, the number of people using the system, and the needs of particular users. Whichever approach is taken, what we are seeing today is the growth of corporate databases in which any individual in the corporation is theoretically able to access information stored by any other part of the organization. (One of the functions of a DBMS is to control who has access to what data.)

Our original definition of database assumed that information is stored once, and only once, in the database. This is seldom the case with real systems, however, because demands for access to particular parts of the data from widely scattered locations may place unduly heavy demands on the data networks. The result of this may be unacceptable delays in accessing the data and high communication costs. It is quite normal, therefore, for local databases to hold separate copies of frequently used data. Here we should make a distinction between a local database that is part of a larger corporate network of databases, and individual databases on personal computers that are created, administered, and used entirely within a single location. The main difference is that an individual database is locally controlled and has no automatic link to other databases in the system. In a (distributed) corporate database, the DBMS is responsible for ensuring that changes made to data in one location are automatically reflected in data held at other locations.

If we think of a database as a critical corporate resource, then it must be managed. This means that it must be

- protected
- usable
- easily located
- cheaply accessible
- in a form that is meaningful, understandable, and easy to use

The benefits a corporation can realize from data are determined by the quality of the data. This implies that the data must be accurate. There are many ways, however, in which the accuracy of data can be compromised; for example, an operator might enter the wrong value into a field, enter the same record twice, or inadvertently delete a record. A program logic error might place incorrect results into the database or fail to update all occurrences of a particular data item. Hardware failures, such as a disk failure, can lead to errors in the values of stored data, or loss of data.

Two terms, *integrity* and *consistency*, are used to describe the quality of data in a database. Integrity describes the accuracy of the data. High integrity implies that the stored values are accurate. Consistency implies we do not have contradictory facts, such as one data item that says there are 100 units of a particular product on hand, and other data items that say there were 500 on hand at the beginning of the month, but that 450 have been shipped and none have been received into stock since then. A consistent database will tend to have high integrity.

Setting up a database is extremely labor-intensive, hence very costly. Once the database is established, however, it is relatively inexpensive to store and to duplicate the data.

In most instances, a corporate database is less than the total corporate data universe. There are a number of reasons for this. One of the most important is complexity: the number of interrelationships among data items, and hence the number of rules governing their storage and use, grows quickly with the number of items in the database. Rather than overwhelm the systems analysts and database administrators with this complexity, many corporate installations maintain databases for different departments, even though the data often is interrelated. Output from one database is then used as input for a database in another department. As the tools for the design and implementation of databases improve, we can expect to see larger and more complex databases developed.

Alternative Types of Data

An organization uses a variety of data in its normal operation. Some of the data is classified as *transient data* in the sense that it is generated, used, and then discarded. Some is classified as *operational data* because it must be maintained by an enterprise to enable the enterprise to carry out its normal operations. The data in a database is referred to as operational data to distinguish it from input data, output data, or other transient data. New data which is entering the system for the first time, often from terminal entry, is transient data, but, after it has been processed, it may become part of the operational data. For example, in the GSL database transient input data could be a loan payment that reduces the amount of the loan balance but that was not specifically stored in the database.

Similarly, output data is not classified as operational data even though it may be derived from operational data contained in the database. For instance, transient output data, such as printed or displayed messages, queues of data awaiting processing, print files, or temporary results are not considered to be operational data. In the GSL database, transient output data could include a report listing total loan amounts for each bank, or an error message generated when a negative number is entered for YEARS in the LOAN file.

Physical vs. Logical Database

There are two distinct *levels* or *views* at which the database can be described: physical and logical.

- The *physical database* is the data as stored on physical media. At this level, to understand the database we need to know such information as the coding method used to represent data (for example, ASCII, EBCDIC, binary integers, binary coded decimal, etc.), record format (the order of data item values within the record), file organization and access paths to records (for example, hashed vs. indexed sequential), and record blocking. While the database designer must understand the physical representation in order to design and tune the database, most of these characteristics should be transparent (invisible) to the user.

- A *logical database* represents the data as seen by the user (described by records, attributes, and relationships) in a form that is independent of the storage device used and the physical organization. For example, the user sees the database as a set of tables with rows representing entities and columns representing attributes. The logical database may show attributes that are not really a part of the stored physical data. In the GSL database a virtual attribute, TOTAL-AMT, which gives the total loan amount for each student, could be added to the STUDENT table. A *virtual attribute* is an attribute that does not really exist; it is materialized by processing (in this case by adding up all the individual loan amounts) and presenting that total on request.

Hardware

The hardware required to support a database consists of storage devices, processors that manipulate the data, and the I/O (Input/Output) channels that transfer data between processor and storage. In this book we are only marginally concerned with the hardware aspects of a database, partly because they constitute a major topic and are fully covered in numerous other books, and partly because the use of a database and DBMS makes a detailed understanding of the hardware less crucial. However, several characteristics of hardware, particularly the organization and access of data on magnetic disk systems, have a strong impact on physical database design. Thus, disk storage devices are reviewed in Chapter 2.

Software

The database management system (DBMS) is a complex software system that interfaces the physical database and the database users. Next to the operating system, the DBMS is usually the most complex software running on a computer.

User requests for data are managed by the DBMS (see Figure 1–5). Operations such as creating files, storing data, retrieving data, or modifying existing data are all performed by the DBMS without involving the user in the details of how the operations are performed. A key function of the DBMS, therefore, is to allow users to use the database without requiring them to be knowledgeable about the details of the physical database. Modern DBMSs also include a selection of tools including report generators and fourth-generation languages for application development.

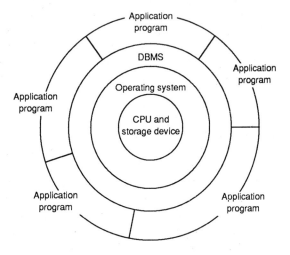

Fig 1-5 Conceptual Architecture of an Information Processing System

People (Users)

People who request data from a database are described as *users*. Broadly speaking, there are three classes of users:
- Analysts and application programmers
- End-users
- Database administrators (DBAs)

Analysts and Application Programmers

Programmers create application software for complex report generation and transaction processing that involves routine and repetitive database updates. Examples of transaction processing for the GSL database would be the entry of new loan data, update of the student address, and recording payments on loans. In most organizations, updates to the operational database are tightly controlled and must be done through specially written programs. Programs may be written in COBOL or, increasingly, in fourth-generation languages.

Database update and access may be performed either on-line or in a batch mode. The choice of method depends on the characteristics of the transactions and the importance of immediacy of output and update. For example, there seems little value in on-line input and update of weekly time cards in a payroll system. A batch process run on a weekly basis with checks ready in a day or two is more cost effective than inputting hours of work for the immediate production of paychecks. By contrast, systems such as those for airline reservations, supermarket scanners, or automatic teller machines clearly require real-time (hence, on-line) access and update.

End-user

An *end-user* is a person who accesses a database either through the UFI (User-Friendly Interface) or through application software. Access is usually via an on-line terminal.

User-Friendly Interface languages are available with DBMSs to assist end-users in data retrieval and report generation. The example given in Figure 1–2 is of the language SQL. While languages such as SQL can be used for updates by end-users, they are usually restricted to read-only usage. This is because of the obvious danger of database corruption if an end-user is given free reign with an update language. For example, the simple SQL statement DELETE FROM LOAN removes every row from the loan table. UFI languages are used for updates on personal computers and for prototyping applications on larger systems. The prototyping, however, uses a test database rather than the actual operational database.

There are two common types of UFI:
- The menu-driven system. This is easier to use by people who have no formal training in the use of databases. The main limitations of using menus are the loss of flexibility and the potential tedium in formulating requests.
- Interactive query languages. Here the user issues high-level commands or statements such as SELECT, INSERT, etc., as shown in Figure 1–2. An interactive query language usually provides a user with more flexibility than a menu-driven system.

Database Administrator

The *database administrator*, or DBA, is the person who is responsible for working with users to define their data needs, creating logical models of the data, designing the database, developing adequate controls and security for the data, and working with information systems management to select suitable hardware and software. The DBA is typically involved with three different interfaces:

1. User-DBA interface. The DBA is the custodian of the data for the users. The DBA enforces user access rights as determined by the data owner, and provides training.

2. Programmer-DBA interface. The DBA controls all data definitions and may assist in the establishment of standards for all applications programs. The DBA also trains programmers in using the DBMS.

3. DBA-DBMS interface. The DBA monitors the performance of the DBMS and "tunes" its physical structure to improve operational characteristics such as response time. The DBA modifies physical structures to reduce response time and increase throughput. The DBA is also responsible for regular database backup, and restoration should it be required.

Data Dictionary

The *data dictionary* (DD), is a supplementary database that contains descriptions of all the data items contained in the database. For example, the DD includes the name of every data item, along with a description of how it is represented in the database, its length, and information for cross-referencing. The data in the data dictionary is called metadata. The word *metadata* is derived from the Greek, prefix *meta*, meaning "behind," "after," or "along with." Metadata, therefore, describes the data behind the data.

Objectives and Advantages of a Database Approach

An organization can choose between two alternative approaches for managing its data. The traditional applications-oriented approach, (or TA), focuses on the procedures used to process the data. With the TA approach, data is processed by a number of essentially independent application programs, each of which uses its own set of files for data storage. For example, in the GSL database, one set of applications might deal with student loan applications processing and therefore need data on both students and loans. Another might determine subsidies due banks and therefore need data on banks and loans. If each of these applications develops its own loan files there will be tremendous redundancy.

In addition, because the output of one application may be the input to another, the designers of each application program must have intimate knowledge of file structures, record layouts, and access paths. There are often situations in which applications that need to work with the same data are unable to do so easily because they cannot access each other's data files. With each application having its own private files, it is difficult to control the data in any systematic way.

In contrast to the TA approach, the database approach integrates the data. This allows sharing of data across applications, reduces the potential for inconsistency and incompatibility, reduces redundancy, and requires that the same data be entered only once. In addition, the DBMS provides an interface between the user and the stored data, so that the user need only be concerned with the logical view of the database and not its physical aspects. The DBMS provides a view to each user of only that subset of the data relevant to the user. In other words, the emphasis is on specifying what data is needed rather than specifying how to access the data. Some examples will help make this clearer.

As an example of the TA approach, consider what is involved in listing the names of all freshmen who have received loans from SEAFIRST, along with the value of the loan. To do this the application program must retrieve and test the data on a record-by-record basis. First it searches the student file for a freshman, then it accesses the loan file for loans with this student's ID to see whether the bank is SEAFIRST. If the conditions are satisfied, the name of the student and the value of the loan are printed. This process requires intimate knowledge of the access paths and file structure, along with programming skills. The following pseudo code, which uses English paraphrasing rather than real query language statements, emphasizes the "record at a time coding" required.

```
For each STUDENT
     If SLEVEL = 1 then
     For each LOAN
               If SID in the LOAN record = SID in the STUDENT record
               and BANK = SEAFIRST then output name and amount
```

Performing the same operation with a DBMS does not require any knowledge of how the data is accessed, how the records are physically structured, or how to perform the necessary selection tests. Instead, a series of conditions are specified in a high-level query language using names for the data items.

```
SELECT NAME, AMOUNT
FROM STUDENT, LOAN
WHERE SLEVEL = 1 AND BANKID = SEAFIRST
AND STUDENT.SID = LOAN.SID
```

Transactions involving additions or deletions in a file-oriented system will often require updates of linkages, or indexes. These updates may require extra programming steps in a file approach but are automatically handled by a DBMS.

The division between file managers and DBMSs is not completely clear. Many file managers masquerade as DBMSs and many DBMSs lack features they should have for full data independence. The difference between the two is basically a question of the degree of data independence that exists. With a file manager the data independence is low, with a DBMS it is high.

Full independence implies that users need not know about details such as:

- location of data items in the record
- physical order of the records
- how data item values are coded
- access paths

The following sections outline some advantages of the database approach.

Centralization of Control and Enforcement of Standards

Because a database places large groups of data within a single system (although not necessarily at the same location), it is possible to place the responsibility for maintaining that data with the database administrator. This centralizes control of the database and makes it easier to enforce standards for handling data. Standards are important for maintaining the quality of the data, for making the structure of the database easier to understand, and as an aid in exchanging data between different divisions or geographical locations of the same organization. A particular installation may be subject to corporate, industry, installation, departmental, national, and international standards. Applicable standards may be adopted in areas such as stored data formats, conventions for naming and documenting data, and data exchange formats.

Less Data Redundancy

Redundancy occurs whenever an organization has the same item of data stored more than once. This is inherent in nondatabase applications since each application maintains its own independent data files. Redundancy results in wasted storage and the possibility of conflicting values for the same stored data item. An ideal DBMS provides controlled redundancy by keeping redundant entries to a practical minimum, while ensuring that there are no discrepancies in the values of the redundant entries. In other words, the DBMS should be aware of the redundancy and ensure that all versions of the data are consistent (see next section) by propagating updates to every occurrence of a particular data item.

Some reasons for data replication:

1. Allowing the same data to be physically stored in more than one way reduces access time. For example, if one application often retrieves all loans for specific banks, then the access time will be reduced if the loans are physically stored in order by bank. However, if another application retrieves all loans for specific students, then that application is better served if the loans are physically ordered by student ID. Since a single copy of the data cannot be stored in more than one way, an alternative is to store two copies in the two different physical orders.

2. Organizations that are geographically dispersed face expensive communication costs if all data access must be from a centralized database. Thus, many organizations are now turning to "distributed database" systems, in which data may be physically replicated at two or more locations. A distributed DBMS is designed to handle replication and to assure that an update to one occurrence of a data item is applied to other occurrences.

3. For decision-support applications, data is often extracted from the central database into personal workstations. An analyst studying the default patterns of loans might extract and download data on defaulted loans to his workstation. There it could be analyzed by decision-support tools such as spreadsheets and statistical systems.

Greater Consistency and Integrity of Data

Whenever more than one copy of a particular data item exists, it becomes difficult to keep all of the copies up to date. It is especially difficult if the copies reside in different files and are processed by different applications programs. When different versions of the same data item exist the data is said to be inconsistent. The database approach reduces the likelihood for inconsistency of the data by reducing the amount of redundancy.

Fewer Problems Correlating Data

Traditional applications-oriented programs often code copies of the same data in different ways, making it difficult and time-consuming to transfer data from one application to another or to carry out processing not envisaged when the coding schemes were developed. For example, if different departments in an organization use different codes to represent similar information, it may be difficult or even impossible to correlate the data on a corporate-wide basis without knowledge of the various coding schemes. The database approach overcomes these difficulties by ensuring that all departments access and work with the same items of stored data.

Data Sharing

Data sharing is the ability of different applications to use the same data. A single database can support many different applications. This eliminates the need to keep separate application-oriented files and, as a consequence, reduces the likelihood of inconsistencies. Data sharing applies not only to existing applications, but also to new applications in which data needs often can be satisfied without the need to create additional stored data.

Easier Access and Use of Data

A database reduces the barrier between the user and the data. Thus, it facilitates using the database for decision support by making data easier to access and use. Whereas the TA approach requires each application program to specify the format and access paths to the data, the database approach requires the application to specify what data is to be found and leaves details of locating and recovering the data to the DBMS. Most DBMSs provide a selection of high-level software tools for data retrieval, report generation, extraction of data for use in other programs (spreadsheets, for example), and graphical displays.

Easier Data Security

An organization creates and stores a great deal of valuable and sensitive data that must be protected against unauthorized access. In the TA approach it is often difficult to provide a high level of security because data occurs in several files and file system security is not as sophisticated as security in a DBMS. In the case of TA, therefore, some responsibility for protecting the data falls to the individual applications programs. It is generally easier to provide security for the data in a database because all access to the data is controlled by the DBMS, and a user must obtain permission for data access from the database administrator. In contrast to file systems that limit access on a file by-file basis, access controls may be specified to rather small units of data in a DBMS. The typical DBMS will allow access types of read-only, update, add and delete to specific attributes and specific rows to be defined for each user. In the GSL database, for example, a given user could be limited to read access for all loans and read or update access for loans from a specific bank.

Data Independence

Types of Data Independence

Most applications programs that deal directly with files are not data-independent because they incorporate specific details about the record organization and access methods of the file. To contrast data-independent and data-dependent systems, here are several examples that illustrate the impact of changes on both. In these examples we will assume that the data-dependent systems manipulate GSL data as three separate files that are accessed directly (as opposed to through a DBMS).

1. Data Item Addition. Assume that the data items CITY and STATE are added to the Student file and the database's Student table.

   Data-dependent approach: This change would most likely necessitate modifying the data description code of each program that used this file. In COBOL this would mean modifying the Data Division, in FORTRAN it would mean changes in FORMAT statements, in BASIC it would mean changes in MAP statements. These programs would then have to be recompiled. When tens or even hundreds of programs are involved, these changes can be expensive, time-consuming, and open to the possibility of error (such as, failure to modify a program).

Data-independent approach: Since data is accessed by data item name and the data description is part of the database, not part of each application program, no recoding or recompilation is necessary.

2. Data Item Deletion. Assume that we start with Student Name stored in the Loan table. Then, due to the high level of redundancy this introduces, it is decided that NAME must be accessed from the Student file only.

Data-dependent approach: Again, the data description code must be changed in the application programs. In addition, programs that relied on NAME from the Loan file must now be further modified to add the description of the Student file, and access NAME from that file.

Data-independent approach: A DBMS provides the means to create a logical database view that makes it *appear* that NAME is still part of the Loan records. Thus, programs that simply accessed NAME from the Loan table will require no modification. However, even a DBMS has trouble with this type of change for programs that performed updates to NAME (in the Loan table).

3. Data Item Representation Changed. Suppose that the Loan date, LDATE, is changed from a YYMMDD form to a *julian date*, that is, a YYDDD form, where DDD is the number of days since the beginning of year YY.

Data-dependent approach: Programs using LDATE must be modified, possibly with statements added to each to translate from the new to the old form (that is, for display in a more user-friendly form). Again, extensive code modification and recompilation is required.

Data-independent approach: A translation routine can be included as part of the database definition so that the new LDATE representation is converted to the old representation before the data item is delivered to the program or to an end-user. Even programs that update LDATE could remain unchanged: a database routine to convert from old (YYMMDD) to the new format could be written. It is important to realize that such a database routine is part of the database description, not part of each application program. It is written once, appears in one place only, etc.

4. Change in Access Paths. Suppose that an index exists for direct access to Student records by AGE. It is subsequently discovered that very few programs ever access by AGE and that it would be cheaper to drop this index, thus saving space and reducing index maintenance costs.

Data-dependent approach: Obviously, programs that used the AGE index will need modification. They now need to sequentially search the Student file to retrieve by AGE. Other programs that accessed Student records but did not retrieve by AGE may need modification in their file description statements, which often include definition of all file indexes.

Data-independent approach: In modern DBMSs, no changes are required, and end-users of UFI languages will not need to change the form of their queries. Those few users who did retrieve by AGE may notice a longer response time.

5. File Partition. Suppose that the Student file and table are vertically partitioned so that SID, NAME, and AGE are in one file/table called SNA, while SID, LEVEL, and ZIP are stored in another file/table called SLZ.

Data-dependent approach: Clearly, this will require major program modification, especially for programs that require data items from both the SNA and SLZ files.

Data-independent approach: A logical view can be created that makes it appear that the two tables are still a single table called Student. This logical view is part of the database description, not part of the application programs.

6. Change in Physical Record Order. Suppose that Loans are ordered by SID, so that all Loans for a given student are in order. It is determined that a more efficient order would be on BID.

Data-dependent approach: A program that retrieved all Loans for a given student previously needed only to locate the first Loan for that Student, then perform "GET NEXTs" to retrieve the rest. Now, its code must change.

Data-independent approach: Modern DBMS manipulation languages do not use or require information about record order. Thus, no changes are required.

7. Changes in File Blocking, Device Assignment, and Device Types. Changes such as these are very low-level changes and include splitting a file across two disk devices, changing the record blocking, replacing disk drives with new models, etc.

Data-dependent approach: Nowadays most file access systems will provide independence for most of these types of change.

Data-independent approach: Users and application programs are insulated from any details or changes at this level.

Benefits of Data Independence

Data independence makes it possible to change many of the physical and logical aspects of a database without having an impact on application programs. For example:

- Physical data can be moved or compacted without affecting the logical database.
- Data items can be added or deleted.
- A variety of data structures (indexed, hashed, linked list) can be used for the physical database. This makes it possible to use data structures ranging from those in which no connection exists between data items to network structures.
- The description of the database and the database itself are not restricted to any particular processing language, and they can therefore be interfaced by a variety of processing languages.
- Separate descriptions are used for the data in the database and the data known to individual programs.

In a truly data-independent system, changes to any of the above features are transparent to the application program.

Overview of Database Design

A successful database implementation relies heavily on careful planning. A major part of this planning involves the development of a preliminary conceptual data model and a schedule for the overall design and implementation of the database.

The creation of a database plan begins with the corporate business plan, and proceeds in a top-down manner to generate definitions of the functions, processes, activities, and events of the enterprise. Working down from the business plan ensures that the design of the database is compatible with the goals and objectives of the enterprise, both now and in the future.

Current design techniques concentrate on the *data* and treat it as a resource that must be managed in the same way as any other resource such as capital or personnel. This produces a database design that is more likely to support the information needs of the organization now and in the future. With modern DBMSs, the database structure may be relatively independent of the languages and programs used to manipulate the database.

An important part of planning a database is the development of a strategic data model, which shows the present and anticipated data needs of the organization. The database plan should reflect the differing information need by level of management. Data needs can be classified into three levels: strategic, tactical, and operational. Strategic planning concerns the overall performance of an enterprise. Tactical management ensures that resources are obtained and used effectively to meet the objectives of the organization. Operational management focuses on the execution of specific tasks and activities such as scheduling and controlling individual jobs, procuring materials, and assigning personnel.

This top-down method assists organizations in establishing a system-architecture plan. The basic assumption is that "an information system plan for a business must be integrated with the business plan and should be developed from the point of view of top management and with their active participation."[1]

Questions

1. What is a database management system, and what capabilities does it include?

2. What kind of operations can be performed by a DBMS?

3. Define and contrast *data* and *information*.

4. Discuss some of the qualities of data as a corporate resource.

5. Define and give several examples of *transient data* and *operational data*.

6. What are the differences between physical and logical databases?

7. Describe the different classes of users.

8. Describe the two different types of database interface commonly available to the end-user.

9. With which aspects of the database system does the database administrator interface?

10. What is a database dictionary?

---

[1] IBM Corporation. *Business System Planning: Information System Planning Guide.*

11. Describe some of the differences between the traditional application-oriented approach and the database approach to data management. What are the strengths and weaknesses of each?

12. With full data independence, what database details are users no longer required to know? What factors contribute to data independence? What benefits result from data independence?

13. Why is it important to reduce data redundancy? What are some good reasons for data redundancy?

14. Define *data consistency* and *integrity*.

References

Bradley, J. *Introduction to Data Base Management in Business.* 2d ed. New York: Holt, Rienhart, and Winston, 1987.

Bryce, M. "The IRM (Information Resource Management) Idea." *Datamation*, vol. 33, no. 8 (April 15, 1987), pp. 89–92.

Cardenas, A. *Data Base Management Systems.* 2d ed. Boston: Allyn and Bacon, Inc., 1985.

Codd, E. "A Relational Model for Large Shared Data Banks." *Communications ACM*, vol. 13, no. 6 (June 1970), pp. 377–387.

Date, C. J. *An Introduction to Database Systems.* Vol. 1. 4th ed. Reading, Mass.: Addison-Wesley Publishing Co., 1985.

IBM Corporation. *Business System Planning: Information System Planning Guide.* Pub.No.GE20-0527-1. White Plains, N.Y., 1975.

Loomis, M.E.S. *The Database Book.* New York: Macmillan Publishing Co., 1987.

Martin, J. *Computer Data-Base Organization.* 2d ed. Englewood Cliffs, N.J.: Prentice-Hall, 1977.

McFadden, F., and Hoffer, J. *Computer Data-Base Organization.* 2d ed. Menlo Park, Calif.: The Benjamin/Cummings Publishing Co., 1988.

2 The Internal Level: Physical File Structures

This chapter provides a summary of the various file structures typically implemented in DBMSs. For readers who have already completed a course in file structures, this will be a review. For the rest, it is an introduction to the physical aspects of storing data. While it is not strictly necessary to understand file structures to *use* a DBMS and to perform logical design, it is essential for physical design and is relevant even to logical database design since logical and physical design are not truly independent in current DBMSs.

The approach used is primarily a generic one in that the specifics of particular operating systems, DBMS file structures, and access methods are not emphasized. Rather, general concepts of linked-list, indexed (B-tree variety), and hashed structures are described.

The emphasis is on B-trees, since they have evolved to be almost the standard file structure for relational DBMSs. The B-tree is very robust— while it is not as fast as hashing for single-record retrieval, it is almost as fast. It is not as efficient as linked lists for retrieval of several records (e.g. "detail") related to another record (the "master"), but again, it is almost as fast. Furthermore, it can support sequential processing and range search, which are not possible with hashed organization. In some cases B-tree performance can improve to be equal or better than the linked organization as the number of detail records retrieved increases. It has the singular feature of dynamic reorganization with file growth—a major deficiency of hashed organizations and a problem with linked lists.

Readers who have already taken a course in file structures could skip this chapter. (On the other hand, if the reader already knows the material then it should make for quick reading.) Nevertheless, it is felt worthwhile to remind the reader of the vast performance difference in secondary and primary memory and why we need be concerned about the choice of file organization and selection of indexes.

A DBMS is commonly organized with a three-level architecture. These levels are also known as *views*. The highest level, called the *external view*, is seen by individual users; the middle level, called the *conceptual view*, provides an overall view of the database in an abstract form; and the lowest level, called the *internal view*, is the low-level representation of the physical database. The view at each level is defined by a *schema*, which is a definition of the structure of the database at that level. The internal and conceptual levels each have a single schema, but, because each database user may be provided with his or her own tailor-made external view of the database, there may be many different external schemas.

In this chapter we are concerned with the internal level in which the database is viewed as a collection of structured records and files. The term *physical file structure* is used to describe the structured arrangement of data on storage media such as disks or tapes.

The selection of a file structure for a particular DBMS is based on a number of important criteria including:

- high throughput for processing transactions
- fast access for retrieval and storage of data
- efficient use of storage space

STUDENT Table

SID	NAME	SLEVEL	AGE	SZIP
9735	ALLEN	1	21	98101
4494	ALTER	2	19	98112
8767	CABEEN	5	24	98118
2368	JONES	4	23	98155
6793	SANDS	1	17	98101
3749	WATSON	5	29	98168

BANK Table

BID	BZIP	TYPE
FIDELITY	98101	MSB
SEAFIRST	98101	BANK
PEOPLES	98109	BANK
CAPITAL	98033	SL
HOME	98031	SL

LOAN Table

LID	LDATE	YEARS	INT_RATE	AMOUNT	SID	BID
27	15-SEP-85	5	8.5	1200	9735	HOME
78	21-JUN-86	5	7.75	1000	9735	PEOPLES
87	07-SEP-83	5	7.0	2000	9735	SEAFIRST
92	12-JAN-85	6	7.5	2100	4494	FIDELITY
99	15-JAN-86	6	9.0	2200	4494	FIDELITY
170	30-APR-83	6	6.5	1900	8767	PEOPLES
490	07-MAY-84	6	6.0	2500	3749	PEOPLES
493	24-JUN-85	7	7.5	3000	3749	PEOPLES

Fig 2-1   GSL Database

- protection from data loss or system failure
- security against unauthorized use
- the characteristics of the secondary storage device on which the files will be stored

Data Hierarchy

Most data used for business applications is organized into a hierarchy of units ranging from characters, at the lowest level, to database at the highest level. For example, the student data of the Guaranteed Student Loan (GSL) database shown in Figure 2–1 would be stored in the STUDENT file. This file contains records. In the case of the student data file, for instance, there is one record for each student. Records themselves are made up of data items. For example, the student record contains the student's identity number (SID), name, level, age and the ZIP (among other data).

Data Items

Consider the row in the STUDENT file for the student with SID = 2368. SID is a data item, which in this case has a value of 2368. NAME is also a data item, which in this case has a value of JONES. Thus data items have names, and occurrences of data items have values. The distinction between the *name* and *occurrence* of a data item is important. In most cases, the context will tell you which is being discussed.

A data item's value is expressed in characters: the single character 5 was used to indicate the SLEVEL of CABEEN. The student name WATSON contains 6 alphabetic characters to represent its value. In most cases, the order of the characters is important; WATSON and WASTON are not the same value.

A data item has a type that limits the values it may assume. Two of the most widely used types are *numeric* and *alphanumeric*. A numeric data type is usually limited to the characters 0123456789,.+. Numeric data types may be further divided into *integers* and *floating point* (or real) types. Integers do not allow a decimal point. Floating point values allow a fractional part, which means they may contain a single decimal point.

Alphanumeric (also called character) data items usually allow both upper and lower case alphabetic symbols, digits, and special symbols such as !@#$%^&*()_+=\{}[]'":;?/><.,. Examples of alphanumeric data items include student name, bank ID, and bank type. This data type is used for values that are not quantities.

Another data type is called *Boolean*. A Boolean data type may have only one of two values, true or false. Boolean types are used where values are naturally true or false, or where a data item may take on only one of two values. Examples include data items indicating married/single, male/female, and taking course for credit or not. An example of a possible Boolean type in the GLS is a "Paid-off" data item in which a true value would indicate that the student completed payment on the loan, and a false value would indicate that the loan still has a positive balance.

Records

Data items are grouped together into a unit called a record. Figure 2–2 shows an example of a record for one student from the GSL database showing the name of each data item, its type, and an example value. This record is an extended example from the the GSL database previously shown. The entry in the parentheses following the word *character* is the length of the item, and following the word *decimal* is the total number of digits, followed by the number of places to the right of the decimal place.

Records also have names (or types) and occurrences. For example, records of this type might be named STUDENT. Records are associated with entities (i.e., things, objects, or events).

Typically, all occurrences of a given record type will have the same set of data items (but clearly not the same set of values). For example, all occurrences of the record LOAN include values for the same set of data items. Since each record occurrence is associated with a single entity, one or more data items uniquely identify the record and the corresponding entity. This data item or set of data items is called a *key*. In the STUDENT record the key is Student Identity Number, or SID; in the BANK record, it is the Bank Identity Number, or BANKID; and in the LOAN record it is the Loan Identity Number, or LID. Note that in the LOAN record the key could also be the pair of data items SID and LDATE (assuming at most one loan for a specific student per day). SID alone would not be sufficient, since,

Data Item Name	Type	Value
Student Number	Integer	9735
Last Name	Character (12)	Allen
First Name	Character (12)	Jonathon
Address	Character (30)	345 Bay St., #344
City	Character (15)	Seattle
ZIP	Character (5)	98101
Date of Birth	Date	09/26/67
Date entered Univ.	Date	09/6/87
Degree Objective	Character (20)	Engineering
State Resident	Boolean	True
Veteran	Boolean	False
Sex	Character (1)	M
Overal GPA	Decimal(3,2)	3.10
Total Credits	Integer	104

Fig 2-2   *Student Record Showing Type and Value of Each Data Item*

while this would associate a given loan with a single student, it would not identify the specific loan.

Files

The collection of all the occurrences of a given record type constitute a file. The file will have a name that is the same as the record type name. Thus the LOAN file would be the collection of all records of the type LOAN. In some computer systems the term *data set* is used instead of *file*.

Databases

A group of related files is termed a *database*. For example, the GSL system maintains data on many different entity types—hence, many different files. There is a clear relationship between the three files STUDENT, BANK, and LOAN. A student takes out a loan which is made by a bank. Thus, these three files would certainly be stored in a single database.

Virtually every file kept by an organization has some relationship, however tenuous, to every other file. Thus, one might be tempted to consider that all files for an organization are a single database; indeed, we sometimes use the terms *corporate database* or *corporate data resource* to collectively refer to all (electronic and manual) corporate files. In practice, attempting to manage all data as one database is impractical; therefore, the files are divided into separate databases of closely interrelated files. Data is then transferred from one database to another for less intimate relationships. In a university information system, when a student graduates, part of his or her records might be transferred into an Alumni Records database that is managed separately from all of the others. In this case, each database in the system is managed independently of the others, even though this may result in some duplication of entries and possible inconsistencies in values (such as, a graduate student who is also an alumni appearing with different addresses in the two databases).

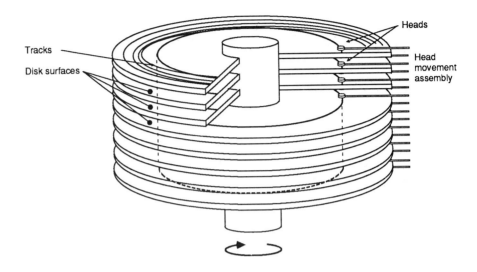

Fig 2-3   Architecture of a Magnetic Disk Device

Storage Device Characteristics

In this section, we give a very brief review of several of the important characteristics of disk storage devices.

A disk storage device has a number of platters, with recording surfaces on one or both sides of each platter as shown in Figure 2–3. Each surface contains a number of data recording *tracks*. Data access (read and write) is by a set of read/write heads mounted on an access arm. The arm is moved in or out to position the heads over the desired track. Electronic switching then selects the read (write) head over one surface for input (output). Note that since the access arm moves all of the read/write heads as a unit, there is a set of tracks, one per surface, which can be accessed without arm movement. All tracks which have the same radius across the several surfaces are called a *cylinder*.

Each track is further subdivided into addressable units called *physical blocks*, *sectors*, or *pages*. We will use the term block. The unit of data transferred between the device and central memory is a block. A block typically contains a number of (logical) records. The device itself, however, has no knowledge of these records. Thus, to access a specific record, the DBMS must actually request transfer of the entire block containing the record. The desired record is then extracted and passed on to the user.

The time required to access a randomly located block includes the time to make a random arm movement, the *seek* time, plus the delay while the desired block rotates into position under the R/W heads, the *rotational* delay or *latency*, plus the time for the actual data transfer from the block. The average seek plus latency time is about 25 milliseconds. Transfer time depends on characteristics of the device and on the size of the block. Typical transfer times are about 1 second for 2 megabytes, or 1 millisecond for 2000 bytes.

The size of the blocks plays a major role in the capacity of the storage device and the speed of data retrieval. First, consider capacity. We will consider a hypothetical device, not unlike several actual devices. Our hypothetical device has 15 surfaces, 1770 usable tracks per surface, and 48,000 bytes per track. Total capacity therefore equals 1770*48,000*15, or 1.27 billion bytes (*gigabytes*). However, this calculation ignores overhead areas. These are areas reserved for system information. The capacity of a track for storage of user data after it has been subdivided into blocks is called the *formatted capacity*. Our hypothetical disk requires an overhead gap of about 500 bytes. Thus, with a block size of 4096 bytes, only 10 blocks per track are possible. (This is determined by finding the largest integral number of blocks of size 4096 bytes plus 500 bytes overhead which will fit in 48,000 bytes — $\lfloor 48,000/4596 \rfloor = 10$.) The formatted capacity of the disk is therefore given by: 10 blocks/track * 1770 tracks/surface *15 surfaces = 265,500 blocks or 265,500 blocks * 4096 bytes/block = 1.087 gigabytes.

If a smaller block size is used, the formatted capacity is lower. For example, with a block size of 512 bytes there is space for only 47 blocks per track (that is, $\lfloor 48,000/(512 + 500) \rfloor = 47$), giving a formatted capacity of 639 megabytes (about 50 percent of the unformatted capacity). From the standpoint of capacity, it would therefore appear that large block sizes are to be preferred. However, this conflicts with the requirements for rapid access to the data.

Obviously, large blocks will take longer to transfer and will require more memory space for storage. Furthermore, since larger blocks hold a greater number of logical records, the "within block" search time to find a specific record will take somewhat longer.

The choice of an appropriate block size depends on the particular application. On-line processes, which necessarily involve random accesses, favor smaller block sizes, since a random retrieval usually needs only a single record of typically 100 to 500 bytes. Thus, setting the block size equal to the record size would avoid transfer of more bytes than necessary. The average time to access and transfer a block of 500 bytes using our hypothetical disk device is 25.25 milliseconds.

On the other hand, a small block size leads to inefficient use of space, as shown by our example calculations above. Thus, there is a space-speed tradeoff. For most on-line retrievals, setting block size at around 5000 bytes results in a good balance. In contrast, for files that are primarily sequentially processed, larger block sizes are advantageous. Finding the overall best block size is not easy. In part it is difficult because the mix of random and sequential processing of a given file will change over time.

Some DBMSs make the decision for the user or give very few choices. For example, IBM mainframe DBMSs usually fix the physical block, called a *page*, at 4096 bytes. While not necessarily optimal, it is seldom a poor choice no matter what the processing characteristics. The choice of a 4096 byte block results in a formatted capacity which is about 86% of the unformatted capacity—a reasonable utilization of the theoretical capacity. The total time to randomly access and transfer the block is on the order of 27 milliseconds—only 8% longer than the time to access and transfer a zero-byte block. While larger block sizes would result in slightly better utilization, the increased transfer time would create a noticeable degradation in total access time.

Physical/Logical Relationships

The relationship between the logical data hierarchy and the physical storage units is described in Figure 2–4. Note that most logical elements do not have a direct physical representation. The disk unit itself knows about tracks and blocks, but it has no information about the division of a block into logical records or the grouping of bytes to create data

Logical Unit	Physical Unit
----	Bit
Character	Byte
Data Item	1+ bytes
Record	Subset of block
Group of records	Block (also called sector or page, depending on the device and operating system)
File	Group of blocks

Fig 2-4   Relationship of Logical and Physical Storage Units

items. Subdividing blocks into logical records is the responsibility of the operating system or the DBMS. Subdividing logical records into data items is the responsibility of the application program or the database management system.

A disk will usually contain a number of files. It will also contain a directory that tells the name of each file, along with such characteristics as blocking factor (number of logical records per block), the type of file, and the starting position on the disk. Files may be segmented (a segment is a group of blocks) in which case the directory will tell the starting location and size of each segment.

File Organization

A file organization is a technique for physically arranging the records of a file on a secondary storage system such as magnetic tape or a magnetic disk. The three commonly used file organizations are called *sequential*, *indexed*, and *direct*.

Sequential File Organization

In a sequential file organization, the records are physically stored in the order they are written to the file, normally in ascending sequence of the primary key. The sequential file organization is rather simple when compared to direct-access organizations. The deciding factors in setting up a sequential file organization include:

- which data items or items are used to sequence records; that is, what is the primary key
- the number of records per block
- whether or not the file should be partitioned

The choice of which data item to use for the primary key is usually obvious: it is the data item that uniquely identifies the records. For example, with the student record the key would probably be the SID. However, a student's social security number might be an alternative.

Most database files will have some need for random access. Because of this, sequential file organization is rarely used for database files. It is most commonly used for archival or backup files.

Indexed Files

One technique for speeding up the process of retrieving records from a file is to use an index. An index may be thought of as a separate file that contains keys and pointers to the individual data records in the main file. A file index is analogous to the index in a book, where page numbers (pointers) point to information in the body of the book (the indexed data file).

Indexed Sequential File Organization

Dense and Non-Dense Indexes

There are two major types of indexes—dense and non-dense—also called *secondary* and *primary*, respectively. Figure 2–5 illustrates (an expanded version of) the STUDENT file with primary index on SID and secondary index on NAME. The non-dense SID index has a index entry, made up of a key value and pointer, to each disk block (sector). Only one entry per sector is required because the file is in order by SID. The entries are the highest SID value from each sector. To locate a record by SID the index is searched for the first entry which is greater than or equal to the desired value; the referenced sector is accessed and the records within the sector are searched internally for a match.

Clearly, a file may have only a single non-dense index—the file may not be ordered on more than one data item. This type of organization is (generically) called *indexed sequential*.

The dense index has an entry for every record as illustrated by the NAME index. Since the records are not in sequential order by name, there is no way to reduce the number of index entries below one per record. In addition, this secondary index illustrates use of a symbolic pointer instead of a sector address. To find a record by name, the index is searched for a match. The resulting SID value is then used to search the primary index.

The properties of primary and secondary indexes are summarized in Figure 2–6 .

A data file may have any number of secondary indexes. Figure 2–5 illustrates only a single secondary index. An index could be constructed for every data item in a record if the extra storage and update processing time were warranted by the way the file is used.

It is also possible to construct an index based on the combined values from two or more data items. For example, Figure 2–7 shows an index to the STUDENT file based on the fields SLEVEL and AGE. This index would be useful for a query that involves finding all seniors within a particular age group. Note that the combined index can also be used as an index on the first field alone, since the first entry in the combined index (SLEVEL) is in consecutive order.

Indexes are sometimes referred to as *inverted lists*. The reason for this is that normal files (such as the STUDENT file we have been discussing) list the values of the data items contained in each record, whereas an index lists, for each value of the indexed data item, the records that contain that value. A file with an index on every data item is said to be *fully inverted*.

The fundamental reason for creating and using an index is to speed up the retrieval of data but, in doing so, there are at least two costs to be considered. First, there is the additional storage space required for the indexes; and second, updating is slower since record additions and deletions will require index updates. Guidelines for the creation of indexes are covered in Chapter 13 in the section on physical database design.

Sector #   **STUDENT MASTER FILE. 4 records/sector**

1	1081 DAVIS 3 22	1147 BAKER 5 37	1256 TYSON 5 24	1533 BECKER 1 19
2	1593 BOWER 4 23	1734 HANNAH 2 20	2080 JESKE 4 25	2368 JONES 4 23
3	2647 SPENCER 1 18	1948 CHASE 3 20	3136 MITO 3 21	3281 MCCLURE 1 19
4	3416 FELDMAN 5 26	3438 PECK 2 24	3609 HARWOOD 3 40	3749 WASON 1 20
5	3822 ALLEN 1 21	4055 SULTAN 2 20	4491 REZNIK 4 29	4494 ALTER 2 19
6	4519 KLEIN 2 20	4701 BARBEE 4 21	4819 ROACH 5 37	4846 FOREST 4 24
7	5070 DAY 5 28	5432 ANDERSON 1 18	6115 GOLDMAN 3 24	6452 SHOR. 5 27
8	5621 VERA 2 26	6755 LEWIS 4 23	6793 SANDS 1 17	7101 TALLMAN 2 19
9	7125 HERMS 3 21	7408 WORTH 5 29	7456 PIKE 2 20	8116 LIPMAN 3 30

RECORD	SIO	NAME
CONTENT	SLEVEL	AGE

PRIMARY INDEX (NON DENSE)

SID	SECTOR #
1533	1
2368	2
3281	3
3749	4
4494	5
4846	6
6542	7
7101	8
8116	9

SECONDARY INDEX (DENSE)

NAME	SID		NAME	SID
ALLEN	3822		KLEIN	3822
ALTER	4494		LEWIS	4494
ANDERSON	5432		LIPMAN	5432
BAKER	1147		MCCLURE	1147
BARBEE	4701		MITO	4701
BECKER	1533		PECK	1533
BOWER	1593		PIKE	1593
CHASE	2948		REZNIK	2948
DAVIS	1081		ROACH	1081
DAY	5070		SANDS	5070
FELDMAN	3416		SHORE	3416
FOREST	4846		SPENCER	4846
GOLDMAN	6115		SULTAN	6115
HANNAH	1734		TALLMAN	1734
HARWOOD	3609		TYSON	3609
HERNS	7125		VERA	7125
JESKE	2080		WATSON	2080
JONES	2368		WORTH	2368

(Continued)

SYMBOLIC POINTERS

Fig 2-5   Example of File with Primary and Secondary Indexes

Primary (Non-Dense) Index

1 key per block.
Records in physical order by key.
Pointer is (usually) directly to record.

Secondary (Dense) Index

1 key per record.
Records not in physical order by key.
Pointer is usually the primary key — a so-called symbolic pointer.

Fig 2-6   Primary and Secondary Indexes

B-tree-based File Structures

There are numerous ways to organize indexed files. While there is no particular method that is best for all applications, the so-called B-tree structure has proven to be one of the best all-around performers. Almost every computer system vendor provides a B-tree-based file organization as part of its operating system. IBM's B-tree file structure is called VSAM for "Virtual (Indexed) Sequential Access Method." Other vendors use terms such as ISAM or simply "indexed" file organization. In addition, the B-tree schemes are widely used in DBMSs—especially in the relational systems which are a major emphasis of this text.

In the last section we saw how an index reduces the number of I/O operations required to retrieve a particular record by removing the need to sequentially scan all of the records in a file. While the use of an index eliminates the need to scan the main file, it is still necessary to search the index file. If the index is large, this operation can also become very time-consuming. One way to reduce the amount of time spent searching an index is to build an index to it, that is, to make an index to the index. This idea can be repeated as many times as desired, with each level of the index providing a nondense index to the level below it. Thus, a tree structure is created. Two to three levels of indexing are normally all that is needed unless you are dealing with a *very* large file.

The uppermost level of the index is called the *root*; entries at the lowest level are called *leaves*. The most widely used form of index tree, known as the B+tree, was introduced in 1972 and is now used in many different variations. In this chapter we present a particular variation known as the B+ tree.

Primary B+tree Index

Figure 2–8 shows a B+ tree structure for the STUDENT file given in Figure 2–5 (for simplicity, only the SID values of each record are shown). Note that the file is physically ordered on SID and the sequence consists of a nondense, or primary, index on SID. Because of the small number of entries in this example, the index consists of only two levels; even so, the treelike structure is obvious. The highest level, called the root of the tree, is on the left; the lowest level, referred to as the leaves, is on the right. Each of the blocks of storage shown on the diagram is called a *node*. The actual data records are stored in the lowest level of the structure. Higher levels contain the index to these records.

SLEVEL	AGE	SID (pointer)	SLEVEL	AGE	SID (pointer)
1	17	6793	3	22	1081
1	18	2647	3	24	6115
1	18	5432	3	30	8116
1	19	1533	3	40	3609
1	19	3281	4	21	4701
1	20	3749	4	23	1593
1	21	3822	4	23	2368
2	19	4494	4	23	6755
2	19	7101	4	23	4846
2	20	1734	4	25	2080
2	20	4055	4	29	4491
2	20	4519	5	24	1256
2	20	7456	5	26	3416
2	24	3438	5	27	6452
2	26	6621	5	28	5070
3	20	2948	5	29	7408
3	21	3136	5	37	1147
3	21	7125	5	37	4819

Fig 2-7   Index on Composite Fields SLEVEL and AGE with Symbolic Pointer, SID

Each data block has a capacity for B records (4 in Figure 2–8) and will typically contain between B/2 and B records. The reasons for the extra space will become obvious as we explain the structure and perform update operations. In practice, data blocks are 1,000 to 4,000 bytes in size and have a typical capacity of five to 40 records.

The index levels contain only keys and pointers to the lower levels. Since the records are maintained in key order, only the highest key from each block is stored in the lowest index level. Similarly, at the next higher index level, only the highest valued key from each of the lowest level blocks is stored along with a pointer. Index blocks are of comparable size to data blocks, but have a larger capacity in terms of number of index entries because index entries are typically much smaller than data records. In this example the index blocking is 6, but in practice it would be on the order of 50 to 500, reflecting a typical block size of 1,000 to 4,000 bytes and index entry sizes of 8 to 20 bytes.

In order for us to compare the performance of the B+tree structure with other file structures, we must look at how common operations are handled. The primary operations that are of interest with any file structure are:

1. Retrieval of a record

2. Addition of a record

3. Deletion of a record

4. Sequential processing

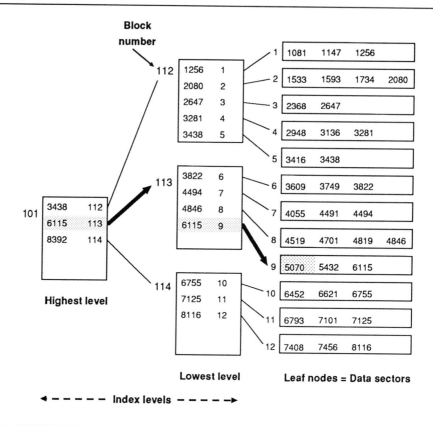

Fig 2-8 STUDENT File Organized with B+tree Index on SID. Highlighted entries show search path for record with SID = 5070—see text.

Each of these operations is described and analyzed in terms of the number of block accesses required. This is followed by an analysis of the structure and its application as a secondary index.

Retrieval of a Single Record

The top level of a B+tree index is usually kept in main memory as a way of reducing the number of physical accesses required to retrieve a record. Retrieval of a record begins with a search of the top level of the index to find the first entry that is equal to or greater than the desired key. When it is located, the entry provides a pointer to the next lower level of the index. This process is repeated until the lowest level of the index is reached. The pointer contained in the lowest level of the index points to the block containing the desired data record. For example, finding the record for SID 5070 with the B+tree shown in Figure 2–8 is performed by searching block 101 (already in memory) and locating the first key equal to or higher than 5070, (that is, 6115, which points to block 113). Block 113 is read into memory (the first disk access) and searched for the first key that is equal to, or higher than 5070. This yields the key 6115, which has a pointer to block 9. Block 9 is read into memory (the second disk access) and searched to find the desired data record with the key 5070. Note that the desired record was found with only two disk accesses.

Generally, the number of disk accesses is one less than the total number of levels in the tree. This is because the single block at the top of the tree is maintained in main memory. The disk accesses are the costly part of the search. A disk access typically requires 5 to 50 milliseconds. In contrast, searching within a block is done at CPU speeds, so that a search through several hundred index entries requires less than a millisecond.

To recap: The B+tree index may have any number of levels. The number of levels will depend primarily on the number of records, their blocking, the size of the index entries, and the index blocking. It is rarely necessary to use an index that is over three levels high. Thus, it is rare that more than three disk accesses are required to retrieve a specific record.

Multiple Record Retrieval: Sequential Processing

An attractive feature of B+trees is that they also support sequential processing. While the index makes it possible to access the blocks in proper logical order, most B+trees also include pointers between sequential blocks at the lowest level of the index (called the *sequence set*). These sequential pointers make it easy to find sequential blocks even when the physical locations of the blocks are different from the logical sequence. Thus, in Figure 2–8, block 112 will point to 113, 113 will point to 114, and so on. As we will discuss below, after a period of use in which records have been added and deleted, index blocks become split; therefore, sequential pointers will not simply point to the next higher block as depicted in Figure 2–8.

B+tree indexed files may also be used in a mode called *skip sequential* processing. In this mode, transaction records are batched and sorted into primary key sequence. Then, rather than accessing every record block, the transaction keys are checked against the keys in the lowest index level. If the index indicates that a particular record block contains no matches with the next transaction key, then that record is skipped. For example, suppose we have the following keys in transaction records:

> 2080, 3416, 4819, 7101, 7125

Examining the lowest index level indicates that only the following record blocks need to be accessed:

> 2, 5, 8, 11

Record Addition

The elegance of B+trees, and the main reason they have become the defacto standard for file indexing, is the manner in which they handle the addition of a record. Two situations can occur when a record is added:

1. There is space for the added record in the appropriate block.

2. The appropriate block is full, in which case it is necessary to perform a *block split*.

Record addition when space exists is straightforward. The record is simply added to the appropriate block. No update of the primary index is needed. To determine where the record for SID 3429 should be added, we search the tree as if we were looking for this record. The search retrieves block 5. Since this block has a capacity of four but presently contains only two records, the new record may be added between 3416 and 3438. (The records are kept in key sequence within the block.)

In the second situation, in which the target block is already full, the elegance of the B+tree becomes apparent. Consider, for example, the addition of a record with the key 4507. As

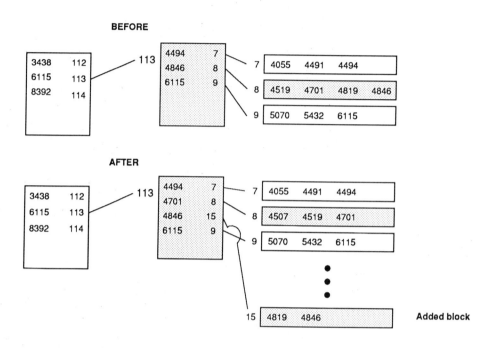

Fig 2-9   Partial B+tree Illustrating Block Splitting on Addition of a Record with Key 4507. Highlighted blocks are those updated by the addition.

we see in Figure 2–8, the new record should be added to block 8, but, because this block is full, it is necessary to split the block. Figure 2–9 shows the result of this operation. The splitting process takes the four records originally contained in block 8 plus the added record and divides them into two roughly equal-sized groups of three and two records, respectively. One group remains in the original block (8), and the other group is assigned to an unused block, say, 15.

Since it is impractical to shift existing records to make space for the new block, no attempt is made to keep the blocks physically in key order. Instead, the index is adjusted to properly sequence the blocks in logical order. To achieve this, the index in block 113 is revised by deleting the key:pointer entry, 4846:8, and adding two new key:pointer pairs, 4701:8 and 4846:15. These are, of course, placed in order within the block. The record with key 4507 can then be added to block 8 without difficulty.

Adding index entries makes it possible that the index block itself will overflow. When this happens, the index block splits and the next higher level of the index is updated. The limiting case, in which the next higher level is the top level of the index and is also full, is handled in exactly the same way as the others: the top level splits into two blocks and a new top-level block is created containing two entries.

In practice, several other tricks are employed to reduce the amount of block splitting and, consequently, increase the percentage utilization of the blocks. One method to reduce block splitting is to look at neighboring blocks for available space when a block overflows.

Rather than splitting block 8 to add the record with SID 4507, the record could have been added to block 7; or record 4846 could have been shifted to block 9, opening up space for the new record in block 8. While either of these would have required an index update, neither would require use of another block.

Record Deletion

When records are deleted a block may *underflow*; that is, end up with less than B/2 records (less than half of its capacity). In formal algorithms which deal with B+trees, this would result in a shifting of records from an adjacent block to bring the block back to at least a half-full state, or, a coallescing of two blocks into a single block. Here is an example. Consider blocks 4 and 5 of Figure 2–8. Suppose record 3416 is deleted causing an underflow in block 5. The four remaining records from blocks 4 and 5 can now be stored in a single block, which frees a block.

In practice, many B+tree file systems ignore underflows unless a block is completely emptied. The evidence is that while coallescing two blocks into one frees storage space temporarily, the added input/output costs do not compensate for the savings in storage costs. Often, coallescing two pages into one page is followed shortly thereafter by a record addition to this same page which causes it to split. The savings in storage are, therefore, often shortlived.

Secondary B+tree Indexes

A secondary index is an index built on a data item other than the primary key. Except by chance, the file will not be in order on this data item, so the index must include every secondary key value in the file and will therefore be a dense index. While the pointer of each key:pointer pair could directly reference the block that contains the data record, it is more common to construct a *cross index* containing primary keys and secondary keys, ordered on the secondary keys. In this arrangement the primary key is called a *symbolic pointer* since it logically points to the desired record but does not physically point to it. This approach ensures that the secondary B+tree index will continue to point to the correct records even when updates have been performed that cause block splitting.

Figure 2–10 shows a secondary index constructed on the student name. This index is also a B+tree which, in this example, has two levels. Note that each entry at the lowest level contains two values: a key (NAME) and a symbolic pointer (SID).

There are several other features of this tree. First, the entries in the top level of this index are abbreviated. This type of B+tree is called a *prefix B+tree*. Index entries can be compressed since the index only guides us to the correct blocks to search. Thus, an index entry need only have enough characters in it to discriminate between the blocks at the next lower level. For example, the (lowest level) index block 201 ends with BARBEE while the next index block (202) begins with BECKER. The entry at the next higher level need only be long enough to guide us to the correct block. While BARBEE could have been entered in the high level block, BC (or BD or BE) is sufficient. This "backend compression" reduces the size of the index entries, hence increases the number of entries per block. The end result may be an index of fewer levels, hence fewer disk accesses.

The index also includes pointers which sequentially link the lowest index blocks. Block 201 points to 202 which, in turn, points to 203 and so forth. This facilitates sequential access to students by name—higher index levels do not need to be accessed.

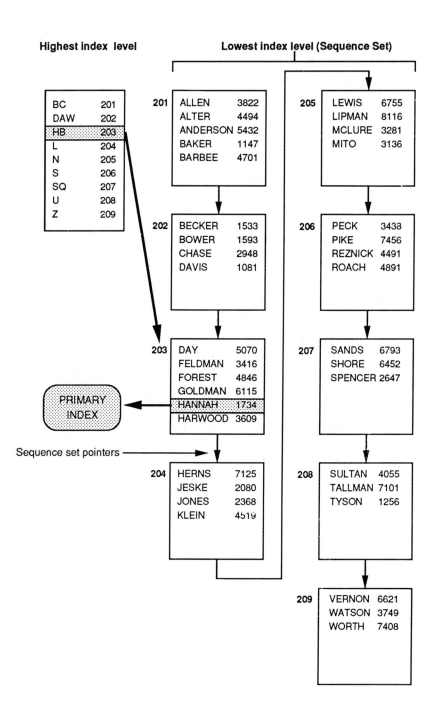

Highest index level   Lowest index level (Sequence Set)

Fig 2-10 *Secondary B+tree Index on Name. Highlighted entries and heavy lines illustrate the search process for student with name HANNAH.*

Example of Secondary Index Search

The bold lines in Figure 2–10 illustrate a search using a secondary B+tree to find the record for the student whose name is HANNAH. This yields the symbolic pointer 1734, which is then used to search the primary index. You should follow this process through and convince yourself that only three disk block accesses are required. Remember that the top level of each index is assumed to be in main memory.

Record Addition

The impact on secondary indexes when a record is added is analogous to the impact on the file itself *if* you view the lowest level of the secondary index as the data level. If there is space in the lowest level index block, the new index entry is simply added. If the added index entry causes the block to overflow, then it splits and the next higher level block is updated. For example, suppose a student with name GOODMAN is added and causes block 203 to overflow. Block 203 is split into two blocks with DAY, FELDMAN, FOREST, and GOLDMAN remaining in block 203; GOODMAN, HANNAH, and HARWOOD move to a new block, say, 210. The top level index must then be updated to reflect this split.

Hashed File Organization

Hashing is a process that uses a mathematical function instead of an index to map a key to an address. The objective of hashing is to translate keys into addresses so that a record can be retrieved with close to a single disk access.

Consider a file with N records, block capacity B, and, number of blocks M equal to N/B. A perfect hash function would translate exactly B of the records to each of the M blocks. While such functions exist, they are extremely difficult to find. Therefore, we look for a function that is good in the sense of distributing records randomly to the available blocks. By randomly, we mean that if there are M blocks, a randomly selected key should have a probability of 1/M of being hashed to any block. As discussed below, when a hashed file is designed, the number of blocks allocated to it will exceed N/B because the hash function will not be perfect. It is typical to allow about 20 percent more blocks than required (that is, $M = 1.2 * N/B$). For example, a file of 100,000 records and blocking 10 might be hashed into 12,000 blocks instead of the absolute minimum of 10,000.

Hash Function

For this discussion we will assume that the file will be stored in consecutive blocks numbered 1 to M, and we will use the following hash function:

Address = (Key MODULO M) + 1

The modulo, or MOD function, is the remainder of the division operation. For example, 30 MOD 13 = 4. The resulting value will range from 0 (if the key is exactly divisible by M), to M-1. Tests have shown that M should be a prime value. As an example of why a non-prime value might be very poor, consider M = 10,000. The hash value of an integer key modulo 10,000 is simply the rightmost four digits of the key. For example, 8,511,234 MOD 10,000 = 1234. Thus, the information in the higher order digits is not used; they have no impact on the address generated. Since the rightmost four digits are probably not randomly assigned, we can hardly expect the function to hash keys to addresses randomly distributed over the range 0 to 9,999. Here are several examples of hashing for specific file parameters:

File Size N =	Blocking B =	Blocks M =	Example keys	Address = Key MODULO M	
25,000	10	3,011	26387	2,299	
			45112	2,968	Synonyms
			48123	2,968	
			78286	0	
100,000	5	25,163	8451293	21,688	
			1293	1,293	
			8551293	21,036	

As shown, it is possible for two keys to be hashed to the same address. In fact, whenever two keys differ by an integer multiple of M they will have the same hash address. Two keys with the same hash address are called *synonyms*. When the number of synonyms of given hash value (that is, number of records which hash to a given location) exceeds the file blocking, an overflow occurs. This means that some of these records must be stored in other than their designated, or *home*, block.

Figure 2–11 is an example hashed file using the hash function *key MOD 17 + 1*. Records are blocked at 3. Records which are not stored in their home block have their home block address indicated in parentheses. From the figure you can see that there are four overflow records, three have been stored in block 12 (which had no records hash to it) and one is in block 14.

Overflow is undesirable because it means that some of the records cannot be retrieved in a single disk access. To retrieve an overflow record we must first access the block at its hash address (its home block), since we have no way of knowing beforehand that a specific record is in overflow. If a record is not found at the expected hash address, and if there are no empty records in the block, then it is necessary to search subsequent blocks until either the desired record is found, or an empty record is found. Methods of handling overflow are described in a subsequent section.

Impact of Blocking and Load Factor

There is no practical way to avoid some overflow. Choices in the file design, particularly the choice of M, the number of available blocks, and B, the blocking, have a major impact on the expected overflow.

Before continuing, use your intuition to answer the following questions:

1. If the total available storage space (M*B) is increased but B remains constant, what is the impact on the number of records that overflow?

2. If the total available storage is maintained constant (M*B is constant) and B is increased, what is the impact on the number of records that overflow?

To answer these questions and analyze the performance of a hashed organization, it is useful to define a parameter called the *load factor*, which is the ratio of the number of records to the file capacity, or:

Load Factor = LF = N/(B*M)

For example, if N = 10,000, B = 10, and M = 1250, then LF = 80 percent. If M increases, and B and N remain constant, then the load factor decreases and the expected overflow will

Block #   **STUDENT MASTER FILE. Blocking = 4**

Block #				
1	1734 HANNAH	3281 MCCLURE		
2	4846 FOREST			
3	7125 HERNS			
4	1533 BECKER	4491 REZNIK		
5	3438 PECK	5070 DAY		
6	3609 HARWOOD	2368 JONES		
7	2080 JESKE	6755 LEWIS	4494 ALTER	
8	2948 CHASE	8116 LIPMAN		
9	1147 BAKER	3136 MITO	4819 ROACH	
10	3749 WATSON	4055 SULTAN	4701 BARBEE	
11	1081 DAVIS	6793 SANDS	7456 PIKE	
12	6621 VERA (9)	5432 ANDERSON (10)	6452 SHOR (10)	
13	1593 BOWER	2647 SPENCER	6115 GOLDMAN	
14	7408 WORTH	7101 TALLMAN (13)		
15	3822 ALLEN	4519 KLEIN		
16	1256 TYSON			
17	3416 FELDMAN			

- Key is the Student ID # (SID)
- Hash function: (Key MOD 17) + 1
- Overflow handling: Sequential Spill
- Entries in ( ) are home block addresses for overflow records

Fig 2-11   Example of Hashed File Organization

also decrease. This is the answer to question 1. To understand why, consider a room partitioned into 1,250 buckets, each with a capacity for 10 balls. Ten thousand balls are randomly tossed into the buckets. If a ball lands in a full bucket, it is placed aside—in overflow. Now suppose we double the number of buckets and hence the amount of room. Clearly the chance that a ball will land in a full bucket is decreased.

To answer question 2, consider keeping the total capacity of all buckets constant by changing the capacity of each bucket to 100 balls but reducing the number to 125. How will this impact the number of overflows? Again, the number of overflows will decrease. To convince yourself, take the extreme case of a single bucket with a capacity of 12,500. Clearly there will be zero overflow in this case.

BLOCK SIZE	LOAD FACTOR									
	0.1	0.2	0.3	0.4	0.5	0.6	0.7	0.8	0.9	1.0
1	4.84	9.37	13.61	17.58	21.32	24.80	28.08	31.17	34.06	36.79
2	0.60	2.19	4.49	7.27	10.36	13.65	17.03	20.43	23.79	27.07
3	0.09	0.63	1.80	3.61	5.99	8.32	11.99	15.37	18.87	22.40
4	0.02	0.20	0.79	1.96	3.76	6.15	9.05	12.32	15.86	19.54
5	0.00	0.07	0.37	1.12	2.48	4.49	7.11	10.26	13.78	17.55
6		0.02	0.18	0.67	1.69	3.38	5.75	8.75	12.24	16.06
7		0.01	0.09	0.41	1.18	2.60	4.74	7.60	11.04	14.90
8		0.00	0.05	0.25	0.84	2.03	3.97	6.68	10.07	13.96
9			0.02	0.16	0.61	1.61	3.36	5.94	9.27	13.18
10			0.01	0.10	0.44	1.29	2.88	5.32	8.59	12.51
11			0.01	0.07	0.33	1.04	2.48	4.80	8.01	11.94
12			0.00	0.04	0.24	0.85	2.15	4.36	7.51	11.44
14				0.02	0.14	0.57	1.65	3.64	6.67	10.60
16				0.01	0.08	0.39	1.28	3.09	6.00	9.92
18				0.00	0.05	0.28	1.01	2.65	5.45	9.36
20					0.03	0.20	0.81	2.30	4.99	8.88
25					0.01	0.09	0.48	1.65	4.10	7.95
30					0.00	0.04	0.29	1.23	3.47	7.26
35						0.02	0.18	0.94	2.98	6.73
40						0.01	0.12	0.73	2.60	6.29
50						0.00	0.05	0.45	2.04	5.63
60							0.02	0.30	1.65	5.14
70							0.01	0.20	1.37	4.76
80							0.01	0.13	1.14	4.46
90							0.00	0.09	0.97	4.20
100								0.06	0.83	3.99

Fig 2-12   Percent Record Overflow as a Function of Load Factor and Block Size

Figure 2–12 illustrates the impact of block capacity and load factor on expected overflow. This graph makes it clear that a low load factor and a large block capacity reduce the probability of overflow. At first sight, we might be led to the conclusion that hashed file design is really quite simple: just select a large value for B and a small load factor. A little reflection shows why this is not a good idea.

First, consider the impact of a low load factor. When a file is created, the cost is in terms of the total file space, not just the space occupied by records. If you create a file with space for 12,500 records you will be charged for 12,500 records even if only 10,000 of the available spaces are full. All available blocks are part of the address space for your file and can't be used by anyone else. Thus, there is a real cost to a low load factor.

Next consider the cost of a large block size. For example, take the extreme of using a single block that will hold the entire file, realizing, of course, that this makes the hashing function rather trivial. The problem is that to find a record, the entire block (which happens to be the whole file) must be read into memory and searched in the same way as a sequential file.

It is obvious, therefore, that there are tradeoffs between the blocking and load factors. From the data in Figure 2–12, we see that blockings of over five and load factors of 80 percent or less produce overflow of under 10 percent, which is generally viewed as acceptable. If the overflow records are retrievable in one extra disk access, then the expected number of accesses to a record will be 1.1, since 90 percent of the records require one access and 10 percent require two—one to determine that overflow exists, and one to retrieve the record. Actual performance may be only slightly poorer than this.

Overflow Handling

There are a number of different schemes for handling overflow. The example of Figure 2–11 uses a simple method called *sequential spill*. In sequential spill, if a record is hashed to a block that is full, we sequentially search forward until a less-than-full block is found and store the record there. The same approach is used during retrieval. If a record is not found in its home block, search ahead until either it is found or a less-than-full block is found, indicating that a record with the desired key does not exist. This method for handling overflow is also called *progressive overflow*.

Referring again to Figure 2–11, the 36 records are hashed into 17 blocks of capacity 3. This is a load factor of 71 percent. To find a record that is not in its home address requires a forward sequential search from its home address. For example, the record with key 6621 hashes to address 9. Block 9 is accessed and searched for this key. It is not present, so blocks at sequentially higher addresses are accessed and searched unitl the records are found in block 12.

The expected performance of the sequential spill method is illustrated in Figure 2–13 where the expected number of accesses is plotted against the load factor for various blockings. For example, with a blocking of 5 and an 80 percent load factor, the expected number of accesses will be about 1.3. With a blocking of 10 or lower, and as load factors increase above 80 to 85 percent, performance deteriorates rapidly. This explains our earlier claim that it is typical to allocate about 20 percent extra space for hashed files.

There are better, but more complicted overflow handling methods. Figure 2–14 graphs the expected performance for a method called *chained overflow*. This method uses pointers to connect the home block to its overflow records. Furthermore, the scheme uses separate overflow blocks. That accounts for the fact that the load factor may be over 100 percent. (The separate overflow blocks are not included in the denominator when computing the load factor.) This type of scheme is the overflow handling method most often used.

Hashed File Processing

The preceding discussion covered operations such as retrieval of a single record by key and record addition. For the sake of completeness, we will review and expand on these operations and cover additional common operations. The following sections include:

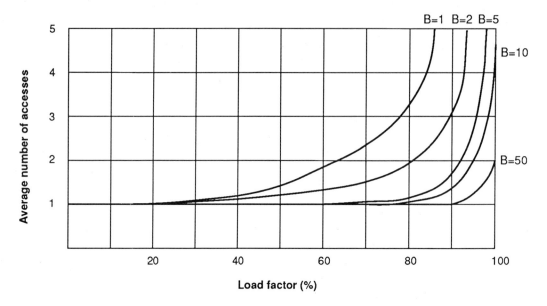

Fig 2-13 Expected number of disk accesses as a function of load factor and blocking, B, for hashed files with overflow handled by sequential spill

- retrieval of a single record by specified key value
- addition of a record
- deletion of a record

Single-Record Retrieval. The key is hashed to a block address and that block is then retrieved. Records within the block are then examined for a match. If the record is not found, additional blocks are accessed until either a match is found or it is established that the record does not exist. The process to locate records in overflow will depend on the overflow handling method. It may involve searching sequentially through blocks, or following a series of pointers that make up a linked list or chain.

Record Addition. The record key is hashed and the home block is accessed. If there is room in the block, the record is added and the block is written back to disk—a total of two disk accesses, one read, and one write. However, if the block is full, then the overflow handling procedure comes into operation to find an available location. In some cases a new block may be added to the file to store the record, and the home block will point to the added block. This bears a crude resemblance to block splitting in B-trees.

Record Deletion. The record is first located as if it is to be retrieved. Depending on the overflow handling scheme, it may be possible to delete the record and make the space available for a subsequent addition. In some cases the record is only marked as deleted. Subsequent file reorganization may be necessary to recover the space occupied by logically deleted but physically present records.

Reorganization Requirements

Conventional hashed files require periodic reorganization with growth. Figure 2–15 illustrates how random access performance deteriorates as a hashed file grows, creating the

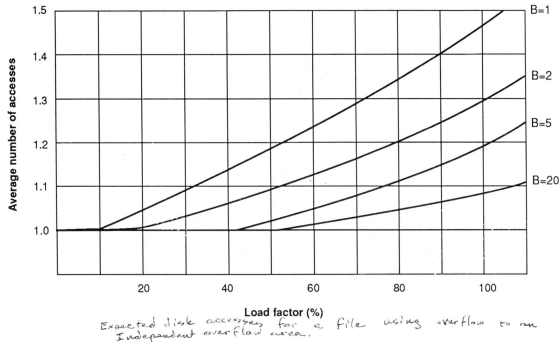

Expected disk accesses for a file using overflow to an
independent overflow area.

Fig 2-14   Performance of a Hashed File with Growth and Periodic Reorganizations

need for periodic reorganization. As the file grows, its expected number of accesses increases because of the increased number of records in overflow. Hashed files have no dynamic reorganization scheme comparable to block splitting in B+trees.

The need for reorganization is a major drawback of the hashed file organization if file growth is significant. It becomes even more of a problem if there is no time to perform the reorganization. For example, it would be extremely difficult to reorganize the files in an application such as an airline reservation system that must be on-line 24 hours a day, seven days a week.

Hashed Indexes

Hashing can also be used to construct a more efficient secondary index. The secondary key is hashed to a block that contains the secondary and primary keys. This type of hashed index provides close to two-access performance to a file via a secondary index— one access to the hashed index, one to the data file.

Extendible Hashed File

Several clever schemes have been developed in the last few years that allow hashed files to dynamically reorganize themselves. These schemes have not yet been implemented in commercial software, but they can be expected to appear soon.

Hashed File Summary

Hashed files provide fast access to single records. With a given blocking and load factor, the expected number of accesses is independent of the number of records. Files of 10,000 records or 10 million records will each have the same number of expected accesses if they

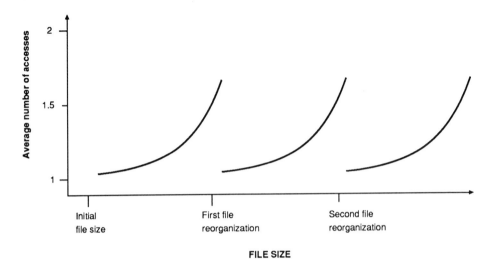

Fig 2-15 Expected Number of Disk Accesses for a File Using Overflow to an Independent Overflow area

have the same blocking, load factor, and overflow handling method. This insensitivity of number of accesses to file size holds for very few file organizations. In fact, hashing is the only practical organization for which it holds.

Hashed files do have several drawbacks, however: they do not support range searches; sequential processing is more complex than for other organizations; and they require reorganization with growth.

Hashed files are most attractive when the following conditions are met:

1. File growth is non-existent to moderate, or else off-hour time is available for reorganization.

2. Very rapid access is needed.

3. The predominance of access is random rather than sequential.

4. Records are small to moderate in size.

5. There are a large number of records.

6. Range search capabilities are not needed.

Summary and Comparison of File Organizations

The table shown in Figure 2–16 summarizes and compares the major file organization methods. As you can see, no method is dominant. That is, each method has at least one important feature in which it excels. Hashed organizations are the best method for single-record processing performance, while sequential methods prevail in processing large subsets and in having no storage overhead. However, as noted earlier, the B+tree-based indexing organization is never very inferior to the best method. If you have to select a single method to use for all files, it is almost always the best choice.

Summary and comparison of major file organization methods

Criterion	File Organization		
	Sequential	Indexed	Hashed
Processing time for:			
Single record	Very poor	Very good	Excellent
Small subset (1%)	Poor	Good (1)	Fair (1)
Mod. subset (10%)	Fair	Good (2)	Fair (1)
Large subset	Excellent	Very Good (3)	Good (1)
Relationship of proc. time to file size (4)	Linear	Logarithmic	Constant
Range search?	No	Yes	No
Space overhead	Zero	10-30%	10-30%
Reorganization required?	Inherent in update process	Very seldom	Frequent with high growth
Backup needed	Inherent in update process	Yes	Yes
Complexity of structure & software	Low	Moderate	Moderate
Storage devices	Tape or DASD (5)	DASD only	DASD only

Notes:
(1) Assumes transactions (or queries) are sorted by file key or hash of file key (as appropriate) prior to processing.
(2) Assumes transactions or queries are sorted by file key and skip sequential processing is used.
(3) Assumes transactions or queries are sorted by file key and sequential processing is used.
(4) Time to access a single record increases directly (linearly) with the number of records, N, for a sequential file, with the log of N for indexed files, and is independent of N for hashed files.
(5) Direct access storage device

Fig 2-16   Summary and Comparison of Major File Organizations

Over time, more and more files will be implemented using direct-access organization. This reflects, of course, the increasing prevalence of on-line systems with their requirement for rapid direct access. Furthermore, as hardware costs decline, the cost of storage space overhead for direct-access organizations also declines. Better operating system software and faster processors encourage the use of more complex organizations, including the increased use of secondary indexes. Finally, the increased emphasis on decision-support applications results in a higher proportion of ad-hoc queries, which often need secondary indexes for efficient processing.

The file organizations described in this chapter are the most common methods but they hardly exhaust the available choices. Many schemes have been developed for rather specialized applications such as searching huge databases of bibliographic data or searching for occurrences of specific character strings in text. Another important, although somewhat limited-purpose method is based on so-called list structures. These are outlined in the next section.

File Organizations Using Linked Lists

Linked List Structure

A linked list is a structure in which each element has a pointer (link) to the next element. In a file system, the element is a record and the pointer is the address of the next record. Records are linked together for one or both of the following two reasons: to create a set of records (those on a common linked list) that have a similar characteristic or to organize the records into some order. In addition to a link from one record to the next, a linked list must also have a pointer to the first record in the set—the so-called list head. Linked lists are also called *chains*.

Figure 2–17 illustrates the use of linked lists for a subset of STUDENT records. For simplicity, only the SID, SLEVEL, and AGE data items plus the link are shown. The links indicate the block number and record within the block; for example, a link value of 4.3 indicates block 4, third record in the block. The linked list in this example is used to both group records by SLEVEL and order records within SLEVEL by AGE. A list head points to the first record for each group of records with given value of SLEVEL. Let's consider the linked list for SLEVEL = 2. The list head points to the fourth record of block 5. That record points to the second record of block 2 which, in turn, points to the second record of block 5. The second record of block 2 points to the second record of block 4, which is the last record on the linked list indicated by its link value is 0. This linked list not only creates a set of all SLEVEL=2 records but the records are also linked in ascending order of age: 19, 20, 20, 24.

Applications and Functions of Linked Lists

A linked list serves the same function as a dense index as seen by the illustration of Figure 2–17. This application allows the DBMS to directly access all STUDENT records of given SLEVEL much as the index of Figure 2–7 provided an index on SLEVEL. The difference between the two structures is, in fact, quite small from one perspective. If the pointers of the linked list are changed to symbolic pointers (SID values) and removed from the records being collected along with the list head, the linked list is transformed into a dense index. Note that since we have used a somewhat larger set of records for Figure 2–7 than for Figure 2–17, performing this transformation on the linked list will create a subset of the entries in the index of Figure 2–7. The set of SIDs for SLEVEL=2 in Figure 2–7 is 4494, 7101, 1734, 4055, 4519, 7456, 3438, 6621. The set of SIDs for SLEVEL=2 in Figure 2–7 is 4494, 4055, 1734, 3438.

Therefore, both linked lists and indexes create *access paths*—ways of retrieving records of some characteristic without resorting to a sequential scan of the file. Linked lists use so-called *embedded* pointers because the pointers are stored in the records; indexes of the B+tree form use *non-embedded* pointers.

One of the most prevalent applications of linked lists in databases is to create sets of records which have "master-detail" or "parent-child" relationships. In the GSL database, a BANK (parent) record is related to zero or more LOAN (child) records. There are several ways to represent this relationship. Simply including the BID of the BANK in the LOAN record captures this relationship. Another way is to create a linked list of all LOAN records belonging to a given bank. In this case the list head usually resides in the BANK record. This is simply another example of using a linked list to group records that have some

BLOCK	SID	SLEVEL	AGE	LINK	LIST HEADS	
					SLEVEL	POINTER
1	1081	3	22	4.3		
	1147	5	37	0	1	3.1
	1256	5	24	4.1	2	5.4
	1533	1	19	3.4	3	3.2
					4	2.4
2	1593	4	23	2.3	5	1.3
	1734	2	20	4.2		
	2080	4	25	5.3		
	2368	4	23	2.1		
3	2647	1	18	1.4		
	2948	3	20	3.3		
	3136	3	21	1.1		
	3281	1	19	4.4		
4	3416	5	26	1.2		
	3438	2	24	0		
	3609	3	40	0		
	3749	1	20	5.1		
5	3822	1	21	0		
	4055	2	20	2.2		
	4491	4	29	0		
	4494	2	19	5.2		

Fig 2-17   Example STUDENT File with Linked-List on SLEVEL. Records are ordered within SLEVEL by AGE.

common characteristic: in this case, the common characteristic is that all the records on the linked list belong to the same bank. Of course, LOAN records for a given bank may then also be ordered on some attribute; for example, in descending order by LDATE so that the bank's most recent LOAN record appears first on the chain.

Figure 2–18 illustrates a single linked list occurrence with BANK Fidelity as the owner record and a set of LOAN records. This figure also illustrates two-way pointers and a form of linked list called a *ring*. A two-way linked list allows moving through the records in either order. It also makes it easy to add a record to the end of the linked list. And, it simplifies deleting a record from the linked list if the record is accessed via other than its owner as discussed in the section below.

Record Retrieval and Physical Organization of a Linked List

The retrieval performance of a linked list depends critically on the *physical* ordering of the records. As seen in Figure 2–17, the records there are physically ordered by SID as they might be if the STUDENT file were organized as a non-dense B+tree file with key SID. There is no physical order by SLEVEL. Thus, to access all STUDENT records of given

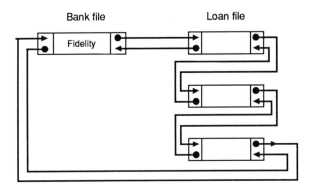

Fig 2-18 *Two-way Linked Lists as Rings*

SLEVEL value we would expect to have to make essentially one disk access per record plus the accesses to retrieve the list head.

In some cases the file on which a linked list is constructed may have no pre-determined physical ordering. That is, the records are not forced into some order by, say, a primary key B+tree or by hashing. In this case we may want to try and keep the records in a physical order that corresponds to the logical ordering of the chains. This is called *clustering*. Figure 2–19 illustrates the records of Figure 2–17, this time clustered on SLEVEL and within SLEVEL on AGE.

Now, retrieval of all records of common SLEVEL value requires about n/B + 1 disk accesses where n is the number of records of common SLEVEL value. (Again, we must add the number of accesses required to determine the list-head pointer value.) For example, to retrieve the four records with SLEVEL=2 requires two disk accesses after list-head retrieval.

As noted, we must also consider the accesses required to retrieve the list head. The list-head access may involve access to a directory of key:pointer pairs as in Figure 2–17 or access to the parent record that contains the list head as would be the case in Figure 2–18. In either event, it is important to realize that access to the list-head pointers may involve one or more disk accesses. For example, to retrieve all loans for a given bank could involve two to three accesses to retrieve the BANK record if the BANK file is structured using a B+tree index.

Adding and Deleting Records

Consider first the case of a one-way (as opposed to two-way) linked-list structure. If there is no prescribed order to the records on a chain, then the easiest place to add a record is at the beginning. The pointer in the added record is first set to the value of the list-head pointer, then the list-head pointer is updated to point to the added record. Figure 2–20 shows relevant blocks from Figure 2–17 and the resulting changes in pointers with the addition of a new record at location 6.1 with SID = 8888, SLEVEL=3, AGE=24. In this case we have not maintained the required ordering of records by AGE within SLEVEL.

BLOCK	SID	SLEVEL	AGE	LINK	LIST HEADS SLEVEL	POINTER
1	2647	1	18	1.2		
	1533	1	19	1.3	1	1.1
	3281	1	19	1.4	2	2.2
	3749	1	20	2.1	3	3.2
					4	4.2
2	3822	1	21	0	5	5.2
	4494	2	19	2.3		
	1734	2	20	2.4		
	4055	2	20	3.1		
3	3438	2	24	0		
	2948	3	20	3.3		
	3136	3	21	3.4		
	1081	3	22	4.1		
4	3609	3	40	0		
	1593	4	23	4.3		
	2368	4	23	4.4		
	2080	4	25	5.1		
5	4491	4	29	0		
	1256	5	24	5.3		
	3416	5	26	5.4		
	1147	5	37	0		

Fig 2-19   STUDENT File with Linked-List Structure on SLEVEL with Physical Order on SLEVEL and AGE

If an ordering is to be maintained within the records in a chain, then the update is more difficult. We must first locate the proper logical position for the addition. This requires searching the linked list for the first occurrence of a record with (in this case) AGE >= 24. Then, the pointer of the previous record is updated to effectively insert the new record in its proper sequence. You should work out the process for adding the above record in proper order.

The number of disk accesses for an addition will depend on two factors—whether the chain has an ordering and, if it does, whether or not the records are clustered. If records have logical order and are clustered, then the number of disk accesses to find the proper place for insertion will average about 0.5*n/B + 1 where n is the number of records on the chain. If the records are not clustered, addition will require an average of 0.5*n + 1 accesses.

When a record is added to a clustered linked list we (or the DBMS) will try to find an open space which at least comes close to maintaining the desired physical order. This may not be possible without shifting existing records and, therefore, adjusting a number of pointers. Many DBMSs will only try to place an added record close to other members of its chain. To restore correspondence between physical and logical ordering the database must be reorganized.

BLOCK	SID	SLEVEL	AGE	LINK	LIST HEADS	
					SLEVEL	POINTER
3	2647	1	18	1.4		
	2948	3	20	3.3	*3*	*6.1*
	3136	3	21	1.1		
	3281	1	19	4.4		
6	*8888*	*3*	*24*	*3.2*		

Fig 2-20   Impact of Addition of a Record to the Beginning of a Linked-List. Updates are shown in italics.

Deleting a record requires first finding the record to be deleted, then updating the pointer of the previous record to the value of the pointer of the deleted record. Deletion can be complex, especially if the deleted record is located by other than traversal of its linked list. Suppose, for example, that the STUDENT record with SID=1533 is to be deleted from the file of Figure 2–17. If the record is accessed by, say, a B+tree index on SID, we have no direct way of knowing which record points to it. The SLEVEL value of 1 tells us which chain the record is on, and we could now search this chain to determine which record points to the deleted record. (From the figure you can see that this is the record at location 3.1.) In some DBMSs the deleted record will be left in place and only marked as deleted. It is left in place to preserve the chain which passes through it. Deleted records are physically removed by a database reorganization.

As we noted above, the presence of two-way pointers can reduce the difficulty of deletion. This is because the two-way pointers tell us not only the location of the following record but also the preceding record. While more pointers must be changed, accesses to the records that must be modified are direct—no further search is required.

Other Characteristics and Features of Linked Lists

As you might expect, if you can have records chained by one characteristic (for example, SLEVEL or BID) you may have them chained by additional characteristics. In the GSL database, LOAN records could be linked by their BANK owner and separately linked by their STUDENT owner. Thus, (with one-way chains) each LOAN record would contain two pointers—one pointing to the next LOAN for given STUDENT owner and the other pointing to the next LOAN for given BANK owner. This is analogous to creating two secondary (dense) indexes to LOAN records, one on SID and the other on BID. Additional chains could be added, for example, to link loans by common year value of LDATE.

When records are linked due to parent-child relationships, the parent identifier in the child record is redundant. For example, if LOAN records are chained by student with list head in the parent STUDENT record, then, strictly speaking, we do not need to store the SID in the LOAN. However, unless access is always to the child (LOAN) record through its parent (STUDENT), eliminating the parent's key (SID) from the LOAN can make it quite expensive to determine its value. For example, suppose we suppress both SID and BID from the LOAN record (and LOANs are on two chains by STUDENT and BANK). If a LOAN record is accessed via its parent STUDENT, the SID will be known but the BID value will not (and vice versa). Therefore, suppressing the parent key values must be done with care.

Linked Lists vs. Indexes

As we have noted, linked lists and dense indexes are topologically analogous. A linked list can be transformed into a dense index by moving the embedded record pointers into the record or directory which stores the list head. The opposite transformation may be performed to transform a dense index into a linked list. While linked lists typically use pointers directly to record location, if the records have a primary index or are hashed on an identifier, this identifier may replace the linked list pointers (turning them into symbolic pointers—the common type of pointer used in a dense index). Since there is an equivalence between the two structures, what are the advantages and disadvantages of each?

The B+tree index has evolved as the generally superior structure—it is more robust. Update of B+tree indexes usually requires the same or fewer disk accesses than update of linked lists. The B+tree performance is better for deletions. (Some of the problems with deletion of records on linked lists were noted earlier.)

Retrieval performance of a B+tree index is usually as good, or almost as good, as the retrieval performance of a linked list. In some cases it may be better. A situation where linked list performance is superior is illustrated by a query which requests a STUDENT record and all related LOAN records. The performances of the linked list and B+tree index are as follows:

- Linked List. With a list head stored in the STUDENT record, no additional accesses are required to know the location of the first LOAN record. Each subsequent LOAN record retrieval will take one access unless they are clustered by SID.
- B+tree INDEX on SID. To detemine the location of the first LOAN requires a search of the index. This could be expected to require two to three disk accesses. These accesses would yield not only the pointer to the first LOAN record but, more than likely, pointers to all LOAN records for this student. Therefore, one added access would be required for each LOAN record.

Therefore, the added cost of the B+tree index is the two to three extra accesses needed to retrieve the LOAN pointers. After these pointers are retrieved, the performance is the same, assuming both structures use the same type of pointers (symbolic or direct) and the LOAN file has the same physical ordering (clustered on SID or not).

While this example illustrates a potential advantage of the linked list, it is not easy to describe a situation where the B+tree will have an advantage. Suppose, for example, that we want to retrieve all LOAN records for a given STUDENT but do not want to retrieve the STUDENT record. In this case the overhead of retrieving the STUDENT record to determine the list head may more than offset the index search time for the B+tree structure.

The issue of which structure is superior may best be decided by looking at industry trends. Older DBMSs, those of the so-called network and hierarchical variety, make extensive use of linked-list structures. The newer (relational) systems employ B+tree based structures almost exclusively.

Conclusion

There are several reasons for understanding physical file structures:

- To appreciate some of the inner workings of a DBMS—the methods and processes used to organize, retrieve, and update data. In many DBMSs it is necessary to understand the performance of various structures in order to code efficient retrievals.
- To provide a basis for physical database design. While the DBMS takes over many tasks previously left to the programmer, many of the choices of physical structures are left to the database administrator.
- To assist in the selection and evaluation of a DBMS. At some point you may be called on to evaluate alternative database management software with the objective of acquiring a new package. One of the evaluation criterion will involve the physical structures supported by the various DBMSs being considered.

Physical database organization will be discussed again in subsequent chapters which present various commercial DBMSs such as ORACLE, INGRES, RBASE, IDMS, and IMS. Chapter 13 will draw heavily on this chapter in its discussion of physical database design.

Questions and Problems

Questions

1. What are some of the factors that affect the selection of a file structure for a particular DBMS?

2. What file organization is often used for periodic backups? Why?

3. What is *blocking*?

4. Why is it impractical if not impossible to store all of an organization's records in main memory? Even if all the records from a file could be stored in main memory, why would there also be a copy on a secondary storage device?

5. Describe the *data hierarchy*.

6. What are some standard data types?

7. Describe the most commonly used file organizations. What are some of the advantages and disadvantages of each?

8. What are the different ways in which indexes can be used?

9. Define a *fully inverted file*.

10. Define *primary*, *secondary*, and *composite key indexes*.

11. What are the impacts of blocking and load factors on performance and space use of a hashed file?

12. Since an index usually points to a relative sector (block) and a hash function produces a relative block number, how is this relative number translated into the actual sector address on the proper storage device?

13. What are the advantages and disadvantages of larger block sizes? What are the factors that influence the choice of block size?

14. What are the factors that discourage implementing a large number of secondary indexes for a file?

15. Why do indexes have multiple levels? (In other words, why not just implement an index as a sequential file?)

16. Can a hashed file have a secondary index? For example, suppose our Student file is hashed on SID and we also want direct access by Name. What would such a secondary index look like?

Problems

The following files are used in many of these problems:

STUDENT with 5-byte key SID, 15-byte Name, and 200-byte total record length. Current file size is 1 million records.

LOAN with 5-byte key LID, 5-byte SID, 12-byte BANKID. Total record size of 150 bytes. Current file size is 3 million records.

1. Consider the disk device described in this chapter. (The device has tracks of 48,000 bytes, 1770 cylinders, 15 surfaces, and a sector overhead of 500 bytes.) Determine the number of cylinders required to store the Student file if records are blocked at (a) 5 per sector; (b) 20 per sector.

2. If the device storing the Student file has random access time of 25 milliseconds to a desired sector and can then transfer a block at the rate of 1000 bytes per millisecond, what is the amount of time to random access a sector if records are blocked at (a) 5 per sector; (b) 20 per sector.

3. Estimate the size in bytes of the lowest level of a primary (non-dense) index on SID to Student, assuming that data and index blocks are 75 percent full and that the index pointer (to a disk sector) requires 4 bytes. Assume the record blocking is 20.

4. Estimate the size of the lowest level of a secondary (dense) index on Name to Student records assuming that the index blocks are 75 percent full.

5. Suppose the Student file is organized as a primary-indexed (B+ tree) file on SID with a secondary index on Name. The secondary index uses a symbolic pointer (SID). The primary index has three levels; the secondary index has four levels. The top levels of both indexes are in main memory.

   a. How many disk accesses are required to retrieve a student by SID?

   b. How many disk accesses are required to retrieve a student by Name (assuming a unique name)?

   c. Suppose that 10 students have the same name: SMITH, JAMES L. They are, of course, not in physical proximity on the disk. How many accesses are needed to retrieve all 10? (Keep in mind that the Name index is in order by name. Thus, the answer to this problem is not simply 10 times the correct answer to part b).

   d. How many disk accesses are required to add a new record, assuming no blocks overflow (that is, no block splits are required)?

6. Refer to Figure 2–8. Show the impact of adding, in turn, four records with SIDs 3396, 1818, 4600, and 6992.

7. Consider the Student file. Which file organization would be best in each of the following situations? If you recommend a direct organization (indexed or hashed), indicate the primary index key, any secondary keys, the hashed key, etc., as appropriate.

   a. The file is almost always processed sequentially but has occasional on-line access by SID.

   b. The file has considerable on-line access by SID. Very fast retrieval is desired, file growth is low.

   c. The file has considerable growth, frequent on-line access by SID, and less frequent on-line access by name.

8. The Loan file has a three-level primary index on the (non-unique) data item, SID. It has a four-level secondary index on LID and another four-level secondary index on BID. Assume that a secondary index has direct sector pointers (that is, symbolic pointers are not used). Loan records are blocked at 20.

   a. How many disk accesses are necessary to retrieve all Loans for a given student assuming the individual has three loans?

   b. How many disk accesses are necessary to retrieve all Loan records for a given BID if the bank has 1000 loans?

9. Assume that the Student file is hashed on SID. Overflow is handled by chaining in a separate area. Records are blocked at 10.

   a. If records are blocked at 5 and the load factor is 90 percent, what is the average number of accesses to a given record?

   b. If the load factor is 90 percent, estimate the minimum blocking that will ensure an average of 1.1 accesses per record.

   c. Suppose the file grows at 1 percent per month. Blocking is 20 and the load factor is initialized at 80 percent. The expected number of accesses is to be a maximum of 1.1. As the file grows (N increases), its load factor also increases, which results in an increase in average accesses. When the average reaches 1.1 accesses, the file is reloaded using a load factor of 80 percent. About how often will the file need to be reorganized? What could be done to reduce the frequency of reorganization (assuming the constraint of 1.1 maximum average accesses)?

10. This problem demonstrates why a sequential file scan is sometimes faster than using an index or linked list. Thus, it also demonstrates why these structures can waste both file space and I/O time. The problem is to retrieve all Freshmen (SLEVEL = 1); assume this amounts to 10 percent of the records in the file. A linked list exists that chains all of the Freshmen records together. This linked list is in no particular logical or physical order. Thus, each next-record access costs a random disk access. A random access plus transfer requires 30 milliseconds.

   For sequential scan, assume each block contains 20 records and each block access averages 10 milliseconds for access and transfer. (This may seem slightly pessimistic, but it allows for the possibility that a disk rotation may occasionally be required to access the next block.)

    a. Compare the total time to randomly access all Freshman records (10 percent of the records in the file) versus full sequential scan of all records.

    b. Assuming that all access times remain constant, what is the blocking at which the two methods require the same total time? (You might first try a few blocking values, for example, 10, then 5, to see how times compare. Then develop a formula that lets you solve for the blocking at which the two methods are equal.)

    c. As you should have discovered, unless the blocking is quite small, the full file scan is cheaper. Thus, we can also say that the linked list would be useful only if records were very _____ (small or large?)

11. The following method provides a reasonable estimate for the number of levels, L, in a primary B+ tree index: Find the smallest integer L such that $(0.75*Bi)^L \geq N/(0.75*B)$ where N is the number of records, Bi is the number of index entries in an index block, and B is the number of records in a data block. The factor 0.75 reflects the fact that due to block splitting, blocks are not full. Assume for the Student file that $B = 20$, $Bi = 133$. What is L? (Hint: Compute $0.75*Bi$ and $N/(0.75*B)$. Then, try increasing values of L starting at 1 until you determine the answer.)

12. If you are familiar with "binary search," try to answer the following. (Answers to these problems should give you an appreciation of why indexes are tree structured.)

    a. Estimate the average number of accesses to a record in the Student file by SID assuming that the file is in order by SID. Remember, the unit of access is a sector that contains 20 records. Searching within a sector requires no accesses.

    b. Suppose that the Student file has an index but it is a flat (one-level) index. Each index block contains 100 (SID-pointer) entries; each record block contains 20 records (in order by SID). Now, if the index is binary searched to yield a pointer to a record block, estimate the total number of disk accesses to a record by SID.

13. An important reason for using two-way chains is that they can speed record deletion. Consider, for example, the GSL Student, Loan, and Bank files with one-way chains from Student to Loan and Bank to Loan. If a Loan record is accessed by traversing the Student-Loan chain and then deleted, why is it difficult to remove it from the Bank-Loan chain? How would the two-way chain facilitate this deletion?

References

Bradley, J. *Introduction to File Management in Business.* 2d ed. New York: Holt, Rinehart and Winston, 1987.

Claybrook, B. G. *File Management Techniques.* New York: John Wiley & Sons, 1983.

Comer, D. "The Ubiquitous B-tree." *ACM Computing Surveys,* vol. 1, (June 1979), pp. 121–138.

Enbody, R. J., and Du, H. C. "Dynamic Hashing Schemes." *ACM Computing Surveys,* vol. 20, no. 2 (June 1988), pp. 85–114.

Fagin, R.; Nieverfelt, J.; Pippenger, N.; and Strong, H. "Extendible Hashing—a Fast Access Method for Dynamic Files." *ACM TODS,* vol. 4, no. 3 (Sept. 1979), pp. 315–344.

Larson, P. A. "Linear Hashing with Overflow Handling by Linear Probing." *ACM Transactions on Database Systems*, vol. 10, no. 1 (1985), pp. 75–89.

Loomis, M.E.S. *Data Management and File Structures.* 2d ed. Englewood Cliffs, N.J.: Prentice-Hall, 1989.

Martin, J. *Computer Data-Base Organization.* 2d ed. Englewood Cliffs, N.J.: Prentice-Hall, 1977.

Peterson, W. W. "Addressing for Random Access Storage." *IBM Journal of R & D.*, vol. 1, no. 2 (1957), pp. 130–146.

Teorey, T. J. and Fry, J. P. *Design of Database Structures.* Englewood Cliffs, N.J.: Prentice-Hall, 1982.

Tharp, A. L. *File Organization and Processing.* New York: John Wiley & Sons, 1988.

3 Data Levels and DBMS System Architecture

The objective of this chapter is threefold: (1) to introduce the concepts of data levels, (2) to show how a DBMS implements the levels, and (3) to give an overview and examples of how various DBMS data manipulation languages (DMLs) work. From this, you will see where subsequent chapters are heading. Due to the importance of this information for understanding database systems, the reader is encouraged to read it twice: once in sequence and then again near the end of the course. This chapter in particular may prove useful as a review or summary.

The concept of levels (or realms, or views) of data is defined in this chapter. We see how four levels can be used to describe data: the real level, the external level, the conceptual (or logical) level, and the internal level. The *real level* is not part of the actual database but consists of the actual entities, their properties, and relationships; in other words, the real level is the "information reality" of the company or organization. The *external level* defines the view of the database provided to each user. The *conceptual*, or *logical*, *level* describes how the real information structure is represented by a particular data model and DBMS. The *internal level* represents the physical organization of the data and storage media.

In this chapter we see how the three levels (external, conceptual/logical, and internal) are incorporated into a DBMS with mappings specified by the subschema (or view) for the external level, the schema for the conceptual level, and the internal data storage description language (or device media control language) for the physical level.

The architecture, components, and flow of control for a DBMS are discussed next. The DBMS languages are described. The DML operations are outlined, and the flow of control is described for an inquiry. The interaction between the user program, the DBMS, and the operating system and how the DBMS uses the schema and subschema are described.

The chapter concludes by showing how the GSL database is represented by the three major conceptual data models: hierarchic, network, and relational. Examples of the data manipulation language for each data model are illustrated.

Brief outlines are given of other software components of the DBMS: various utilities and ancillary packages for communications, report generation, and graphics generation. We see how the DBMS is used as the core for many of the so-called fourth-generation languages. Software systems that began as DBMSs have now been enhanced with such a wide variety of packages and features that they have evolved into complete system-development tools.

The Three Levels of Database Architecture

Figure 3–1 shows the ANSI/SPARC (American National Standards Institute/Standards Planning and Requirements Committee) model of a database, which is based on three levels of abstraction. These levels provide external, conceptual, and internal views of the database. The *external level* is concerned with the way a particular user sees the data he or she is interested in. Since individual users are likely to need their own individual view of specific

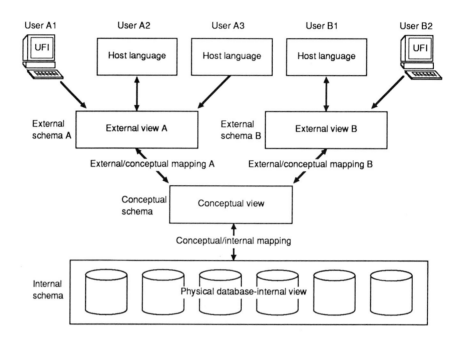

Fig 3-1 Three Levels of a Database

small sections of the data, there will usually be many different external views. The *conceptual level* provides a single overall, logical view of the entire database. This includes the union of all the user external levels. The *internal level* provides a single view of the way the data is physically stored in the database. This view is more or less hidden from the end-user, and may only be partially revealed to the system analyst/programmer, but is quite evident to the database administrator.

Reality

Reality consists of the things and events described by the information in the database. This includes the organization and its components, such as employees, facilities, and activities, and the environment in which it operates. The *environment* consists of everything that influences the organization or is influenced by the organization. Before a database can be used to store information about an organization, it is necessary to have a way to describe all of the objects and events that make up the organization.

It should be noted that the real level and the conceptual level differ in that reality is much richer. When mapping reality to the conceptual level we leave out a lot of details in terms of properties that are not included, resulting in less precision in the representation (for example, age is usually represented only by date of birth). We also completely ignore some entity classes, often overwrite when we update (for example, when a student changes his or her address we may not maintain the old address), and lose subtle associations (for example, a student receiving a loan might also be an employee of the federal agency administering the GSL program. While it is sometimes implied that the computer database stores everything, this is obviously not true. Database designers are faced with tough decisions involving (1) what to store, (2) the level of detail, and (3) what data to maintain temporarily rather than as a full history.

Entity

An entity is any object that is relevant to an organization. This can include tangible objects, such as students, teachers, banks, university buildings, and books; intangible objects such as loans, grades, and school histories; or events, such as class schedules, payments, and extra-curricular activities.

Entity Class

An *entity class*, also known as an *entity set* or *entity type*, is a collection of entities, all of which have similar qualities. For example, all of the students in a university belong to a single entity class, STUDENT.

Attributes

Attributes are the properties of individual entities that are relevent to the organization. For example, the attributes recorded for a loan might include loan date, loan amount, and interest rate. The number of attributes in each entity class may range from a few to hundreds. For example, in the GSL database the entity class LOAN PAYMENT would have the attributes of the loan ID, the loan payment amount, and the date on which the payment was received. The entity class STUDENT could have over a hundred attributes, including address, historical data on schools attended, extensive financial information, major, GPA, and so on. When all of the entity classes are taken into account, a large organization would typically have thousands of attributes in its database.

Identifier

An *identifier* is an attribute or combination of attributes that distinguish one entity from all others in its entity class. An identifier is necessary for the user to be able to refer to a particular entity and for the computer to be able to locate information for the entity. For example, a social security number uniquely identifies a person, and a part number uniquely identifies a stock item. In some instances it is necessary to use more than one attribute to identify an entity. For example, since a student may have several loans, to identify a loan payment it is necessary to know the values of both the LID and the PAYMENT_DATE. This assumes that each student will only make one payment on a given loan on a given day.

Relationship

When two entity types are associated, the term *relationship* is used. For example, because a student takes out a loan, relationships exist between students and loans. Relationships may be given a name. For example, we might call the student-loan relationship *holds*. Another relationship in the GSL database is between banks and loans—a bank *makes* a loan.

Relationships themselves occasionally have attributes. For example, suppose a bank can sell a loan to another financial institution. The date of sale might be recorded as an attribute of the relationship between bank and loan.

Entity models

Understanding the information reality of an organization is the first step in database design. Database designers may use one or more of several approaches to describe this reality ranging from an English language description to various formal models such as the extended entity relationship model (the E-ERM) described in Chapter 11. This representation of reality is then transformed into a form acceptable to the DBMS.

Conceptual (or Logical) Level

The *conceptual* or *logical* level is a representation of that subset of reality that is stored in the database. The conceptual view is defined to the DBMS by a *conceptual schema*, using the DBMS's data definition language (*DDL*). The conceptual schema includes definitions for the various types of conceptual records.

The conceptual schema describes how the actual information structure is represented by a particular data model. This model may be hierarchical, network, or relational. Ideally, the conceptual schema will be independent of the manner in which the data is actually stored at the internal level (linked lists, B-trees, etc.).

Internal Level

The internal level is a low-level representation of the entire database consisting of multiple occurrences of multiple types of *internal records*. (Internal record is the ANSI/SPARC term for a stored record.) In most cases, the internal level is still one level removed from the physical level since it usually does not deal in terms of physical records or device-specific properties such as tracks or cylinders. Instead, in most cases, it assumes an infinite linear address space, which is mapped to the physical address space. This mapping provides the bridge between the logical view of the data and the physically stored data. The internal level includes the ordering of records, access paths (indexes, linked lists), and blocking. The language at this level defines how records are grouped, and how the data is to be addressed.

External Level

The external level or view is the level at which individual users see the database. Each user may have a completely different view of the database; consequently, there may be many different external views. For example in the GSL database, the business office would have a view of the database that included the student ID and loan information, while the dean of students would only see the student name and level. Both would be using the same database, but would only see those parts that were applicable to their own tasks.

DBMS Languages and Operation

The Data Sublanguage (DSL): DDL and DML

The data sublanguage (DSL) is the totality of statements used to both define and manipulate a database. One or more data definition languages (DDL) will be available to the database administrator, and to some extent to the users, to define external, conceptual, and internal levels of the database. The other component of the DSL is the language used to manipulate the database—that is, to retrieve, add, delete, and update data. The set of statements for these operations form the Data Manipulation Language (DML). (Note that the reason for *sub* in data *sub* language is that the DDL and DML are often embedded in a standard language such as COBOL or PL/I. Thus, the DDL and DML statements constitute a subset of the full language.)

Data Definition Language (DDL)

A data definition language is a set of commands that is used by database designers to write the schemas (conceptual, external, and internal). The DDL provides for the descriptions of data items, records, primary keys, and record relationships, but it also includes access paths, etc. In some systems the DDL is also used to describe integrity constraints and access controls.

Since the ANSI/SPARC model of a database allows three different views, there are three different schemas, one for each view. Each schema is generally written with a different DDL. It should be noted, however, that these three levels often overlap. This is particularly true of the internal and conceptual levels. For instance, many CODASYL DBMSs include physical aspects in the conceptual schema. SQL-based systems include conceptual and physical definitions in SQL, although the physical definitions are transparent to the user.

DBMS products tend to have their own distinct data definition languages, but there are similarities among families of DBMSs. For example, hierarchical DBMSs use schemas to describe fields, segments, and databases. Network DBMSs use schemas to describe data items, records, sets, and user views (called subschemas), while relational DBMSs describe attributes, domains, relations, and views.

DML Capabilities

Typical *data manipulation language* (DML) commands fall into three broad classifications: data retrieval statements, data modification statements, and control statements. These enable an application programmer or end-user to specify operations such as opening a database; retrieving, modifying, storing, or deleting specific records; and closing the database. As an example, let's look at typical SQL DML commands.

Retrieval commands in SQL include:

SELECT	Retrieves record(s) in a relation;

This command is able to retrieve a unique record, a group of records, and data items from records in more than one relation or file.

Modification commands in SQL include:

INSERT	Inserts a new record or set of records into a relation ;
UPDATE	Changes the values of data in an existing record or set of records;
DELETE	Removes records(s) from a relation;

Control commands in SQL include:

COMMIT	Makes permanent all updates performed since the last COMMIT;
ROLLBACK	Restores the database to the status existing at the time of the last COMMIT;
LOCK	Places concurrent access controls on database tables to prevent simultaneous use or modification of a single record.

DBMS Operation and Data Realms

The DBMS processes a user request in, say, the form of a SQL SELECT statement by using the external, conceptual, and internal schemas to map the user request into the necessary low-level file accesses and data manipulations necessary to materialize the request. A request may be either interpretively processed or compiled (much as an interpretation or compilation is used to convert high-level language source code into machine-level object code). The interpretation or compilation requires, of course, reference to the various schemas in order to produce the proper (machine level) operations.

As an example of this process, consider what is involved in the retrieval of a particular external record. Assume that the external record occurrence will require fields from several conceptual record occurrences. Each conceptual record occurrence may, in turn, require fields from several stored record occurrences. For the DBMS to provide a user with a specified conceptual record occurrence it must first retrieve the necessary stored record occurrences, using whatever access paths are available. From this it constructs the conceptual record occurrences, and from these, the required external record occurrences. Conversions may be required at each stage of this process, including data type conversions.

The Three Data Models

A database representation at the conceptual and external levels falls into one of three major classifications: relational, network, or hierarchical. Representations at both the external and conceptual levels will reflect the particular data model. The internal representation is however, somewhat independent of the data model.

Relational Model

Relational Database Structure

With a relational database, data is organized into *relations* (also called *tables* or *flat files*). Relations are formal mathematical structures and have precise rules for their organization. They will be covered in more depth in Chapter 4.

The rows of a relation are called *tuples* (rhymes with couples), the formal term for row or record. Likewise, columns are known as *attributes*. Figure 3–2 reproduces the example GSL database with labels to illustrate these terms.

Rather than representing associations between tuples with pointers, the relational model represents associations strictly through attributes of relations. For example, the student ID number appears in the Student table and in the Loan table. As you can tell from the example data in Figure 3–2, the student who holds the loan with LID = 92 has SID = 4494. Since the SID attribute also appears in the STUDENT table, you can determine the name of this student (ALTER), age (19), and so forth. Thus, the student ID number provides the relationship between the Student table and the Loan table. Another example of this is the bank ID, where BID provides the relationship between the Loan and the Bank tables.

STUDENT Table

Attributes (columns)

SID	NAME	SLEVEL	AGE	SZIP
9735	ALLEN	1	21	98101
4494	ALTER	2	19	98112
8767	CABEEN	5	24	98118
2368	JONES	4	23	98155
6793	SANDS	1	17	98101
3749	WATSON	5	29	98168

Tuples (rows)

BANK Table

BID	BZIP	TYPE
FIDELITY	98101	MSB
SEAFIRST	98101	BANK
PEOPLES	98109	BANK
CAPITAL	98033	SL
HOME	98031	SL

LOAN Table

LID	LDATE	YEARS	INT_RATE	AMOUNT	SID	BID
27	15-SEP-85	5	8.5	1200	9735	HOME
78	21-JUN-86	5	7.75	1000	9735	PEOPLES
87	07-SEP-83	5	7.0	2000	9735	SEAFIRST
92	12-JAN-85	6	7.5	2100	4494	FIDELITY
99	15-JAN-86	6	9.0	2200	4494	FIDELITY
170	30-APR-83	6	6.5	1900	8767	PEOPLES
490	07-MAY-84	6	6.0	2500	3749	PEOPLES
493	24-JUN-85	7	7.5	3000	3749	PEOPLES

Fig 3-2   Sample Student Loan Database

An important characteristic of the relational approach is that all data is uniformly stored as tables regardless of whether it represents entities or relationships. Pointers are not used to represent associations. As we shall see later, this is not so with hierarchical and network approaches.

DML Operations

A major advantage of having uniformity of data is that it leads to a corresponding uniformity of the operator set. For example, only one operator is needed for each of the basic functions of retrieval, insertion, update, and deletion. The following examples illustrate simple insert, delete, and retrieval operations using the SQL relational DML. These operations are covered in detail in Chapters 4 through 7.

Retrieval

A SQL statement to retrieve student name and age along with loan identifier and amount for graduate students (SLEVEL=5) is written as:

```
SELECT NAME, AGE, LID, AMOUNT
    FROM STUDENT, LOAN
    WHERE SLEVEL = 5
        AND STUDENT.SID = LOAN.SID;
```

The resulting output relation is:

NAME	AGE	LID	AMOUNT
CABEEN	24	170	1900
WATSON	29	490	2500
WATSON	29	493	3000

This query illustrates several features of the relational DML:

· The query states *what* is wanted as opposed to *how* to obtain the result.

· The statement deals with the data on a relation by relation basis as opposed to a record-at-a-time basis.

· The output is also a relation. In fact, the retrieval results could be stored in another relation for subsequent manipulation.

· The "connection" between the two tables is explicitly stated in the query by requiring that the two SIDs be equal.

Adding Tuples

To add a new tuple to a relation the INSERT command is used. The following adds a new freshman student with SID 8888, name JOHNSON, age 20, and ZIP code 01201:

```
INSERT INTO STUDENT VALUES (8888, 'JOHNSON', 1, 20, 01201);
```

As noted in the example retrieval, the results of a retrieval can be saved in a relation for later manipulation. The following statement saves the example retrieval results above in a table named GR_LOAN.

```
INSERT INTO GR_LOAN
SELECT NAME, AGE, LID, AMOUNT
FROM STUDENT, LOAN
WHERE SLEVEL = 5
    AND STUDENT.SID = LOAN.SID;
```

We could now use the SELECT command to retrieve from GR_LOAN or use the INSERT, UPDATE, or DELETE to modify it.

Deleting Tuples

One or more tuples can be dropped from a single table with the DELETE command. The following, while it might not be sensible, eliminates all loans from FIDELITY bank:

```
DELETE FROM LOAN WHERE BID = 'FIDELITY';
```

Updating Attribute Values

Values of attributes are updated with the UPDATE command. The following command reduces the interest rate by 1% for all loans with current interest rate over 7%:

```
UPDATE LOAN
    SET INT_RATE = INT_RATE - 1
    WHERE INT_RATE > 7;
```

Hierarchical Model

Hierarchical Database Structure

In the hierarchical model, data is represented in the form of a tree. Data for an entity is recorded in a record-like unit called a *segment*. For the GSL database, there will be a segment for student data, another for bank data, and a third for loan data. These segments will then be arranged in the form of a hierarchy with segments in parent-child relationships.

One possible arrangement of the GSL segments as a hierarchy is shown in Figure 3–3. The figure shows only a subset of the segments' attributes for simplicity. In this hierarchy, the BANK segment is the so-called root segment and is the parent of the (child) STUDENT segment. STUDENT in turn is the parent segment of the (child) LOAN segment. The arrangement is not, of course, arbitrary. The choice of LOAN as the lowest level segment in this hierarchy is obvious since there are one-to-many relationships from both STUDENT to LOAN and BANK to LOAN segments. That is, each STUDENT segment occurrence has zero to many LOAN segment occurrences; each BANK segment has zero to many LOAN segment occurrences.

The choice of BANK as the root segment is not at all obvious nor is it the only reasonable choice. STUDENT could also have been made the root segment with BANK as its child. The design difficulty arises because the three segments do not have a natural hierarchical ordering. In particular, the LOAN segment causes difficulty because it has two immediate parents—a STUDENT and a BANK. Since both STUDENT and BANK are immediate parents of LOAN, they cannot be in a parent-child relationship with each other.

Some of the difficulties of representing data in a strict hierarchical model are illustrated by our example database:

- Where do we place a student who has no loan, hence no BANK parent? You will note that student JONES does not appear in Figure 3–3.

- It is necessary to replicate some segments. In this example, any student who has loans with more than one bank must appear once for each bank. Student 9735 appears three times.

- Due to the replication, updates are apt to create inconsistencies. Suppose, for example, that ALLEN gets married and has a name change. We must assure that the name is changed in all occurrences of this student's segments.

The data manipulation language in a hierarchical model includes the following types of commands:

Retrieval

Segment retrieval in the hierarchical model has three forms, depending on the type of retrieval to be performed, each of which is followed by a condition that is used to navigate through the database. The first form is GET FIRST (GU), which finds the first occurrence of a segment meeting specified criteria. GET NEXT (GN) retrieves the next segment occurrence, possibly also meeting specified criteria. The third retrieval command is GET NEXT WITHIN PARENT (GNP), which is similar to GN except that it searches through only those segments that are children of the current parent segment.

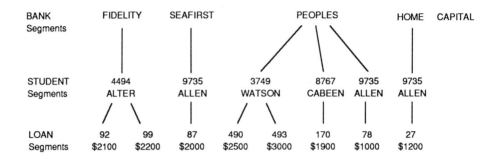

Fig 3-3   Hierarchical Representation of the Sample GSL Database

DML operations in hierarchical DBMSs are usually segment-at-a-time operations. Unlike the relational languages which specify the desired result of the operation, hierarchical DMLs must specify *how* to create the desired result. The following is an example sequence of statements in pigeon-DML to retrieve the names and loan amounts for all graduate students with loans from PEOPLES bank.

```
GU BANK (BID = 'PEOPLES')
      WHILE EXISTS
            GNP STUDENT (SLEVEL = 5)
            OUTPUT NAME
            WHILE EXISTS
                  GNP LOAN
                  OUTPUT AMOUNT
            ENDWHILE
      ENDWHILE
```

The user must explicitly "navigate" through the tree structure, accessing parent then child segments which meet the desired search criteria.

Segment Addition, Deletion, Update

Modification of a hierarchical database first requires identifying the specific segment to be deleted or updated or the specific location for segment addition. After the relevant segment is retrieved, commands exist to delete or modify it. These commands are described in more detail in Chapter 10.

Summary of Hierarchical Model

Here is a brief summary of the features of a hierarchical model and its DML:

- Relationships are explicitly represented by the hierarchical, parent-child, ordering of segments.
- It is difficult to transform most real information structures into the hierarchical structure unless all relationships are strictly one-to-many and each segment has only one

immediate parent segment. (The GSL model does not transform easily because each LOAN segment has two immediate parents—STUDENT and BANK.)

- Representation of segments in a strict hierarchy may result in replication of data with concomitant space costs and potential inconsistencies.
- Operations are segment-by-segment. The user must specify how, not what, is desired.
- Results of DML retrievals are segments, but the result is not in the same form as the database—the result is not itself a hierarchy.

The restriction of one parent record per segment is so limiting that there are very few pure hierarchical DBMSs in use. Widely used systems, such as IBM's IMS, extend the model to support semi-network structures at the conceptual level. The external model remains, however, a hierarchy.

Network Model

Network Database Structure

The network and hierarchical models are similar in many respects—both have explicit connections between segments and the DML is of the navigation (how) variety. The important difference between the two is that the network model allows a segment to have more than a single-parent segment.

Before continuing the discussion, we note that there are a number of differences in terminology between the network and hierarchical models. These differences are, for the most part, just that—different words used with virtually identical meanings. The correspondences are as follows:

- Hierarchical segments are termed records.
- The parent-child designations become *owner-member*.
- In a network, the owner-member relationship is called a *set* and the set is given a name. A set occurrence is one owner and all of its member records. For example, FIDELITY along with its two loans (LID 92 and 99) constitute an occurrence of the BANK-LOAN set.

Figure 3–4 illustrates the GSL database as a network. Note how each LOAN record occurrence has two parent record occurrences—one BANK and one STUDENT. Also note that the STUDENT records are not replicated. Now we can include the student, JONES, in the database even though he has no loan.

Data Manipulation

Data manipulation in the network model is similar in principal to hierarchical data manipulation; that is, the user must explicitly program the navigation through the data, moving from record to record and from set owner to member. Since a record may have more than a single owner, the network DML also includes a command to move to the owner record within a specified set. Here is an example query to retrieve names and loan amounts for graduate students with loans from PEOPLES bank. Again, a pigeon-DML is used for illustration:

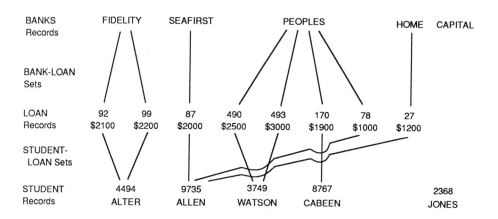

Fig 3-4 Network Representation of the Sample GSL Database

```
GET BANK (BID = 'PEOPLES')
      WHILE EXISTS
            GET NEXT LOAN IN BANK-LOAN SET
            GET OWNER IN STUDENT-LOAN SET
                  IF SLEVEL = 5 THEN OUTPUT NAME, AMOUNT
      ENDWHILE
```

While in the hierarchical model the navigation paths were obvious (enter through BANK, search STUDENT for SLEVEL=5, get LOANs), there are (at least) two alternative approaches for this query in the network. We could navigate as illustrated above or we could begin with STUDENT records, looking for graduate students. When a graduate student is found, his loans are retrieved one by one and for each loan the owner BANK is retrieved and examined to see if it is PEOPLES. The method illustrated is clearly superior. But, there will be situations where the best navigation paths are not obvious.

Leaving the choice of navigation path up to the user can be a blessing because it affords the skilled navigator the opportunity to write highly efficient DML. But, for the novice or even the experienced user on a bad day, the flexibility can lead to disaster. Poor navigation can result in orders of magnitude greater processing costs. We point this out because choice of navigation is not an option to the relational system user. Remember, the relational DML specifies desired results, not methods of obtaining them.

Update commands and methods in the network model are similar to the hierarchical approach—navigate to identify the record to update or delete, then issue the update or delete command. Adding a record in the network model can be somewhat simpler depending on the particular DBMS implementation. Details are left to Chapter 9.

Product Name:	Type:	Vendor:
ADABAS	Inverted List	Software AG
DATACOM/DB	Inverted List	Applied Data Research
DB2	Relational	IBM
DMS1100	Network	Sperry
IMS	Hierarchical	IBM
IDMS	Network	Cullinet
INGRES	Relational	Relational Technology
MODEL 204	Inverted List	CCA
Oracle	Relational	ORACLE Corp
Rd/VMS	Relational	DEC
SQL/DS	Relational	IBM
System 2000	Hierarchical	Intel
TOTAL	Network	Cincom Systems

Fig 3-5   Database Products

Commercial DBMSs

There are two broad classes of commercial DBMSs: (1) relational DBMSs, in which all data is stored in tables and nothing but tables; and (2) nonrelational DBMSs, in which explicit connections are used to represent relations. Included in the nonrelational DBMSs are hierarchical and network. Another class of DBMS is termed *inverted list*. Inverted list systems are similar to network and hierarchical DBMSs although some, such as ADABAS, also incorporate relational features (see Figure 3–5) .

Other DBMS Software Components

The DBMS facilitates the conversion of data into information, but it does not, and indeed it should not, serve as the only tool for information processing. Providing information for functions ranging from everyday operational data processing (accounting, payroll, purchasing, and so on) to long-range planning by the organization's top-level management requires capabilities never intended for the DBMS. The data extracted and possibly summarized by the DBMS is subsequently processed by specialized application programs or other software packages such as report writers, statistical forecasting, simulation, optimization, spreadsheets, and graphics systems.

Most DBMS now include, or have as optional modules, software packages such as report writers, communications managers, and graphics. In addition, the DBMS may provide tools to assist both in the initial design of the database and in the creation of specialized application programs. The program generators often use so-called fourth-generation languages.

Data Communications

The users of a large database are often situated at some distance from the physical location of the database. In the past, many of the decision-support functions were based on printed reports that were produced and distributed daily, weekly, monthly, and so on. This approach resulted in both information overload ("I know the answer is in there somewhere but I don't have the time or the inclination to find it") and reliance on outdated figures. Currently, most users prefer to use the database in an online, or interactive, manner through a remote terminal that communicates with the DBMS over a telecommunications system.

All data communications are handled by a data communications (DC) manager. This is a separate component to the DBMS but should be seen as an equal partner, providing a user with access to on-line applications. The DC manager handles all messages from users to applications programs (which in turn interact with the DBMS) and send responses back to the users.

Utilities

The database administrator requires a variety of utility programs to perform tasks related to setting up and maintaining the database. Examples of these utilities include:

- *Load routines*, which create database files from nondatabase files.
- *Dump/restore routines*, which dump the contents of a database to backup storage for recovery purposes and reload the database from the backup storage if the data is somehow damaged.
- *Reorganization routines*, which rearrange data within the database either to improve the performance of particular operations or to reclaim space held by obsolete data.
- *Statistics routines*, which compute performance statistics for monitoring the operation and usage of the DBMS. The sort of information gathered includes file sizes, data-value distributions, and frequency and type of user requests.

Applications Tools

Data Dictionary

The *data dictionary* is a database which describes the content and organization of the database proper. The data dictionary includes information about tables, views, indexes, users, access privileges, and other inportant system information. This information is often called *metadata*, or data about data. The data dictionary can be used to inspect the database system, particularly when changing or tuning the database.

Report Writers

A *report* is a set of formatted output from a database; it may be either displayed by the terminal or printed. A *report writer*, or report generator, is software that creates reports based on specifications. A report writer typically uses the DML to retrieve relevant data. It then formats and summarizes the output.

Application Generators

Application generators are rapid application development tools which are an advance over conventional high-level languages such as COBOL and PL/1, in the same ways that high level languages are an advance over assembler language. Application generators are often referred to as fourth-generation languages (4GL). An application generator may convert programs into COBOL. It removes details from the user, simplifies screen and output formatting, and automates edit checks.

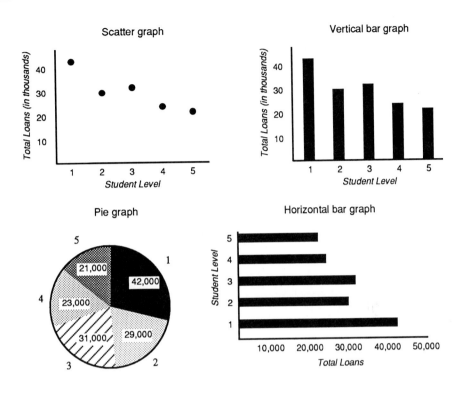

Fig 3-6   Same Numerical Information Shown in Several Different Graphical Forms

Graphics Generators

Graphics generators are analogous to report generators except that their output is in a graphical form. The choice of an appropriate graphical form makes particular features easier to see and understand. To graph data from the database, the user must first generate a table containing the information to be graphed. The graphics generator is then instructed by the user to draw the data as a designated type of graph such as bar, pie, line, scatter, or histogram (see Figure 3–6).

Questions

1. Describe the levels of a database.

2. Define *entity, entity class, atttribute, identifier,* and *relationship.* Give examples of each.

3. What is the data definition language? What are its components and their respective capabilities?

4. In what ways do the facts and relationships that exist at the real level of data differ from what is represented in the database at the conceptual level?

5. What is a *subschema* or *view*?

6. List and describe some of the applications modules that are often supported by the DBMS.

7. a. What are the major differences in the data manipulation languages of the three data models?

    b. What are the major differences in the way data is represented by the three data models?

8. Define *table*, *relation*, and *tuple*.

References

Date, C.J. *An Introduction to Database Systems,* Vol. 1. 4th ed. Reading, Mass.: Addison-Wesley Publishing Co., 1985.

Martin, J. *Computer Data-Base Organization.* 2d ed. Englewood Cliffs, N.J: Prentice-Hall, 1977.

McFadden, F., and Hoffer, J. *Computer Data-Base Organization.* 2d ed. Menlo Park, Calif.: The Benjamin/Cummings Publishing Co., 1988.

Tsichritzis, D.C., and Klug, A., eds. "The ANSI/X3/SPARC DBMS Framework: Report of the Study Group on Data Base Management Systems." *Information Systems*, vol. 3, 1978.

PART II

The Relational Model and Relational DBMSs

4 *The Relational Model and Relational Algebra*

Relational Structure: Example and Overview

This chapter introduces the relational database model. The underlying theory is explained and the methods used to define and manipulate relational databases are described. This chapter does not describe a specific DBMS, but rather a model for both the representation and manipulation of data. Subsequent chapters will give examples of specific implementations of relational DBMSs (RDBMSs).

A relational database is one that is perceived by its users as a collection of tables and nothing but tables. Operators in a relational system generate new tables from old. The relational model applies to both the conceptual and external levels—the internal level is relatively independent of the conceptual level.

The relational model consists of three major parts: one part handles data structure, one handles data integrity, and one handles data manipulation.

In addition, there are three fundamental properties of relational databases outlined below. These points are well illustrated by the GSL database. Refer to Figure 4–1.

First, the tables contain only one data value in each row and column position; that is, data values are *atomic*. If, for example, a given bank had multiple branches, hence multiple values for ZIP, then multiple rows would be required, one for each branch.

Second, all of the information contained in the database is represented as explicit data values in column positions within rows of tables. This is the only method of representation allowed in a relational system. Unlike other database models, there are no pointers at the conceptual or external levels connecting one table to another. For example, there is an association between ALLEN in the STUDENT table and HOME in the BANK table. That connection is made, not by pointers, but by entries in the LOAN table. The row in the LOAN table containing the value 9735 in the SID column and HOME in the BID column provides a connection between ALLEN in the STUDENT table and HOME in the BANK table. In nonrelational systems, such connections are usually represented by some form of pointer or physical link.

The third point is that each table contains a column or set of columns in which the values in each row are unique with respect to all such values appearing in the table. In the table STUDENT, the unique column is SID; in the table BANK it is BID; in the table LOAN it is LID. In formal relational terminology, these unique identifiers are called *primary keys*. We will look at primary keys in more detail later in this chapter.

A *relation* is a mathematical term for a table. In most situations the terms *relation* and *table* are synonymous and are used interchangeably. Relational systems are based on the relational model of data introduced in 1969–70 by Dr. E. F. Codd, a mathematician at IBM. Codd was the first to recognize that the discipline of mathematics could be applied to the field of database management. His ideas were published in what has become a classic paper, "A Relational Model of Data for Large Shared Data Banks" (*Communications of the ACM*,

STUDENT Table

SID	NAME	SLEVEL	AGE	SZIP
9735	ALLEN	1	21	98101
4494	ALTER	2	19	98112
8767	CABEEN	5	24	98118
2368	JONES	4	23	98155
6793	SANDS	1	17	98101
3749	WATSON	5	29	98168

BANK Table

BID	BZIP	TYPE
FIDELITY	98101	MSB
SEAFIRST	98101	BANK
PEOPLES	98109	BANK
CAPITAL	98033	SL
HOME	98031	SL

LOAN Table

LID	LDATE	YEARS	INT_RATE	AMOUNT	SID	BID
27	15-SEP-85	5	8.5	1200	9735	HOME
78	21-JUN-86	5	7.75	1000	9735	PEOPLES
87	07-SEP-83	5	7.0	2000	9735	SEAFIRST
92	12-JAN-85	6	7.5	2100	4494	FIDELITY
99	15-JAN-86	6	9.0	2200	4494	FIDELITY
170	30-APR-83	6	6.5	1900	8767	PEOPLES
490	07-MAY-84	6	6.0	2500	3749	PEOPLES
493	24-JUN-85	7	7.5	3000	3749	PEOPLES

Fig 4-1   GSL Database

vol. 13, no. 6, June 1970). Since that time, Codd's ideas have had a major influence on many aspects of database technology.

When Codd defined the relational model, he deliberately used terms that were not widely used in data processing. This was because many of the existing terms were used in a variety of contexts and were therefore fuzzy in their meanings (think of the different ways the word *record* is used). Codd adopted mathematical terms to provide the precision necessary to formally define the data structures he proposed in the new database model. Figure 4–2 shows the most commonly used formal relational terms alongside the more commonly used informal equivalent terms. Notice that the terms *row* and *record* are used interchangeably, as are *column* and *field*. When used in this way *record* is used to mean "record occurrence."

Here are some other definitions that will be important in the following discussions:

- A *relation* is the formal term for describing what we have been calling a table.

- A *tuple* is a row of a relation.

Formal Relational Term	Informal Equivalent Term
Relation	Table
Tuple	Row or record
Attribute	Column or field
Primary key	Unique identifier
Domain	Pool of legal values

Fig 4-2   Some Relational Terminology

- An *attribute* is a column of a relation.
- A *primary key* is the unique identifier for the relation. It is a column (or combination of columns) in which no two rows of the relation contain the same value in that column (or combination of columns).
- A *domain* is a "pool of values" from which one or more columns draw their values. For example, the SID domain is the set of legal student identity numbers. The SID values that occur in the STUDENT relation are a subset of all the possible values in the domain. Similarly, the attribute SID in the relation LOAN is also a subset of values from the SID domain.

We will now look at each of these in greater detail.

Domains

A *domain* is a set of all possible values of the same type. These values should be "atomic" values, such as student ID or loan amount, that cannot be reduced into smaller parts. For example, the domain of ZIP codes consists of all values for a five-digit ZIP code as defined by the U.S. Postal Service. Both the student SZIP and bank BZIP attributes are defined over this same ZIP domain. Thus a single domain can support more than one attribute. Typically, all values of a domain do not occur as attribute values. For example, there will be many ZIP codes with no bank in that postal area.

Domains are generally not stored in the database. Therefore, domains must usually remain conceptual in nature. The formal relational model requires that they be specified as part of the database definition. As yet, only a few databases support domains.

Figure 4–3a shows how the domains of the GSL database might be defined in a system that supports domains. The specification DECIMAL (s) or (s,d) is a decimal value of s digits, with d digits to the right of the decimal point. Thus, the domain of SID is all seven-digit decimal numbers. The domain of INT_RATE is all four-digit values with two digits to the right of the decimal point (for example, 8.75, 9.00, 11.25). The parameter RANGE allows further limiting of the allowable values. For example, INT_RATE values must be a minimum of 1.00 and a maximum of 12.00. A range limitation would be appropriate where GSL program regulations limit the allowable interest rates that can be charged on loans. DATE specifies a date data type. The system will check for invalid dates (for example, it would not allow a value of Sept. 31, 1988 or Feb. 29, 1991).

```
CREATE DOMAIN SID        DECIMAL(7);
CREATE DOMAIN NAME       CHAR (20);
CREATE DOMAIN SLEVEL     DECIMAL(1), VALUES 1,2,3,4,5;
CREATE DOMAIN AGE        DECIMAL(2);
CREATE DOMAIN ZIP        DECIMAL(5);
CREATE DOMAIN BANKID     CHAR(15);
CREATE DOMAIN TYPE       CHAR (5), VALUES "MSB", "SL", "BANK",
                         "CU";
CREATE DOMAIN LID        DECIMAL (6);
CREATE DOMAIN LDATE      DATE;
CREATE DOMAIN YEARS      DECIMAL(2), RANGE 1 TO 15;
CREATE DOMAIN INT_RATE   DECIMAL(4,2), RANGE 1.00 to 12.00;
CREATE DOMAIN AMOUNT     MONEY(6,2);
```

Fig 4-3a   Domain Definition Using Pseudo DDL

```
CREATE TABLE STUDENT
    ( SID DOMAIN ( SID ), NOT NULL,
      NAME DOMAIN ( NAME ),
      SLEVEL DOMAIN ( SLEVEL ),
      AGE DOMAIN ( AGE )
      SZIP DOMAIN (ZIP));

CREATE TABLE BANK
    ( BID DOMAIN ( BANKID)   NOT NULL,
      BZIP DOMAIN (ZIP ),
      TYPE DOMAIN ( TYPE ));

CREATE TABLE LOAN
    ( LID DOMAIN ( LID) NOT NULL,
      LDATE DOMAIN ( LDATE ),
      YEARS DOMAIN (YEARS),
      INT_RATE DOMAIN ( INT_RATE),
      AMOUNT DOMAIN (AMOUNT),
      SID DOMAIN (SID),
      BID DOMAIN (BANKID));
```

Fig 4-3b   The GSL Database Definition Using Domain Support

Where there is a small set of allowable values, they can be explicitly listed with the VALUES clause. The definition of the SLEVEL domain limits values to the integers 1 through 5. Allowable values in the TYPE domain are "MSB," "SL," etc. A MONEY data type is a subset of the DECIMAL(s,2) specification. MONEY might also imply that the output of values from a MONEY domain would include a dollar sign.

Relations

Figure 4–3b includes definitions of three relations. A relation consists of a heading and a body. The heading includes the table name and the definitions of the attributes included in the table. These attributes are each defined on a particular domain. The body of a relation is the set of tuples.

Relation Definition

The definition begins with naming the relation, followed by attribute definition as seen in part b of Figure 4–3. Usually an attribute is assigned the same name as its underlying domains, but that is not a requirement. See, for example, attribute BID defined over domain BANKID, and BZIP and SZIP both defined over domain ZIP. Different names are required when more than one attribute in the same relation shares a domain. For example, suppose the LOAN relation contains two dates: one that is the creation date of the loan, and another that is the date of the last payment. Both of these attributes are defined over the same domain, LDATE. Since two attributes of a given relation may not share the same name, at least one of the attribute names must differ from the domain name. When it is impossible for the attribute to have the same name as the corresponding domain, an attempt should be made to include part of the domain name in the attribute name.

Formally, values of two attributes can be compared only if they are drawn from the same domain. For example, we could not compare the value of SID with LID, or SLEVEL with AGE. In most cases this makes sense. Such comparisons are the proverbial "apples" and "oranges" comparisons. But, there are some situations in which the comparison of values from different domains does make sense. For example, suppose we want to retrieve all "young" students. "Young" is defined as an age that is less than 16 plus SLEVEL. Thus, 16-year-old freshmen (SLEVEL=1) are young, as are 20-year-old graduate students. But unless the restrictions on comparing values from different domains is relaxed, we could not write a predicate (comparison) such as "AGE < 16 + SLEVEL."

In fact, most DBMSs are quite liberal with the comparisons they allow. They insist only that the underlying data *types* of the values be comparable; that is, they allow comparison of numeric values to each other, character strings to character strings, and dates to dates. They would not allow the comparison of a string to a date, a date to a number, etc. (However, we will see in our study of SQL that there are ways around even these restrictions. For example, suppose AGE is represented, as it should be, by birthdate defined over a date domain. Then, to identify "young" students we would need to compare BIRTH_DATE with SLEVEL—attributes of two different data types. A DBMS will allow this by providing functions that convert from one data type to another.)

Relation Body

Each tuple or row is a set of attribute-value pairs, with one value for each attribute in the heading. The values must be from the domain associated with that particular attribute. The body of the relation STUDENT consists of a set of tuples (six in Figure 4–1, but the number varies with time as updates are made to the relation); and each tuple consists of five attribute-value pairs, one such pair for each attribute in the heading. For example, the tuple for student Sands consists of the following pairs:

```
(SID :    6793 )
(NAME:    SANDS)
(SLEVEL: 1    )
(AGE :    17   )
(SZIP:    98101)
```

Normally, the attribute names are not displayed in informal contexts. Attribute values are simply listed in the same order as the attributes are listed in the heading. The above tuple from STUDENT would then be represented simply as (6793, SANDS, 1, 17, 98101).

Properties of Relations

As mentioned earlier, relations have several important properties:

- There are no duplicate tuples in a relation.
- Tuples are unordered. This means that there is no top-to-bottom ordering in a relation.
- Attributes are unordered. In other words, there is no left-to-right ordering of a relation.
- All attribute values are atomic.
- A relation has a set of attributes that uniquely identify the rows.

These properties are described in greater detail in the following sections.

Properties of Tuples: Primary Key. In a mathematical set, no duplicate elements are allowed. Because a relation is a mathematical set, all rows must be unique, and there should always be a set of attributes that can serve as the primary key. In the extreme case, all attributes serve as the primary key. Typically, one or two attributes provide the primary key. Note that a primary key depends on more than just an attribute (or set of attributes) being unique at a given point of time. The attribute (or set) must be unique over all time and all possible tuples. As it currently stands, the STUDENT relation has three columns that are unique: NAME, SID, and AGE. But for all columns except SID, this is just chance. There is nothing in the GSL rules and regulations that restricts participation to students with unique names. (If there were such a regulation, a lot of JAMES L. SMITHs would be very upset.)

Primary keys are fundamental to the operation of the relational model because they provide tuple-level addressing. In fact, they are the only means by which tuples can be addressed within the relational model. For example, suppose that the STUDENT table does not contain SID and that we try to use NAME as the key. Consider what happens if a tuple is added that duplicates an existing name (say, JONES, MARY). If one of the MARY JONESes has a change in the value of SLEVEL, how do we access the desired tuple? Remember, we can't use position—for example, we can't tell the DBMS we want to update the "first occurrence" of "JONES, MARY." We are stuck. Clearly, similar problems will arise if we want to perform deletions and there is no unique key. This type of addressing, in which values, not positions, determine the address of a tuple, is called *associative addressing*.

There are two more restrictions for primary keys that are composite. Suppose that in place of SID, students are identified by a pair of attributes: school ID and a school-assigned number, ST#. Since schools do not coordinate the assignment of ST# values, ST# by itself may not be unique. The restrictions are:

- No part of a composite key may be null. This restriction avoids complications in database manipulations.

• No subset of a key may itself be unique. For example, the pair of attributes school ID and social security number are unique (if a student attends only a single school at a time). But the SSN by itself is unique, hence the pair does not qualify as a key.

Lack of Order. Mathematical sets are unordered. Relations are mathematical sets, therefore their tuples are also unordered. For instance, the STUDENT relation in Figure 4–1 would be the same relation even if its tuples were completely reordered. What this means is that we cannot process tuples of a relation one by one and expect them to occur in any particular order. If we want tuples to be displayed in a particular order, then a data manipulation command must be used to sort the output.

Properties of Attributes: Lack of Order

Attributes are unordered from left to right. Because the heading of a relation is also a set—in this case a set of attributes—and a set is unordered, the attributes are unordered. The position of the attribute in a relation is an artificial property that arises as a consequence of displaying or printing the relation as a table arranged in rows and columns. (Here we see a distinction between a table and a relation. The columns in a table do have left-to-right ordering, but the attributes in a relation do not.) Strictly speaking, the position of any particular column is totally arbitrary. Attributes are always referenced by name, never by position.

Atomic. All attribute values are atomic. In other words, a set of values is never allowed for any particular attribute in any particular tuple. A single value is the only valid possibilty. Thus, relations do not contain "repeating groups." When data occurs with repeating groups as shown in Figure 4–4a, it must be reorganized, or "flattened," as shown in Figure 4–4b.

The conversion of a relation with repeating groups to a relation without repeating groups is called *normalization*. In the relational model, normalization simplifies the structure of a relation and consequently leads to fewer and simpler operations. Without normalization, separate operators would be required to manipulate structures with repeating groups. For example, consider the two following transactions:

T1. Create a new loan for SID 9833, name JONES, loan ID 783, loan amount $4,000, bank Seafirst.

T2. Create a new loan for SID 9735, name ALLEN, loan ID 102, loan amount $4,000, bank Seafirst.

With the normalized relation in Figure 4–4b, both transactions are performed with the same single-tuple insert operator. With the structure of the table in Figure 4–4a, different operators would be required for the two transactions. T1 uses the same single-tuple insert operator as before, but T2 requires a different insert operator, which appends a new entry to a set of entries within an existing tuple. Thus two different forms of insert are required to work with unnormalized structures.

Terminology: Degree and Cardinality

The *degree of a relation* is defined as the number of attributes in a relation. A unary relation is of degree one, a binary relation is of degree two, a ternary relation is of degree three, and an n-ary relation is of degree n. The relations STUDENT, BANK, and LOAN of the GSL database have degrees of five, three and seven, respectively.

The *cardinality* is the number of rows in the relation. In the GSL database the cardinalities are six for STUDENT, five for BANK, and eight for LOAN.

ST-LOAN

SID	NAME	LID	BID	AMOUNT	
9735	ALLEN	27	HOME	1200	
		78	PEOPLES	1000	⎦ repeating group
		87	SEAFIRST	2000	
4494	ALTER	92	FIDELITY	2100	
		99	FIDELITY	2200	⎦ repeating group
8767	CABEEN	170	PEOPLES	1900	repeating group
3749	WATSON	490	PEOPLES	2500	
		493	PEOPLES	3000	⎦ repeating group

Fig 4-4a   Loan Table with Repeating Groups

LOAN

SID	NAME	LID	BID	AMOUNT
9735	ALLEN	27	HOME	1200
9735	ALLEN	78	PEOPLES	1000
9735	ALLEN	87	SEAFIRST	2000
4494	ALTER	92	FIDELITY	2100
4494	ALTER	99	FIDELITY	2200
8767	CABEEN	170	PEOPLES	1900
3749	WATSON	490	PEOPLES	2500
3749	WATSON	493	PEOPLES	3000

Fig 4-4b   Data Represented without Repeating Groups

The degree of a relation tends to remain constant for long periods of time. A change in degree implies a change in the definition of a relation. Definitions of relations are not changed frequently; however, most RDBMSs provide for definition change (such as adding a new attribute to a relation). On the other hand, the cardinality changes frequently due to the addition or deletion of tuples.

Alternate and Candidate Keys

As stated above, each relation contains a primary key. An alternate key is any other column (or combination of columns) that are unique valued. Relations do not require alternate keys; typically there is no alternate. If the STUDENT relation also included the social security number, then the SSN would be an alternate key.

The term *candidate key* is used for a collection of all possible keys for a relation, including the primary key and all alternate keys. Since any candidate key may be designated as the primary key, the restrictions for a primary key also apply to candidate keys:

- No part of a candidate key may be null.
- For a group of attributes to qualify as a candidate key, no subset of the group may itself be unique.

Foreign Keys

In the GSL database (Figure 4–1), the value of each SID attribute in the LOAN table must match exactly one of the SID values in the STUDENT relation. A match must exist in order for the database to be in a state of integrity. In other words, it only makes sense to have a loan in the database if the student who holds the loan is already in the database. For example, the ID value of 9735 in LOAN matches the SID value for ALLEN in the STUDENT relation. It would make no sense to have an SID value of 1684 in the LOAN relation since there is no matching value in the STUDENT relation. Attribute SID in the LOAN relation is an example of a foreign key.

An attribute in a relation that matches the primary key of another relation is called a *foreign key*. A foreign key can, of course, be a composite. The same underlying domain should be used to define both the foreign key and its primary key.

In some situations, a null foreign key may exist. For example, suppose that when a loan goes into default, we assign a collection agent to pursue payment on the loan. Thus, a table is added, AGENT, with key (say) A_ID which is the agent's employee number. A_ID is also added to LOAN. But most loans are not in collection and have no assigned agent; hence, a null value (nonexistent value) for A_ID is the appropriate entry.

It is also possible for the foreign key and the matching primary key to be contained in the same relation. For example, suppose that a bank is actually a branch of another bank. To relate it to its home office, another column is added to the BANK table:

```
BANK (BID, TYPE, HOME_ID, BZIP)
```

The primary key is BID. The ID of the home bank, HOME_ID, is a foreign key. In this case, the foreign key matches the primary key of the same relation. Both the BID and HOME_ID attributes are from the same domain. A null value for HOME_ID indicates that this bank is the home office.

For simplicity, we will show here only the two attributes: BID and HOME_ID. The example shows that bank PEOPLES is a home office, the banks PEOPL02 and PEOPL07 are branches with home office PEOPLES; and FEDDC and FEDNY have home office FEDCU. Banks FIRSTBANK and LASTBANK are home offices and have no branches.

```
BID             HOME_ID
---------       -------
PEOPLES
PEOPL02         PEOPLES
PEOPL07         PEOPLES
FEDCU
FEDDC           FEDCU
FEDNY           FEDCU
FIRSTBANK
LASTBANK
```

Foreign keys are, of course, the "glue" that provides the connections between tuples. The SID in LOAN is there because loans are related to students. Similarly, the BID in LOAN provides the association of a given loan with the bank that made the loan. Note, however, that relational systems are not limited to associations from one relation to another via a foreign key. It is also possible, for example, to associate students and banks on their ZIPs. Such a situation might arise if we wanted to provide a list of "nearby" banks to each student. Sharing the same ZIP would mean that the bank was geographically close to the student.

Integrity Rules

Data integrity is the second part of the relational model. (Several of these rules have been described earlier but are repeated here.) The relational model has two general integrity rules: the entity integrity rule, which has to do with the consequences of primary keys, and the referential integrity rule, which has to do with foreign keys. These rules help ensure that the data in the database makes sense. Any database that claims to conform to the relational standard must satisfy these two rules. Of course, there may be other rules that are specific to a particular database (for example, that a student is limited to 10 loans). Such additional rules are not an inherent part of the relational model.

Entity Integrity

The entity rule states that no null values are allowed in any part of the primary key. The entity rule is based on the fact that relations are tables of data about entities, each of which is in some way unique, and each of which is uniquely identified by its primary key. For example, the relation STUDENT represents the students who have applied for loans underwritten by the GSL program. Each of these entities has some unique identifying feature, in this case SID. In the relational model, primary keys are used to uniquely identify entities. Therefore, as long as an entity exists, it will have some value for the primary key. A null value would indicate that the entity did not exist. For this reason, primary keys will not contain null values.

Referential Integrity

In the same way that there are restrictions on the values of candidate keys (uniqueness, non-null), there are also restrictions on the values of foreign keys. In particular, the value of a foreign key must exist as a value of a primary key or be null. This is known as *referential integrity*. Referential integrity applied to the GSL database says, for example, that every value of SID in the LOAN table must exist as a value of SID in the STUDENT table. Similarly, the value of every BID in LOAN must exist as a value of BID in BANK. Consider what it would mean to have a loan with SID value (say, SID = 9999) that does not exist in STUDENT. We now have a loan that either has no student owner, or the data about this student (such as name, age, etc.) is not in our database. This does not make sense.

Referential integrity is, therefore, simply a commonsense restriction to avoid one type of inconsistency—tuples that should be, but are not, related to some other tuple. A "good" DBMS will enforce referential integrity. Enforcement means that four types of updates must be monitored to assure that referential integrity is not violated:

- Addition of a tuple with a foreign key value that does not exist as a primary key value. For example, addition of a loan with BID = "NOBANK."
- Change in a foreign key value to a value that does not exist as a primary key value. For example, change of SID in LOAN from 4494 to 9949.
- Deletion of a tuple with a primary key value that exists as the value of one or more foreign keys. For example, deletion of the STUDENT tuple with SID = 4494.

• Change of a primary key value where the original primary key value exists as a foreign key value.

An interesting problem is presented in a DBMS that enforces referential integrity if a tuple exists with incorrect primary key value. For example, suppose we discover that the tuple with SID = 4494 should actually be 9949. If this is discovered before any loans are stored with SID = 4494, it is easy to correct. But if a loan with SID = 4494 exists, then correcting the database is tricky. This is left as an exercise.

Relational Algebra

Introduction

Previous sections have dealt with *database definition* and certain integrity constraints of the relational model. We turn now to *database manipulation* using the relational algebra language.

Relational Algebra: Definition

There are eight operators in the relational algebra for data manipulation. Four of them are based on the traditional set operations of union, intersection, difference, and Cartesian product. The other four are the special relational operators: *select, project, join, and divide*. Each operator takes one or two relations as its input and produces a new relation as its output. The relational operators allow rows meeting specified conditions (for example, all rows of STUDENT where SLEVEL equal to 5) to be selected, display specified columns (such as SID and NAME), and bring together data from two relations (such as STUDENT and LOAN). We will deal with these operators more or less in the order of their frequency of use—select, project, and join (especially the so-called "natural join"), next the *union, intersection and difference* are described. The infrequently used *Cartesian product* and *divide* are explained last. The data of Figure 4–1 will be used to illustrate the results of these operations.

SELECT

Rows are extracted from a relation with the *select* operator. All rows may be selected, or a condition can be defined so that only specific rows are selected. The result of the select operation is then a new relation:

```
R1 (condition);
```

Those rows of R1 that are selected must meet the stated conditions. All duplicate rows are removed from the result. For example, when the statement

```
STUDENT(WHERE SLEVEL=5)
```

is applied to the GSL database, it creates a new (temporary) relation containing the same attributes as the STUDENT table. However, only those tuples in which the SLEVEL equals 5 are included in the new relation.

```
8767    CABEEN    5    24    98118
3749    WATSON    5    29    98168
```

In this case there are no duplicate rows, but if there were, they would be discarded.

The result from the above query can also be assigned to a new permanent table. For instance:

```
GRAD_STUDENT:=STUDENT(WHERE SLEVEL=5)
```

would create a new table called GRAD_STUDENT with only graduate students. This table could then be manipulated like any other table.

Multiple comparisons can also be included in a select condition. For instance, to find all students with a level greater than or equal to 2, and a ZIP code of either 98101 or 98112:

```
STUDENT(WHERE (SZIP=98101 OR SZIP=98112) AND SLEVEL ≥ 2)
```

The result is:

SID	NAME	SLEVEL	AGE	SZIP
4494	ALTER	2	19	98112

Notice that parenthesis are used to specify the order of the operations.

PROJECT

Projection extracts attributes (columns) from a relation. The columns to be extracted are shown in brackets: [ ]. Once again, the result will be a new relation. A command with both selection and projection will have the form:

```
R1 (condition) [A1,A2, ... ,An]
```

The attributes A1, A2, through An of the relation R1 are extracted to form a new relation. As with the select operation, duplicate rows are discarded from the new relation, as shown in this example:

```
LOAN [SID, BID]
```

This creates a new relation containing a list of all the student IDs and their loan BIDs:

SID	BID
9735	HOME
9735	PEOPLES
9735	SEAFIRST
4494	FIDELITY
8767	PEOPLES
3749	PEOPLES

The command to select students with a level of at least 2, and a ZIP of either 98101 or 98112, but to display only the SID and NAME columns is:

```
STUDENT(WHERE (SZIP=98101 OR SZIP=98112) AND SLEVEL ≥ 2)[SID, NAME]
```

It is also possible to use a selection as part of the condition. Suppose that only the loans for graduate students are needed:

```
LOAN(WHERE SID=STUDENT(WHERE SLEVEL=5)[SID])
```

In this case the selection of graduate SIDs from the STUDENT relation is first performed, and the result of this is then used to select only those loans that are for graduate students.

LID	LDATE	YEARS	INT_RATE	AMOUNT	SID	BID
170	30-APR-83	6	6.5	1900	8767	PEOPLES
490	07-MAY-84	6	6.0	2500	3749	PEOPLES
493	24-JUN-85	7	7.5	3000	3749	PEOPLES

Natural Join

Except for the immediately preceding example, which selected loans for students who have SLEVEL=5, the queries have involved only a single table. It is very common to want data from two or more related columns. Suppose that we want to display the bank TYPE and ZIP along with the LID and AMOUNT columns for loans with SID < 9000. In this case, the result is:

```
LID        AMOUNT    TYPE    BZIP
---        ------    ----    -----
 92         2100     MSB     98101
 99         2200     MSB     98101
170         1900     BANK    98109
490         2500     BANK    98109
493         3000     BANK    98109
```

Data from the two relations are brought together with the *join* operator, which forms a new relation by extracting and "matching" rows from two relations. The (general) join operation joins together two tables on the basis of some condition. The natural join is a special version of the join operation. It is used to combine the rows of two relations in which there is a primary key–foreign key match. In other words, a natural join can be performed when the primary key of one relation is a foreign key in the other relation. The natural join appends (or concatenates) a row from one relation to each row of the other relation for which the rows have the same values of the common columns. Most often there is a single column over which the match is performed, but there can be more. The syntax for the natural join is:

```
R1 JOIN R2;
```

In this case R1 and R2 are joined, resulting in a new relation. Duplicate rows are eliminated from the result. All columns from both relations are included, with only one occurrence of the common columns. Here is a simple example of the join of two relations.

R1	A	B
	1	x
	2	y
	3	x

R2	A	C	D
	1	m	3
	1	n	1
	2	q	3

R1 JOIN R2	A	B	C	D
	1	x	m	3
	1	x	n	1
	2	y	q	3

To create the above result, we need to join BANK and LOAN—as in BANK JOIN LOAN—but we must also restrict SID values to those less than 9000 and project only columns LID, AMOUNT, TYPE, and BZIP. The final form is:

```
BANK JOIN LOAN (WHERE SID < 9000)[LID, AMOUNT, TYPE, BZIP]
```

The result is as shown above.

As a slightly more complex example, consider how we would display the names of students and IDs of banks for loans made during 1985 to students who are undergraduates.

The query requires a join, selects on both the STUDENT and LOAN relations, and a projection. The result is assigned to the relation 1985_UG_LOANS:

```
1985_UG_LOANS:=(LOANS (WHERE LDATE ≥ 1-JAN-85 AND LDATE ≤ 31-DEC-85)
    JOIN STUDENT (WHERE SLEVEL ≤ 4))[NAME, BID]
```

Other Joins

While the natural join is the most commonly used form of join, there are several other types. The other varieties of joins differ in that you must explicitly state the attributes that are being compared and the type of comparison: equal to (=), not equal to (≠), greater than (>), greater than or equal to (≥), less than (<), and less than or equal to (≤). The form of these joins is:

```
R1 JOIN (condition) R2
```

The condition may be quite complex, as subsequent examples will demonstrate. First, though, consider the case in which the condition involves a simple equality comparison of two attributes. In this case the operation is called an *equijoin* and is almost identical to the natural join except that all columns, including the common joined column or columns are included in the result. For example, an equijoin of BANK and LOAN with selection of banks of TYPE = BANK and projection over SID and BID is expressed as:

```
(BANK (WHERE TYPE = 'BANK') JOIN (BANK.BID =LOAN.BID) LOAN)
    [SID,BANK.BID]
```

The result is:

```
SID         BID
----        -------
9735        PEOPLES
9735        SEAFIRST
8767        PEOPLES
3749        PEOPLES
```

Note the necessity to qualify attribute names whenever there is potential ambiguity. The join condition, which compares two BID attributes, must explicitly indicate which relation each attribute is from. It makes no sense to say BID = BID. The projection also requires qualification because the result of the join includes the BID columns from both BANK and LOAN. The result drops a duplicate of the row (3749, PEOPLES).

The use of an equijoin instead of a natural join is rare—why bother with expressing the join condition if a match over common columns is being performed? The preceding query would be cleaner if the natural join were used:

```
(BANK (WHERE TYPE = 'BANK') JOIN LOAN) [SID, BID]
```

Following is a situation in which the equijoin is required. We want to provide each student with a listing of all banks that share the same ZIP code—this might be termed the "nearby" bank listing. Thus STUDENT and BANK are to be joined over the attributes SZIP and BZIP. Since the natural join operates only over like-named columns, the command: STUDENT JOIN BANK will give a null result. The equijoin must be used in this situation:

```
STUDENT JOIN (SZIP = BZIP) BANK
```

Self-Joins. A self-join is a join of a relation with itself. At first this might not seem to make sense, but here are a couple of realistic examples. Recall the case in which a bank is a branch and has a home office designated by an attribute HOME_ID. Here are some example data:

BID	BZIP	HOME_ID
PEOPLES	98109	
PEOPL02	98040	PEOPLES
PEOPL07	99120	PEOPLES
FEDCU	20201	
FEDDC	20016	FEDCU

We want to list each branch bank with its home office bank and the ZIP of the home office. The result should be:

BID	BZIP	HOME_ID	BZIP
PEOPL02	98040	PEOPLES	98109
PEOPL07	99120	PEOPLES	98109
FEDDC	20016	FEDCU	20201

The second BZIP column is the ZIP code of the home office bank. The problem with attempting a join of a relation with itself becomes apparent in the following:

```
BANK JOIN (BID = HOME_ID) BANK
```

The condition, BID = HOME_ID, is ambiguous. To make it unambiguous, we need to associate a temporary name with BANK, say B2. We then write:

```
BANK JOIN (BANK.HOME_ID = B2.BID) B2 [BANK.BID, BANK.BZIP,
     B2.BID, B2.BZIP]
```

to produce the desired result. The way that the temporary name, or *alias*, is assigned to BANK is by the statement:

```
ALIAS B2 FOR BANK
```

You can visualize this as creating a copy of the BANK relation with the name B2. Then the two relations are joined over BID and HOME_ID. You should work out the details of this by actually writing down a copy of BANK, then performing the specified equijoin.

Here is another example of a self-join that also illustrates the use of a greater-than join. A listing is desired of SIDs for all students who have two or more loans with YEARS ≥ 6. The LIDs of these loans are also desired. To illustrate how this may be done, first consider two projections of the LOAN relation for loans with YEARS ≥ 6, one called L1 and the other L2, with attributes LID and SID:

L1 Table		**L2 Table**	
LID	SID	LID	SID
92	4494	92	4494
99	4494	99	4494
170	8767	170	8767
490	3749	490	3749
493	3749	493	3749

The appropriate condition for students with two or more loans is a join of L1 and L2 where the SIDs are equal but the LIDs are not equal. Here is one way to produce the desired result:

```
L1 JOIN (L1.LID ≠ L2.LID AND L1.SID = L2.SID) L2
[ L1.SID. L1.LID, L2.LID ]
```

The result is:

```
L1.SID    L1.LID    L2.LID
------    ------    ------
 4494        92        99
 4494        99        92
 3749       490       493
 3749       493       490
```

Only one row for each student is needed—the other is redundant. By using a greater-than join, the redundant rows can be eliminated:

```
L1 JOIN (L1.LID > L2.LID AND L1.SID = L2.SID) LOAN
      [ L1.SID. L1.LID, L2.LID ]
```

The result is:

```
L1.SID    L1.LID    L2.LID
------    ------    ------
 4494        99        92
 3749       493       490
```

The same result can be produced without first physically creating the new relations L1 and L2 by using an alias as follows:

```
ALIAS L1 FOR LOAN

L1 JOIN (L1.LID > LOAN.LID AND L1.SID = LOAN.SID) L2
      [ L1.SID. L1.LID, LOAN.LID ]
```

Union, Intersection, and Difference

The next set of operators discussed are the traditional set operations of *union, intersection,* and *difference.* Two operands are required for each operation.

UNION. A UNION B results in a new relation that contains all the rows from either relation A or relation B, or both. Duplicate rows are discarded.

To determine the SIDs of students who are grad students *or* have a loan greater than $2,000 requires obtaining SID values from two different relations: STUDENT and LOAN. We will illustrate this by a three-step approach first, then a single-command operation. First we obtain the SIDs of graduate students:

```
GRADS:=STUDENT (WHERE SLEVEL=5)[SID]
```

The result is:

```
SID
-----
8767
3749
```

Next, the SIDs of students with loans over $2,000:

```
BIG_LOAN:=(LOAN (WHERE AMOUNT > 2000)) [SID]
```

The result is:

```
SID
----
4494
3749
```

The union of these two sets is created by:

```
     BIG_LOAN_OR_GRAD:=GRADS UNION BIG_LOAN
```

The result is:

```
SID
----
8767
4494
3749
```

This could also be accomplished with a single nested query:

```
BLOG:=(STUDENTS (WHERE SLEVEL=5) [SID]) UNION (LOAN (WHERE   AMOUNT
> 2000) [SID])
```

Union Compatibility. In fact, there is a constraint on the two relations that must be met before we can form their union. They must both have the same number of attributes, and the attributes must be from the same domains. In the example above, we could take the union of GRADS and BIG_LOAN because each had a single column from the SID domain. If the relational expression that defined GRADS did not include the projection over SID, then it would not have been possible to union it with BIG_LOAN.

Union compatibility is required for the intersection and difference operations also. Essentially, union compatibility says that we cannot perform these set operations unless the tuples from the two relations have identical domain definitions for their attributes. Here is another example. We want LIDs, LDATEs, INT_RATEs and YEARSs for loans with YEARS greater than 5 or INT_RATE greater than 8 percent. The simple way to do this is with selection/projection operations, but union may also be used:

```
     LOAN (INT_RATE > 8) [LID, LDATE, INT_RATE, YEARS] UNION
     LOAN (YEARS  > 5) [LID, LDATE, INT_RATE, YEARS]
```

The result is:

LID	LDATE	INT_RATE	YEARS
27	15-SEP-85	8.5	5
92	12-JAN-85	7.5	6
99	15-JAN-86	9.0	6
170	30-APR-83	6.5	6
490	07-MAY-84	6.0	6
493	24-JUN-85	7.5	7

Note how union differs from join. Union can be thought of as appending one relation to another, with elimination of duplicated rows. Join concatenates tuples from one relation to tuples from another relation based on the join condition. With union, the number of columns in the result is the same as the number of columns in the two operand relations; the number of rows is the sum of the rows in each relation less duplicated rows. The number of columns resulting from a join is the sum of the number of columns of the two operand relations (less duplicated columns if it is a natural join). The number of rows in the result cannot be easily stated—it can range from as low as zero if no tuples from the two relations satisfy the join condition, to as high as the product of the number of rows in both relations. For example, suppose relation A has three rows, relation B has four rows. If every row of relation A is joined with every row of relation B, then the resulting relation will have three times four, or 12 rows.

Here is a more complex example that requires use of join and union as well as selection and projection operations: We want not only SIDs of graduate students with loans of over $2,000, but also their names. Note that the following does not work

```
STUDENT (WHERE SLEVEL = 5) [SID, NAME]
     UNION
LOAN (WHERE AMOUNT > 2000) [SID]
```

because the two relation operands are not union compatible—the first relation has two columns, SID and NAME; the second has only a single column, SID. The way to answer the query requires union to be applied just to SIDs, then the SIDs are joined with STUDENT and SID and NAME projected:

```
( STUDENT (WHERE SLEVEL = 5) [SID]
     UNION
LOAN (WHERE AMOUNT > 2000) [SID] )
     JOIN
STUDENT [SID, NAME]
```

INTERSECTION. A INTERSECT B results in a new relation containing all the rows that appear in both relation A and relation B. Relations A and B must be union compatible.

An example of INTERSECT would be all grads with loan amounts greater than $2,000. Using the GRADS and BIG_LOAN determined above, the expression is:

```
GRADS INTERSECT BIG_LOAN
```

with a single resulting row:

```
SID
----
3749
```

Once again this could be written as a single query:

```
STUDENT (WHERE SLEVEL=5) [SID]
INTERSECT
LOAN (WHERE AMOUNT > 2000) [SID]
```

DIFFERENCE. A MINUS B results in a new relation that contains all the rows that are in relation A but not in relation B. A and B must be union compatible.

Grads with no loans over $2,000 would be an example of the MINUS operation:

```
GRADS MINUS BIG_LOANS
```

which results in the single row, SID=8767. As a nested query, this can be written:

```
STUDENT (WHERE SLEVEL=5)[SID]
     MINUS
LOAN (WHERE AMOUNT > 2000)[SID]
```

Extended Cartesian Product

A TIMES B results in a new relation containing every row from relation A concatenated with every row from relation B. Note that if the cardinality (number of tuples) of A is M and the cardinality of B is N, then the cardinality of A times B is M times N.

To illustrate the Cartesian product we first do selections and projections on the two operand relations in order to reduce the size of the result. First we select the graduate students:

```
GRADS:=STUDENT(WHERE SLEVEL=5)[SID, NAME]
```

The result is:

```
SID        NAME

----       -------

8767       CABEEN
3749       WATSON
```

We also select all the loans over $2,000 projecting LID and SID:

```
BIG_LOANS:=LOAN(WHERE AMOUNT > 2000) [LID, SID]
```

The result is:

```
LID  SID
---- ------
92   4494
99   4494
490  3749
493  3749
```

Then the product of GRADS and BIG_LOAN is:

```
GRADS TIMES BIG_LOAN
```

with the result:

```
SID        NAME      LID  SID
---        ------    ---  ----
8767       CABEEN     92  4494
8767       CABEEN     99  4494
8767       CABEEN    490  3749
8767       CABEEN    493  3749
3749       WATSON     92  4494
3749       WATSON     99  4494
3749       WATSON    490  3749
3749       WATSON    493  3749
```

This can also be done with the following nested query:

```
STUDENT (WHERE SLEVEL = 5) [SID, NAME] TIMES
LOAN (WHERE AMOUNT > 2000) [LID, SID]
```

A join can always be replaced by a Cartesian product and appropriate SELECT. For example, to obtain the names and IDs of all grads with loans greater than $2,000, we could project SID and NAME from the Cartesian product found above with the condition that the two SID columns must have the same value. The relational algebra expression is:

```
(STUDENT (WHERE SLEVEL = 5) [SID, NAME] TIMES
LOAN (WHERE AMOUNT > 2000) [LID, SID])
    (WHERE STUDENT.SID = LOAN.SID) [STUDENT.SID, NAME]
```

The result would be the single row: SID=3749, NAME = WATSON. The equivalent join approach is:

```
STUDENT (WHERE SLEVEL=5) JOIN LOAN (WHERE AMOUNT>2000) [SID, NAME]
```

Clearly, the join approach is cleaner. The primary reason for these examples is to show that there are equivalent operations—for example, a join can always be replaced by a Cartesian product and a select. The Cartesian product equivalent also, in a sense, defines how the join operation works.

Division

Suppose we want to find all SIDs for students with loans from the two banks Peoples and Seafirst. One way of getting the desired result is to join LOAN with itself over equal SID values but unequal LID values.

The result of the self-join is then tested for rows with both BID values—that is, SEAFIRST and PEOPLES. The operations are shown in steps to illustrate:

```
ALIAS L1 FOR LOAN
ALIAS L2 FOR LOAN

L1 JOIN (L1.SID = L2.SID AND L1.LID < L2.LID) L2
      [L1.LID, L2.LID, L1.SID, L1.BID, L2.BID]
```

The result is:

L1.LID	L2.LID	L1.SID	L1.BID	L2.BID
27	78	9735	HOME	PEOPLES
27	87	9735	HOME	SEAFIRST
78	87	9735	PEOPLES	SEAFIRST
92	99	4494	FIDELITY	FIDELITY
490	493	3749	PEOPLES	PEOPLES

This has identified everyone with two or more loans (which is a necessary condition in order for each person to have one or more loans from each of the two banks, Seafirst and Peoples). The desired rows are those where L1.BID = PEOPLES and L2.BID = SEAFIRST or vice-versa. Here is the complete expression with slight changes (which you should work through):

```
( L1 (WHERE BID = 'PEOPLES')
JOIN (L1.SID = L2.SID AND L1.LID ≠ L2.LID)
L2 (WHERE BID = 'SEAFIRST') )
[L1.SID]
```

The result is the single row, SID = 9735.

This query can be solved with the division operator. First, we need to create a relation with a single column containing the desired values of BID. Call this relation BID_SEL; it contains:

```
BID
--------
PEOPLES
SEAFIRST
```

BID_SEL is now divided into the projection of LOAN over SID, BID:

```
LOAN [SID, BID] DIVIDEBY BID_SEL
```

The result is the single row, SID = 9735.

Magic? Not quite. The division operation can be thought of as first grouping rows of the dividend relation (the projection of LOAN over SID and BID) by the attribute that does not appear in the divisor relation. That is, since BID_SEL has the single column BID, LOAN [SID,BID] is divided into groups of rows by SID. To make our example a bit more interesting, we have added another row to LOAN with LID = 888, SID = 3749, BID = CAPITAL.

```
LOAN [SID, BID]

SID        BID
----       -----
9735       HOME
9735       PEOPLES        ] "9735 Group"
9735       SEAFIRST

4494       FIDELITY         "4494 Group"

8767       PEOPLES          "8767 Group"

3749       PEOPLES        ] "3749 Group"
3749       CAPITAL
```

For a group to appear in the result (the quotient), its set of BID values must contain all of those BID values in the dividend (BID_SEL) relation—that is, both PEOPLES and SEAFIRST. For the given data, the result is the single row, SID = 9735.

In general, the division operator divides a relation A by a relation B. The relation A is the dividend relation and is of degree m+n. The relation B is the divisor relation and is of degree n. The result will be a quotient relation of degree m.

The previous example of division had M = 1 and N = 1. That is, the dividend relation A (in general) or the projection of LOAN over SID, BID (for our example) has two columns (M + N = 2); the divisor relation, B or BID_SEL, had a single column. Examples with M and N greater than one are more complex. The following query would have N = 2: Are there any students with a five-year loan from HOME and a six-year loan from FIDELITY? The first step would be to create the two-column divisor relation, BID_YR:

```
YEARS      BID
-----      --------
    5      HOME
    6      FIDELITY
```

The division is:

```
LOAN [SID, YEARS, BID] DIVIDEBY BID_YR
```

The dividend relation, LOAN[SID,YEARS,BID], is partitioned (again) by SID values since SID does not appear in the divisor relation. For each set of rows in LOAN[SID,YEARS,BID] with common SID value that contain the rows in BID_YR, the SID value will appear in the result. For our sample data the result is null.

Database Updates

Of course, in addition to being able to manipulate data in relations a DBMS must also be able to add and delete rows and update values. The relational algebra operators are sufficient to perform these operations, although they are quite clumsy. (Note: Remember, the relational algebra language is a theoretical language—it is not intended that it be directly implemented but rather to serve as a guideline. This is not unlike the way standard algorithmic languages such as PASCAL, FORTRAN, and BASIC implement algebraic expression. On paper we write expressions such as:

$$\frac{-B + \sqrt{B^2 - 4AC}}{2A}$$

The expression in a computer language would be similar to:

```
( -B + SQR(B**2 - 4*A*C))/(2*A)
```

Furthermore, just as conventional algebra makes no provision for input, neither does the relational algebra conveniently provide for additions, deletions, or updates.)

Additions

To add a row to a relation, we take the *union* of the relation with the row and assign the result to the relation. For example, to add the bank FIRSTBANK with BZIP = 10216, TYPE = 'SL' to the BANK relation we write:

```
BANK := BANK
        UNION
        {BID = 'FIRSTBANK', BZIP = 10216, TYPE = 'SL' }
```

Deletions

To delete a row, take the *difference* of the relation and the row. To delete the bank with BID = FIDELITY write:

```
BANK := BANK MINUS BANK (WHERE BID = 'FIDELITY')
```

Updates

Updates of the attribute-value-changing variety are possible also but are rather messy. To change a value the row is deleted using the MINUS operator, then added back with UNION. For example, to change the BZIP of PEOPLES from 98109 to 99163 write:

```
BANK := BANK MINUS BANK (WHERE BID = 'PEOPLES')
        UNION {BID='PEOPLES',BZIP=99163, TYPE = 'BANK'}
```

It is easy to devise a set of straightforward insertion, deletion, and update commands. For example, to add a row to STUDENT we might write:

```
INSERT STUDENT(1224, PUCKETT, 2, 25, 88001)
```

To delete specified rows from a relation, the command might have the form:

```
DELETE STUDENT (WHERE SID=4494)
```

and to update values, the form:

```
UPDATE STUDENT (SET AGE=24, SZIP=98040) (WHERE SID=2368)
```

Definition of a Relational System

To sum up this chapter we briefly review the definition of a relational database management system (RDBMS). At this time there is no commercial system that has completely implemented the relational model, but there are many products that come close. There is general agreement that it is not essential for a product to provide all of the features specified in the relational model for it to be able to provide many of the benefits of the relational approach. However, there are two properties of the relational model that must be present before a product can call itself relational. First, a relational system supports databases that are perceived by the user as tables and nothing more. And second, the system is able to perform, without requiring the user to define physical access paths, the operations select, project, and natural join.

Some of the products that are marketed as relational systems do not meet the criteria outlined above. Broadly speaking, the so-called relational databases fall into four categories.

The first catagory is database products that have a tabular data structure. However, the set-level operators are tabular rather than relational. Included in the list are inverted-list data structures.

The next category includes tabular data structures and some of the relational operators. Operators included are usually the SELECT, PROJECT, and the JOIN operators. Because of this, these systems, which include some of the microcomputer database systems, are considered *minimally relational.*

The third category includes many relational products, among them ORACLE, INGRES, DB2 and SQL/DS. These systems support tabular data structures and all of the relational operators. However, domains are not supported. Systems in this category are classified as *relationally complete.*

The fourth and final category is those systems that implement the entire relational model. This includes tables, the relational operators, domains, and the two integrity rules. These systems are considered fully relational. While some products are approaching these criteria, none are yet *fully relational.*

Commercial Relational Products

There are now many commercial database products based on the relational model. Much of the original relational model research was done on System R, developed during the 1970s at IBM's San Jose Research Laboratory. This research included not only the structure and operations for a relational model, but also concurrency control, access methods, and the interface between the relational system and the user. However, System R was never a commercial product.

IBM introduced two commercial derivatives of System R in the early 1980s: SQL/Data System (SQL/DS) in 1982, and Database 2 (DB2) in 1984. SQL/DS and DB2 are designed to run on different sizes of machines. SQL/DS was particularly designed for the intermediate range of IBM computers, including System/370, 303x, 43xx, and compatible DOS/VSE processors. DB2, on the other hand, was designed for the larger IBM systems. These include the MVS/370 and MVS/XA computers.

Another early relational database, called ORACLE, was produced by Relational Software, Inc. (now called Oracle, Inc.). Originally implemented on a DEC VAX, ORACLE is now available for a wide spectrum of computers ranging from mainframes down to desktop PCs. INGRES, from Relational Technology, was also developed on a VAX and is based on work originally done at the University of California, Berkeley. INGRES is now available on a range of machines from mainframes down to PCs. ORACLE and INGRES are both used extensively on UNIX-based multiuser systems.

Some of the popular relational database products are listed in Figure 4–5.

System	Vendor	Hardware	Operating System
DB2	IBM	IBM	MVS
SQL/DS	IBM	IBM	VM,DOS
AIM/RDB	Fujitsu	Fujitsu	OS IV/F4
ORACLE	ORACLE	IBM, DEC, DG, Macintosh	
		INTEL, MC68000	MANY
PDQ	Honeywell	Honeywell	GCOS 8
INGRES	Relational	IBM PC	MS DOS
	Technology	DEC, MC68000	VMS, UNIX
dBASE	Ashton-Tate	IBM PC	MS DOS
R:BASE	MicroRIM	IBM PC	MS DOS
INFORMIX	Relational		
	Database		
	Systems	DEC, IBM PC	UNIX, MS DOS

Fig 4-5   Some Relational Database Products

Questions and Problems

Questions

1. Define *table*, *relation*, *tuples*, and *domains*, and their respective properties.

2. Why are domains important?

3. What is a normalized relation? What are the advantages of normalization?

4. What are the degree and cardinality of a relation?

5. Why are repeating groups not allowed in a relational system?

6. Explain the integrity rules for a relational model.

7. What are the differences between a primary key, a candidate key, an alternate key, and a foreign key?

8. What kind of tuple-level addressing is used in a relational model?

9. What are the eight operators of the relational algebra, and what does each do?

10. Define and contrast the various forms of relational JOIN operators.

Problems

The following questions use the GSL database with example data as shown in Figure 4–1.

1. As shown in Figure 4–1, there are no duplicated values for NAME. Therefore, why isn't it a candidate key?

2. Why isn't the composite attribute, BID:LID, a candidate key in LOAN?

3. Suppose that the LOAN identifier is not unique—rather, LID is a "sequence" number that begins at one and counts up for each loan held by a given student. For example, since student 9735 holds three loans, their LIDs would be 1, 2, and 3. What are the candidate keys in LOAN? What are the foreign keys?

4. The SID 4494 was entered incorrectly in both STUDENT and LOAN relations. All occurrences of SID = 4494 should be changed to 9949. Given that referential integrity is enforced, what steps are necessary to make this change?

For each of the following relational algebra queries on the GSL database, show the output:

5. LOAN (WHERE YEARS > 5 AND AMOUNT < 2000)

6. Assume that arithmetic expressions are allowed in the WHERE condition, such as used in this query:

   STUDENT (WHERE AGE < SLEVEL + 16) [SID, NAME]

7. (STUDENT (WHERE SLEVEL = 1 OR SLEVEL = 2) JOIN LOAN (WHERE INT_RATE > 8.0)) [SID, AMOUNT]

8. ((STUDENT (WHERE SLEVEL = 1) JOIN LOAN) JOIN BANK) [NAME, SZIP, BZIP]

9. (STUDENT (WHERE SLEVEL = 1) [SID]) UNION (LOAN (WHERE BID = "PEOPLES") [SID])

10. (STUDENT (WHERE SLEVEL = 1) [SID]) INTERSECT (LOAN (WHERE BID = "PEOPLES") [SID])

For the following, you are to write the query using the relational algebra and show the result.

11. Display names and SZIPs of students of age less than or equal to 21.

12. Display names and SZIPs of students of age less than or equal to 21 who have one or more loans. (For example, this will exclude SANDs from the output.)

13. Display names of students who have loans with banks located in ZIP code 98101.

14. Display names and SIDs of students who do not have a loan.

15. For each student produce a list of banks that are located close to the student. A bank is "close to" a student if their respective ZIP codes differ by 10 or less. For example, ALTER is close to PEOPLES bank. (See question 6 above to see how arithmetic expressions may be used in a condition.)

16. First add the following tuple to the STUDENT relation: 1234, JONES, 3, 22, 89101. Then display the names and SIDs of all students with a non-unique name.

The following example database (see Figure 4–6), with CUSTOMER, ORDER, INVEN-TORY, and LINE ITEM relations, will be used for questions 17 through 26. The semantics (meanings) of the data are as follows. The database is for a wholesale supplier of electronics components. Virtually all sales are to a more or less fixed group of retail customers. The Customer relation holds data on these customers, including an identifier assigned by the wholesaler (CID), a name, and a location (CITY). Each customer has been assigned a credit rating (RATING). When a customer places an order, a tuple in the ORDER relation is created that includes a (unique) order number (ORD#), the identity of the customer (CID), the date of the order, and the name of the salesperson. An order is made up of one or more LINE ITEMS: one for each different part ordered. The LINE ITEM indicates the order it belongs to (ORD#), which line of the order it is (LINE), the identity of the part ordered (PART #), and the quantity ordered. The INVENTORY relation maintains data on the current quantity on hand (QTY), the part's identifier (PART #), a descriptive name of the part (NAME), and its selling price.

17. Identify the candidate keys for each relation.

18. a. Identify the foreign keys for each relation.

    b. If the first column (attribute) of LINE ITEM were named Order-No, would that attribute be a foreign key?

19. Consider the addition of the following tuples to LINE ITEM. Values are listed in the order ORD#, LINE, PART#, QTY. For each addition, indicate if there is anything that will prevent the entry.

    a. (108, 2, P8, 10)
    b. (108, 5, M7, 10)
    c. (108, 5, M4, 20)
    d. (103, 3, N2, 20)
    e. (112, 2, P4, 100)

20. Suppose another relation is added—EMPLOYEE (EID, NAME, JOB)—in which EID is the employee's number, NAME is his or her name, and JOB is his or her position (for example, salesperson, clerk, president). Given this change, how would you modify the current database?

Write relational algebra statements for each of the following queries and indicate the results.

21. Display customer names and ratings for all Chicago customers.

22. Display all order data for orders taken in March by salesperson Strong.

23. Display names of all salespeople who have taken orders during March from customers with less than A ratings.

24. Display names of customers with B ratings or who have placed an order with salesperson Strong.

25. Display any customer names that are not unique (for example, Myers).

26. Demonstrate two ways (such as using JOIN and Cartesian product) to list ORD#, PART#, and PART NAME for all parts with LINE_ITEM.QTY > 100.

CUSTOMER

CID	NAME	CITY	RATING
21	ADAMS	LOS ANGELES	A
24	MYERS	NEW YORK	A
29	HALL	CHICAGO	B
34	LEWIS	DENVER	A
39	HAMMER	CHICAGO	C
40	ENGLE	AUSTIN	B
42	MYERS	OAKLAND	B
46	ABLE	NEW ORLEANS	A
50	STROM	BOSTON	C

ORDER

ORD#	CID	DATE	SALESPERSON
102	42	860207	JOHNSON
103	39	860211	STRONG
104	24	860228	BOGGS
105	42	860303	STRONG
107	34	860308	WEST
108	46	860308	WEST
110	24	860312	BOGGS
111	21	860318	STRONG
112	29	860320	CLARK

INVENTORY

PART#	NAME	QTY	PRICE
M2	64K PROM	2000	10.00
SM1	64K STATIC RAM	500	5.00
M4	64K X 4 RAM	100	8.00
M7	64K RAM	1500	2.00
M10	256K RAM	500	5.00
P3	8088 CPU	120	8.00
P4	8086 CPU	40	11.00
P8	80286 CPU	70	100.00
N2	8087 NUMERIC CHIP	10	129.00
P5	68000 CPU	25	10.00

LINE ITEM

ORD#	LINE#	PART#	QTY
102	1	P4	20
102	2	M7	100
102	3	N2	7
103	1	P5	10
104	1	M2	100
104	2	M7	500
105	1	M7	100
105	2	N2	5
105	3	P4	20
107	1	P8	10
108	1	SM1	100
108	2	M7	400
108	3	P3	20
108	4	N2	4
111	1	P8	20
111	2	M10	100
112	1	N7	200

Fig 4-6 Electronic Components Wholesaler Database

References

Brodie, M. L., and Schmidt, J. W. eds. "Final Report of the ANSI/X#/SPARC DBS-SG Relational Database Task Group." *ACM SIGMOD Record*, vol. 12, no. 4 (July 1982).

Date, C. J. "A Formal Definition of the Relational Model." *ACM SIGMOD Record*, vol. 13, no. 1 (Sept. 1982), pp. 18–29.

_____. *An Introduction to Database Systems*. Vol. 1, 4th ed. Reading, Mass.: Addison-Wesley Publishing Co., 1985.

Loomis, M. E. S. *The Database Book*. New York: Macmillan Publishing Co., 1987.

Pirotte, A. "A Precise Definition of Basic Relational Notions and of the Relational Algebra." *ACM SIGMOD Record*, vol. 13, no.1 (Sept. 1982), pp. 30–40.

5 An SQL-based System: ORACLE

The objective of this chapter is to present the general architecture, operation, and capabilities of SQL-based relational database management systems.

Many commercial RDBMSs are based on SQL. ORACLE, a product of Oracle, Inc., is typical of several SQL-based products such as IBM's DB2 and SQL/DS products and Relational Technology, Inc.'s, INGRES. One of the attractive features of ORACLE and INGRES is that they run on a wide range of computer systems, from PCs to mainframes. ORACLE is used in this chapter to illustrate SQL concepts and operations.

In addition to basic DBMS functions, many add-on products are available for ORACLE and other products, to allow users to perform specialized functions such as graphics, report generation, and application generators. These features are not discussed here.

Note: This chapter involves learning a language. As with any language, the only real way to gain confidence and competence is to actually use it. Therefore, we suggest that you read through the section "SQL SELECT Statement, Simple Form," then read the appendix to this chapter, "Editing SQL Commands." If you don't have on SQL DBMS, stop at that point and try to work problems 1 through 14.

Introduction and Overview of SQL-based Systems

Structured Query Language (SQL) is a nonprocedural data definition and manipulation language that is part relational calculus and part relational algebra. A standard for SQL was approved by the American National Standards Institute (ANSI) in 1986. This standard, proposed by the X3H2 Technical Committee on Databases, specifies the functions and language syntax for SQL-based systems.

SQL's origins were in IBM's research relational DBMS, System R. System R was developed beginning in the early 1970s, following Dr. E. F. Codd's publication of a seminal paper ("A Relational Model of Data for Large Shared Data Banks", *Communications of the ACM*, Vol. 12, No. 6, June 1970). Work continues on System R in such areas as distributed databases and storage of nontraditional types of data.

The so-called User-Friendly Interface (UFI) of SQL is designed for interactive use by noncomputer specialists. SQL also can be embedded in a host language such as COBOL, PL/I, or FORTRAN. An attractive feature of SQL is that its UFI and embedded forms are virtually identical. Thus, to make the transition from the UFI to the embedded version does not require learning an entirely new language, a problem with many earlier DBMS languages and even with many of the new PC-based DBMSs.

SQL supports all of the relational algebra operations, including selection, projection, join, and union. In addition, it has statements for tuple addition, deletion, and update.

SQL's data definition language is used to define relations called *base tables*. It is also used to create virtual tables called *views*. Views are subsets of one or more real tables. Queries can be directed to view tables in the same way that they are directed to real (base) tables. (There are, however, some limitations on updates of views; see Chapter 6.)

The data definition language is also used to define database access rules. These are used to provide security and privacy for selected portions of the database.

Data Definition Language

The SQL data definition language supports the creation, alteration, and removal of tables through the following statements:

- CREATE TABLE
- ALTER TABLE
- DROP TABLE

The first step in defining a SQL database is to define the base tables. Base tables constitute the conceptual, or logical, level of a database. We will illustrate ORACLE/SQL by defining the GSL database. Example data for the database appear in Figure 5–1. This database will be used throughout the remainder of this chapter, as well as in parts of Chapter 6, to show how basic database functions are carried out using SQL.

Relation: LOAN

LID	Unique loan identifier; one to six digits.
LDATE	Year, month, and day the loan began.
YEARS	Term of the loan; integer values up to 20.
INT_RATE	Loan interest rate in percent; a four-digit number with up to two digits to the right of the decimal point.
AMOUNT	Initial amount of a loan; integer values up to $9999.
SID	Identifier of student to whom a loan was made; one to six digits.
BID	Identifier of the bank that made the loan; up to 16 characters.

Relation: STUDENT

SID	Unique student identifier; one to six digits.
NAME	Student name; up to 16 characters.
SLEVEL	1=Freshman, 2=Sophomore, 3=Junior, 4=Senior, 5=Graduate. (LEVEL is a reserved word in SQL.)
AGE	Age in years; two digits.
SZIP	ZIP code of student's residence; five-digit integer.

Relation: BANK

BID	Unique bank identifier; up to 16 characters.
BZIP	ZIP code of bank's location; five-digit integer.
TYPE	SL=Savings & Loan, MSB=Mutual Savings Bank, BANK=full service bank, CU=Credit Union.

Fig 5-1 Student-Loan Database Design

Note the shared attributes of SID in the LOAN and STUDENT relations, and BID in the LOAN and BANK relations. Both of these attributes, SID and BID, are foreign keys in the LOAN relation.

Defining a Relation

The CREATE TABLE *table_name* statement is used to define a base table. For example:

    CREATE TABLE LOAN

The table name is then followed by attribute definitions of the form: *name, data_type, length*. The allowable data types are completely defined in the following subsection. The most commonly used types include:

- A variable-length character string defined by CHAR(len) where len is the maximum length.
- A decimal data type defined by NUMBER (d) or NUMBER(d,s) where d is the total number of digits and s is the number to the right of the decimal point. For example, NUMBER(5,2) would define a numeric value of five digits, with two to the right of the decimal (for example, 123.56, -9.02, 999.99).
- A *date* data type, defined by specifying DATE.

An optional parameter, NOT NULL, can also be used to specify whether missing values are allowed. The GSL database is defined using these three data types in Figure 5–2. Note that it is not necessary to start each column definition on a new line as is done for the STUDENT and LOAN tables. In fact, spacing is somewhat arbitrary, and lines can be broken almost anywhere. The command is ended with a semicolon; see, for example, the definitions of LOAN and BANK.

```
CREATE TABLE STUDENT
      (SID NUMBER(6) NOT NULL,
      NAME CHAR(16),
      SLEVEL NUMBER(1),
      AGE NUMBER(2),
      SZIP NUMBER(5));

CREATE TABLE LOAN
      (LID NUMBER(6) NOT NULL,
      LDATE DATE,
      YEARS  NUMBER(2),
      INT_RATE NUMBER(4,2),
      AMOUNT NUMBER(4),
      SID NUMBER(6),
      BID CHAR(16));

CREATE TABLE BANK
      (BID CHAR(16) NOT NULL, BZIP NUMBER(5), TYPE CHAR(4));
```

Fig 5-2 Student-Loan Database Definition

Data Types

Despite the presence of SQL as a standard, not all of the various commercial implementations of RDMSs provide for the same set of data types. ORACLE, for example, supports three data types: number, character, and date.

- CHAR(c)—CHAR fields vary in length up to c characters. Allowable characters are digits, upper- and lower-case letters, and special characters such as +, -, %, $, & etc. The maximum value of c is determined by the operating environment and hardware (typically about 255 characters). The default length is 22 characters (bytes). Thus, a definition such as NAME CHAR without a length is also valid.
- NUMBER(d) or NUMBER(d,s)—Numeric values are stored as decimal data types. The total number of digits is specified by d, and s represents the number of digits to the right of the decimal point. NUMBER attributes may contain the digits 0–9 and a plus (+) or minus (-) sign.
- DATE—The standard format for DATE fields is DD-MON-YY for day, month, and year, for example, 12-AUG-86. It is possible to alter this format; see the ORACLE manual.
- LONG—A special long character string data type for strings up to about 64,000 characters. However, there are severe limitation on the types of operations supported for this data type. In general, it can only be displayed and updated; that is, it is not possible to search on data of this type.

In fact, ORACLE has a rather limited set of data types. IBM's DB2 implementation supports decimal and binary numeric data types, two types of character strings, and a date data type. Numeric data types are:

- INTEGER—A 32-bit word, 31-bit binary representation plus a sign bit. Range: $\pm 2^{\pm 31}$ - 1.
- SMALLINT—A 16-bit word, 15-bit binary representation plus a sign bit. Range: $\pm 2^{\pm 15}$ - 1.
- DECIMAL(d,s)—A packed decimal number, in which d represents the total number of digits and s represents the number of digits to the right of the decimal point. The maximum value of d is 15.
- FLOAT—A 64-bit binary floating point with 15 digits of precision.

There are two string data types, a fixed and a variable-length character type:

- CHARACTER(n)—This is a fixed-length string in which n represents the number of 8-bit characters and can vary from 0 to 255.
- VARCHAR(n)—A variable-length string of up to n characters in which n must be greater than zero. The upper limit of n depends on the pagesize, either 4096 or 32768 characters. As with ORACLE, strings longer than 254 characters have restrictions on where they may be used.

Modifying the Database Definition

An important feature of SQL is that base tables can be defined dynamically or altered at any time using the CREATE TABLE and ALTER TABLE statements. Tables may be removed at any time using the DROP TABLE statement. This eliminates the need to dump all, or a large portion of, an existing database and then reload it under a new definition when columns are added or tables deleted. (Note that a column may not be dropped, dynamically, from a table. To drop a column, a new table is defined without the column in question, then data is loaded from the current table to the new table, omitting the dropped column.)

Adding columns and deleting tables has no effect on the operation of application programs that do not reference the added columns or deleted tables. This provides a degree of data independence not found in most network and hierarchical systems.

Both DB2 and ORACLE support adding columns to an existing table; only ORACLE supports modifying an existing column.

To add the column STATUS to the (existing) LOAN table, the statement is:

```
ALTER TABLE LOAN
    ADD (STATUS CHAR(1));
```

To increase the width of the STATUS column:

```
ALTER TABLE LOAN
    MODIFY (STATUS CHAR(5));
```

Tables can be dropped at any time with the DROP TABLE statement. When a table is dropped, its definition, and any existing associations such as views, indexes, and the like are also removed from the system. In addition, the storage space for the tuples of the dropped table is released. To remove the LOAN table from the Student-Loan database:

```
DROP TABLE LOAN;
```

Data Retrievals

The SQL data-retrieval statement is SELECT, which, through its various clauses and ability to nest multiple SELECTs, can perform very complex queries. The result of a query is another table, which, if not otherwise specified, is displayed on the user's screen. SELECT can perform relational algebra selections, projections, joins, unions, and Cartesian products. Output can be sorted, and several simple statistical operations (such as MAX, MIN, AVG, and SUM) can be performed. The relational algebra set intersections and difference operations are not supported directly but can be performed using other operations, as demonstrated below.

Various forms of SELECT are illustrated in the following sections using the GSL database with example data shown in Figure 5–3. (Here we assume that data already exists in the three tables. Methods for inputting and updating data are described in the "Updates" section.)

The SQL SELECT Statement, Simple Form

An SQL SELECT statement specifies the columns to be displayed (that is, projected), the table from which the columns are obtained, and an optional restriction (selection) in a WHERE clause. A simple form of the SELECT follows. The brackets around the so-called WHERE clause indicate that it is optional. The vertical bar, I, is read "or." Three dots (...) mean that the previous element may repeat.

```
SELECT [DISTINCT] col_name [,col_name] ... | *
    FROM table_name
    [ WHERE col_name comparison_operator col_name
        | constant ] ;
```

STUDENT Table

SID	NAME	SLEVEL	AGE	SZIP
9735	ALLEN	1	21	98101
4494	ALTER	2	19	98112
8767	CABEEN	5	24	98118
2368	JONES	4	23	98155
6793	SANDS	1	17	98101
3749	WATSON	5	29	98168

BANK Table

BID	BZIP	TYPE
FIDELITY	98101	MSB
SEAFIRST	98101	BANK
PEOPLES	98109	BANK
CAPITAL	98033	SL
HOME	98031	SL

LOAN Table

LID	LDATE	YEARS	INT_RATE	AMOUNT	SID	BID
27	15-SEP-85	5	8.5	1200	9735	HOME
78	21-JUN-86	5	7.75	1000	9735	PEOPLES
87	07-SEP-83	5	7.0	2000	9735	SEAFIRST
92	12-JAN-85	6	7.5	2100	4494	FIDELITY
99	15-JAN-86	6	9.0	2200	4494	FIDELITY
170	30-APR-83	6	6.5	1900	8767	PEOPLES
490	07-MAY-84	6	6.0	2500	3749	PEOPLES
493	24-JUN-85	7	7.5	3000	3749	PEOPLES

Fig 5-3   Sample Student-Loan Database

The form SELECT * FROM table_name specifies all columns and rows. For example:

```
SELECT * FROM STUDENT;
```

would display the entire contents of the STUDENT base table. An example with row restrictions and column projections is:

```
SELECT SID, NAME
     FROM STUDENT
        WHERE SZIP = 98101;
```

SID	NAME
9735	ALLEN
6793	SANDS

As with the CREATE statement, it is not necessary to start each clause (SELECT, FROM, WHERE) on a new line. The above query could just as well have been written:

```
SELECT SID, NAME FROM STUDENT WHERE SZIP = 98101;
```

Also note the output formatting: right justify "RJ" and align decimal points, character strings are left justified. Chapter 6 describes methods for controlling output form. A message indicating the number of records that satisfied the query may also be displayed. In the following examples, we won't display that line.

The following sections describe the SQL language in some detail, primarily through the use of examples.

Single Relation Queries

Single-relation queries retrieve data from one database table. As shown in the example above, the SELECT statement without any row or column qualifiers results in the broadest type of search, that is, one that retrieves all columns and rows of a table. The resultant display is thus the original table. A shorthand method to specify all the columns of a table is the asterisk (*) as in:

```
SELECT *
        FROM LOAN;
```

To limit the number of columns in the result table (projection), the desired column names are listed:

```
SELECT LID, INT_RATE
        FROM LOAN;
```

LID	INT_RATE
27	8.5
78	7.75
87	7
92	7.5
99	9
170	6.5
490	6
493	7.5

The result is every row, but only the LID and INT_RATE columns.

The order of columns specified in a SELECT statement does not have to be the same as the order in the original table. Thus, the SELECT statement could be used to change the order of columns appearing in a result table.

Many queries will result in duplicated rows. For example, suppose we simply want a list of all the SIDs for students with loans:

```
SELECT SID
        FROM LOAN;
```

SID
9735
9735
9735
4494
4494
8767
3749
3749

If we have no interest in the number of loans each student has, there is probably no point in printing duplicated SIDs. The DISTINCT operator will restrict the output to unique occurrences. Thus:

```
SELECT DISTINCT SID
    FROM LOAN;

SID
-----
9735
4494
8767
3749
```

Note that only one DISTINCT may appear in each SELECT.

Examples: WHERE Clause, Ordering Result

To restrict the rows retrieved from a table, a WHERE clause followed by a predicate is added:

```
SELECT SLEVEL, NAME
    FROM STUDENT
    WHERE AGE >= 23;

SLEVEL    NAME
------    -------
     5    CABEEN
     4    JONES
     5    WATSON
```

The result is a subset of the original table containing only the specified columns and those rows that meet the selection criteria. In this example, the predicate—a statement about the values of a tuple that must be true—consists of a column name, a comparison operator (>=), and a numeric constant. If the comparison involves a character data type, the value must be between apostrophes, not quotation marks, as follows:

```
SELECT SLEVEL, NAME
    FROM STUDENT
    WHERE NAME < 'B';

SLEVEL    NAME
------    -----
     1    ALLEN
     2    ALTER
```

Comparisons may be combined using the Boolean operators AND, OR. When more than one of the AND/OR logical operators appear, the default evaluation sequence of this type of expression is AND before OR, left-to-right. That is, AND logical operations are performed first, beginning with the left-most AND. Then, OR operations are performed, left to right. The following example retrieves students who meet one or both of the following conditions: (1) an ID greater than or equal to 7000 and a ZIP equal to 98101; (2) a ZIP equal to 98112.

```
SELECT NAME, SID
    FROM STUDENT
    WHERE SZIP = 98112 OR SZIP = 98101 AND SID >= 7000;
```

```
NAME      SID
-----     ----
ALLEN     9735
ALTER     4494
```

Parentheses may also be used to explicitly specify the order of operations. For example, the following retrieves only those students who meet *both* of the following conditions: (1) having a ZIP of 98101 or 98112; (2) an ID greater than or equal to 7000. Note the difference in the result.

```
SELECT NAME, SID
     FROM STUDENT
     WHERE (SZIP = 98101 OR SZIP = 98112) AND SID >= 7000;

NAME      SID
-----     ----
ALLEN     9735
```

Allowable Forms of a Predicate. To provide a more formal definition of a predicate, a few other definitions are needed. First, in addition to columns and constants, an operand (a thing being compared) may be an arithmetic expression. An expression is similar to the usual definition of an expression in a language such as FORTRAN, BASIC, or PASCAL. For example, 2*SLEVEL + AGE is a valid expression. To select all young students, defined as those whose age is less than 17 plus their student level, the SELECT is:

```
SELECT *
     FROM STUDENT
     WHERE AGE < 17 + SLEVEL;

SID     NAME     SLEVEL     AGE  SZIP
----    -----    ------     ---  -----
6793    SANDS         1      17  98101
```

Quite complex predicates are possible, including the use of parentheses and a wide variety of both string and numeric functions. A definition of all available functions is beyond the scope of this text, but a number of the more widely used functions appear in the appendix to this chapter and are used in several of the examples in this and the following chapter.

To retrieve all student tuples where AGE plus the square root of AGE exceeds SLEVEL + 25 we write: (Note: Keep in mind that this query may not make sense. Subsequent, but more complex, examples will make use of functions for sensible problems.)

```
SELECT *
     FROM STUDENT
     WHERE AGE + SQRT(AGE) > SLEVEL + 25:

SID     NAME     SLEVEL     AGE  SZIP
----    ------   ------     ---  -----
3749    WATSON        5      29  98168
```

To summarize, the definition of an operand may be stated as:

operand := column | constant | expression

The vertical line separates options.

A *condition* is the next component of a predicate. A condition has one of the following forms:

```
condition := operand operator operand |
            operand BETWEEN operand AND operand |
            operand NOT BETWEEN operand AND operand |
            operand IN (value_list) |
            operand NOT IN (value_list)
```

The allowable comparison operators are:

<	less than
<=	less than or equal to
=	equal to
!=	not equal to
>=	greater than or equal to
>	greater than

As an example of the BETWEEN and IN operators, suppose we want to retrieve all banks with a zip code in the range 98101 through 98112. While we could write the predicate as BZIP >= 98101 and BZIP <= 98112, it is probably easier to write:

```
SELECT * FROM BANK WHERE BZIP BETWEEN 98101 AND 98112;

BID             BZIP        TYPE
--------        -----       ----
FIDELITY        98101       MSB
SEAFIRST        98101       BANK
PEOPLES         98109       BANK
```

As an example of the IN operator, suppose we want to retrieve all banks in the geographical vicinity of a student who lives in ZIP code 98102. We know that this includes ZIP codes 98101, 98102, and 98112. However, other ZIPs in the range 98101 through 98112 are not necessarily nearby. Thus, it is not satisfactory to use a predicate of the form BZIP BETWEEN 98101 AND 98112. Clearly, we could use a (messy) predicate, of the form BZIP = 98101 OR BZIP = 98102, etc. A simpler method is provided by using the *value_list* form of operand and the IN operator:

```
SELECT * FROM BANK WHERE BZIP IN (98101, 98102, 98112);

BID             BZIP        TYPE
--------        -----       ----
FIDELITY        98101       MSB
SEAFIRST        98101       BANK
```

The definition of a predicate can now be based on the definition of a condition:

```
predicate := condition |
        predicate logical_operator condition
```

This is a so-called *recursive definition*, since the thing being defined, a predicate, appears in the definition itself. What the definition says in words is that (1) a predicate may be simply a condition; or (2) it may be anything that meets the definition of a predicate (for example, a condition), followed by a logical_operator (that is, AND, OR) and a condition. The result is that we can combine conditions. (Observant readers will note that our definition is not 100 percent precise. For example, we have omitted the parentheses that can be included.)

Finally, note that an expression may also appear in the list of columns to display. As a simple example, suppose we want to calculate and display the amount of interest that occurs in the first month of a loan's life. This is the annual interest rate divided by 1,200 (to convert from a percentage to a fraction and from annual to monthly interest) times the initial amount of the loan. The SELECT to do this for loans of AMOUNT greater than $2,000 is:

```
SELECT LID, YEARS, INT_RATE, AMOUNT, INT_RATE * AMOUNT/1200
       FROM LOAN
       WHERE AMOUNT > 2000;
```

LID	YEARS	INT_RATE	AMOUNT	INT_RATE*AMOUNT/1200
92	6	7.5	2100	13.125
99	6	9	2200	16.5
490	6	6	2500	12.5
493	7	7.5	3000	18.75

This column heading for expressions is not particularly attractive. Chapter 7 will show how to clean it up.

Ordering the Output. By default, an SQL retrieval operation prints the rows selected in the order in which they appear in the database. To sort the result on some attribute, the ORDER BY clause is used. For example:

```
SELECT BID, TYPE
       FROM BANK
       ORDER BY BID;
```

The default sort order is in normal (ascending) alphabetic order. This can be changed to descending by adding DESC following the column name, for example, ORDER BY BID DESC. Ordering based on a combination of two or more fields is possible. To sort loans with a date prior to 1986, by SID and within SID in descending order by date (that is, the most recent loans first for each student), we write:

```
SELECT *
       FROM LOAN
       WHERE LDATE < '01-JAN-1986'
       ORDER BY SID, LDATE DESC;
```

LID	LDATE	YEARS	INT_RATE	AMOUNT	SID	BID
493	24-JUN-85	7	7.5	3000	3749	PEOPLES
490	07-MAY-84	6	6	2500	3749	PEOPLES
92	12-JAN-85	6	7.5	2100	4494	FIDELITY
170	30-APR-83	6	6.5	1900	8767	PEOPLES
27	15-SEP-85	5	8.5	1200	9735	HOME
87	07-SEP-83	5	7	2000	9735	SEAFIRST

LIKE and NULL

It is often desirable to establish selection criteria for character strings based on partial rather than complete matches to specified values. Such "generic" searches are supported in SQL by the LIKE operator followed by a character string constant enclosed in single quotes.

Inside the string, the wildcard character (%) represents any string of zero or more characters. The underline character (_) is used to represent any single character. For example, to select students who have A and N as the second and third characters of their name, followed by any characters, we write:

```
SELECT SID, NAME
       FROM STUDENT
       WHERE NAME LIKE '_AN%';
```

```
SID      NAME
----     -----
6793     SANDS
```

A pair of comparison operators, IS NULL and IS NOT NULL, can be used with the WHERE clause to control the retrieval of null, or missing, values. Assume that students ALLEN and ALTER have no SLEVEL values assigned in the STUDENT table. The following query would produce the result shown:

```
SELECT SID, NAME
     FROM STUDENT
     WHERE SLEVEL IS NULL;

SID      NAME
------   -------
9735     ALLEN
4494     ALTER
```

Complete Examples. We conclude this section with several rather complex examples that demonstrate the power and flexibility of SQL. If this is your first reading of the chapter, and you haven't yet tried SQL on a computer, these examples may prove to be difficult to follow. Again, the only real way to become proficient with SQL is to use it.

Example 1. Suppose that we want to perform an audit of our database that will include a careful study of the records of freshmen students. The staff of the Office of GSL will contact students to confirm the values stored in the database. Suppose further that there are literally millions of students in the table and that even for a single level there will be hundreds of thousands. Not having the resources to contact every student, we wish to restrict the output in two ways. First, we will begin by studying only those students in the state of Washington. They have ZIP codes beginning 98 and 99. Second, a sample of roughly one out of every 100 students, all of whom meet the freshmen and Washington state conditions, will be made. Finally, the output will be ordered by ZIP code and, within ZIP code, by name.

There is nothing particularly tricky about this retrieval except the condition that 1 percent of the qualified records is to be retrieved. How can we manage this? One approach would be to select only those students whose SID ends with a particular two digits. The right-most two digits of a numeric value can be isolated using the TRUNC function and following expression:

```
SID - 100*TRUNC(SID/100,0)
```

The *TRUNC (numeric value, d)* function truncates the numeric value to *d* places to the right of the decimal. (See the appendix for details of several functions.) For example, suppose SID equals 493282. Then TRUNC (SID/100,0) equals 4932. Multiplying by 100 gives 493200; subtracting from the original value gives the right-most two digits, 82. Thus, the SELECT could be written as:

```
SELECT * FROM STUDENT
     WHERE SLEVEL = 1 AND ZIP BETWEEN 98000 AND 99999 AND
          SID - 100*TRUNC(SID/100,0) = 67;
```

This would select all freshmen in the state of Washington whose student ID ends with 67. This seems okay, except for the possibility that student IDs (remember, these are actually social security numbers) may not be randomly distributed over the 100 possible last two digits. Selecting those ending with 67 might give too many, too few, or a nonrandom sample of students.

A result that will be closer to random and assure close to a 1 percent sample, can be achieved if we first "randomize" the student number. A good randomizing function can be based on the typical hashing function of *value modulo divisor*. We will then select from the result two digits that equal a specified value. To obtain a satisfactory randomization, the divisor should be a moderately large prime value, for example, 58231. The result (that is, the remainder of dividing the SID by 58231) will be a value in the range 0 to 58230. Finally, multiplying the result by 100/58231, truncating to an integer, and selecting those that equal any particular two-digit value will assure not only a reasonably random result but also very close to 1 percent of the otherwise qualifying records. The SELECT is

```
SELECT *
    FROM STUDENT
    WHERE SLEVEL = 1 AND ZIP BETWEEN 98000 AND 99999 AND
        TRUNC(MOD(SID,58231)*100/58231,0) = 16;
```

Using our (tiny) example database the result is:

SID	NAME	SLEVEL	AGE	SZIP
9735	ALLEN	1	21	98101

Example 2. This query will select loans with an initial date in January of any year and print their monthly payment amounts. The output will be LID, SID, and payment amount. Assume that the output is to be ordered by descending amount of monthly payment.

First, to select on a particular month we need to "mask" off the month value from the LDATE. Several string functions are listed in the appendix to this chapter. The appropriate one is TO_CHAR, which has the form: TO_CHAR (string, picture). The string may be a date column. Options for the picture are also described in the appendix. The picture we want is MM, which will mask out the month as a two-character month number. For example, TO_CHAR('01-FEB-88','MM') gives '02'.

The monthly payment on a loan of initial amount A, paid off over years Y, with annual interest rate R (as a fraction) is given by the following formula (see an accounting or finance text for annuity formulas):

Monthly Payment = $A*(R/12)/(1 - (1 + R/12)-12*Y)$

Writing this formula in SQL using AMOUNT, YEARS, and INT_RATE for A, Y, and R respectively gives:

```
AMOUNT*(INT_RATE/1200)/(1 - POWER(1 + INT_RATE/1200,-12*YEARS) )
```

Note that there is no exponentiation operator in SQL; the function *POWER (number, p)* serves this purpose by raising *number* to the *p*th power.

Finally, the ORDER BY clause can indicate the column number of the output on which to sort as opposed to the column name. (This overcomes the problem of having no column name when we are sorting on an expression value.) For example, the following SELECT sorts on SZIP and within that on AGE:

```
SELECT NAME, SZIP, SLEVEL, AGE
    FROM STUDENT
    ORDER BY 2, 4;
```

The final form of the query for this problem is:

```
SELECT LID, SID,
    AMOUNT*(INT_RATE/1200)/(1 - POWER(1 + INT_RATE/1200, -12*YEARS) )
    FROM LOAN
    WHERE TO_CHAR(LDATE,'MM') = '01'
    ORDER BY 3;

LID  SID     AMOUNT*(INT_RATE/1200)/(1-POWER
                ((1+INT_RATE/1200),-12*YEARS))
---  ----    -------------------------------
 92  4494                         36.3092358
 99  4494                         39.6561818
```

Example 3. Suppose that the student name is actually a last name followed by a comma and a first name (as is more likely the case in the actual database). We want to prepare mailing labels for a set of students and would like the first line of output to be arranged as first name, last name. Furthermore, suppose that our student relation also has the column SEX with M for male, F for female. We want male's names to be preceded by MR., females by MS. Before going any further, here is our revised student relation:

SID	NAME	SLEVEL	AGE	SZIP	SEX
9735	ALLEN,JAMES	1	21	98101	M
4494	ALTER,CARL	2	19	98112	M
8767	CABEEN,JULIE	5	24	98118	F
2368	JONES,FRANK	4	23	98155	M
6793	SANDS,LINDA	1	17	98101	F
3749	WATSON,SUSAN	5	29	98168	F

There are numerous string functions. To reverse the name order to first-last, the needed functions are INSTR, which will locate the comma in the NAME column; SUBSTR, which extracts a substring from a string; and LENGTH, which gives string length. In particular, the (string) expression to extract the last name is:

```
SUBSTR(NAME,1,INSTR(NAME,',')-1)
```

To explain this, take the name WATSON,SUSAN and work from the inside out. INSTR(NAME,',') gives the position of the comma in NAME—7 for this example; thus, SUBSTR(NAME ...) extracts the first character up to the comma from NAME; that is, the last name.

The string expression to extract the first name is:

```
SUBSTR(NAME, INSTR(NAME,',') + 1,LENGTH(NAME) - INSTR(NAME,','))
```

Working from the inside out again, INSTR(NAME,',') gives the position of the comma in NAME; subtracting INSTR(NAME,',')from LENGTH(NAME) gives 5, the number of characters in the first name. Thus, SUBSTR(NAME ...) extracts the seventh through twelfth character from NAME, that is, SUSAN. To print the first name followed by the last name we need to append the last name to the first in the output, with an intervening blank. To append one string to another the operator || is used. The appropriate expression is:

```
SUBSTR(NAME, INSTR(NAME,',')+1,LENGTH(NAME) - INSTR(NAME,','))
        || ' ' || SUBSTR(NAME,1,INSTR(NAME,',')-1)
```

ORACLE/SQL provides a function called DECODE, which will translate a value to another value. The form is *DECODE (column_name, value-1, constant-1, value-2, constant-2, ..., default string)*. If a column value matches value-i, then the output is constant-i.

If no match occurs, the output is the default string. For example, using the tuple for WATSON, SUSAN again, DECODE (SEX, 'M','MR.', 'F', 'MS.', ' ') results in translating "F" to "MS".

The full SELECT for this problem is:

```
SELECT DECODE (SEX, 'M','MR.', 'F', 'MS.', '  '),
    SUBSTR(NAME, INSTR(NAME,',')+1,LENGTH(NAME) - INSTR (NAME,','))
    || ' ' || SUBSTR(NAME,1,INSTR (NAME,',')-1)
FROM STUDENT;

DEC  SUBSTR(NAME,INSTR(NAME,',')+1,LEN
---  -------------------------------
MR.  JAMES ALLEN
MR.  CARL ALTER
MS.  JULIE CABEEN
MR.  FRANK JONES
MS.  LINDA SANDS
MS.  SUSAN WATSON
```

As you can see, there is considerable flexibility both in the output and in the selection. Subsequent sections will describe some additional controls over output form available to the user. For example, column headings, formatted numeric values (with dollar signs, commas, etc.), and many other options are possible. But, before getting bogged down in such details, we will turn to a discussion of one of the most important capabilities of a relational DBMS: the join.

Queries Using Joins

The ability to join one or more tables on any column is one of the more distinguishing features of relational systems. Formally, to join two columns they must be defined on the same domain. However, in practice few RDBMs support domains. Therefore, in most systems columns can be joined if they are of the same data type. With the use of various functions that convert from one data type to another, it is even possible to join two columns of different data types.

A join is implemented in SQL by specifying the column names and joining criteria in the WHERE clause. All of the standard join types are possible, such as equijoin, greater-than join, not-equal join, etc.

Equijoins. The equijoin is the simplest and most common type of join. The first example involves an equijoin of the loan and student tables with output of NAME and LID. (No other restrictions are included in the WHERE.) The joining condition is specified by the condition that two tuples are joined only if the two student IDs match. This is expressed by STUDENT.SID = LOAN.SID. Note the necessity of qualifying each column name with the name of the table if there is a possibility of ambiguity. Also note that the FROM clause must include the names of all tables involved in the query, whether their columns are used in the WHERE or in the projected output. The full query is:

```
SELECT NAME, LID
    FROM STUDENT, LOAN
    WHERE STUDENT.SID = LOAN.SID;
```

```
NAME      LID
-----     ---
ALLEN      27
ALLEN      78
ALLEN      87
ALTER      92
ALTER      99
CABEEN    170
WATSON    490
WATSON    493
```

A qualified form of reference to a column is always required when there is ambiguity. The qualified form precedes the column name by the table name and a period. For example, suppose the output of the above query is to include SID, and we want the join only for SIDs greater than 7000. The query is:

```
SELECT STUDENT.SID, NAME, LID
    FROM STUDENT, LOAN
    WHERE STUDENT.SID = LOAN.SID and STUDENT.SID > 7000;
```

```
SID      NAME     LID
----     ------   ---
9735     ALLEN     27
9735     ALLEN     78
9735     ALLEN     87
8767     CABEEN   170
```

In the above query, SIDs must be qualified in both the projected column reference and in the WHERE clause, because the SID could come from either STUDENT or LOAN.

The natural join is not supported directly, but this is of little consequence. Since there is no natural join, the SELECT using * will produce all columns from both tables, including the duplicated SID column. Following is the unedited output produced. Since the width of the output is too long for a screen, each output row requires two lines. (Hard to read? Chapter 7 will give us tools to clean it up.)

```
SELECT *
    FROM STUDENT, LOAN
    WHERE STUDENT.SID = LOAN.SID and STUDENT.SID > 7000;
```

```
SID NAME     SLEVEL    AGE      SZIP      LID
--------     -------   -------  -----     ---------
LDATE        YEARS     INT_RATE AMOUNT    SID BID
--------     -------   -------- -----     --------
9735 ALLEN         1   21       98101       27
15-SEP-85          5    8.5      1200     9735 HOME
9735 ALLEN         1   21       98101       78
21-JUN-86          5    7.75     1000     9735 PEOPLES
9735 ALLEN         1   21       98101       87
07-SEP-83          5    7        2000     9735 SEAFIRST
8767 CABEEN        5   24       98118      170
30-APR-83          6    6.5      1900     8767 PEOPLES
```

Any number of tables may be joined in a single query. For example, suppose we want SID, NAME, AMOUNT, and TYPE in the output for all loans with SID ≥ 7000. Thus, two joins are required: an equijoin of STUDENT and LOAN and an equijoin of LOAN and BANK:

```
SELECT STUDENT.SID, NAME, AMOUNT, TYPE
    FROM STUDENT, LOAN, BANK
    WHERE STUDENT.SID = LOAN.SID AND LOAN.BID = BANK.BID
        AND STUDENT.SID >= 7000;

SID       NAME       AMOUNT    TYPE
-----     -----      -------   ----
9735      ALLEN        2000    BANK
9735      ALLEN        1000    BANK
8767      CABEEN       1900    BANK
9735      ALLEN        1200    SL
```

Joins can be performed over attributes other than the usual primary key-foreign key. The following produces a listing of each student and the banks which share his or her ZIP code. To do this the join of STUDENT and BANK is over SZIP and BZIP. Since the two ZIP columns have different names it is not necessary to qualify them. The query is:

```
SELECT SID, NAME, BID FROM STUDENT, BANK
    WHERE SZIP = BZIP;

SID       NAME       BID
----      -----      --------
9735      ALLEN      FIDELITY
6793      SANDS      FIDELITY
9735      ALLEN      SEAFIRST
6793      SANDS      SEAFIRST
```

This ability to "connect" tables over attributes other than primary and foreign keys is one of the important features of the relational model. Earlier DBMSs (based on network and hierarchical models) required the DBA to determine, at the time of database design, the connections that might be made between two files. It is very unlikely that the designer would anticipate the connection over ZIP codes that this query illustrates. Yet, it is not a pathological example. The author's experience is that database users, especially in decision-support applications, need to be able to perform these types of queries quite frequently. In fact, in practice there are many queries that you might think were contrived if you didn't know they were from the "real world." (Note: Lest you suspect that queries such as this are contrived, we pass on the following: when IBM tested their research DBMS, System R, at several large companies, the users created queries for real problems that were so complex they overflowed the memory space the software designers had allowed for parsing and interpreting the query itself; that is, it was not the result of the query that was so large, but the actual SQL command itself. The solution was to allow more space. Other user needs resulted in extensions and refinements to SQL. The resulting language, we can safely say, is powerful and can handle virtually all real query problems.)

Joins Other Than Equijoin. While in practice most joins are equijoins, there are some situations where other varieties of joins are needed. Consider first a simple, if somewhat nonsensical problem. Suppose we want a listing of banks of type SL and the BID and AMOUNT of loans which do not belong to that bank—that is, a listing in which the BID in BANK does not match the BID in LOAN.

```
SELECT BANK.BID, LOAN.BID, AMOUNT
    FROM LOAN, BANK
    WHERE TYPE = 'SL' AND BANK.BID != LOAN.BID;
```

```
BID              BID              AMOUNT
-------          --------         ------
CAPITAL          HOME               1200
CAPITAL          PEOPLES            1000
CAPITAL          SEAFIRST           2000
CAPITAL          FIDELITY           2100
CAPITAL          FIDELITY           2200
```

As a more realistic example of non-equijoins, let's return to the problem of identifying banks that are near students. Suppose we define *near* as ZIPS that are within 20. A student with ZIP = 98112 would be considered to be near a bank with ZIP = 98101. The query is:

```
SELECT NAME, BID
     FROM STUDENT, BANK
     WHERE SZIP BETWEEN BZIP - 20 AND BZIP + 20;

NAME       BID
------     --------
ALLEN      FIDELITY
ALTER      FIDELITY
CABEEN     FIDELITY
SANDS      FIDELITY
ALLEN      SEAFIRST
ALTER      SEAFIRST
CABEEN     SEAFIRST
SANDS      SEAFIRST
ALLEN      PEOPLES
ALTER      PEOPLES
CABEEN     PEOPLES
SANDS      PEOPLES
```

One way to visualize any join operation is to consider the Cartesian product of two tables; that is, a table containing every row from one table combined with every row from another table. Then eliminate all those rows not meeting the specified selection criteria. The result is the desired join.

For additional examples of non-equijoins see the section on self-joins.

Subqueries

There is an alternative way of expressing joins that uses the capability of SQL to nest queries. *Nesting* means the capability to include another SELECT within the WHERE clause. For example, the value list supplied explicitly following the IN operator described above, may be replaced with a SELECT to produce a nested query, or subquery. Consider the problem of listing the SID and NAME of all students who have a loan. The "explicit" join form used in the previous section would be expressed in the following way using nesting/subqueries:

```
SELECT SID, NAME
     FROM STUDENT
     WHERE SID IN
          (SELECT SID FROM LOAN);

SID        NAME
----       ------
9735       ALLEN
4494       ALTER
8767       CABEEN
3749       WATSON
```

When a subquery is executed, it produces (of course) a relation. In the above example, the subquery result is a unary (one-column) relation of SIDs. The outer query is then executed and rows of STUDENT are selected which have SID values in the column produced by the subquery. Note that with the subquery it is not necessary to qualify SID. In the outer SELECT, all columns are from STUDENT; in the subquery all columns are from LOAN.

As a more complex nested-query example, the following query lists SID and NAME for all students who have loans with AMOUNT over $2,000 from banks of type BANK. This query demonstrates that nesting can be to several levels; the limit is usually large enough that it is not of concern for anything except "pathological" problems.

```
SELECT NAME, SID FROM STUDENT
    WHERE SID IN
    (SELECT SID FROM LOAN WHERE AMOUNT > 2000 AND BID IN
        (SELECT BID FROM BANK WHERE TYPE = 'BANK') );

NAME      SID
------    ----
WATSON    3749
```

You should also try writing this as a non-nested query. Which appears easier? While the developers of SQL seemed to prefer the nested variety, the author's experience is that most people seeing SQL for the first time find the explicit join easier. An interesting question is, even though the results from two queries might be the same, will the DBMS be smart enough to use the "optimal" method for processing each different form? The answer is *no*. Thus, the time required to process two different but logically equivalent forms might differ. With large relations and frequently repeated queries, experimentation with alternative forms is recommended to determine the faster method. (Note: With some DBMSs it is possible to request a display of the method the DBMS devised to process a query: the "plan." By looking at the plans for alternative equivalent queries, you may be able to determine which will execute faster without actually trying the queries out. Another highly recommended approach when dealing with large databases is to maintain a test database whose size is 1 to 5 percent of the real database's size. The test database is then used not only for performance estimation but also to check the semantics of queries.)

As another example of nested queries, consider the problem of listing all students who do not have loans. At first blush you might be tempted to use the following explicit, non-equijoin form to solve this problem:

```
SELECT STUDENT.SID, NAME
    FROM STUDENT, LOAN
    WHERE STUDENT.SID != LOAN.SID;
```

We will leave as an exercise determining why this query doesn't work. The correct result is produced by using the subquery form with the NOT IN operator:

```
SELECT SID, NAME FROM STUDENT
    WHERE SID NOT IN
        (SELECT SID FROM LOAN);

SID     NAME
----    -----
2368    JONES
6793    SANDS
```

In fact, the NOT IN operator performs essentially the equivalent of the relational algebra difference operator. The result of the inner query, the set of all SIDs with loans, is subtracted from the result of the outer query, the set of all SIDs.

Self-Joins

Tables can be also joined to themselves. A *self-join*, also called a *recursive join*, is another example of relational system flexibility that is seldom shared by DBMSs based on other models. (Note: In fact, some relational systems choke on self-joins. The self-join is one of the acid tests of a DBMS—if it can't do a self-join, chances are that there will be other queries that will be clumsy to code at best.) This is the situation where joins other than equijoins are most likely to be used. For example, suppose we want to find all banks that share a ZIP code with another bank. Thus, an equijoin of the BANK relation with itself is involved, matching on BZIP. Two problems arise. The following doesn't make sense:

```
SELECT * FROM BANK
      WHERE BZIP = BZIP;
```

This is simply going to produce the original table. We need a way of creating a "virtual" copy of the BANK table that can be joined with itself. This is done using the "alias" feature, as illustrated below:

```
SELECT A.BID, A.TYPE, B.BID, B.TYPE, B.BZIP
      FROM BANK A, BANK B
      WHERE A.BZIP = B.BZIP;
```

The form *table_name alias* specifies an alternative name for the table. Note that there is a space, not a comma, between the table name and the alias. The alias feature can be thought of as creating a copy of the table with the new name alias. In fact, no copy is actually created—the alias just allows an alternative way of referring to the table and allows us to distinguish two different occurrences of the same column value (that is, to compare or list values from a single column but two different rows). The query above works, except that in addition to listing every bank with its ZIP neighbor, it also lists every bank with itself:

BID	TYPE	BID	TYPE	BZIP
FIDELITY	MSB	FIDELITY	MSB	98101
FIDELITY	MSB	SEAFIRST	BANK	98101
SEAFIRST	BANK	FIDELITY	MSB	98101
SEAFIRST	BANK	SEAFIRST	BANK	98101
PEOPLES	BANK	PEOPLES	BANK	98109
CAPITAL	SL	CAPITAL	SL	98033
HOME	SL	HOME	SL	98031

Clearly, those rows where the two BIDs are equal are not informative. A simple modification gets rid of these uninteresting rows:

```
SELECT A.BID, A.TYPE, B.BID, B.TYPE, B.BZIP
      FROM BANK A, BANK B
      WHERE A.BZIP = B.BZIP AND A.BID > B.BID;
```

BID	TYPE	BID	TYPE	BZIP
SEAFIRST	BANK	FIDELITY	MSB	98101

(You should consider what the result would be if instead of the greater-than operator on BIDs, the not-equal-to-operator were used.)

Aliases can also be used to shorten table references, even if they are not required to differentiate column occurrences. The following query is written first without, then with, the use of aliases.

```
SELECT STUDENT.SID, NAME, LID
    FROM STUDENT, LOAN
    WHERE STUDENT.SID = LOAN.SID AND STUDENT.SID > 7000;
```

```
SELECT S.SID, NAME, LID
    FROM STUDENT S, LOAN L
    WHERE S.SID = L.SID AND S.SID > 7000;
```

Queries with EXISTS and NOT EXISTS

To motivate the EXISTS operator, consider an example. Suppose we want to retrieve *all* graduate students if *any* graduate student is more than 25 years of age. (While this might not seem to make sense, bear with us for a moment—more sensible situations that demand the EXISTS operator exist!) The following is clearly not correct, since it simply retrieves each graduate student who is more than 25 years of age:

```
SELECT SID, NAME
    FROM STUDENT
    WHERE SLEVEL = 5 AND AGE > 25;
```

We want not only the tuple for WATSON, but also the tuple for CABEEN, another graduate student but one who is not over 25 years of age. The proper query is:

```
SELECT SID, NAME
    FROM STUDENT
    WHERE SLEVEL = 5 AND EXISTS
    (SELECT SID FROM STUDENT
    WHERE SLEVEL = 5 AND AGE > 25);
```

SID	NAME
8767	CABEEN
3749	WATSON

The result is clearly what we were looking for—but how and why did it work? The EXISTS operator returns a value of TRUE if the subquery returns anything at all. Note that the columns projected from the subquery are immaterial: SID works fine, and the use of * would also work fine.

If no tuples qualify for the subquery, the EXISTS will be false. For example, the subquery in the following returns no tuples since there are no students with SLEVEL = 1 and with AGE > 25.

```
SELECT SID, NAME
    FROM STUDENT
    WHERE SLEVEL = 1 AND EXISTS
    (SELECT * FROM STUDENT
        WHERE SLEVEL = 1 AND AGE > 25);
```

Here is a somewhat more complex example. Suppose we want to examine all loans for a bank if that bank has any loan with an interest rate greater than 8 percent. For our sample

LOAN tuples, you can see that all loans for two banks should be returned: HOME, which has a single loan with an interest rate of 8.5 percent and FIDELITY, which has two loans, one with a rate of 9 percent. The loans for PEOPLES and SEAFIRST all have interest rates of 8 percent or less. The following is almost, but not quite correct:

```
SELECT LID, INT_RATE, BID
      FROM LOAN
      WHERE EXISTS
      (SELECT LID FROM LOAN
            WHERE INT_RATE > 8);
```

LID	INT_RATE	BID
27	8.5	HOME
78	7.75	PEOPLES
87	7	SEAFIRST
92	7.5	FIDELITY
99	9	FIDELITY
170	6.5	PEOPLES
490	6	PEOPLES
493	7.5	PEOPLES

Everything is returned. The problem is that we want to consider loans for one bank at a time. Note the added condition below, that BID equal FIDELITY:

```
SELECT LID, INT_RATE, BID
      FROM LOAN
      WHERE BID = 'FIDELITY' AND EXISTS
      (SELECT LID FROM LOAN
            WHERE BID = 'FIDELITY' AND INT_RATE > 8);
```

LID	INT_RATE	BID
92	7.5	FIDELITY
99	9	FIDELITY

This is fine, but it works only for one bank at a time. We need a scheme that will somehow cycle through the BID values one at a time—or in other words, that will examine the same BID value in both the inner and outer queries. We can make use of the alias to make a link from the outer to the inner query as follows:

```
SELECT LID, INT_RATE, BID
      FROM LOAN L1
      WHERE EXISTS
      (SELECT LID FROM LOAN L2
            WHERE L2.BID = L1.BID AND INT_RATE > 8);
```

LID	INT_RATE	BID
27	8.5	HOME
92	7.5	FIDELITY
99	9	FIDELITY

One way of imagining how this query works is to consider that the outer query loops through the tuples in the LOAN relation, with alias L1, one at a time. Each tuple in L1 has, of course, a specific BID: the first tuple has BID = HOME. Now, the subquery executes substituting HOME for L1.BID. This execution of the subquery finds no tuples that satisfy its predicate; that is, there are no tuples in LOAN that satisfy BID = HOME and INT_RATE

>8. Therefore, the EXISTS evaluates False and the first tuple is not displayed. The outer query now moves to the next tuple with BID = PEOPLES. The inner query executes again, with predicate BID = PEOPLES and INT_RATE > 8. Again, no tuples result from the inner query, so the second tuple is not displayed. When the outer query reaches the fourth tuple we finally hit pay dirt. The inner query predicate is BID = FIDELITY and INT_RATE > 8, and it produces a single LID (99). The EXISTS is True, and the LID, INT_RATE, and BID for the fourth tuple are displayed.

The NOT EXISTS operator simply *nots* the result of the EXISTS. That is, if the subquery returns something, the NOT EXISTS evaluates false; if nothing is returned, it evaluates true. Suppose that we want names and ages of all students of a given level only if everyone at his or her level is 20 years of age or younger.

```
SELECT NAME, AGE
    FROM STUDENT S1
    WHERE NOT EXISTS
    (SELECT SID FROM STUDENT S2
        WHERE S1.SLEVEL = S2.SLEVEL AND AGE > 20);

NAME      AGE
-----     ---
ALTER     19
```

The output excludes SANDS, even though he is under 20 years of age, because he is a freshman (SLEVEL = 1) and at least one freshman has age greater than 20.

When forms of the SELECT get messy or very complicated, it is usually interesting to determine if there is an alternative that is superior in any way. Here are several alternatives to the above examples using different approaches:

To display all graduate students if any of them have age > 25, we can also write:

```
SELECT SID, NAME
    FROM STUDENT
    WHERE SLEVEL IN
    (SELECT SLEVEL FROM STUDENT
        WHERE SLEVEL = 5 AND AGE > 25);

SID      NAME
----     ------
8767     CABEEN
3749     WATSON
```

To display all loans for a bank if any of that bank's loans have an interest rate over 8 percent:

```
SELECT LID, INT_RATE, BID
    FROM LOAN
    WHERE BID IN
    (SELECT BID FROM LOAN
        WHERE INT_RATE > 8);

LID      INT_RATE     BID
---      --------     --------
 27        8.5        HOME
 92        7.5        FIDELITY
 99        9          FIDELITY
```

We stress that while the EXISTS and NOT EXISTS are seldom needed, at times they may provide the simplest or, in a few cases, the only way to solve a particular query. Whenever you are tempted to use EXISTS or NOT EXISTS, carefully think through how it will work to see if it is appropriate. A couple of examples were given above that at first seem to provide the correct solution but, in fact, do not. On a database of 10 to 20 tuples, the wrong answer is usually easy to detect. On a database of 100,000 tuples, an improperly formed query may be expensive to execute, producing prodigous undesired output or output that appears correct but is not. (Note: A query that appears to produce the correct output but does not is probably the worst situation. Again, we recommend keeping a small sample database around—even smaller than the one suggested for performance testing. This sample should be rich—that is, it should have enough tuples to provide nontrivial output—but it should also be small enough so that the desired results can be determined manually.)

Using GROUP BY and Aggregate Functions

SQL provides a method of obtaining summary information such as count, sum, average, minimum, and maximum over a set of rows from a table. These are the "aggregate" or "grouping" functions since they operate over rows, as opposed to functions such as SQRT, TO_CHAR, etc., which operate on columns within a single row. The following aggregate functions are supported:

- COUNT (*) Counts number of rows in result.
- COUNT (col_name) Counts number of rows in result.
- COUNT (DISTINCT col_name) Counts number of unique values in specified column.
- SUM (col_name) Computes sum of values in specified column.
- AVG (col_name) Computes average of values in specified column.
- MAX (col_name) Computes maximum of values in specified column.
- MIN (col_name) Computes minimum of values in specified column.

For example, to produce a report showing the total number of loans, total amount, and average interest rate charged for loans the query is:

```
SELECT COUNT(*), SUM(AMOUNT),AVG(INT_RATE)
    FROM LOAN;

COUNT(*) SUM(AMOUNT)   AVG(INT_RATE)
-------- -----------   -------------
       8       15900         7.46875
```

To obtain these statistics for a specific bank, such as PEOPLES, we could obviously add a predicate to the query to restrict it to that bank. For example:

```
SELECT COUNT(*), SUM(AMOUNT),AVG(INT_RATE)
    FROM LOAN
    WHERE BID = 'PEOPLES';

COUNT(*) SUM(AMOUNT)   AVG(INT_RATE)
-------- -----------   -------------
       4        8400          6.9375
```

Suppose that we want to find these statistics for each bank. The above query could be run once for each bank in the table, but this will become quite tedious if there are more than a few banks. The solution is provided by the GROUP BY operator. First, the query:

```
SELECT BID, COUNT(*), SUM(AMOUNT),AVG(INT_RATE)
     FROM LOAN
     GROUP BY BID;
```

BID	COUNT(*)	SUM(AMOUNT)	AVG(INT_RATE)
FIDELITY	2	4300	8.25
HOME	1	1200	8.5
PEOPLES	4	8400	6.9375
SEAFIRST	1	2000	7

Conceptually, the GROUP BY can be considered to rearrange the rows of a table based on the value of the specified grouping column—BID in this case. Then, the functions are applied within each group. Following is the LOAN table grouped by BID:

LID	LDATE	YEARS	INT_RATE	AMOUNT	SID	BID
27	15-SEP-85	5	8.5	1200	9735	HOME
87	07-SEP-83	5	7.0	2000	9735	SEAFIRST
92	12-JAN-85	6	7.5	2100	4494	FIDELITY
99	15-JAN-86	6	9.0	2200	4494	FIDELITY
170	30-APR-83	6	6.5	1900	8767	PEOPLES
490	07-MAY-84	6	6.0	2500	3749	PEOPLES
78	21-JUN-86	5	7.75	1000	9735	PEOPLES
493	24-JUN-85	7	7.5	3000	3749	PEOPLES

Of course, the DBMS does not actually rearrange the rows of the table in this order. There are any number of ways it might produce this logical grouping (for example, by sorting the relevant columns on BID, using internal tables to accumulate sums and counts, etc.).

The GROUP BY can be applied to more than a single column. Suppose we want to produce these same statistics for loans by bank and by the year part of the LDATE column. Recall that there is a function, TO_CHAR, that allows us to mask off part of a date field. Specifically, TO_CHAR(LDATE,'YY') will return the two-digit year value of LDATE. The proper query is:

```
SELECT BID, TO_CHAR(LDATE,'YY'),COUNT(*),SUM(AMOUNT),
     AVG(INT_RATE)
          FROM LOAN
          GROUP BY BID, TO_CHAR(LDATE,'YY');
```

BID	TO_CHAR(LDATE,'YY')	COUNT(*)	SUM (AMOUNT)	AVG (INT_RATE)
FIDELITY	85	1	2100	7.5
FIDELITY	86	1	2200	9
HOME	85	1	1200	8.5
PEOPLES	83	1	1900	6.5
PEOPLES	84	1	2500	6
PEOPLES	85	1	3000	7.5
PEOPLES	86	1	1000	7.75
SEAFIRST	83	1	2000	7

Note that all columns following SELECT that appear outside of arguments of aggregate functions must appear in the GROUP BY. In the above query, the columns following

SELECT are BID and TO_CHAR(LDATE,'YY'). Thus, these same two columns must appear in the GROUP BY. Here is an example, that does not work because SID does not appear in GROUP BY:

```
SELECT BID, SID, COUNT(*)
    FROM LOAN GROUP BY BID;
```

Computer response:

```
SELECT BID, SID, COUNT(*) FROM LOAN GROUP BY BID
       *
ERROR at line 1: not a GROUP BY expression
```

Here is the corrected version and output:

```
SELECT BID, SID, COUNT(*)
    FROM LOAN GROUP BY BID, SID;

BID              SID          COUNT(*)
--------         ----         --------
FIDELITY         4494                2
HOME             9735                1
PEOPLES          3749                2
PEOPLES          8767                1
PEOPLES          9735                1
SEAFIRST         9735                1
```

Grouping can be performed on joins. For example, to find the total number and average amount of loans by student level:

```
SELECT SLEVEL, COUNT(*), AVG(AMOUNT)
    FROM STUDENT S, LOAN L
    WHERE S.SID = L.SID
    GROUP BY SLEVEL;

SLEVEL    COUNT(*) AVG(AMOUNT)
------    -------- -----------
     1           3 1400
     2           2 2150
     5           3 2466.66667
```

A common mistake is to write the WHERE and GROUP BY in the wrong order. The GROUP BY appears after the WHERE clause.

The WHERE clause can, of course, contain other than explicit joins. And the ORDER BY clause may also be used to order output. It appears following GROUP BY. For example, to produce the above report, but only for undergraduates (that is, SLEVEL <= 4), and to order the results by SLEVEL:

```
SELECT LEVEL, COUNT(*), AVG(AMOUNT)
    FROM STUDENT S, LOAN L
    WHERE S.SID = L.SID AND SLEVEL <= 4
    GROUP BY SLEVEL
    ORDER BY SLEVEL;

SLEVEL    COUNT(*)      AVG(AMOUNT)
------    --------      -----------
     1           3             1400
     2           2             2150
```

The aggregate functions can be combined as shown in the following examples. Furthermore, the argument of a function can be an expression, and/or the aggregate function may appear in an expression. A simpler way of saying all this is that you may use an aggregate function just about any place that it makes sense. Let's consider a more complex query to illustrate. Suppose we want to find the weighted average interest rate over all loans, where the weighting is by loan amount. If we have two loans with amounts of $1,000 and $2,000 and interest rates of 6 percent and 9 percent, the weighted average interest rate will be ($1000*6% + $2000*9%)/($1000 + $2000) = 8%. It is not the average of 6 percent and 9 percent.) The query is:

```
SELECT SUM(AMOUNT*INT_RATE)/SUM(AMOUNT)
    FROM LOAN;

SUM(AMOUNT*INT_RATE)/SUM(AMOUNT)
--------------------------------
                      7.38050314
```

As an even more complex example, suppose we want the (nonweighted) average monthly payment for each level of student. Recall that from an earlier example the monthly payment can be computed from by the following expression:

```
AMOUNT*(INT_RATE/1200)/(1-POWER(1+INT_RATE/1200),-12*YEARS))
```

Therefore, the average payment by SLEVEL is given by:

```
SELECT SLEVEL,
    AVG(AMOUNT*(INT_RATE/1200)/(1 - POWER
    (1 + INT_RATE/1200,-12*YEARS) ) )
    FROM STUDENT S, LOAN L
    WHERE S.SID = L.SID
    GROUP BY SLEVEL;

SLEVEL          AVG(AMOUNT*(INT_RATE/1200)/(1-POWER
                ((1+INT_RATE/1200),-12*YEARS)))
------          -----------------------------------------------------
     1                                                     28.1263981
     2                                                     37.9827088
     5                                                     39.7953045
```

Specifying a Restriction by GROUP: The HAVING operator

Suppose that we want to apply aggregate functions only to groups that meet certain conditions. For example, we want counts and average loan amount by bank, but only banks that have two or more loans. (From the sample loan table you can see that this will exclude HOME and SEAFIRST banks from the output.) The inclusion or exclusion of a specific group is specified by a HAVING operator. HAVING performs the same function for groups that WHERE performs for rows; that is, it eliminates (restricts) groups. The query solution is:

```
SELECT BID, AVG(AMOUNT)
    FROM LOAN
    GROUP BY BID
    HAVING COUNT(*)>= 2;

BID             AVG(AMOUNT)
--------        -----------
FIDELITY               2150
PEOPLES                2100
```

The COUNT(*) aggregate function in the HAVING predicate counts the number of rows in each group. If that count is greater than or equal to two, the group qualifies for output.

A SELECT with GROUP BY...HAVING may be used as a subquery. For example, to display the names of students with two or more loans, a subquery is used to determine those SIDs with COUNT greater than or equal to two:

```
SELECT NAME
      FROM STUDENT
      WHERE SID IN
      (SELECT SID
            FROM LOAN
            GROUP BY SID HAVING COUNT(*)>= 2);

NAME
------
WATSON
ALTER
ALLEN
```

UNION Operator

The previous examples were designed to produce a subset of an original table or joins of original tables by selectively eliminating columns and rows. The UNION operator combines rows from one SELECT with rows from another SELECT. (Note: At the time of writing, ORACLE does not support the UNION operator.) Thus, the sets of rows from the two SELECTs must be UNION compatible; that is, they must contain the same number of columns whose data types and widths are the same. Here is an example. We want names of all students with ZIP = 98101 or who have a loan with a bank that has ZIP = 98101. The approach is to write two separate (not nested) SELECTs, then UNION the results:

```
SELECT NAME
      FROM STUDENT
      WHERE SZIP = 98101
UNION
      SELECT NAME
            FROM STUDENT S, LOAN L, BANK B
            WHERE S.SID = L.SID AND L.BID = B.BID AND BZIP = 98101;

NAME
-----
ALLEN
ALTER
SANDS
```

Updates

The SQL data manipulation language can update table values. Rows can be deleted, added, and column values changed. Examples are first given for single-row operations. A subsequent section deals with updates on multiple rows.

Single-Row Update, Addition, Deletion

The general format of the command for changing the value of an attribute in a row is:

```
UPDATE relation_name
      SET col_name1 = value1 [, col_name2 = value2] ...
            WHERE table key = value;
```

By "table key" we mean that column, or possibly set of columns, that uniquely identifies a single row of the table; that is, a candidate key. For example, to change the number of years and interest rate of the loan with LID = 134:

```
UPDATE LOAN
    SET YEARS = 6, INT_RATE = 11
        WHERE LID = 134;
```

The general form of a single-row insertion is:

```
INSERT
    INTO relation_name
    VALUES   (value1, value2, ... valueN);
```

The values must be in the order corresponding to the column order for the table. For example, to add a row to the bank table with BID = MONEYBANK, ZIP = 19530, and TYPE = BANK:

```
INSERT BID, BZIP, TYPE
    INTO BANK
    VALUES ('MONEYBANK',19530,'BANK');
```

The general form of a single-record delete is:

```
DELETE
    FROM relation_name
    WHERE table key = value;
```

To delete the record for PACIFIC bank from the BANK table:

```
DELETE
    FROM BANK
    WHERE BID = 'PACIFIC';
```

Note that all the rows of a table would be deleted if no WHERE clause were to be specified above. The table would then be empty. This is not the same as DROPping a table. When a table is DROPped, its definition as well as its data no longer exists. When it is empty as a result of a total delete, its definition still exists; it simply does not contain any data.

Batch operations can also be performed to add, change, or delete data. These are not discussed in this text, although Chapter 7 shows how they are done using embedded SQL.

ORACLE contains a global command that governs when changes to a database take place. To have changes take place immediately, the statement SET AUTOCOMMIT IMM is issued. To defer "hard update" of the table, use SET AUTOCOMMIT OFF. When AUTOCOMMIT OFF is in effect, changes are not made permanent until the statement COMMIT WORK is issued. Therefore, changes made prior to executing a COMMIT WORK may be canceled ("undone") by issuing the ROLLBACK WORK statement. If the user terminates the session before issuing any COMMIT WORK commands, then the system automatically performs that function.

Here is a simple example:

```
SET AUTOCOMMIT OFF

INSERT INTO BANK VALUES ('TEST1', '11111', 'BANK');
```

This first insertion is made permanent, followed by insertion of another row:

```
COMMIT WORK

INSERT INTO BANK VALUES ('TEST2', '22222', 'BANK');
```

A query on BANK shows that both inserted rows are present:

```
SELECT * FROM BANK WHERE TYPE = 'BANK';

BID          BZIP      TYPE
--------     -----     ----
SEAFIRST     98101     BANK
PEOPLES      98109     BANK
TEST1        11111     BANK
TEST2        22222     BANK
```

Now, we undo the second insertion, then query the BANK table again:

```
ROLLBACK WORK

SELECT * FROM BANK WHERE TYPE = 'BANK';

BID          BZIP      TYPE
--------     -----     ----
SEAFIRST     98101     BANK
PEOPLES      98109     BANK
TEST1        11111     BANK
```

Note that bank TEST2 is gone. The same type of undo is possible for deletes and updates. The safe way of operating is to use SET AUTOCOMMIT OFF. Then, only after you are certain that changes are appropriate, issue COMMIT WORK.

Multiple-Record Updates

The syntax for multiple-record updates and deletes is identical to single-record updates except that the WHERE clause is broadened. To delete from the LOAN table all the instances of loans for the student whose name is ALLEN:

```
DELETE FROM LOAN
     WHERE LID IN
     (SELECT LID FROM STUDENT
          WHERE NAME = 'ALLEN');
```

A query on LOAN using ALLEN's SID (9735) reveals that those three loans are gone.

As the preceding example illustrates, the syntax for the DELETE is quite general. Following the DELETE FROM ... WHERE, we may have any predicate—including nested SELECTs—that is allowed for the SELECT command. This illustrates, again, the beauty of SQL. We don't have to continually learn complex new syntax for new operations. To perform updates we only need to learn several minor additions to what has already been covered in dealing with SELECT. This is not generally the case with other DBMS manipulation languages.

Changes to multiple rows can be performed in a similar manner. For example, to decrease the interest rate on all loans for FIDELITY bank by .5 percent:

```
UPDATE LOAN
     SET INT_RATE = INT_RATE - 0.5
     WHERE BID = 'FIDELITY';
```

The update is verified by the following query:

```
SELECT LID, INT_RATE, SID FROM LOAN;

LID      INT_RATE    SID
---      --------    -----
 27        8.5       9735
 78        7.75      9735
 87        7         9735
 92        7         4494
 99        8.5       4494
170        6.5       8767
490        6         3749
493        7.5       3749
```

Before going on, assume that the above updates are undone. The following examples, unless otherwise noted, will deal with the original form of the LOAN table.

As a more involved example, suppose a regulation is passed saying that the maximum permissible interest rate is 8 percent unless the loan is held by an individual who has three or more loans. If you look at the LOAN table you will see that the interest rate for the loan with LID 99 should be reduced from 9 to 8 percent, since the student holding this loan has only two loans. (However, the other loan in the table with a rate over 8 percent is held by a person with three loans, therefore, no interest rate change is required.)

```
UPDATE LOAN
     SET INT_RATE = 8
     WHERE INT_RATE > 8 AND SID IN
          (SELECT SID FROM LOAN
               GROUP BY SID HAVING COUNT(*) < 3);
```

The following query validates that the update worked as specified—in particular, that the interest rate for the loan with LID 99 was reduced from 9 to 8 percent because this student, SID=8767, had less than three loans.

```
SELECT LID, INT_RATE, SID FROM LOAN;

LID      INT_RATE    SID
---      --------    ----
 27        8.5       9735
 78        7.75      9735
 87        7         9735
 92        7.5       4494
 99        8         4494
170        6.5       8767
490        6         3749
 93        7.5       3749
```

Assigning Results to a Relation: Multiple-Row Insertion

The default output for an SQL query is the user's display screen. Thus, the result table does not exist in memory or on any permanent storage media. To "hold" the result table for future use, an INSERT... SELECT form of the INSERT is used.

Before saving results in a table, that table must be created (that is, defined) using the CREATE TABLE statement. For example, suppose we want to create a table of all graduate students. Furthermore, this table will only have rows SID, NAME, and SZIP. The table, called GRAD_ST, is first defined:

```
CREATE TABLE GRAD ST
     (SID NUMBER(6),
     NAME CHAR(16),
     GZIP NUMBER(5));
```

Data is now inserted into GRAD_ST by the following:

```
INSERT INTO GRAD ST (SID, NAME, GZIP)
     SELECT SID, NAME, SZIP
          FROM STUDENT
          WHERE SLEVEL = 5;
```

The following SELECT on GRAD_ST shows that we were successful:

```
SELECT * FROM GRAD ST;

SID       NAME      GZIP
----      ------    -----
8767      CABEEN    98118
3749      WATSON    98168
```

As you might expect, since a result column can be an expression, its value may be inserted into a new table. To illustrate, suppose a frequent application needs the loan identifier, corresponding SID, and monthly payment amount for all loans from the bank PEOPLES. While this application could compute the payment each time it is needed, that would be time-consuming. Therefore, a new table, PEO_LOAN_PAY, is defined with three columns: LID, SID, and PAYMENT.

```
CREATE TABLE PEO LOAN PAY
     (SID NUMBER(6),
     LID NUMBER(6 )
     PAYMENT NUMBER(5,2));
```

The PAYMENT will be rounded to integral cents using the ROUND(value,d) function, which rounds value to d places to the right of the decimal.

```
INSERT INTO PEO LOAN PAY (LID, SID, PAYMENT)
     SELECT LID, SID,
          ROUND(AMOUNT*(INT RATE/1200)/
              (1-POWER((1 + INT RATE/1200),-12*YEARS)),2)
          FROM LOAN WHERE BID = 'PEOPLES';
```

Here is the result:

```
SELECT * FROM PEO LOAN PAY;

SID       LID       PAYMENT
----      ---       -------
9735       78        20.16
8767      170        31.94
3749      490        41.43
3749      493        46.01
```

Keep in mind that when data from one table is inserted into another, any changes to the original table are not reflected in the other table, and vice versa. The table of extracted, and possibly recomputed values, is based on the original table(s) at the time the insert is executed. The result table is also termed a database "snapshot" because, like a photograph, it does not reflect changes to its subject that take place later in time.

Concluding Comments

The above examples should impress you with the extensive capabilities of SQL. Without resorting to the use of a host language (such as COBOL, PL/I, or FORTRAN), it is possible to perform very complex queries and even manipulate output to a considerable extent. The next chapter will describe SQL features that can be used to improve the appearance of output and to generate subtotals and totals (that is, report-writing capabilities). That chapter will also describe the SQL approach to the creation of the external level.

While SQL is both very powerful and very well designed, its design could have been better. One of its deficiencies was noted above: the ability to write a given query in more than one form might seem desirable at first but results in the user experimenting with different versions (for example, explicit join versus nested query) to see which one performs best. The objective of the relational approach is to free the user from concerns about how a query is processed. That was supposed to be the job of the DBMS and, in part through his or her responsibility for the physical database design, of the database administrator. An interesting article by C. J. Date provides additional examples and criticism of the language ("Where SQL Falls Short." *Datamation*, May 1987, pp. 83ff.).

SQL is not all-powerful (although we could argue that any system that tries to do too much will either fail or be so complex that it will be very unfriendly). There are many situations in which additional processing of the result of a query is necessary and the capabilities of SQL will not suffice. The user then has several choices: SQL can be embedded in the programming language as described in the next chapter or the output from SQL can be transferred to a standard file that is subsequently input and processed by a programming language or some other tool such as a spreadsheet.

APPENDIX: ORACLE SQL Functions and Manipulating Date Data Types

In this appendix we describe a few of the many functions that are available in the ORACLE implementation of SQL. Also described are several of the types of operations that can be performed on values of data type *date*. Many of these functions and date operators are supported by other implementations, but you should check manuals for your specific system.

The functions can be divided into those which are more or less standard arithmetic functions, and those that deal with string and date data types.

Arithmetic Functions

In the following table, X, Y, D, and P, are arithmetic expressions; that is, they range from simple constants and attribute names to complex expressions involving constants, attributes, and both arithmetic and string/date functions. Brackets are used for optional arguments. The default value is given in parentheses under the explanation.

Function Reference	Explanation
POWER (X, P)	Raise X to the P power, i.e., XP.
ROUND (X [, D])	Round X to D digits to the right of the decimal. (D=0).
TRUNC (X [, D])	Truncate X at D digits to right of decimal (D=0).
ABS (X)	Absolute value of X.
MOD (X, Y)	X modulo Y.
SIGN (X)	+1 if X positive, 0 if X=0, -1 if X negative.

Character String Functions

The following functions operate on strings and/or numeric values returning either a character string or a numeric result. In the following, S and T are character valued, B and L are numeric valued.

Function Reference	Result	Explanation and Example
LENGTH (S)	Numeric	Length of S LENGTH ('TO BE OR NOT TO') = 15
SUBSTR (S, B, L)	Char	The L characters beginning at the Bth character of S. SUBSTR ('TO BE OR NOT TO',4, 5) = 'BE OR'
INSTR (S, T [,B])	Numeric	Position of the first occurrence of the string T in S starting at B. If T is not in S, the result is 0 (B = 1). INSTR ('TO BE OR NOT TO','TO') = 1 INSTR ('TO BE OR NOT TO','TO',5) = 14 INSTR ('TO BE OR NOT TO','XX',1) = 0
TO_NUMBER(S)	Numeric	The numeric value of S (if S has the form of a valid numeric constant). See additional discussion below. TO_NUMBER('18.45') = 18.45
TO_CHAR (X)	Char	The character representation of X.(See below.) TO_CHAR(18.45) = '18.45'
DECODE	See below.	

The TO_NUMBER and TO_CHAR functions also have the ability to translate dates to string or numeric types according to a specified *picture*. First, we give a couple of examples:

Function Use	Value	Explanation/Comment
TO_CHAR ('07-MAY-41','MM/DD/YY')	'05/07/41'	MM, DD, YY are two-digit values of month, day, and year.
TO_CHAR ('07-MAY-41','YYYY-DDD')	'1941-127'	YYYY is four-digit year; DDD is the day of the year.

TO_CHAR ('07-MAY-41','MONTH')	'MAY'	MONTH is the name of the month.
TO-NUMBER ('07-MAY-41','DDD')	127	Numeric result.

A few of the available pictures are:

Picture	Meaning (and Examples)
YY	Two-digit year
YYYY	Four-digit year
MM	Two-digit month
DD	Two-digit day
DDD	Day of year
D	Day of week
MONTH	Full month name, all caps (JANUARY, FEBRUARY)
Month	Full month name, first letter capitalized (March)
MON	Three-letter month abbreviation (APR, MAY, JUN)
DAY	Name of day (SUNDAY, MONDAY)

(Note: Refer to your system manual for other picture specifications.)

Date Arithmetic

Limited arithmetic can be performed on dates. For example, you can add or subtract a number to a date: '01-MAR-89' + 60 = '30-APR-89'. A date may be subtracted from another date, with the result being the number of days between them: '30-APR-89' - '01-MAR-89' = 60.

Date functions are also available that provide the ability to perform more complex operations on dates and numbers. For example, the function MONTHS_BETWEEN (*date1*, *date2*) determines the numeric value of the number of months between two dates; NEXT_DAY (date1, day) gives the next date following date1 on which the day (for example, MONDAY) occurs. Again, you are referred to an SQL manual for details.

APPENDIX: Editing SQL Statements

ORACLE includes a simple editor which can be used on the "current" SQL command. Generally, the current command is the one just entered. The "current line" is the line just listed (with the LIST) command. The available editor operations are:

- LIST[n]—Lists the current command or its *nth* line.
- APPEND *text*—Appends *text* to the right of the current line of the command.
- DEL—Deletes the current line.
- CHANGE /*old* / *new*/—Changes the first occurrence of text *old* to *new* in the current line.
- INPUT—Allows insertion of new line(s) after the current line.
- RUN—Executes the current command.

Here are several examples of these edit commands on the GSL tables. Note that the line numbers entered by ORACLE are included in the listing. Furthermore, to clearly distinguish between user input and computer response, the user input is underlined. However, output from execution of the SQL commands has been suppressed.

First, a SQL command is entered:

```
SELECT SID, NAME
2      FROM STUDENT
3      WHERE AGE > 24;
```

The above command is now the current command and can be displayed:

```
UFI > LIST

1      SELECT SID, NAME
2      FROM STUDENT
3*     WHERE AGE > 24
```

A specific line can be listed by specifying the line number after LIST. In addition, commands can be abbreviated—L is equivalent to LIST.

```
UFI > L3

3*     WHERE AGE > 24
```

We now use the CHANGE command to change 24 to 29:

```
UFI > C/24/29/

3*     WHERE AGE > 29
```

The command is executed by entering RUN. (Output is suppressed.)

```
UFI > RUN

1      SELECT SID, NAME
2      FROM STUDENT
3*     WHERE AGE > 29
```

The predicate is altered to add a condition on SLEVEL (at the end of line 3).

```
UFI > APPEND AND SLEVEL <= 4

3*     WHERE AGE > 29 AND SLEVEL <= 4
```

The LOAN table with alias L and an alias S for STUDENT are added to the second line:

```
UFI > L2

2*     FROM STUDENT

UFI > C/ENT/ENT S, LOAN L/

2*     FROM STUDENT S, LOAN L
```

A join of STUDENT (alias S) and LOAN (alias L) is added plus a condition on AMOUNT. The command is then executed and an error results. The error is then corrected.

```
UFI > APPEND AND S.SID = L.SID AND AMOUNT > 3000

3*     WHERE AGE > 29 AND SLEVEL <= 4 AND S.SID = L.SID
       AND AMOUNT > 3000
```

```
UFI > RUN
        1     SELECT SID, NAME
        2     FROM STUDENT S, LOAN L
        3*    WHERE AGE > 29 AND SLEVEL <= 4 AND S.SID = L.SID
                  AND AMOUNT > 3000
SELECT SID, NAME
       *
ERROR at line 1: column ambiguously defined
UFI > L1
        1*    SELECT SID, NAME
UFI > C/SID/S.SID/
        1*    SELECT S.SID, NAME
UFI > RUN
        1     SELECT S.SID, NAME
        2     FROM STUDENT S, LOAN L
        3*    WHERE AGE > 29 AND LEVEL <= 4 AND S.SID = L.SID
                  AND AMOUNT > 3000
```

A line is inserted between the first and second lines. To terminate the input mode, a carriage return is entered (i.e., after the 3i below). The result is then executed.

```
UFI > INPUT
        2i  , AMOUNT
        3i
UFI > RUN
        1     SELECT S.SID, NAME
        2       , AMOUNT
        3     FROM STUDENT S, LOAN L
        4*    WHERE AGE > 29 AND LEVEL <= 4 AND S.SID = L.SID
                  AND AMOUNT > 3000
```

The second line is deleted. Note that the abbreviation D for DELETE does not work:

```
UFI > D
unknown command.
UFI > DEL
UFI > LIST
        1     SELECT S.SID, NAME
        2     FROM STUDENT S, LOAN L
        3*    WHERE AGE > 29 AND LEVEL <= 4 AND S.SID = L.SID
                  AND AMOUNT > 3000
```

Questions and Problems

Questions

1. What database definition statements are introduced in this chapter? Give a brief description of each one.

2. Describe the data types available in ORACLE. What are the differences in the CHAR and LONG types?

3. Give examples of four data types found in other RDBMSs which are not available in ORACLE.

4. All CHAR types are stored in ORACLE as (fixed, variable) length strings.

5. (True, False) You cannot add a column to an existing table if data has already been stored in the table.

6. Describe how ORACLE supports each of the following (if it does):

   a. Domains

   b. Non-null primary key

   c. Unique values for primary key

   d. Referential integrity

7. What is (are) the SQL statement(s) corresponding to the following relational algebra operations: select, project, join?

8. A join in SQL is specified by _____.

9. How does SQL handle sorting rows in each of the following cases:

   a. Sort on a single column (say) x in descending order

   b. Sort in ascending order on a pair of columns (say) x and y

   c. Sort on a column which is an expression (say) x-y

10. Are *null* and blank values equivalent? Discuss.

11. What is the difference in the IS NOT IN and != operators?

12. What is the difference in the meaning of XYZ in the following two SELECTs:

```
SELECT * FROM ABC, XYZ;
SELECT * FROM ABC XYZ;
```

13. What is the difference in the EXISTS and IS IN operators? (See also subsequent problems.)

14. What is the major difference in functions such as POWER, ABS, SIGN and SUM, AVG, MAX?

15. Can a WHERE clause be applied to the results of a GROUP BY? Discuss. How do you restrict output to groups with specific characteristics?

16. Describe the effects of commands

```
SET AUTO COMMIT OFF
COMMIT WORK
```

17. Why is the DELETE a potentially dangerous command?

18. Since there is no explicit *difference* operator in SQL, how is this operation handled?

Problems

1. Define appropriate ORACLE data types for each of the following:

   a. Customer name of up to 24 characters. Null values are allowed.

   b. Patient's temperature to accuracy of tenths of degrees, maximum value 110.

   c. Date of birth.

   d. Result of multiplying COST times QTY where COST is defined as NUMBER (5,2), QTY as NUMBER (3).

2. Consider the Customer-Order-Part-Line Item database described in the problems of Chapter 4. Create four ORACLE base tables with appropriate column definitions for that database. Make reasonable assumptions for sizes of character attributes and range and precision (number of digits to right of decimal point) for numeric data types.

   The remaining problems refer to the GSL model as defined in Figure 5-2 (unless otherwise specified).

3. Write a statement which would add a new column called STREET to the BANK table. This column may have up to 25 characters.

4. Write SQL statements for the following single-relation queries:

   a. All columns from LOAN with INT_RATE over 8%.

   b. Columns LID, LDATE, YEARS and BID for rows of LOAN with INT_RATE between 7 and 8% (inclusive) and AMOUNT over $2,000.

   c. All columns from LOAN for rows which satisfy either of the following conditions:

      (1) YEARS > 6 and INT_RATE over 7%

      (2) INT_RATE over 8%

   d. Write a statement to display the (unique) BID values of banks which have one or more loans.

   e. Repeat part d, with output ordered by BID.

   f. Display SID and name of all students whose name ends with 5.

   g. Select a 10% random sample of rows from STUDENT where SLEVEL equals 5.

   h. Display SID and name of all students who have the digit 9 anywhere in their SID. (Hint: see the function TO_CHAR in the appendix.)

5. Write SQL statements for the following multiple-table queries.

   a. Display unique BID and TYPE for all banks with loans. Write this query two ways — using an explicit join and using nesting.

   b. Display SID and NAME for all students who have a loan from bank PEOPLES or SEAFIRST.

   c. Display SID, NAME, AMOUNT and LID for all students' loans where the loan is from a bank of type MSB or SL. Can the nested form of the SELECT be used for this query? Discuss.

   d. Display BID, LID, and AMOUNT for all loans made to freshmen or sophomores in the year 1985.

6. Write SQL statements for the following queries which use the GROUP BY clause.

   a. Determine total loan amount and number of loans by bank. Display BID, BZID and the aggregates.

b. Display total loan amount, SID and NAME for every student who has one or more loans of amount over $2,000. (The total, however, is over all loans for the student.) Write this two ways — using HAVING and not using HAVING.

c. Display SID, NAME, and number of loans for every student who has one or more loan with LDATE in 1983 or 1984.

d. Display the name and SID of the student who has the maximum loan total.

7. Rewrite the following using IS NOT IN instead of NOT EXISTS:

```
SELECT NAME, AGE FROM STUDENT S1
    WHERE NOT EXISTS
        (SELECT SID FROM STUDENT S2
            WHERE S1.SLEVEL = S2.LEVEL AND AGE > 20)
```

8. What is the result of the following query:

```
SELECT SID, NAME
    FROM STUDENT, LOAN
        WHERE AGE > 21 AND AMOUNT >= 2500;
```

(Be careful — there is a trick here.)

9. Suppose there are two tables of student data. One table is for graduate students, the other for undergraduates. While many of the columns of the two tables are identical, each table has columns which do not appear in the other. We want to display names and ages of all students (from both tables) who have three or more loans. What operator is required for this query? Can you devise a method to write the query without this operator?

10. The following SELECT was shown to illustrate an *incorrect* method of displaying data for students with no loans:

```
SELECT STUDENT.SID, NAME
    FROM STUDENT, LOAN
        WHERE STUDENT.SID != LOAN.SID;
```

11. What is wrong with the following:

```
SELECT SID, NAME, COUNT(*)
    FROM STUDENT S, LOAN L
        WHERE S.SID = L.SID
            GROUP BY S.SID;
```

(There are at least two errors.)

12. Translate the following relational algebra queries to SQL:

a. (STUDENT [SID] MINUS LOAN [SID]) JOIN STUDENT (WHERE SLEVEL ≤ 4)

b. (STUDENT (WHERE SLEVEL = 5) [SID] UNION
LOAN JOIN BANK (WHERE TYPE = 'MSB') [SID]) JOIN STUDENT [SID, NAME, AGE]

13. Perform the following update:

a. Add a new bank with ID BANKAMER, BZIP = 90056, type BANK.

b. Decrease loan amount by $100 for all loans with INT_RATE over 7.5%.

   c. Decrease the amount of the loan which has maximum amount (over all loans) by $500. (For the sample data, the result should be a decrease in AMOUNT to $2,500 for loan with LID = 493.)

14. A statistician wants to analyze all loans held by undergraduates. Data needed for analysis includes LID, LDATE, YEARS, INT_RATE, AMOUNT, and SLEVEL. Define a table UG_LOAN and load this table with appropriate data.

References

Ageloff, R. *A Primer on SQL*. St. Louis, Mo.: Times Mirror/Mosby College Publishing, 1988.

American National Standards Institute. *Database Language SQL*. Document X3.135–1986.

Bradley, J. *Introduction to Data Base Management in Business*. 2d ed. New York: Holt, Reinhart and Winston, 1987.

Date, C.J. *A Guide to The SQL Standard*. Reading Mass.: Addison-Wesley Publishing Co., 1987.

_____. *An Introduction to Database Systems*. Vol. 1. 4th ed. Reading, Mass.: Addison-Wesley Publishing Co., 1985.

Oracle Corporation. *ORACLE for Macintosh: Primers*. 1988.

Oracle Corporation. *ORACLE for Macintosh: References*. 1988.

Oracle Corporation. *ORACLE UFI Terminal User's Guide*.

Oracle Corporation. *ORACLE UFI Terminal User's Reference*.

6 Additional Features and Characteristics of ORACLE

This chapter describes additional features of SQL-based relational DBMSs, again using ORACLE as an example. These features include:

- The creation of so-called views, which is the term used for the external data level in the relational model.
- Formatting output and report generation.
- Obtaining "meta data"; that is, information about tables, views, attributes, and other system information.
- Using SQL from a host language: "embedded SQL."
- Defining indexes.
- Optimizing the execution of queries.

The beauty of SQL is that view definition, formatting, report generation, and embedded SQL are simply extensions of the SQL explained in the last chapter, not entirely new languages as is the case with most non-relational DBMSs.

Views

Views are virtual tables that do not contain any actual data in the sense in which a base table does. However, a view can be treated as if it were a real table as far as retrievals (SELECTs) are concerned, and in some cases a view can be updated as if it were a real table. The simplest views are those that are subsets of base tables; that is, they involve only (relational algebra) restriction and projection operations. For example, the view mechanism can be used to restrict an end-user to columns SID, NAME and SLEVEL of the STUDENT table and to only those rows for students aged 23 or older.

Once again we will use the GSL database to illustrate many of the concepts in this chapter. For your convenience, this data is shown again in Figure 6–1.

Defining Views

The CREATE VIEW command defines the external view that will be seen by a user, and thereby defines the mapping from the conceptual to the external level. The general form is:

```
CREATE VIEW view_name [(col_name, ... )] AS select-statement
```

where the *select-statement* is just that: an SQL SELECT statement with WHERE, GROUP BY, ... clauses. About the only restriction on the SELECT statement is that it may not include an ORDER BY clause. The col_name gives new names to the columns in the view. First we'll illustrate a form without the optional column names. The following view named OLDER_ST addresses the situation suggested above: it creates a row and column subset consisting of the SID, SLEVEL, and NAME for all students aged 23 or over. The

STUDENT Table

SID	NAME	SLEVEL	AGE	SZIP
9735	ALLEN	1	21	98101
4494	ALTER	2	19	98112
8767	CABEEN	5	24	98118
2368	JONES	4	23	98155
6793	SANDS	1	17	98101
3749	WATSON	5	29	98168

BANK Table

BID	BZIP	TYPE
FIDELITY	98101	MSB
SEAFIRST	98101	BANK
PEOPLES	98109	BANK
CAPITAL	98033	SL
HOME	98031	SL

LOAN Table

LID	LDATE	YEARS	INT_RATE	AMOUNT	SID	BID
27	15-SEP-85	5	8.5	1200	9735	HOME
78	21-JUN-86	5	7.75	1000	9735	PEOPLES
87	07-SEP-83	5	7.0	2000	9735	SEAFIRST
92	12-JAN-85	6	7.5	2100	4494	FIDELITY
99	15-JAN-86	6	9.0	2200	4494	FIDELITY
170	30-APR-83	6	6.5	1900	8767	PEOPLES
490	07-MAY-84	6	6.0	2500	3749	PEOPLES
493	24-JUN-85	7	7.5	3000	3749	PEOPLES

Fig 6-1 GSL Database

ORACLE/SQL response is the simple message "view created" if the view definition is valid. This message is suppressed in subsequent CREATE VIEW statements.

```
CREATE VIEW OLDER_ST AS
    SELECT SID, SLEVEL, NAME
        FROM STUDENT
        WHERE AGE >= 23;

View created.
```

The effect of this view definition is to create a table (but not a base table) that can be considered to mask off those rows and columns that are not selected and projected by the SQL SELECT statement. Here is the virtual effect indicating by graying out those rows that are not in the OLDER_ST table:

```
OLDER_ST Table

SID      NAME       SLEVEL AGE      SZIP
9735     ALLEN          1 21        98101
4494     ALTER          2 19        98112
8767     CABEEN         5 24        98118
2368     JONES          4 23        98155
6793     SANDS          1 17        98101
3749     WATSON         5 29        98168
```

As far as the user is concerned, the table OLDER_ST contains only those rows and columns that have not been darkened. For example, look at the result of the following:

```
SELECT * FROM OLDER_ST;

SID      SLEVEL    NAME
----     ------    ------
8767          5    CABEEN
2368          4    JONES
3749          5    WATSON
```

It is very useful to understand how a view works. When the query, SELECT * FROM OLDER_ST, is executed, the DBMS converts it into a new query on a base table or tables by substituting the definition of OLDER_ST into the query. Thus, the following two queries are equivalent.

```
SELECT *                    SELECT SID, SLEVEL, NAME
     FROM OLDER_ST;             FROM STUDENT
                               WHERE AGE >= 23;
```

The columns in OLDER_ST are in a different order from the columns in STUDENT. The equivalent query on the STUDENT base table reflects this.

As you might expect, the query on a view can be almost any valid SELECT.[1] The following displays only the names of undergraduate students from OLDER_ST:

```
SELECT NAME
     FROM OLDER_ST
     WHERE SLEVEL <= 4;

NAME
-----
JONES
```

Again, the query is processed by merging it with the definition of the view, OLDER_ST, to create the following equivalent query on the STUDENT base table:

```
SELECT NAME
     FROM STUDENT
     WHERE AGE >= 23 AND SLEVEL <= 4;
```

Of course, the user could have written the query directly on the STUDENT base table; the equivalent base-table query is only slightly more complex than the view-table query. It is not hard to imagine considerably more complex queries, in which defining a view would

---

[1] There are a few restrictions on such queries, but they are encountered very rarely in practice and are beyond the scope of this text. Check relevant manuals if you run into trouble with a SELECT on a view.

make subsequent queries of the view much simpler than using the base tables directly. Furthermore, there are other reasons for using views. Suppose, for example, that we don't want a particular user accessing any data about students other than SID, NAME, and SLEVEL and then only for those students aged 23 or over. To impose this restriction we do not tell the user about the base STUDENT table; that is, we do not give the user access permission to the base table, only to the OLDER_ST view table.

When updates are made to base tables, those updates are in the view since a view is simply a mask over a base table (or, equivalently, a window into parts of a base table). Note that we are speaking here of direct updates to the underlying base table on which the view is defined. The problems with updates of views will be addressed later.

The view definition can rename columns. If no column names are specified within parentheses following the view name, then the column names from the underlying base table or tables are used, as you can see from the above example. But, this will work only as long as no name conflicts arise. If in the previous example we wanted the view to have different column names, the definition could be:

```
CREATE VIEW OLDER_ST2 (OLD_ST_SID, OLD_ST_LEVEL, OLD_ST_NAME) AS
    SELECT SID, SLEVEL, NAME
        FROM STUDENT WHERE AGE >= 23;
```

Note the change in column headings resulting from the following query.

```
SELECT * FROM OLDER_ST2;

OLD_ST_SID     OLD_ST_LEVEL   OLD_ST_NAME
----------     ------------   -----------
      8767                5   CABEEN
      2368                4   JONES
      3749                5   WATSON
```

While the columns have been given different names in the view, they still contain the same information. Of course, we can rearrange the column order in the view, repeat a column, and even put a constant value into the view. If a view has a column that is an expression, then that column *must* be named in the view definition. Look at the following definition and its result. Subsequent examples will illustrate other situations in which renaming a column is mandatory.

```
CREATE VIEW
    OLDER_ST3(OLD_ST_LEVEL,OLD_ST_NAME,LEV_LABEL,ST_LEVEL) AS
        SELECT SLEVEL, NAME, 'LEVEL = ', SLEVEL
            FROM STUDENT
            WHERE AGE >= 23;

SELECT * FROM OLDER_ST3;

OLD_ST_LEVEL   OLD_ST_NAME    LEV_LABE     ST_LEVEL
------------   -----------    --------     --------
           5   CABEEN         LEVEL =             5
           4   JONES          LEVEL =             4
           5   WATSON         LEVEL =             5
```

These have been rather simple examples to help you understand the view concept. But, as stated above, the definition of the view is essentially unlimited: almost any SELECT can be used. That means that views can involve joins, aggregations (GROUP BY), and expressions in either the projected columns or in the WHERE clauses. And views may be defined on views. Again, the simplicity and power of SQL come through. The simple clause CREATE VIEW *view-name* was essentially the only addition to either the language or your understanding necessary to create any view. While the following examples are therefore somewhat redundant (you have, in effect, already seen them in the previous chapter), they are provided to illustrate applications of views and to emphasize their value.

Views Involving Joins. Suppose a user always needs to see the student's name and level when looking at loan data. If this user writes queries directly on the base tables, then both the STUDENT and LOAN tables must be referenced in the FROM clause, and they must be joined in the WHERE clause by writing STUDENT.SID = LOAN.SID. By defining a view, this user's queries need only reference the single view table. Suppose further that the only attributes in addition to student name and level that are relevant to this user's job are AMOUNT, LDATE, and BID. A view definition called ST_LOANS is created by:

```
CREATE VIEW ST_LOANS AS
     SELECT NAME, SLEVEL, AMOUNT, LDATE, BID
          FROM STUDENT S, LOAN L
          WHERE S.SID = L.SID;
```

A query to display ST_LOANS for loans from PEOPLES is written:

```
SELECT *
     FROM ST_LOANS
     WHERE BID = 'PEOPLES';
```

NAME	SLEVEL	AMOUNT	LDATE	BID
ALLEN	1	1000	21-JUN-86	PEOPLES
CABEEN	5	1900	30-APR-83	PEOPLES
WATSON	5	2500	07-MAY-84	PEOPLES
WATSON	5	3000	24-JUN-85	PEOPLES

You should write down the equivalent query on the base tables to see how the view definition pays off in simplicity. Of course, if a view is referenced only once, it doesn't make much sense from a work-saving standpoint to first create the view, then to write a single SELECT using it. The payoff comes from repeated use of the view. Note that there may be other reasons for creating a view even if it is only used once. One reason is privacy: to hide rows or columns that are not relevant to a user.

Views with Virtual Columns. Virtual columns can also be defined in views. A very simple example was given earlier, when a column was defined as a string constant (LEVEL =). Several more interesting examples follow. Suppose that a group of people are involved with review and approval of loans. They need to see the total loan amount for each student but do not need data on each separate loan. The query to produce a loan total involves a join of STUDENT and LOAN, with an aggregation of AMOUNT using the GROUP BY. The view definition is built on top of this. Since the loan total column involves a function, it must be named.

```
CREATE VIEW ST_TOT (SID, NAME, TOT_AMT) AS
     SELECT S.SID, NAME, SUM(AMOUNT)
          FROM STUDENT S, LOAN L
          WHERE S.SID = L.SID
          GROUP BY S.SID, NAME;
```

Display of all data from this view follows:

```
SELECT * FROM ST_TOT;

SID       NAME      TOT_AMT
----      ------    -------
3749      WATSON     5500
4494      ALTER      4300
8767      CABEEN     1900
9735      ALLEN      4200
```

The column TOT_AMT doesn't really exist; it is defined by the view and dynamically created as required at runtime. Thus, it cannot be updated.

Views Defined on Views. In addition to creating views based on joins of base tables, it is also possible to create views based on views. This includes, of course, the definition of a view that is a join of a base table and a view, and even a view defined on the joins of other views. If, in the previous example, one employee in the group of users was interested in the loan totals only for older students, it would be possible to join the view defined earlier of older students with the ST_TOT view. This new view also adds SLEVEL. We repeat the definition of OLDER_ST for convenience:

```
CREATE VIEW OLDER_ST AS
    SELECT SID, SLEVEL, NAME
        FROM STUDENT
            WHERE AGE >= 23;
```

The new view (older students with loan total) is:

```
CREATE VIEW OLDER_ST_TOT (SID, NAME, SLEVEL, TOT_AMT) AS
    SELECT S.SID, S.NAME, SLEVEL, TOT_AMT
        FROM OLDER_ST S, ST_TOT ST
            WHERE S.SID = ST.SID;
```

Display of data defined by the view follows:

```
SELECT * FROM OLDER_ST_TOT;

SID       NAME      SLEVEL    TOT_AMT
----      ------    ------    -------
3749      WATSON      5        5500
0767      CABEEN      5        1900
```

Restrictions

One restriction on view definition was noted earlier: the ORDER BY clause is not permitted. That is because a view defines a relation and relations have no order. Some versions of SQL place restrictions on the operations that can be performed on a column based on an aggregate function. For example, suppose we want rows from the view ST_TOT but only if the total amount, TOT_AMT, exceeds $5,000. The following query works in ORACLE but not in every other SQL implementation:

```
SELECT *
    FROM ST_TOT
        WHERE TOT_AMT > 5000;

SID       NAME      TOT_AMT
----      ------    -------
3749      WATSON     5500
```

Let's consider why this query fails in some SQLs. First recall that the definition of ST_TOT is:

```
CREATE VIEW ST_TOT (SID, NAME, TOT_AMT) AS
    SELECT S.SID, NAME, SUM(AMOUNT)
        FROM STUDENT S, LOAN L
        WHERE S.SID = L.SID
        GROUP BY S.SID, NAME;
```

When the query to display only those with TOT_AMT > $5,000 is merged with the definition of ST_TOT, the following query is the result:

```
SELECT S.SID, NAME, SUM(AMOUNT)
    FROM STUDENT S, LOAN L
    WHERE S.SID = L.SID AND SUM(AMOUNT) > 5000
    GROUP BY S.SID, NAME;
```

When the above query is entered directly, ORACLE responds with:

```
WHERE S.SID = L.SID AND SUM(AMOUNT) > 5000
                          *

ERROR at line 3: set function is not allowed here
```

The error occurs because this is not valid SQL: a condition on an aggregate function must appear in a HAVING clause. The proper way to write the query in SQL is:

```
SELECT S.SID, NAME, SUM(AMOUNT)
    FROM STUDENT S, LOAN L
    WHERE S.SID = L.SID
    GROUP BY S.SID, NAME
    HAVING SUM(AMOUNT) > 5000;
```

Thus, it is surprising that ORACLE lets us get away with using a column based on an aggregate function (i.e., TOT_AMT) in a WHERE clause. It suggests that ORACLE does not actually merge the view definition and query on the view into a single SQL statement that is then processed. The view definition and query must be kept somewhat separate.

Dropping Views

Like tables, views can be DROPped. For example:

```
DROP VIEW OLDER_ST;
```

But remember that there is a big difference in dropping a view and dropping a base table. Dropping a view drops its definition—no data disappears. Dropping a table not only removes the definition but also all the associated data. Thus, keeping an unneeded view around is "inexpensive"—a few bytes for storage of its definition. The expense of keeping a no-longer-relevant table around is directly dependent on its size.

Examples. We will conclude these examples of view definition and manipulation with several comprehensive problems and solutions.

1. Suppose that a more convenient representation of loan interest rate (INT_RATE) for many users would be in the form of a monthly fraction. Thus, an annual percentage of 12 percent would be transformed to 0.01 as a monthly interest fraction. A view over the entire LOAN relation with INT_RATE transformed is:

```
CREATE VIEW LOAN_M
    (LID,LDATE,YEARS,MON_RATE,AMOUNT,SID,BID) AS
        SELECT LID, LDATE, YEARS, INT_RATE/1200, AMOUNT, SID, BID
            FROM LOAN;
```

An example query and output follow:

```
SELECT LID, MON_RATE FROM LOAN_M WHERE SID = 9735;

LID         MON_RATE
---         ----------
27          .007083333
78          .006458333
87          .005833333
```

2. Building on example 1, suppose that a number of applications need not only the interest rate as a monthly fraction but also need to compute the monthly payment amount on a loan. The following query was developed in Chapter 5 to display LID, SID, and payment amount:

```
SELECT LID, SID,
    AMOUNT*(INT_RATE/1200)/(1 - POWER(1 + INT_RATE/1200,
        -12*YEARS) )
    FROM LOAN;
```

To remove the burden of writing this complex payment calculation formula, a view is defined over the entire LOAN table that adds the virtual column PAYMENT. We can use the view defined in example 1 to somewhat simplify this view definition, since it performs the transformation of interest rate from annual percentage to monthly fraction.

```
CREATE VIEW LOAN_P
(LID,LDATE,YEARS,MON_RATE,AMOUNT,SID,BID,PAYMENT) AS
    SELECT LID, LDATE, YEARS, MON_RATE, AMOUNT, SID, BID,
        AMOUNT*MON_RATE/(1 - POWER(1 + MON_RATE,-12*YEARS))
    FROM LOAN_M;
```

A query on LOAN_P to display LID, MON_RATE, and PAYMENT for loans for graduate students is:

```
SELECT LID, MON_RATE, PAYMENT
    FROM LOAN_P L, STUDENT S
    WHERE L.SID = S.SID AND SLEVEL = 5;

LID         MON_RATE        PAYMENT
---         ----------      ----------
170         .005416667      31.9388663
490         .005            41.4322197
493         .00625          46.0148276
```

The section in this chapter on formatting output and the report writer will help clean up the appearance of output.

3. A common application of views is to simplify translating a code value into its corresponding full text. Suppose, for example, we would like to give the user the impression that a student's level is stored as FRESHMAN, SOPHOMORE ... instead of 1, 2, ... A view is the way to do this. One approach is to use the DECODE string function (see example 4), but a more general way is to create a table with numeric and corresponding text values of level. The table definition is:

```
CREATE TABLE LEVEL_CODE (SLEVEL NUMBER(1), LEVEL_NAME CHAR(10));
```

The table will contain:

```
SLEVEL    LEVEL_NAME
------    ----------
     1    FRESHMAN
     2    SOPHOMORE
     3    JUNIOR
     4    SENIOR
     5    GRADUATE
```

The view is defined as a join of LEVEL_CODE and STUDENT, with the LEVEL_NAME column replacing SLEVEL in the definition.

```
CREATE VIEW STUDENT_L (SID,NAME, LEVEL_NAME, AGE,SZIP) AS
     SELECT SID, NAME, LEVEL_NAME, AGE, SZIP
        FROM STUDENT S, LEVEL_CODE LC
        WHERE S.SLEVEL = LC.SLEVEL;
```

The following query on STUDENT_L displays rows in which the student level name contains the character M:

```
SELECT SID, NAME, LEVEL_NAME
FROM STUDENT_L WHERE LEVEL_NAME LIKE '%M%';

SID       NAME      LEVEL_NAME
----      -----     ----------
9735      ALLEN     FRESHMAN
6793      SANDS     FRESHMAN
4494      ALTER     SOPHOMORE
```

4. In the previous chapter a query was developed that would separate names stored in the form *last name, first name* into a "friendlier" form of *first name last name* and also add a title of MR. or MS. depending on the value of the SEX. (We expanded the STUDENT table to add a column containing M or F to indicate sex; the names were also updated so that the first name followed the last name.) Several string functions were used to find the comma separating the names, to extract the substrings from NAME that correspond to first and last names, and to translate the value of SEX into MR. or MS. The query was:

```
SELECT DECODE (SEX, 'M','MR.', 'F', 'MS.', ' '),
     SUBSTR(NAME, INSTR(NAME,',')+1,LENGTH(NAME)
        - INSTR(NAME,',')) ||
     ' ' || SUBSTR(NAME,1,INSTR(NAME,',')-1)
     FROM STUDENT;
```

Here is what the revised table looks like:

```
SELECT * FROM STUDENT;
SID       NAME             SLEVEL   AGE  SZIP      S
----      ------------     ------   ---  -----     -
9735      ALLEN,JAMES           1    21  98101     M
4494      ALTER,CARL            2    19  98112     M
2368      JONES,FRANK           4    23  98155     M
8767      CABEEN,JULIE          5    24  98118     F
6793      SANDS,LINDA           1    17  98101     F
3749      WATSON,SUSAN          5    29  98168     F
```

Now, suppose a user needs a view of the STUDENT table that has names in the "friendly" form preceded by MR. or MS. In addition, the columns SID and SZIP are also desired. The view definition is:

```
CREATE VIEW ST_FRIENDLY (F_L_NAME, SID, SZIP) AS
    SELECT DECODE (SEX, 'M','MR.','F','MS.', ' ')|| ' ' ||
    SUBSTR(NAME, INSTR(NAME,',')+1,LENGTH(NAME)
        - INSTR(NAME,',')) ||
    ' ' || SUBSTR(NAME,1,INSTR(NAME,',')-1),SID, SZIP
FROM STUDENT;
```

This is messy, but certainly not as bad as having to enter the query every time the user wants to transform the output into this form. The result of a query on this view is shown below:

```
SELECT SID, F_L_NAME
    FROM ST_FRIENDLY
    WHERE ZIP BETWEEN 98101 AND 98119;

SID        F_L_NAME
----       ----------------
9735       MR. JAMES ALLEN
4494       MR. CARL ALTER
8767       MS. JULIE CABEEN
6793       MS. LINDA SANDS
```

Updates of Views

The forms of the various statements to update views (that is, UPDATE, DELETE, and INSERT) are identical to the forms for a base table update except that a view name is used instead of a base table name. Here is a simple example. The ORACLE response to the update and the subsequent query on the base table show that the update worked.

```
UPDATE OLDER_ST
    SET LEVEL=5
    WHERE SID = 2368;

1 record updated.

SELECT * FROM STUDENT WHERE SID = 2368;
SID      NAME      SLEVEL     AGE       SZIP
----     -----     ------     ---       -----
2368     JONES          5      23       98155
```

There are restrictions on updating views. A view that is a row and column subset of a base table presents no problems for value-changing updates. However, updates that add rows, INSERTs, will not work if the view does not include columns that are defined as NOT NULL. For example, here is a simple view on STUDENT that is a projection of the NAME and AGE columns.

```
CREATE VIEW N_A AS
    SELECT NAME, AGE FROM STUDENT;
```

While the following value-change update works, as seen from the output, the attempt to insert a row fails because the N_A view does not contain the attribute SID, which is defined as NOT NULL.

```
UPDATE N_A SET AGE = 22 WHERE NAME = 'ALLEN';

1 record updated

SELECT NAME, AGE FROM STUDENT WHERE SID = 9735;
```

```
NAME      AGE
-----     ---
ALLEN     22


INSERT INTO N_A VALUES ('SMITH',99)
                *

ERROR at line 1: missing mandatory column during insert
```

Views involving joins, virtual columns, or an aggregation cannot be updated. Clearly, it makes no sense to update a view with a virtual column or a view with a column based on an aggregate function except in very special cases. Most join views also create clear problems if an update is attempted. For example, consider the following view, ST_LOAN, based on the join of STUDENT and LOAN.

```
CREATE VIEW ST_LOAN (SID, NAME, LID, AMOUNT) AS
    SELECT S.SID, NAME, LID, AMOUNT
       FROM STUDENT S, LOAN L
       WHERE S.SID = L.SID;
```

Suppose we now try to insert the following row to ST_LOAN:

```
(9735, 'ALLEN', 323, 8888);
```

How would you interpret this insertion? Should both a new STUDENT row with SID = 9735 and NAME = ALLEN and a new LOAN row with LID = 323 and AMOUNT 8888 be inserted, or only the new LOAN row since we already have a STUDENT with this SID and NAME? Suppose the INSERT specifies SID = 9735 but NAME = SIBLEY? Now what is the appropriate action? There are no good and consistent answers to these types of updates; thus, they are not allowed.

There are, however, cases of views based on joins in which it makes sense to perform value-change updates. It would be unambiguous to change LOAN amounts in ST_LOAN if the LID is specified. But if this is attempted, ORACLE gives an error message:

```
UPDATE ST_LOAN SET AMOUNT = 9999 WHERE LID = 27
               *

ERROR at line 1: table or view does not exist
```

The message is a bit strange since the underlying tables and the view do, in fact, exist. Of course, the data in any view can always be updated if we resort to updating the underlying base table.

The "state of the art" in database theory with regard to the update of views is somewhat ahead of the implementation. Database theorists can prove, for example, that certain classes of views and certain types of updates make sense. These include updates of join views in a few cases. The theorists can also prove that certain types of updates usually make no sense, such as the update of virtual columns and columns based on aggregates. (Note: A virtual column can be updated when the definition of the values in the virtual column are one to one with the values in underlying columns. For example, suppose we define a view on LOAN with the virtual column MONTHS defined as 12*YEARS. Now, the values of YEARS and MONTHS are one to one: YEARS = MONTHS/12. A change in the value of MONTHS could be reflected unambiguously as a new value of YEARS. But how would we handle an update to the virtual column PAYMENT defined in the view LOAN_P in this chapter?) There are a few situations in which the theorists are not sure whether updates can be unambiguously performed or not.

The DBMS designers take a conservative approach and allow updates of views only under more restrictive conditions. ORACLE views may have value updates (UPDATE) or row insertions (INSERT) only when they (1) are not based on joins, virtual columns, or aggregates; and (2) do not insert tuples in which the view definition excludes columns defined as NOT NULL.

No row deletions from views (that is, DELETE operations) are allowed.

Objectives and Benefits of Views

The previous discussion of views has included some of the reasons for using views, particularly the added simplicity and security, or privacy, afforded by views. More generally, the primary objectives of creating a view are:

- To provide for logical data independence so that, to some extent, the database may be restructured without impact on the user. (See details below.)
- To provide for alternate views of the same data at the same time to facilitate database sharing.
- To simplify the user's perception of the database.
- To provide for security and privacy of selected parts of a database by hiding data; that is, not including it in a view.

Data Independence

You will recall from Chapter 3 that one of the most important objectives and features of the database approach is data independence (DI). DI allows the user to deal with data by name instead of physical characteristics. A high degree of DI allows the user to be unaffected by changes in the logical structure of the database. For example, deleting tables that are not referenced by the user, adding a column to a table or deleting an unused column should not affect the user view of the database. Many of these changes can be made "transparently" to the user in relational DBMSs even without the view mechanism. But, other changes will have impact; that is, they will change how the user sees the logical database and will thus require changes in the form of queries.

As an example of changes that will affect the user (unless a view is used), suppose that in order to decrease the response time of an online transaction processing system it is determined that an existing base table should be split into two parts. This is a restructuring and would certainly affect the users of that table. However, through the view mechanism the database administrator can partition the table and then create a view that joins the two parts back together. The name used for the view is the original table name. Now, at least for those applications that do not update the table, there is no impact on the user.

Suppose that the STUDENT table, in a much expanded form, is suffering from reduced transaction times and needs to be split into two smaller tables. One table, STUDENT_PERS, could hold all the personal information about a student, including age, sex, location, next of kin, etc. The other table, STUDENT_ED, could hold all information about the student relating to his or her tenure at the school, including level, GPA, major, total credits, etc. Both tables would include SID as the primary key. To recreate the original STUDENT table, the following view could be defined:

```
CREATE VIEW STUDENT AS
    SELECT SP.SID, ...
        FROM STUDENT_PERS SP, STUDENT_ED SE
        WHERE SP.SID = SE.SID;
```

This view would then be used by all applications requiring the complete STUDENT table, removing the necessity of altering all the applications to reflect the change in base tables. Applications that require columns from only one of the tables should have views (also called STUDENT) defined that reference only the single base table. (Note that each different application may have its own set of views with view names that duplicate the names of other applications while having different definitions. Shared views may also be created.)

Another reason to partition a table vertically is to create "static" or almost static tables. If a group of columns are largely read-only (that is, they are updated only infrequently and then usually by batch processes), there may be a performance gain if these columns are placed in a separate table. Some of these physical design issues are dealt with in Chapter 13.

Report Writer

While SQL as discussed thus far is quite powerful and flexible, the format of the output is not always particularly attractive. A number of features are available to enhance output appearance and add additional summarization beyond that provided by the aggregate functions. These features include column formatting and the addition of column headings, page headings, page footings, computed columns, totals, and subtotals. Enhancing the output involves writing definitions that are then applied to the output generated by an SQL command. The added statements are called "UFI" commands—they are not part of SQL. It is important to note that you do not need to learn a new query language to generate reports, nor are SQL commands burdened with additional syntax.

The format and report generation definitions use the following statements. Examples of use and more complete definitions are given later.

• To control the appearance of values in a column and to change the column heading:

```
COLUMN col_name HEADING 'character_string' FORMAT format_mask
```

• To cause output to skip lines or move to a new page when a column value changes:

```
    BREAK ON col_name [SKIP n] [PAGE]
```

• To compute totals on a column and indicate the "break" column—that is, which column controls when the totals are output— a BREAK ON statement is required in conjunction with the COMPUTE directive:

```
    COMPUTE SUM OF sum_column ON break_column
```

• To place titles at the top and bottom, respectively, of a report:

```
    TTITLE 'character_string'
    BTITLE 'character_string'
```

These statements are entered first to describe the form of the output, then followed by the SELECT query to specify the content of the output. The following example illustrates the use of a number of these options.

Suppose we wanted to create a report showing all the loans held by each student with the total amount of his or her loans. Note that we cannot quite accomplish this with a SQL command. While SELECTs could be written for either individual loan data listing or for loan amount total by student (using GROUP BY), there is no way to get both detail and summary with a single SELECT. The following UFI COMPUTE directive causes the AMOUNT column to be summed. The BREAK directive causes the total to be printed and a blank line inserted (SKIP 1) whenever SID changes.

```
COMPUTE SUM OF AMOUNT ON SID
BREAK ON SID SKIP 1
```

A title is entered at the top of the report using TTITLE (for Top Title).

```
TTITLE 'STUDENT LOAN REPORT'
```

Loan amounts are displayed in a format of dollar sign followed by five digits. This is a format picture of $99,999. The column will be headed LOAN AMOUNT.

```
COLUMN AMOUNT HEADING 'LOAN AMOUNT' FORMAT $99,999
```

Now the SQL statement is entered to specify report content. To assure that all of the loans for a student are grouped in the output, the ORDER BY clause is used.

```
SELECT S.SID, NAME, AMOUNT
    FROM STUDENT S, LOAN L
    WHERE S.SID = L.SID
    ORDER BY S.SID;
```

```
Mon Oct 31                        page 1
         STUDENT LOAN REPORT
SID        NAME      LOAN AMOUNT
---        -------   -----------
3749       WATSON    $2,500
           WATSON    $3,000
*******              ---------------
                     $5,500

4494       ALTER     $2,100
           ALTER     $2,200
*******              ---------------
                     $4,300

8767       CABEEN    $1,900
*******              ---------------
                     $1,900


9735       ALLEN     $1,200
           ALLEN     $1,000
           ALLEN     $2,000
*******              ---------------
                     $4,200
```

There are a very large number of alternative formats for columns. Here are a few with example values and the resulting output form.

Numeric Format	Value	Displayed as:
999.99	123.456	123.46
9,999.99	1234.7	1,234.70
09999	82	00082
999MI	-123.56	123-
$9,999.99	123.5	$123.50
999.99	123456	###.##

There is also a format for character strings, the An format. The n indicates the column width. Look at what happens with the following 10-character width specified for the student name column (using data with first and last names):

```
COLUMN NAME FORMAT A10
SELECT NAME FROM STUDENT;

NAME
----------
ALLEN,JAME
S

ALTER,CARL
JONES,FRAN
K

CABEEN,JUL
IE

SANDS,LIND
A

WATSON,SUS
AN
```

Sort of messy, isn't it? If what we really want is just the first 10 characters of a name, then the SUBSTR function should be used. To control the heading for the SUBSTR function column, we will specify a format and heading for it and rename it in the SELECT.

```
COLUMN SHORT_NAME HEADING 'NAME' FORMAT A10
SELECT SUBSTR(NAME,1,10) SHORT_NAME FROM STUDENT;

NAME
----------
ALLEN,JAME
ALTER,CARL
JONES,FRAN
CABEEN,JUL
SANDS,LIND
WATSON,SUS
```

In the above example, note how the heading of NAME and the 10-character output format for the column called SHORT_NAME in the SELECT are determined by the preceding COLUMN directive.

There are many fancy things that you can do to control the content and format of output. Here is a final example, with an explanation. To appreciate the full capabilities of DBMS report writers you will need to refer to their manuals.

We want to produce a report for each bank, listing loan summary data for each student level along with an overall total for the bank. Note that individual loan data is not wanted—just counts, total amounts, and average amounts by level. First, a view is created that contains the specified data, including counts and loan totals.

```
CREATE VIEW L_STATS (SLEVEL, BID, L_NO, L_TOT) AS
    SELECT SLEVEL, B.BID, COUNT(LID), SUM(AMOUNT)
    FROM STUDENT S, BANK B, LOAN L
    WHERE S.SID = L.SID AND B.BID = L.BID
    GROUP BY B.BID, SLEVEL;
```

To make the output more interesting, we have considerably extended the database for this example. There are about 60 loan records and 14 banks. Here is a query on this view for banks beginning with letters P through Z:

```
SELECT * FROM L_STATS
    WHERE BID >= 'P';
```

SLEVEL	BID	L_NO	L_TOT
3	PACIFIC	3	4500
4	PACIFIC	1	1000
1	PEOPLES	1	1000
4	PEOPLES	2	2100
5	PEOPLES	4	4850
3	QUEENCITY	1	1450
4	QUEENCITY	1	1400
3	RAINIER	1	1750
5	RAINIER	2	2600
1	SEAFIRST	2	2800
2	SEAFIRST	1	1400
5	SEAFIRST	3	4400
4	WASHINGTON	2	2600

Now the report specifications are added, starting with top and bottom titles:

```
TTITLE 'LOAN REPORT BY BANK AND STUDENT LEVEL | FOR BANKS
STARTING P'
BTITLE 'HAPPY HALLOWEEN'
```

The vertical line in the TTITLE directive will cause the title to be printed on two lines. Column formats and headings are specified next. The vertical line is used again to place several headings on two lines. The heading and format for a column that will be called AVG_AMT in the SELECT is also specified.

```
COLUMN L_NO HEADING 'NUMBER |OF LOANS' FORMAT 999999999
COLUMN L_TOT HEADING 'TOTAL AMOUNT' FORMAT $999,999,99
COLUMN SLEVEL HEADING 'STUDENT| LEVEL' FORMAT 99999999
COLUMN BID FORMAT A12
COLUMN AVG_AMT HEADING 'AVERAGE LOAN | AMOUNT' FORMAT $9,999.99
```

The COMPUTE and BREAK directives are:

```
COMPUTE SUM OF L_NO ON BID
COMPUTE SUM OF L_TOT ON BID
BREAK ON BID PAGE
```

The SELECT for the computation of the average-amount column, with an output only for banks beginning with letter P, is:

```
SELECT BID, SLEVEL, L_NO, L_TOT, L_TOT/L_NO AVG_AMT
    FROM L_STATS
    WHERE BID >= 'P';
```

In the interest of reducing the output, only two pages are shown:

```
Mon Oct 31                                              page 2
            LOAN REPORT BY BANK AND STUDENT LEVEL
                    FOR BANKS STARTING P
    BID        STUDENT  NUMBER        TOTAL        AVERAGE
               LEVEL    OF LOANS      AMOUNT       LOAN AMOUNT
    --------   -------  ---------     -------      --------------
    PEOPLES       1         1         $1,000       $1,000.00
                  4         2         $2,100       $1,050.00
                  5         4         $4,850       $1,212.50
    ********   -------  ---------     -------
                            7         $7,950

            HAPPY HALLOWEEN

Mon Oct 31                                              page 3
            LOAN REPORT BY BANK AND STUDENT LEVEL
                    FOR BANKS STARTING P
               STUDENT  NUMBER   TOTAL    AVERAGE
    BID        LEVEL    OF LOANS AMOUNT   LOAN AMOUNT
    ----------- -------- ------- -------  ----------
    QUEENCITY      3        1 $1,450      $1,450.00
                   4        1 $1,400      $1,400.00
    ********    -------- ------- -------
                           2    $2,850

            HAPPY HALLOWEEN
```

When you are done with a report generation, you need to clear out the COMPUTEs and BREAKs and turn the titles off with the following statements:

```
CLEAR COMPUTES
CLEAR BREAKS
TTITLE OFF
BTITLE OFF
```

Here is what happens if they are not cleared:

```
SELECT * FROM STUDENT;
Mon Oct 31                              page 1
LOAN REPORT BY BANK AND STUDENT LEVEL
        FOR BANKS STARTING P

STUDENT
SID      NAME     LEVEL    AGE  SZIP
----     ------   ------   ---  ----
9735     ALLEN      1      21   98101
4494     ALTER      2      19   98112
8767     CABEEN     5      24   98118
2368     JONES      4      23   98155
6793     SANDS      1      17   98101
3749     WATSON     5      29   98168
         HAPPY HALLOWEEN
```

You can see what a title is and its status (off or on) by entering TTITLE or BTITLE:

```
BTITLE

btitle ON and is the following 15 characters:
     HAPPY HALLOWEEN
```

System Catalog

The system catalog of an SQL RDBMS contains a built-in data dictionary capability with information about the tables, columns, views, indexes, access rights, etc., of a database. In true relational fashion, this catalog is maintained as a set of system tables that are created and maintained automatically by the system.

The system tables may be queried, just as if they were user created. In practice, the entire set of system tables may consist of as many as 25 or 30 tables, depending upon the implementation.

Contents and Organization of the Catalog

Since the system catalog contains information specific to the system as well as user data structures, the details of the system catalog vary from one implementation to another. Information about which tables are in the catalog is contained in the table DTAB. We have listed several of the tables that are relevant to the user.

SELECT * FROM DTAB;

TNAME	REMARKS
CATALOG	Profile of tables accessible to user, excluding data dictionary
COL	Specifications of columns in tables created by the user
COLUMNS	Specifications of columns in tables (excluding data dictionary)
DTAB	Description of tables and views in ORACLE data dictionary
SYSCATALOG	Profile of tables and views accessible to the user
SYSCOLAUTH	Directory of column-level update grants by or to the user
SYSCOLUMNS	Specifications of columns in accessible tables and views
SYSTABAUTH	Directory of access authorization granted by or to the user
SYSUSERLIST	List of ORACLE users
TAB	List of tables, views, clusters, and synonyms created by the user
TABALLOC	Data and index space allocations for all user's tables
TABQUOTAS	Table allocation (space) parameters for tables created by user
VIEWS	Quotations of the SQL statements on which views are based

A detailed examination of the data in these tables is beyond the scope of our discussion here. In general, they track information such as the creator of a table, table type (real or view), and statistics such as the number of columns in a table or the date it was last accessed. Since these tables are just like any other tables, the SELECT statement can be used to display any or all of the rows and columns. Several of these tables are particularly useful and are described with examples below.

The TAB table is helpful for beginning to find out what you have created. Here is an edited list of some of the tables and views created in this and the previous chapter:

```
SELECT * FROM TAB;

TNAME                TABTYPE
------------         ------
CLASS_CODE           TABLE
MINOR_ST             VIEW
ST_LOAN              VIEW
L_STATS              VIEW
LOAN                 TABLE
STUDENT              TABLE
BANK                 TABLE
GR_ST_TOT            VIEW
OLDER_ST             VIEW
LOAN_P               VIEW
ST_FRIENDLY          VIEW
```

Let's suppose we want to determine the definition of the LOAN table; that is, what are its column names and their data types. This information is in the COL table. One of the columns of that table is the table name. Thus, rather than display the entire COL table, the following will select only those rows that describe the columns of the STUDENT table:

```
SELECT * FROM COL
     WHERE TNAME = 'STUDENT';

TNAME     COLNO   CNAME    COLTYP    WIDTH   SCALE   NULLS
-------   ------  ------   -------   -----   -----   -----
STUDENT      1    SID      NUMBER       6       0    NOT NULL
STUDENT      2    NAME     CHAR        16            NULL
STUDENT      3    SLEVEL   NUMBER       1       0    NULL
STUDENT      4    AGE      NUMBER       2       0    NULL
STUDENT      5    SZIP     NUMBER       5       0    NULL
```

The output tells us that the column for ZIP code is called SZIP, is of the type *number*, and is five digits long with null values allowed. The SCALE column indicates the number of digits to the right of the decimal point in columns of the type NUMBER.

Miscellaneous SQL/UFI Features: Help, Convenience, Data Transfer

Need help? ORACLE has an extensive set of on-line explanations. The HELP HELP command will let you see what is available. Here are a few of the options in two groups—help for SQL statements and clauses and help for UFI commands:

```
SQL Help:

Query          Joins          Outer Join    Subquery         Repeating
SELECT         FROM           WHERE         GROUP BY         HAVING
ORDER BY       DELETE         INSERT        ALTER TABLE      UPDATE
CREATE TABLE   CREATE INDEX   CREATE VIEW   CREATE SYNONYM   GRANT
DROP TABLE     DROP INDEX     DROP VIEW     DROP SYNONYM     REVOKE
LIKE

UFI Help:

Editing    Titles     HELP            SET
ECHO       NEWPAGE    PAGESIZE        LINESIZE     WRAP
START      PAUSE      SPACE           NUMWIDTH     FEEDBACK
BREAK ON   COMPUTE    SUM OF COLUMN   FORMAT       SPOOL
```

Here is an example of the response to help for the GROUP BY clause:

```
HELP GROUP BY
Syntax

SELECT [ DISTINCT ] { * | select_list } FROM [creator.]table_name
[ WHERE predicate ]
GROUP BY column_name [ HAVING predicate ]

Examples
SELECT JOB, MAX(SAL), MIN(SAL), AVG(SAL) FROM EMP
   GROUP BY JOB
SELECT JOB, COUNT(*), COUNT(COMM) FROM EMP GROUP BY JOB
SELECT DEPTNO, SUM(COMM) FROM EMP WHERE JOB='Salesperson'
   GROUP BY DEPTNO
Queries may return composite results by organizing the table into
groups of rows with the same value for a particular column(s).
For each group (or set) of rows, one or more of these SQL set
functions, SUM, AVG, MAX, MIN, COUNT, are applied, resulting in a
single row as a composite result for the group.

The SELECT clause must include the columns mentioned in GROUP BY
as well as those to be processed by the calculation functions.
Rows in the base table can be eliminated before the group is
formed, by using the WHERE clause. The HAVING clause may be used
to exclude entire groups by specifying qualifying conditions.

The expression COUNT(*) will return the number of rows in each
group irrespective of null values, while COUNT(column) will only
count the number of non-null entries in that column for each
group. COUNT (DISTINCT column) will ignore duplicate values in
that column.
```

Convenience Features

ORACLE and other SQL systems provide several features to simplify the preparation of SQL and UFI statements. These include the ability to declare a synonym for a table or view name, to save and execute (saved) queries, and to define a limited form of macro.

Saving, Retrieving, and Running Queries

Suppose you have created an especially complex query that you know will be required again. You could, of course, have defined it as a view—that is one way of avoiding the reentry of a complex statement. In addition, the current SQL command (the one just entered) may be stored for later use with the SAVE command. It is retrieved with the GET command, then RUN is entered to execute it. Here is an example of entry, saving a command, and subsequent retrieval and execution. The string following SAVE is any valid file name for your system.

```
SELECT SID, NAME
    FROM STUDENT
    WHERE SID IN
        (SELECT SID FROM LOAN);

SAVE ST_W_LOANS

saved to file ST_W_LOANS.UFI

GET ST_W_LOANS
```

ORACLE responds:

```
1 SELECT SID, NAME
2    FROM STUDENT
3    WHERE SID IN
4*           (SELECT SID FROM LOAN)

RUN
```

ORACLE responds:

```
1 SELECT SID, NAME
2    FROM STUDENT
3    WHERE SID IN
4*           (SELECT SID FROM LOAN)

SID      NAME
----     ------
9735     ALLEN
4494     ALTER
8767     CABEEN
3749     WATSON
```

Since the command is stored in a standard computer file, this also means that you can create a complex statement by using (say) an editor. Then the statement is retrieved with the GET command. The command can now be executed (RUN), or you can use the ORACLE editor to make changes prior to its execution.

Synonyms. It is often a good idea to create descriptive names for tables, especially for complex views. The problem is that such names are usually long and clumsy to enter. There is a compromise. You can create a long name such as LOAN_STATS_BY_BANK, then define a shorter name, L_STATS, using the CREATE SYNONYM statement. (Note that this is an SQL statement, not a UFI command.)

```
CREATE SYNONYM L_STATS FOR LOAN_STATS_BY_BANK
```

The name L_STATS may then be used instead of LOAN_STATS_BY_BANK in any SQL command.

Saving Output. The results of a database query are often just the first step in transforming data into information. Users may want to cut and paste output into a word-processing document, or to transfer data to some other software system, such as a spreadsheet, for subsequent analysis. ORACLE and other RDBMSs now have rather fancy procedures to perform such transfers, including mainframe-to-PC links and conversion of output to specialized formats for input to other software systems.

A simple way to obtain output in text form is to use the *spool* feature. Prior to running a SELECT, the command SPOOL *file name* is entered. Subsequent output is then stored in the specified file until the command SPOOL OFF is entered. The output can then be edited, if necessary, so that it may be input to another software package.

The use of SPOOL is also a good way to create a file of a complete terminal session, which can then be printed for hardcopy output.

Embedded SQL

SQL statements may be included in host-language programs written in COBOL, FORTRAN, PL/1, and others, with only minor modification. That is another beauty of SQL:

it is not necessary to learn a new language in order to access a database from within a high-level language.

First, we'll discuss how to embed SQL in a FORTRAN program for queries and updates that operate on only a single record at a time. Then we will deal with the more complex situation of statements that result in multiple-row results. We warn the reader that even though the embedded language is quite similar to the UFI version, there are considerable complexities involved in creating production programs with embedded SQL. While the programs are much simpler than equivalent programs using file-access systems, there are still a number of details, some of which are quite specific to the particular DBMS, operating system, and computer model being used.

Furthermore, even though COBOL is the more widely used language for database processing, our examples use FORTRAN because of its relative simplicity and because of its greater similarity to languages such as PASCAL and BASIC. Thus, if you know any of these languages (COBOL, PASCAL, BASIC, FORTRAN), you should be able to follow our examples.

There are several possible ways to embed one language (SQL) within a host. One is to modify the host language compiler so that it understands SQL. Then, a program containing SQL is simply compiled directly by the (extended) FORTRAN compiler. But this requires extensive modification to every version of the FORTRAN compiler in which the DBMS will be used, and therefore is not the method followed.

The approach adopted is a "precompiler" approach. The SQL statements are flagged, then source code is preprocessed by a special SQL precompiler that converts the SQL statements into valid FORTRAN statements. Essentially what happens is that the SQL statements are translated into FORTRAN CALL statements to either general-purpose SQL subroutines or to specially generated SQL subroutines that carry out the specific SQL operations (such as SELECTs, INSERTs, UPDATEs, etc.) that are specified in the source code. The converted FORTRAN (with CALLs to SQL subroutines) can then be compiled by the standard FORTRAN compiler. Further discussion of this process follows our examples.

The method used to flag SQL code so that it can be recognized by the SQL precompiler is to preface a single statement with EXEC SQL or to begin a block of SQL code with EXEC SQL BEGIN and end with EXEC SQL END.

Single Row Manipulations

Retrieve One Row

Programs that deal with a single row at a time require only minor changes to the UFI SQL commands when they are embedded in a host language. The first program retrieves rows one at a time from the STUDENT table; see Figure 6–2, which is keyed to the following discussion. Note in particular the statements beginning EXEC SQL and the blocks set off by EXEC SQL BEGIN and EXEC SQL END.

A. The first step is to "connect" the program to ORACLE. The statement

```
EXEC SQL INCLUDE SYS&ORACLE:SQLCA.FOR
```

does this. It will be converted to a CALL, to a standard SQL subroutine that sets up the communication area (SQLCA) between the program and the DBMS.

```
                    PROGRAM RETSTD
                    IMPLICIT INTEGER (A-Z)

        C Call the Fortran program that allows ORACLE to interface with your program.
A                   EXEC SQL INCLUDE SYS$ORACLE:SQLCA.FOR

        C RETSTD: A program which retrieves student records from the Student Table of
        C          the GSL Database.  To end the program enter 0 for Student ID.

        C All Host variables in the program must be named between the EXEC SQL DECLARE
        C statements. If a Host variable is used in a SQL statement but not DECLAREd,
        C you will receive an error message.
                    EXEC SQL BEGIN DECLARE SECTION
                    LOGICAL*1    NAME(16)
B                   CHARACTER*30 USERN, PSWD
                    INTEGER      SID, LEV, AGE, ZIP
                    EXEC SQL END DECLARE SECTION

        C The CONNECT statement establishes a connection between the Program and the
        C Tables in ORACLE. A password of X must be used no matter what your password
        C may be.
                    USERN = 'OPS$8431806'
C                   PSWD  = 'X'
                    EXEC SQL CONNECT :USERN IDENTIFIED BY :PSWD

        C Prompt the user (Via dev. 6) for the ID of the Student to be Retrieved.
            10  WRITE(6,20)
            20  FORMAT(' Enter ID number of Student you wish to Retrieve ',
               +       '[0 to EXIT]:')
                    READ(5,30,ERR=10) SID
            30  FORMAT(I4)
                    IF (SID .EQ. 0) THEN
                        GOTO 1000
                    END IF
                    PRINT *

        C Execute the Retrieval of Information by putting the matching column values
D       C into their relative :Host variables.
                    EXEC SQL WHENEVER NOT FOUND GO TO 10
                    EXEC SQL SELECT NAME, SLEVEL, AGE, SZIP
D1          1       INTO :NAME, :LEV, :AGE, :ZIP
            2       FROM STUDENT
D2          3       WHERE SID = :SID
        C Output all information to the screen pertaining to the Retrieved Student
            40  WRITE(6,50)
            50  FORMAT(1X,'STUDENT #',5X,'NAME',11X,'LEVEL',5X,'AGE',5X,'ZIP')
            60  WRITE(6,70) SID,(NAME(J),J=1,16), LEV, AGE, ZIP
            70  FORMAT(1X,I4,10X,16A1,2X,I1,8X,I2,5X,I5)
                    PRINT *

        C Signal end of a Logical Unit of Work. Protects from rollback of data in
        C case of an error.
D3                  EXEC SQL COMMIT WORK
                    GOTO 10
          1000  STOP 'EXIT FORTRAN/ORACLE PROGRAM'
                    END

        $ RUN RETSTD
        Enter ID number of Student you wish to Retrieve [0 TO EXIT]: 9735

E
        STUDENT #    NAME           LEVEL     AGE      ZIP
        9735         ALLEN            1        21       98101

        Enter ID number of Student you wish to Retrieve [0 TO EXIT]: 0
        EXIT FORTRAN/ORACLE PROGRAM
```

Fig 6-2   FORTRAN Get Rows

B. These statements are processed by the SQL precompiler, which plants an SQL CALL and also leaves the data declarations intact for the FORTRAN compiler. The character variables USERN and PSWD will contain the user account number and password, respectively. Any valid FORTRAN variable names could be used for these two variables. The variable NAME, declared to be a 16-element array of one-byte logical values, corresponds to the ORACLE data type CHAR(16). Note that any valid FORTRAN variable name could be chosen—it does not need to be the same as the column name used in the definition of the STUDENT relation.

C. Values for the user account number and password are assigned and then a call is made to ORACLE. This essentially corresponds to the UFI act of "signing on" to ORACLE. The colon (:) in front of a variable signals SQL that this is, in fact, a standard FORTRAN variable.

D. This block of code inputs the SID of the row to be retrieved, executes SQL to retrieve a row, and loops until an SID of zero is entered. (Admittedly, this is not the best program organization that could have been achieved—the extensive use of GOTOs is not recommended.)

D.1. Here are two SQL statements. The first handles the case of any attempted retrieval for a nonexistent SID, sending the program back to statement 10 to request the input of another SID.

D.2. This single statement is identical to standard UFI SQL if the line beginning INTO is dropped and :SID in the WHERE clause is changed to a constant. (Note: If you are not familiar with FORTRAN, the entries 1, 2, 3 in column 6 indicate that a statement is continued. Thus, no BEGIN and END are required.) The INTO clause tells SQL where to put the results of the query: column NAME is stored in (FORTRAN variable) NAME, SLEVEL into LEV, AGE into AGE, and SZIP into ZIP. In the WHERE clause, the :SID indicates the FORTRAN variable that supplies the value for comparison.

The retrieved row is then displayed using standard FORTRAN.

D.3. This final SQL statement signals ORACLE that our retrieval is done. It prevents tying up (locking) the database and preventing other users (the database can be shared) from manipulating the STUDENT table.

E. This is the result of executing the program. No surprises here.

Insert One Row

The next example program adds one row at a time to the database. The program is in Figure 6–3. Our comments are briefer because the program is quite similar to the previous example.

A. This is standard FORTRAN to input values for SID (SID=0 terminates the program), NAME, etc. In the interests of economy, code to input other variables has been edited out.

The integer variables SID, LEV, AGE, and ZIP will be used to accept input values, which are then inserted into the STUDENT table. Again, the choice of variable names is up to you, but the type must be numeric since that is the type of the columns in the STUDENT relation. Of course, not all of the columns in STUDENT need to

```
            PROGRAM ADDSTD
            IMPLICIT INTEGER (AZ)

C Call the Fortran program that allows ORACLE to interface with your program.
            EXEC SQL INCLUDE SYS$ORACLE:SQLCA.FOR

C ADDSTD: A program which adds new student records to the Student Table of the
C         GSL Database.  The program doesn't check for data integrity or error.

C All Host variables in the program must be named in the SQL Declare Section
            EXEC SQL BEGIN DECLARE SECTION
            LOGICAL*1    NAME(16)
            CHARACTER*30 USERN, PSWD
            INTEGER      SID, SID1, SLEVEL, AGE, SZIP
            EXEC SQL DECLARE SECTION

C The CONNECT Statement establishes a connection between the program and ORACLE
            USERN = 'OPS$8431806'
            PSWD  = 'X'
            EXEC SQL CONNECT :USERN IDENTIFIED BY :PSWD

C Prompt the user (Via dev. 6) for information about the student
       10   WRITE(6,20)
       20   FORMAT(' Enter students ID number [0 TO EXIT]:')
            READ(5,30,ERR=10) SID
       30   FORMAT(I6)
            SID1=SID
            IF (SID .EQ. 0) THEN
                GO TO 1000
            END IF
       40   WRITE(6,50)
       50   FORMAT(' Enter student's Name       : ')
            READ (5,60)(NAME(J),J= 1,16)
       60   FORMAT(16A1)
            PRINT *

(Additional statements here to prompt for and input values for LEV, AGE, and ZIP.)

C Execute the insertion of :Host variables into names of the STUDENT Table.
            EXEC SQL INSERT INTO STUDENT(SID,NAME,SLEVEL,AGE,SZIP)
       1       VALUES (:SID, :NAME, :LEV, :AGE, :ZIP)

C Signal end of Logical Unit of Work.  Protects from rollback in case of error
            EXEC SQL COMMIT WORK

C Tell the user that the row has been added to the GSL Student Table
       160  WRITE(6,170) (NAME(J),J =1,16), SID1
       170  FORMAT(1X,16A1,'added to GSL STUDENT TABLE as student #',I6)
            PRINT *
            GO TO 10
      1000  STOP 'END OF THE FORTRAN/ORACLE PROGRAM'
            END

 $ RUN ADDSTD
 Enter students ID number [0 TO EXIT]: 8431
 Enter students Name      : LORENGO
 Enter students Level     : 4
 Enter students Age       : 21
 Enter students ZIP code : 98031

 LORENGO          added to GSL STUDENT TABLE as student #  8431

 Enter student's ID number [0 TO EXIT]: 0
 END OF THE FORTRAN/ORACLE PROGRAM
```

A —

B

Fig 6-3   FORTRAN Add Row

be retrieved. If we wanted only the NAME and SLEVEL columns from STUDENT, then only two FORTRAN variables would be declared to receive values from those two columns.

B. Again you see an almost–UFI/SQL statement for adding a row to a table. The only difference is the use of FORTRAN variables to supply the values instead of the constants that would be used in UFI/SQL.

Multiple-Row Manipulations

A problem arises when manipulations involve more than a single row because most languages, FORTRAN included, cannot deal with a multirow structure (an array of records) of an unknown number of rows. The problem is solved through the use of what is called a *cursor*, which works as follows:

1. An SQL statement that retrieves multiple rows is executed. For example:

```
SELECT LID, LDATE, YEARS, INT_RATE, AMOUNT, BID
    FROM LOAN
    WHERE SID = 1234
    ORDER BY LID
```

2. The resulting rows are stored in a temporary file (relation) and a pointer (the cursor) is set to the first row.

3. The program fetches one row from this file. Each time a row is fetched, the cursor advances to the next row.

The program in Figure 6–4 retrieves data for a single student and all of his or her loans. It implements the immediately preceding SQL SELECT with the specific value for SID (1234) replaced by a variable.

A. FORTRAN variables are defined. The program will retrieve columns from LOAN, thus variables BANK (to receive BID values), INTRT (to receive INT_RATE values), and others are declared. Note that in the interest of simplicity, the LOAN table used in this example is slightly different from that used with previous UFI/SQL. In particular, the loan date has been changed to a simple four-digit value with year preceding month (e.g., 8009), and the interest rate is a single-digit integer.

B. Here is where a significant difference between UFI and embedded SQL occurs. This block of code *defines* the multiple-row query on the LOAN table, but it does not actually *execute* it at this time. The cursor is called C1 for this query. If several multiple-row queries occurred in one program, each cursor would be given a different name.

C. This SQL is a single-row retrieval. Nothing new here.

D. This statement actually causes execution of the SQL query with a cursor named C1. It is at this point that the database is accessed and the temporary file (which we might think of as the C1 file) is created.

E. This block of code retrieves rows from the C1 file, one at a time, into FORTRAN variables.

E.1. The EXEC SQL FETCH statement causes data to be moved from the C1 file into the FORTRAN variables. This statement and the statement at B are

```
            PROGRAM RETROW
            IMPLICIT INTEGER (A-Z)

  C Call the Fortran program that allows ORACLE to interface with your program.
            EXEC SQL INCLUDE SYS$ORACLE:SQLCA.FOR

  C RETROW: A program which retrieves student records from the Student Table of
  C         the GSL Database. To end the program enter 0 for Student ID.

  C All Host variables in the program must be named between the EXEC SQL DECLARE
  C statements.  If a Host variable is used in a SQL statement but not DECLAREd,
  C you will receive an error message.
            EXEC SQL BEGIN DECLARE SECTION
            LOGICAL*1               NAME(16), BANK(12)
A           CHARACTER*30            USERN, PSWD
            INTEGER SID, LID, DATE, YEARS, INTRT, AMOUNT
            EXEC SQL END DECLARE SECTION

  C The CONNECT statement establishes a connection between the Program and the
  C Tables in ORACLE.  A password of X must be used no matter what your password
  C may be.
            USERN = 'OPS$8431806'
            PSWD  = 'X'
            EXEC SQL CONNECT :USERN IDENTIFIED BY :PSWD

  C The DECLARE statement allows you to define a cursor by assigning it a name
  C associated with a query.  The cursor may return many rows from the data base.
  C These rows are referred to as the Active Set of the cursor.
            EXEC SQL DECLARE C1 CURSOR FOR
          1     SELECT LID, LDATE, YEARS, INT_RATE, AMOUNT, BID
B         2     FROM LOAN
          3     WHERE SID = :SID
          4     ORDER BY LID

  C Prompt the user (Via dev. 6) for the ID of the Student to be Retrieved
     10  WRITE(6,20)
     20  FORMAT(' Enter ID of Student for Retrieval of ',
         +       'Loan Records [0 TO EXIT]: ')
            READ(5,30,ERR=10) SID

     30  FORMAT(I4)
            PRINT *
            IF (SID .EQ. 0) THEN
                GOTO 1000
            END IF

  C Execute the Retrieval of Students name corresponding to ID selected
            EXEC SQL WHENEVER NOT FOUND GO TO 100
            EXEC SQL SELECT NAME
C         1         INTO  :NAME
          2         FROM  STUDENT
          3                         WHERE SID = :SID

     35  WRITE(6,37)NAME,SID
     37  FORMAT(1X,'NAME: ',16A1,'ID #: ',I4)
            PRINT *
     50  WRITE(6,55)
     55  FORMAT(1X,'LID   DATE   YEARS   INTRT   AMOUNT   BANK')
     57  WRITE(6,58)
     58  FORMAT(1X,'---------------------------------------------')

  C The OPEN statement examines the contents of the input host variables in the
  C WHERE clause of the query.  The cursor is then placed in the active state.
```

Fig 6-4 FORTRAN Many Rows

```
D         EXEC SQL OPEN C1

      C The FETCH statement advances the position of the cursor to the next row
      C of its Active Set and delivers the selected fields of throw into the Host
      C variables.  WHENEVER NOT FOUND provides the exit from the loop.
         60  EXEC SQL WHENEVER NOT FOUND GO TO 100
E.1          EXEC SQL FETCH C1 INTO :LID, :DATE, :YEARS,
           1                              :INTRT, :AMOUNT, :BANK

E ──
      C Output all information to the screen pertaining to the Retrieved Student
         70  WRITE(6,80) LID,DATE,YEARS,INTRT,AMOUNT, BANK
         80  FORMAT(1X,I3,3X,I4,5X,I1,7X,I1,5X,I5,4X,12A1)
         90  GO TO 60
        100  PRINT *
             GO TO 10


      C Signal end of a Logical Unit of Work.  Protects from rollback of data in
      C case of an error.  And CLOSE the Cursor.
       1000  EXEC SQL COMMIT WORK
             EXEC SQL CLOSE C1
             STOP 'EXIT FORTRAN/ORACLE PROGRAM'
             END

       $ RUN RETLNS
      Enter ID of Student for Retrieval of Loan records [0 to EXIT]: 9735

      NAME: ALLEN         ID #: 9735

      LID   DATE   YEARS   INTRT   AMOUNT   BANK
      ----------------------------------------------------------------------
       27    8509     5       9      1200    HOME
       78    8606     5       8      1000    PEOPLES
       87    8309     5       7      2000    SEAFIRST

      Enter ID of Student for Retrieval of Loan records [0 to EXIT]: 8767

      NAME: CABEEN ID # 8767

      LID   DATE   YEARS   INTRT   AMOUNT   BANK
      ----------------------------------------------------------------------
      170    8304     6       7      1900    PEOPLES

      Enter ID of Student for Retrieval of Loan records [0 to EXIT]: 0
      EXIT FORTRAN/ORACLE PROGRAM
```

Fig 6-4   FORTRAN Many Rows (cont.)

closely tied together. The order of FORTRAN variables in the FETCH must correspond to the order of variables in the SELECT. Each time the FETCH is executed, the cursor is advanced by one row. When the end of the file C1 is reached, the program branches to line 100, then to 10 to repeat.

We have not shown all of the "bells and whistles" of embedded SQL. For example, after each execution of an SQL statement, values are placed in a communication area that can be examined by the program to determine the status of the result: success, failure, warning, etc. In a production program, this communication area would be monitored carefully.

We will conclude with a few comments about data independence, and the lack of it, in embedded SQL. There is both logical and physical independence between the program and the database in the following ways:

- There could be more columns in the STUDENT table than this program references.
- The program does not need to know the order of the columns in STUDENT.
- The program does depend on the column names being NAME, SLEVEL, etc. But if we wanted to use different names in the program (for example, ST_NAME, ST_AGE), a view could be written and the SELECT could reference that view instead of the base table.
- If a column were added to STUDENT, no change would be required in the program unless we wanted to retrieve that column.
- No information is required about the access path to the STUDENT table. There might be an index on SID.

The program depends on the characteristics of the STUDENT table in the following ways:

- It must know the data types. The declaration of NAME as a 16-element array of one-byte logical type is dependent on the fact that the NAME column of STUDENT is of type CHAR(16). However, we could get around this to some extent with a view. For example, suppose that NAME in STUDENT is defined as CHAR(24), but that for some reason this program only wants to work with the first 16 characters. A view could be defined to extract only the first 16 characters of NAME by using SUB-STR(NAME,1,16).
- It must know the table name. But even this could be overcome by using the SYNONYM statement so that the program could call the STUDENT table by a synonym.

Physical Structure of SQL Databases

The placement of data onto a physical storage device in a relational database system is controlled by the internal-level software. In general, SQL-based systems store data physically as variable-length rows (records) on direct-access pages. By default, most of these SQL systems store rows from a single table in each page unless the database designer has created a "cluster" (described later). There are two types of pages: data pages that store rows of base relations, and pages that contain internal-directory and index entries.

Figure 6–5 shows the organization of a data page and an index entry (described later). A data page is divided into three sections: header, body, and slot pointers. The page header contains the number of the page and other system information. The body contains rows

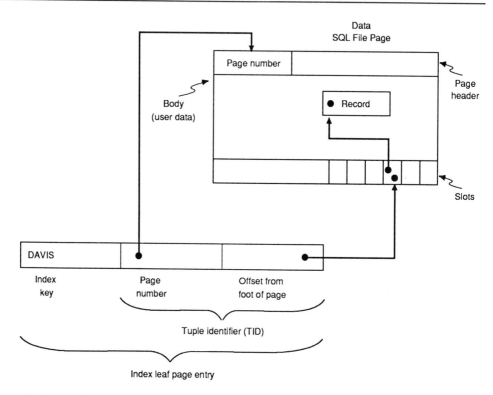

Fig 6-5 Data Page Structure

from one or more base tables. The slot pointers contain pointers into the body of a page. Slot pointers begin at the end of a page and grow toward the beginning. There is one slot for each row on the page. Each slot contains the offset, in bytes, of the beginning of the row from the top of the page.

Associated with each row of data in a database is a tuple identifier (TID), made up of a page number and an offset. The TID thus points to a slot pointer, which in turn points to a row. The TID is not accessible for use by end-users. Since the beginning of each row is indicated by a slot pointer, variable-length records are easily supported. In addition, each field of a row has a prefix that contains the length of the field.

SQL systems allow the database designer to define indexes on single or combined attributes. An index in ORACLE, DB2, and other RDBMSs is a dense B-tree with TIDs as pointers. Figure 6–6 shows a B+tree file structure, which would result if an index were created on name. The lowest-level index pages contain the key and TID pairs, which point to data pages. Higher levels of the tree contain key prefixes and pointers to lower-level pages.

Note in the figure how the pointers from the leaf pages do not point to data pages in any particular order. This is the general situation that results from defining an index. The indexes are dense and thus have one pointer to each row.

ORACLE allows an index to be created for every column in a database. Indexes should be selected carefully, however, due to the additional amount of space required and the I/O

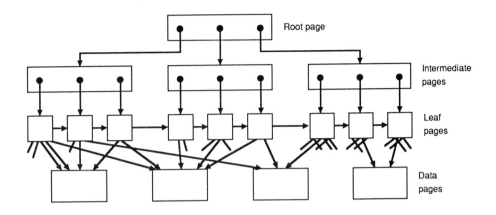

Fig 6-6   SQL B+Tree File Index Structure

and processing time for their maintenance. Criteria for selection of indexes are detailed in Chapter 13.

Defining Indexes

To create an index, the SQL statement is:

```
CREATE [UNIQUE] INDEX index_name ON table_name(col_name);
```

For example, to create an index to loans by LID:

```
CREATE INDEX LIDX ON LOAN(LID);
```

The somewhat amazing thing is that an index may be created at any time—it does not have to be created prior to loading data into tables as is the case with older, nonrelational DBMSs. Thus, the designer has considerably greater flexibility. He or she can modify the physical data structure (to some extent) as necessary to meet changing needs.

You will recall from the definition of the formal relational model that every relation must have a primary key: a set of attributes that are uniquely valued within the relation. Most RDBMSs do not provide for the definition of a primary key. But by creating an index on the primary key and using the UNIQUE option, essentially the same result is achieved. For example, to assure that LID is unique in LOAN, the LIDS index should be created by:

```
CREATE UNIQUE INDEX LIDS ON LOAN(LID)
```

Dropping Indexes

Indexes, just like tables and views, can be removed when they are no longer cost effective by the statement:

```
DROP INDEX index_name;
```

You might consider how this affects previously compiled programs with embedded SQL—do we need to recompile them? We will address this later.

Clustering

One technique for improving system response is to physically store rows from separate tables, which are frequently retrieved together, on the same disk page. This approach is implemented by creating a *cluster*. The general form varies somewhat from one implementation to another, but in ORACLE a cluster is first defined by:

```
CREATE CLUSTER cluster_name, column
```

For example:

```
CREATE CLUSTER L_SID, L_SIDX
```

This sets up the cluster, but as yet nothing physical has happened. Before showing the next step, consider the following situation:

Suppose a very frequent query requests a list of all the loans for a specific student. Without clustering, the loans for one student would, most likely, be scattered across several disk pages. What we would like is to have all loans for a student appear in a single page—or if a student has too many loans for one page, to store them in the minimum number of pages. That is, if the page capacity for loans is B, and a student has n loans, then at most the number of pages required would be the smallest integer greater than or equal to n/B.

To actually group loans for one student into a page (or pages), the following statement is entered:

```
ALTER CLUSTER L_SID
    ADD TABLE LOAN WHERE SID=L_SIDX
```

Now all loans of a given SID value are moved to a page. The page itself will indicate the SID value of all the loans stored in it; therefore, it is not necessary to store (physically) the SID with each loan.

It is possible to carry the clustering beyond the physical grouping of rows from one table to the grouping rows from several tables. For example, suppose that not only are all loans for a single student accessed together, but the student row is also accessed with them as shown in the following query:

```
SELECT S.SID,NAME, LID, AMOUNT
    FROM STUDENT S, LOAN L
    WHERE S.SID=L.SID
    AND NAME='JOHNSON, SALLY'
```

The student rows can be clustered with their loans by executing:

```
ALTER CLUSTER L_SID
    ADD TABLE LOAN WHERE SID=L_SIDX
```

Now, in a sense, students and their loans are "pre-joined."

Compiling Queries

The research into relational DBMSs (System R) at IBM led to a number of significant findings. One of these was made by Ron Fagin, who proved that any SQL query could be decomposed into machine-language fragments (from a library) to create code for the SQL statement. Compilation is particularly beneficial in circumstances in which the same statement is used repetitively. But it is also cost effective for UFI/SQL when the query is other than very simple.

When the SQL statement occurs in a host language, the compilation process begins with a precompiler. The precompiler removes the SQL statements from the source code, replacing them with CALL statements. Using the SQL statements, a database request module (DBRM) is created.

The next step is called *binding*. The bind component compiles the DBRMs created in the precompiler to construct internal control structures. These structures are essentially compiled versions of the original SQL statements. Then the compiled DBRMs and the compiled host language code (with DBRM calls) are loaded and execution begins.

The runtime supervisor is responsible for interacting with the application program at runtime. It receives control whenever the application program requests a database operation. The runtime supervisor then calls the data manager to perform the requested operations using the compiled DBRMs. The data manager performs the normal database functions such as retrievals, updates, deletions, and insertions. Other system components, responsible for data locking, logging, and physical I/O operations, are called by the data manager as necessary. The end result is the delivery of attribute values to the program.

A similar process takes place if the SQL statement is from the UFI. The statement is compiled in DBRM object code, loaded, and executed. The DBMS formats the output and sends it back to the user terminal.

Since an application program containing SQL statements is preprocessed, the overhead of parsing each statement, selecting access paths, etc., is removed from the execution process. As a result, the application program interacts only with its DBRMs and not with the SQL interpreter.

We turn now to a question raised earlier. Suppose that the following events occur in the indicated order:

1. An index on student by SID is created:

   ```
   CREATE INDEX SIDX ON STUDENT(SID)
   ```

2. A program with embedded SQL is coded, compiled, and executed. The program has the following statement:

   ```
   SELECT NAME, SLEVEL
          INTO :NAME, :LEV
          FROM STUDENT
          WHERE SID=:SID_FIND;
   ```

   Of course, the SQL module for the statement uses the SIDX index.

3. The index is dropped:

   ```
   DROP INDEX SIDX;
   ```

4. The program is run again. What do you suppose happens?

   A. The program executes but crashes when it executes the SQL statement. It must be recompiled before it will work.

   B. The program will not even go into execution.

   C. The program works because you cannot drop an index that any existing program uses.

   D. None of the above.

The answer is D. How can that be? When the index is dropped all DBRMs that relied on that index are marked as invalid. When a program is executed that used one of the modules, the module source code is retrieved and recompiled. Thus, the rather dramatic change at the internal level is transparent at the conceptual level and even transparent to programs that have already been compiled.

While a DBRM is recompiled at runtime if changes occur to the database structure, it does not automatically use "new" indexes. The procedure must be recompiled if an index is created. Of course, high-level SQL queries, entered interactively through the UFI, use whatever indexes currently exist that will reduce page accesses. The queries are also compiled into an access module and executed, but this is done at the time of the query.

The Optimizer

In the introduction to SQL we stated that relational systems suffer to some extent in transaction processing compared with network and hierarchical systems. Because of this, it is essential that a relational system provide as much performance optimization as possible.

Query processing, including optimization and compilation, is performed when the DBRM is compiled. Almost any query can be performed in a number of ways, some of which are more efficient than others. The query compiler is responsible for finding the most efficient method for performing any particular query. The following describes some of the steps taken automatically by the DBMS to optimize performance, as well as steps the application designer and end user can take to improve efficiency.

As an example of alternatives considered by the optimizer, consider the following query:

```
SELECT * FROM LOAN
      WHERE SID=9876 AND BID='PEOPLES'
```

Possible alternative ways to process the query include:

1. Scanning the LOAN relation and checking each loan to see if it satisfies the predicate.

2. Using an index on BID to select rows having BID= 'PEOPLES', then retrieving the rows, examining each for SID = 9876.

3. Using an index on SID to select rows having SID = 9876, then retrieving the rows, examining each for BID = 'PEOPLES'.

If both indexes do exist, the selectivity and clustering of each alternative would be taken into account to choose between alternatives 2 and 3. The selectivity of an index is the percentage of rows in the relation that have a common value of the indexed attribute. For example, suppose our database has 1,000 students and 100 banks. Then the SID index has an average selectivity of $1/1000 = 0.1\%$, and the BID index an average selectivity of $1/100 = 1\%$. Suppose further that there are 10,000 rows in the LOAN table. The index on SID would (on the average) point to 10 loans for each given SID value and 100 loans for each given BID value.

At first blush you are probably tempted to suggest that the SID index should be used for this query since that would mean only 10 rows need to be retrieved. But suppose that the BID index clusters rows and that the average page (or physical block) contains 25 LOAN rows. What this means is that the 100 loans for Peoples Bank are probably stored in only four pages—thus, after (probably) two accesses within the index, only four additional data pages are accessed, and these will be in physical proximity to each other. By contrast, we can be pretty certain that the 10 Loans for SID = 9876 are in 10 separate pages (since they cannot also be clustered on SID). Using the SID index will require two index accesses plus 10 data page accesses. The optimizer will probably perform this same estimate of the number of page accesses and chose the BID index.

Here is a summary:

INDEX	SELECTIVITY	CLUSTERING	ESTIMATED RECORDS	ACCESSES OF: PAGES
SID	0.1%	NO	10	12
BID	1%	YES	100	6

The optimizer is also called into play for more complex queries, such as those involving joins. Note that the choice of access paths is left to the system rather than the user. This approach provides a significant degree of data independence.

In addition to estimating "costs" associated with the alternative access paths, the query optimizer also considers alternative orders of operations.

The general strategies for reducing processing time are:

1. Perform selections and projections first to reduce the number of rows and the number of attributes in each row that need to be dealt with in a subsequent join.

2. Defer join operations; that is, do them as late as possible.

In theory, two equivalent SQL queries should be compiled into the same (near optimal) DBRM object modules. For example, both of the following retrieve all student rows for graduate students with loans of $3,000 or more.

```
SELECT * FROM STUDENT S, LOAN L
    WHERE SLEVEL = 5 AND S.SID=L.SID
    AND AMOUNT >=3000;

SELECT * FROM STUDENT
    WHERE SLEVEL=5 AND SID IN
    SELECT SID FROM LOAN
        WHERE AMOUNT >=3000;
```

Unfortunately, the current technology is not sophisticated enough to assure that both queries create the best DBRM. Thus, a user might want to try both queries on a sample database and examine the "cost" (or CPU and I/O times) to see which is more efficient. The query with the lower cost could then be run against the full database.

In addition, some SQL-DBMSs allow you to interrogate the system to determine how the query was compiled. By looking at the order of operations, access paths, and processes used (for example, sorting vs. index access), you may be able to figure out which query will execute more efficiently.

Conclusion

By now you should have begun to appreciate the power, flexibility, and complexity of an RDBMS. Fortunately, much of the complexity of an RDBMS, such as query optimization, is hidden from the user, so that he or she is able to focus on data needs rather than on how to obtain that data. In the next chapter we will describe some alternative RDBMS implementations and their features.

Questions and Problems

Questions

1. What is a view? What are the reasons to create a view?

2. In a three-level DBMS, a view represents the _____ level.

3. Describe the conditions under which an update can and cannot be performed on a view in most RDBMS implementations?

4. What enhancements does the report writer provide?

5. In general terms, what types of information are included in the system catalog? Which table provides column type data for columns you have created?

6. Briefly describe how to embed SQL statements into a host language program when the SQL statement retrieves or adds a single row.

7. Answer question 6 for the case of SQL statements which retrieve multiple rows.

8. Describe the three sections of a data page.

9. What structure is created by the CREATE INDEX statement?

10. What is a *cluster*? Why is a cluster used?

11. What are some of the different means of improving performance?

12. Describe the compilation process. What happens when a previously referenced index is dropped?

Problems

1. Define a view named LOAN_85 which includes LID, LDATE, YEARS, AMOUNT, and SID for loans with LDATE in 1985. Can this view be updated (e.g. could AMOUNT be changed)?

2. Define a view named MSB_ST which includes all columns of STUDENT for those people who have a loan with a bank of type MSB.

3. Consider the following view:

```
CREATE VIEW UG234 AS
    SELECT SID, NAME, AGE
        FROM STUDENT
        WHERE SLEVEL BETWEEN 2 AND 4;
```

   a. Given the following query on UG234, write the equivalent query directly on base tables.

```
SELECT SID, LID, AMOUNT
    FROM LOAN L, UG234 U
WHERE L.SID = U.SID
    AND YEARS >=6;
```

   b. Use UG234 to create a view named UG_LOAN which includes SID, NAME, and all columns from LOAN for students with AGE ≥ 21 who have SLEVEL = 2, 3, or 4.

c. Use UG234 to create a view named UG_TOT which includes SID, NAME, and total amount of loans for students in levels 2, 3, and 4. Call the loan total column TOTAL.

d. With UG_TOT as defined in part c, why is it surprising that the following works in ORACLE:

```
SELECT * FROM UG_TOT
       WHERE TOTAL > 3000;
```

4. Define a view TOT_PYMT which has all columns from STUDENT plus a column giving the total of monthly loan payments. You may use any view defined in this chapter to simplify your CREATE VIEW statement.

5. Using the definition of base tables STUDENT, LOAN, and BANK from Chapter 5, describe the types of updates (additions, value updates, deletions) possible for each of the following view definitions.

```
CREATE VIEW BIG_LOAN AS
       SELECT * FROM LOAN
       WHERE AMOUNT >= 2500;

CREATE VIEW ZIP_TYPE AS
       SELECT DISTINCT BZIP, TYPE
       FROM BANK;

CREATE VIEW LSB AS
       SELECT LID, SID, BID
       FROM LOAN;
```

6. Create a report which lists the BID, SID, AMOUNT, YEARS, and INT_RATE for each loan. Order the output by BID and within BID by SID. Compute and display total of AMOUNT for each different BANK. Include headings, title and appropriate formats.

7. Create the same report specified in question 6 except that it will show one line for each student with loans from a given bank. That is, each line will be an aggregate of several rows from LOAN if a student has multiple loans from one bank.

8. Suppose a view has been created and you can no longer recall its name. How might you find out its name?

9. How could you determine which tables include columns where the column name includes the string ZIP?

10. Use the SAVE and RUN feature to create the view of question 2 and then execute a query which displays NAMEs from that view.

11. Outline the code in a host language with which you are familiar to input a loan ID, retrieve that loan, and display its SID, BID, and AMOUNT columns.

12. Outline the code in a host language of your choice to retrieve and display names of all students who have two or more loans from a bank whose BID value is input to the program.

13. Determine the specifics of a SQL-based system available to you and create host language programs for questions 11 and 12.

14. Use the SPOOL feature or similar feature on your SQL system to extract all rows of LOAN and load into a spreadsheet system such as LOTUS 1-2-3 or EXCEL.

15. Use the example CLUSTER named L_SID with rows from LOAN and STUDENT to illustrate the probable physical arrangement of STUDENT and LOAN rows using the data of Figure 6-1. Assume each page has capacity for 3 rows.

16. Suppose that an extended STUDENT table has indexes on SZIP and MAJOR. There are 100 different values of MAJOR. Assume that students are evenly distributed over the 100,000 possible values for SZIP (i.e., *all* five digit numeric values for ZIP code are valid). Rows of STUDENT are not clustered by either MAJOR or SZIP. For each of the following queries, which index should the query optimizer choose and why?

   a. ```
       SELECT * FROM STUDENT
            WHERE MAJOR = 'MKTNG';
       ```

   b.  ```
       SELECT * FROM STUDENT
            WHERE MAJOR = 'ARCHJ'
            AND SZIP BETWEEN 88000 AND 90000;
       ```

   c. ```
       SELECT * FROM STUDENT
            WHERE MAJOR IN ('MKTNG', 'ACCTG',
            'FINAN', 'MIS', 'PROD') AND
            SZIP < 00500
       ```

17. Answer question 16 under the assumption that rows of STUDENT are clustered on SZIP.

18. If you have the larger version of the GSL Database available to you (provided with the Instructor's Manual for this text), create an index to LOAN on LID and perform queries by specific LID value to see if response time is affected.

19. Given an available database, empirically evaluate the impact of response time for join queries if indexes are created on join attributes. For example, compare response time for the following SELECT with and without indexes on SID:

   ```
   SELECT * FROM STUDENT S, LOAN L
        WHERE S.SID = L.SID;
   ```

References

See Chapter 5 References.

Codd, E. F. "Fatal Flaws in SQL: Part 1." *Datamation*, vol. 34, no. 16 (Aug. 15, 1988), pp. 45ff.

_____. "Fatal Flaws in SQL: Part 2." *Datamation*, vol. 34, no. 17 (Sept. 1, 1988), pp. 71–74.

Date, C. J. "Where SQL Falls Short." *Datamation*, vol. 33, no. 9 (May 1, 1987), pp. 83–86.

Sither, M. "Oracle Extends DBMS Reach into On-line Processing." *Mini-Micro Systems*, (Feb. 1988), pp. 15–16.
   ```

7 *Other Relational Systems and Capabilities*

RDMSs include both SQL-based systems and non-SQL systems. This chapter gives an overview of DB2, SQL/DS, INGRES, and QBE. Both DB2 and SQL/DS, from IBM, are based on the SQL standard. INGRES, from Relational Technology, Inc. (RTI), has both an SQL interface and its own language, QUEL. In QBE (Query By Example), users make entries into a table to specify a query.

Important Features and Characteristics of DB2 and SQL/DS

The data manipulation languages (DML) and data definition languages (DDL) of DB2, SQL/DS, and ORACLE are very similar since they are all SQL-based systems and share a common ancestor, System R. The major difference between them is that they are designed to run on different hardware or with different operating systems.

IBM DATABASE 2 (DB2) runs on large mainframes under IMS (Integrated Management System), CICS (Customer Information Control System), and the TSO component of MVS. DB2 can run either in a batch mode or interactively under IMS and MVS/TSO, while under CICS it can only run interactively. Figure 7–1 shows a general block diagram of the DB2 operating environment.

When running under IMS, in either mode, IMS is the controlling system. In the batch mode, a conventional IMS batch application program can access DB2 data via SQL statements, and IMS data via DL/1 database calls. In the online mode, a DB2 application program is invoked from an IMS data communications terminal and uses the data communications facilities of IMS to exchange messages with the DB2 application.

When running under TSO, again either in batch or online mode, DB2 is the controlling system, but in this case it cannot access IMS files.

All of the variations discussed above are able to run concurrently and are able to share the same DB2 files. In addition, IMS files may be shared where permitted by IMS and MVS. Thus, an interesting feature of DB2 is its ability to access both newer DB2 databases and older IMS databases. (IMS, a hierarchical database, is discussed in Chapter 10.)

SQL/DS (Structured Query Language/Data System) is designed to run under the DOS/VSE and VM/CMS operating environments. While, logically speaking, SQL/DS and DB2 are very similar, DB2 was designed to run on very large systems, while SQL/DS was designed to run on smaller mainframe and mini computers. This is reflected in the more elaborate access procedures available for DB2 (to handle a larger number of users) and in the amount of online storage supported. DB2 is limited only by operating system and hardware constraints, while SQL/DS has a built-in limit.

Since SQL/DS and DB2 can not share each other's files, IBM provides a product, DXT (Data Extract), to move data from one system to the other.

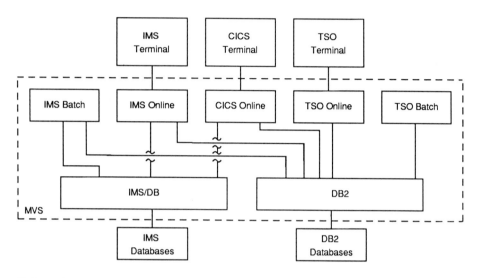

Fig 7-1 DB2 Operating Environment

INGRES

INGRES is a relational database management system that supports both SQL and its own language, QUEL. QUEL (Query Language) is based on the relational calculus, and can be invoked from a host language via EQUEL (Embedded Query Language).

Introduction

INGRES (Interactive Graphics and Retrieval System) was initially developed at the University of California, Berkeley, to run on DEC PDP machines under UNIX. It has found wide acceptance in the university environment and is marketed commercially by Relational Technology, Inc. The commercial version runs on DEC VAX machines under UNIX or VMS; IBM 43xx and 30xx machines under VM/CMS or MVS; a number of computers based on the Motorola MC6800 microprocessor family; IBM-PCs and compatibles.

The INGRES language is QUEL (although SQL is now supported as well). While SQL is a mixture of relational calculus and relational algebra, INGRES is a nearly pure implementation of relational calculus. Even though the data manipulation language is somewhat similar to SQL, there are other important differences in how multiple-relation updates, join operations, and the programming language interface are implemented.

The QUEL Data Definition Language

Our goal here is not to teach QUEL, but to point out the important and interesting differences between QUEL and SQL. For instance, the CREATE statement, used to define a table, is virtually identical to the SQL CREATE TABLE statement. The statement to create the STUDENT table of Figure 6–1 in INGRES is:

```
CREATE STUDENT (SID = I2,
     NAME = TEXT(16),
     LEVEL = I1,
     AGE = I2,
     SZIP = I5)
```

The data types supported by INGRES include binary integer, floating point, money, fixed and variable-length text, and date.

The INGRES MODIFY statement is used to change the storage structure (that is, the physical organization and ordering of records) of a table and is not used to change table specifications or data values. The general form is:

```
MODIFY base_table_name TO structure [UNIQUE] [ON col_name
[, col_name]..] index_name
```

where structure is one of the following:

- BTREE B-tree Index
- HASH Computed Storage Location
- ISAM Indexed Sequential Access Method
- HEAP Records added where there is room
- HEAPSORT Sorted when the MODIFY statement is executed, but subsequent insertions added where there is room.

Both the ORACLE and the IBM products support only the BTREE structure. In addition, INGRES's BTREE structure is comparable to the ORACLE and IBM product's clustering index . The INGRES HEAP is comparable to having no clustering index, so that the records are stored wherever there is space. HASH and HEAPSORT have no comparable structures in the ORACLE and IBM products. In the HASH structure, a hashed file is used, while the INGRES HEAPSORT is a sorted heap. ISAM is similar to the clustered BTREE structure.

For example, to store the student table as a hashed storage structure (file), with hashing on SID, the appropriate statement is:

```
MODIFY STUDENT TO HASH UNIQUE ON SID
```

Indexes are created by writing:

```
INDEX ON base_table_name IS index_name (col_name
[, col_name]...)
```

For example, to create an index on SID of the STUDENT table:

```
INDEX ON STUDENT IS SNUMBER (SID)
```

Both tables and indexes may be removed from the system with the statement DESTROY *name*.

The QUEL Data Manipulation Language

QUEL has statements equivalent to the SQL statements for the following operations:

```
QUEL          SQL
--------      ------
RETRIEVE      SELECT
REPLACE       UPDATE
DELETE        DELETE
APPEND        INSERT
```

One difference between SQL and QUEL is the absence of a FROM clause. For this reason, field names in INGRES retrievals are always qualified, in contrast to SQL where this is only necessary to avoid ambiguity.

The general form of an INGRES query is:

```
RETRIEVE [UNIQUE] (col_name1 [, col_name2] ...])
    [WHERE predicate]
    [SORT BY col_name1 [, col_name2] ...]
```

To retrieve all students with a 98102 ZIP code from the GSL database, we would write:

```
RETRIEVE (STUDENT.NAME, STUDENT.SID)
    WHERE STUDENT.SZIP = 98102
```

Another example, again using the GSL database:

```
RETRIEVE INTO OLDER_STUDENTS (STUDENT.LEVEL, STUDENT.NAME)
    WHERE STUDENT.AGE >= 23
```

This query retrieves all students age 23 or older, and places the result of the query in a new table named OLDER_STUDENTS with columns LEVEL and NAME.

Although there are minor differences in the actual words used, INGRES retrievals are similar enough to SQL so that only a few retrieval types, those with interesting differences, will be repeated in INGRES. There are, however, some minor differences in creating views and some more significant differences in embedded QUEL that we will explore briefly.

To perform a join of the STUDENT and LOAN tables the QUEL statement is:

```
RETRIEVE (STUDENT.NAME, LOAN.LID)
    WHERE STUDENT.SID=LOAN.SID
```

In INGRES, a self-join is written by first defining range variables (which are similar to SQL synonyms):

```
RANGE OF X IS BANK
RANGE OF Y IS BANK
```

Having defined range variables, the following command uses them to retrieve all banks that share the same ZIP code:

```
RETRIEVE (X.BID, X.TYPE, Y.BID, Y.TYPE, Y.BZIP)
    WHERE X.BZIP = Y.BZIP AND X.BID>Y.BID
```

The general form of the statement to create a view is:

```
DEFINE VIEW view_name
    (view_col_name = base_relation_col_name, ...)
    WHERE predicate
```

For the GSL database, the statement to create a view of graduate students projected over NAME, SID, and ZIP code is:

```
DEFINE VIEW GRAD_STUDENTS
    (GNAME = STUDENT.NAME, GSID = STUDENT.SID,
        GZIP = STUDENT.SZIP)
    WHERE STUDENT.SLEVEL = 5
```

Embedded QUEL

As in SQL, INGRES employs a preprocessor to strip out the INGRES code of an application program. INGRES code is identified to the preprocessor by placing "##" in columns 1 and 2 of the host language source code.

A ## DECLARE statement is used to inform the preprocessor that a block of data type declarations follows. This must be done before any processing can occur. Once a variable is declared, values may be passed freely between the host language and INGRES. To accomplish this, host language statements may be interspersed between INGRES retrieval lines, as shown in this FORTRAN example:

```
## DECLARE CHARACTER * 25 PRED
    PRED = 'BANK.TYPE = "MSB"'
## RETRIEVE (BANK.BID)
##   WHERE PRED
```

The reason this flexibility is possible in INGRES and not in SQL is that SQL is compiled separately, then run in the compiled form until recompiled. In contrast, INGRES does not compile until runtime and is recompiled at every runtime thereafter; however, recompilation does not occur on each execution of a statement—only on its first execution.

QUEL vs. SQL

QUEL was the language used with the original INGRES product. It became apparent that SQL would probably be adopted as a national standard relational language, so RTI also implemented SQL. Because ANSI adopted SQL as the standard relational language, RTI supports both the QUEL and the SQL languages.

QUEL is thought by some database experts to be a superior language to SQL, in part because of its more direct implementation of the relational calculus. However, with the ANSI adoption of SQL as the standard relational language, it is probable that SQL will become more comercially successful.

INGRES System Architecture

As in SQL, each row of every table is associated with a tuple identifier (TID). In a *nonkeyed* file, the TID represents the byte offset of the tuple into the file. Each new tuple added to the database is inserted at the end of the file.

All of the keyed storage structures use the value of a row's primary key to determine the actual storage location. If the HASH structure is chosen, the field's primary key is used to compute the storage address. ISAM and BTREE provide both sequential and direct access, based on a relation's primary key values. Generally the BTREE structure is superior to ISAM unless the file has very few additions or deletions.

In contrast to SQL, INGRES allows only one type of relation to appear on a given file page.

Conclusion

INGRES also includes the ability to access a database through a menu, a report writer, and graphics capabilities. In addition, INGRES has recently been expanded to support a database that is distributed across several physical locations.

QBE

QBE (Query By Example) is actually part of an IBM add-on product for DB2 called QMF, Query Management Facility. QBE is significantly different from the other relational languages discussed so far. In general, the end-user interacts with the RDBMS through the use of blank tables. Cells in the blank tables are filled in with relation names, column values, and comparison operators in order to specify a query.

Although QBE is very user-friendly and easy to learn, it does have certain limitations: it does not support the creation of relations, views, and indexes, and it can not be called from a host language. Tables, views, and indexes must be created by the SQL portion of QMF, either in interactive or batch mode.

QBE uses a two-dimensional syntax. The end-user enters an example of the desired result onto input forms to specify the retrieval, rather than entering a command in a linear form.

The QBE data manipulation operations available are P., I., U., and D., which are analogous to the SQL operations of SELECT, INSERT, UPDATE, and DELETE respectively. The P. operator is shorthand for *print* or *present*. As shown in the examples below, additional options may be concatenated to these four basic operators to eliminate duplicates, to aggregate values by groups, and to order the results.

To begin the retrieval process, the user enters the command DRAW *relation_name*. This causes the system to draw a blank form for the desired relation on the screen, with only the table name and column names filled in. Next, the user types a P. in each column that is to be displayed in the result table, or, to display all columns, in the first column of the input form, under the table name. This is the QBE equivalent of SELECT * FROM STUDENT:

```
DRAW STUDENT

STUDENT  | SID    | NAME    | SLEVEL | AGE    | SZIP
         -------------------------------------------------
P.       |        |         |        |        |
```

To implement AND restrictions, comparison operators are simply placed in each of those columns on the same line. To implement an OR operation, comparison operators are placed on separate lines of the input form, in the desired columns.

For example, suppose we wanted to display the names for all the graduate students. The QBE entry is:

```
DRAW STUDENT

STUDENT  |SID     |NAME    |AGE |SLEVEL  |SZIP
         ---------------------------------------------
         |        |P.      |    |5       |
```

The result is:

```
NAME
------
CABEEN
WATSON
```

To further restrict the list to include only those graduate students with a zip code of 98168:

```
DRAW STUDENT

STUDENT  |SID |NAME     |AGE |SLEVEL   |SZIP
---------------------------------------------
         |    |P.       |    |5        |98168
```

To select rows which meet predicates with *or* conditions, multiple lines are filled in. To print the names of students where SLEVEL = 3 OR SZIP = 98102:

```
DRAW STUDENT

STUDENT  |SID |NAME     |AGE |SLEVEL   |SZIP
---------------------------------------------
         |    |P.       |    |3        |
         |    |P.       |    |         |98102
```

The following illustrates how comparison operators such as greater-than-or-equal-to may be specified. This query displays all students with SLEVEL in the range 2 to 4.

```
DRAW STUDENT

STUDENT  |SID |NAME     |AGE |SLEVEL   |SLEVEL   |SZIP
-----------------------------------------------------
         |P.  |P.       |P.  |>=2      |<=4      |
```

In this case a second column named SLEVEL was added to specify the AND condition.

To produce a list of unique IDs of students with loans, the UNQ. operator is used:

```
DRAW LOAN

LOAN |LID |DATE    |YEARS   |INT_RATE   |AMOUNT   |SID    |BID
-------------------------------------------------------------
UNQ. |    |        |        |           |         |P.     |
```

Results can be sorted in ascending order, using the AO. operator, or in descending order using the DO. operator. Major and minor sort fields may be specified by numbers in parentheses, for example AO(1). or DO(2). Thus, to sort LOAN data in descending order by date and within date in ascending order by SID:

```
DRAW LOAN

LOAN |LID |DATE     |YEARS   | INT_RATE   | AMOUNT | SID      | BID
------------------------------------------------------------------
     |    |P.DO(1). |        |            |        |P.AO(2).  |
```

Negation operations are supported with the "not" operator, ¬ . To list all the lending institutions that are not of TYPE = BANK:

```
DRAW BANK

BANK |BID | BZIP   | TYPE
-------------------------
     |P.  |        |¬ BANK
```

To provide for more complex selection criteria than can be entered into a single form, the command COND is used to draw a condition box. A condition box is a separate area on the monitor and may contain operators such as:

• AND

• OR

- NOT
- IN (value_list)
- LIKE
- NULL

For instance, the AND operator could be used in the following query:

```
STUDENT   |SID |NAME      |AGE |SLEVEL    |SLEVEL |SZIP
          ----------------------------------------------------
          |        |P.        |      |          | _AG       |
     |   CONDITIONS                  |
          --------------------------
     |  _AG>=2 AND  _AG<=4    |,
```

This is a different way of specifying the query for all students in levels 2 through 4, in which the SLEVEL column was duplicated in order to enter the AND condition.

A powerful feature of QBE is the capability to declare variables that can then be used in the conditions box, to create computed columns, or to link columns together. A variable is identified by beginning it with an underline. For example, in the preceding example, _AG is a variable used in the condition box to select ages within a certain range. The value for the variable _AG in the SLEVEL column must satisfy the conditions specified for _AG in the CONDITIONS table. Thus, SLEVEL must be in the range 2 to 4.

Next consider a simple join of STUDENT and LOAN with display of name and SID for every student who has a loan with amount greater than $2500. The forms are filled in as follows:

```
STUDENT   |SID       |NAME
          ------------------------
          |P._S      |P.
LOAN      |SID       |AMOUNT
          ------------------------
          |_S        |>2500
```

The variable _S is used in these two forms to provide the join—to be displayed, the row in STUDENT must have SID value, _S, which equals the SID value, _S, in LOAN and the AMOUNT must exceed 2500.

When results are displayed from more than a single table a *result* form must be created. The result form indicates the columns to be displayed. The following query displays SIDs, NAMEs and LIDs for loans of AMOUNT >2500.

```
STUDENT   |SID       |NAME
          ----------------------
          |_S        |_N
LOAN      |SID       |AMOUNT  |LID
          --------------------------------
          |_S        |>2500   |_L
RESULT    |          |        |
          --------------------------------
          |_S        |_N      |_L
```

Note that the column names of the RESULT table are supplied by the column names of its variables (e.g. _S is the SID column).

The following sections give additional examples using variables.

Suppose that all the loans in the LOAN table were variable-rate loans and that every lending institution was going to increase its rates by 0.25 percent. To produce a report showing the adjusted rate of each loan by LID (partial table shown):

```
DRAW LOAN

LOAN |LID |INT_RATE    |SID |NEW_RATE
-----------------------------------------------
     |P.  |P._OLDRATE  |    |P._OLDRATE + 0.25
```

Aggregation of values by group is performed by aggregation operators in conjunction with the group indicator, G. These are:

```
CNT.ALL. or CNT.UNQ.ALL.
SUM.ALL. or SUM.UNQ.ALL
AVG.ALL. or AVG.UNQ.ALL.
MAX.ALL
MIN.ALL.
```

To count the total number of students with loans at each lending institution another column must be created as shown below:

```
DRAW LOAN

LOAN |YEARS    |INT_RATE    |AMOUNT  |SID |BID  |TOTAL
---- ------    ----------  ---------  ------  ----  ---------------
     |         |            |_TAMT   |    |P.G.|P.SUM._TAMT
```

To insert a record, the I. command is entered in the column under the table name and values entered into the columns. Columns with null values are left empty. As an example, to enter a new freshman student DOUGHERTY, with ID 6449, age 18, and ZIP code 88001:

```
STUDENT  | SID    | NAME       | SLEVEL | AGE    |SZIP
-------------------------------------------------------
I.       | 6449   | DOUGHERTY  | 1      | 18     |88001
```

To update a record, the U. command is used. Suppose that student ID 6449, entered above, is actually a graduate student and 25 years old. This update is accomplished as follows:

```
STUDENT  | SID    | NAME   | SLEVEL | AGE     | SZIP
-----------------------------------------------------
         | 6449   |        | U.5    | U.25    |
```

If student ID 6449 were to graduate and repay his or her loan, he or she could then be deleted using the D. command:

```
STUDENT  | SID    | NAME   | SLEVEL | AGE     | SZIP
-----------------------------------------------------
D.       | 6449   |        |        |         |
```

QBE Summary

Various studies have indicated the superiority of this approach to data retrieval over command structured languages, particularly for users who are not data-processing professionals. The learning time is considerably shorter, partly because there is a smaller set of operations to learn and partly because the retrieval process is easier to visualize. However, as queries become more complex, QBE also becomes more difficult to use, and at some point SQL or QUEL- type languages are simpler.

RDBMS Products

Many relational DBMSs have been enhanced with a variety of products designed to increase user effectiveness and ease of use. For instance, IBM has developed a wide variety of relational database management products. This Relational Productivity Family includes tools to facilitate database operations such as:

- Application Development
- End-User's Tasks
- Database Administration
- Data Extraction

For INGRES, RTI has developed an Application Development System that includes the following:

- INGRES/MENU
- INGRES/QUERY
- INGRES/FORMS
- INGRES/REPORTS
- INGRES/GRAPHICS
- INGRES/APPLICATIONS

INGRES/MENU is a frontend to INGRES. INGRES/MENU uses forms to execute queries, reports, and graphs that have been previously defined. Forms are the basis for much of the Application Development System, and are defined and edited using IN-GRES/FORMS.

INGRES/QUERY uses forms for data entry, update, and retrieval. This is accomplished through the use of Query By Forms (QBF). These forms can either be predefined or automatically generated by QBF.

Reports in INGRES/REPORTS use forms to define and generate reports, The reports are created using Report By Forms (RBF) and are then displayed using the Report Writer. INGRES/GRAPHICS supports user-defined graphical output.

INGRES/APPLICATIONS is another forms-based system for the development of simple applications.

All together, these products significantly extend the capabilities of INGRES. One other product deserves mention. This is INGRES/STAR, which allows one database to be distributed across any number of physical locations. These locations can have different computers and operating systems. Distributed databases are one of the latest developments in database technology, and will be discussed in more detail in Chapter 15.

Questions and Problems

Questions

1. Why does IBM have several different DBMSs?
2. Describe some important differences in QUEL and SQL.
3. What INGRES data types exist that are not available in ORACLE/SQL?

4. Why are field names always qualified in INGRES? Why is this not required in SQL?

5. What storage structures are available in INGRES that do not exist in ORACLE?

6. What is the effect of the following statement?

```
MODIFY LOAN TO BTREE ON BID, LID
```

7. What is the difference in the effect of the MODIFY and INDEX statements? For example, what do each of the following accomplish?

```
MODIFY LOAN TO BTREE ON LID
INDEX ON LOAN IS LID_X (LID)
```

8. Cite several important limitations of QBE.

9. Describe the use of the condition box in QBE.

Problems

1. Write a QUEL statement to display the names of students who are age 21 or less and have a loan amount of over $2,000.

2. What is the output, using the sample GSL database, from the following QUEL statement?

```
RETRIEVE (STUDENT.NAME, LOAN.AMOUNT, BANK.TYPE)
    WHERE STUDENT.SID=LOAN.SID AND BANK.SID=LOAN.SID
        AND STUDENT.SLEVEL <=4 AND LOAN.YEARS>5
```

3. Show the form of a QBE query to display all loan LIDs, AMOUNTs, and YEARS for graduate students. Is a result table needed for the output?

4. Show the form of a QBE query that is equivalent to the QUEL query in question 2.

5. What is the output from the following QBE query (look out—this is trickier than it might appear):

```
STUDENT  | SID     | NAME    |SLEVEL  | AGE      | SZIP
----------------------------------------------------------
         | P.      | P.      | <=4    |          |
         | P.      | P.      | >=1    |          |
```

6. What is the output from the following QBE query? (Compare this output to the output from question 5).

```
STUDENT  | SID     | NAME    |SLEVEL  | SLEVEL | AGE    |SZIP
----------------------------------------------------------
         | P.      | P.      | <=4    | >=1    |        |
```

References

Blasgen, M. W. et al. "System R: An Architectural Overview." *IBM Systems Journal*, vol. 20, no. 1 (1981), pp. 41–62.

Browning, D., and Blasdel, H. "Managing Databases, Mainframe Style." *PC Tech Journal*, (December 1987), pp. 106ff.

Date, C.J. *A Guide to INGRES*. Reading, Mass.: Addison-Wesley Publishing Co., 1987.

_____. and White, Colin J. *A Guide to DB2*. 2d ed. Reading, Mass.: Addison-Wesley Publishing Co., 1988.

Fosdick, H., and Garcia-Rose, L. "DB2 Users Stand Up to be Counted." *Datamation*, vol. 34, no. 20 (Nov. 15, 1988), pp. 45–54.

Gulo, K. "New DB2 Migration Facing Roadblock?" *Datamation*, vol. 34, no. 11 (June 1, 1988), pp. 28–31.

IBM Corporation. *Query-by-Example Terminal User's Guide*. Form SH20-2078, Irving, Texas, 1980.

Martorelli, W. P. "IBM Users Take DB2 to its Outer Limit." *Information WEEK*, (Jan. 14, 1985), pp. 82–84.

Moad, J. "DB2 Performance Gets Kick with Closer Ties to 3090S, ESA." *Datamation*, vol. 34, no. 18 (Sept. 15, 1988), pp. 19–20.

Myers, E. D. "The Long Shadow of DB2." *Datamation*, vol. 33, no. 19 (Oct. 1, 1987), pp. 110–114.

Pascal, F. "Relational Power, PC Ease." *PC Tech Journal*, (December 1987), pp. 74ff.

8 R:BASE: A Personal Computer Relational DBMS

Introduction to R:BASE

The purpose of this chapter is to provide an overview of a microcomputer-based relational DBMS. R:BASE is one of several DBMSs targeted for the personal computer user and the small organization. The other major product in this arena is dBASE. Most of these database management systems were developed at a time when personal computers still had a very limited memory, which essentially precluded successful adaptation of mainframe DBMSs. Today, the situation has changed, and many of the mini and mainframe DBMSs, such as ORACLE and INGRES, are now available on PCs. Nevertheless, the PC-based DBMSs have interesting features that make their study worthwhile. Most of them take advantage of the excellent graphics capabilities of PCs and provide a friendly user interface.

R:BASE is a relational system that fairly faithfully implements relational algebra. It is one of the easiest relational DBMSs to learn because it makes extensive use of menus to reduce the number of commands a user must enter. It also has a comprehensive help system that provides online instructions. It is constructed as a variety of modules, which collectively make it a powerful system. In its latest version, R:BASE for DOS, a version of SQL has been implemented. This has helped the system to overcome a number of problems with its earlier query language.

But R:BASE still has shortcomings. Several of its problems can be traced to deficiencies in its initial design. It evolved from a product called Relational Information Manager, RIM. As we describe R:BASE, we will expand on some of these problems. Understanding the deficiencies as well as the strong points of a system is very important if you are faced with the problem of selecting a DBMS. Thus, looking at R:BASE has a secondary objective of providing insight into how to evaluate a DBMS.

Our primary objective is to provide enough information so that you can use R:BASE to create and manipulate a simple database. But we will only scratch the surface of the system's many features and capabilities. To appreciate its full capabilities, you will need to consult R:BASE manuals and, more important, use the system. As noted above, the system's extensive hand-holding features will let you initially develop and manipulate a database almost without reference to the manuals.

Early sections of this chapter introduce the main features of the R:BASE system, including simple database definition and manipulation using the model GSL database. Later sections present more advanced features of both definition and manipulation and describe some of the alternative modes of R:BASE usage.

```
                              R:BASE
                        Prompt By Example
                  Copyright (c) Microrim, Inc., 1987

       (1)  Define or modify a database
       (2)  Create or modify an R:BASE application
       (3)  Open an existing database
       (4)  Add data to a database
       (5)  Modify data
       (6)  Query a database
       (7)  SQL (Structured Query Language) commands
       (8)  R:BASE and operating system utilities
       (9)  Exit from R:BASE




  [ESC] Done      [F10] Help
  Database:
```

Fig 8-1   Initial R:BASE Menu

R:BASE Modules

R:BASE consists of eight major components: R:BASE Commands, Application EXPRESS, Definition EXPRESS, Forms EXPRESS, Report EXPRESS, RBEDIT, File Gateway, and CodeLock. Access to these modules is via a menu, shown in Figure 8–1, which is the R:BASE menu presented when you start up the system.

The *R:BASE Commands* module enables a user to define or redefine databases and the information contained within them, to assign security passwords, to define data-entry rules, and to build command files. As suggested by the name of the module, the approach is command-driven—very similar to SQL.

The *Application EXPRESS* module is an application development tool that guides a developer through the tasks involved in developing a user application and then automatically generates the application program in internal R:BASE code.

Definition EXPRESS is the R:BASE database definition module. It guides the user through the definition and redefinition of a database that can then be accessed with R:BASE Commands or via applications developed using Application EXPRESS. We will use EXPRESS for defining the GSL database and also illustrate how it can be defined from the command module.

Forms EXPRESS is a data-entry module that enables a developer to create a variety of forms for data entry. Forms EXPRESS supports entry of new data, modification of existing data, creation of menus, and definition of data-entry screens.

STUDENT Table

SID	NAME	SLEVEL	AGE	SZIP
9735	ALLEN	1	21	98101
4494	ALTER	2	19	98112
8767	CABEEN	5	24	98118
2368	JONES	4	23	98155
6793	SANDS	1	17	98101
3749	WATSON	5	29	98168

BANK Table

BID	BZIP	TYPE
FIDELITY	98101	MSB
SEAFIRST	98101	BANK
PEOPLES	98109	BANK
CAPITAL	98033	SL
HOME	98031	SL

LOAN Table

LID	LDATE	YEARS	INT_RATE	AMOUNT	SID	BID
27	15-SEP-85	5	8.5	1200	9735	HOME
78	21-JUN-86	5	7.75	1000	9735	PEOPLES
87	07-SEP-83	5	7.0	2000	9735	SEAFIRST
92	12-JAN-85	6	7.5	2100	4494	FIDELITY
99	15-JAN-86	6	9.0	2200	4494	FIDELITY
170	30-APR-83	6	6.5	1900	8767	PEOPLES
490	07-MAY-84	6	6.0	2500	3749	PEOPLES
493	24-JUN-85	7	7.5	3000	3749	PEOPLES

Fig 8-2   GSL Database

The *Report EXPRESS* module enables a developer to create custom reports. It supports a number of relational operations including selection, projection, and joins, as well as total and subtotal calculation.

The *RBEDIT* module is a screen editor designed to help a developer enter program code into a file. It operates independently of the R:BASE database and is provided mainly as a convenience.

The *File Gateway* module is a data-transfer package that copies and formats data between R:BASE and other popular systems such as Lotus 123, dBASE II, dBASE III, and pfs:FILE.

The *CodeLock* module is an application encoder that translates completed application files in ASCII into a more compact and secure binary format.

Before getting into the system, we will review the GSL database structure and content.

Database Structure

The GSL system has three tables: a STUDENT table, a LOAN table, and a BANK table. The STUDENT table includes data about a student—specifically: student identifier (SID), name, age, level (SLEVEL: from freshman=1 to graduate student=5), and ZIP code (ZIP). The LOAN table includes an identifier (LID), loan date (LDATE), number of years, the loan amount (AMOUNT), interest rate (INT_RATE), the ID of the student receiving the loan (SID), and the identifier of the bank making the loan (BID). The BANK table includes the bank's ID, the type of the bank, and the bank's ZIP code. The information in these tables can be seen in Figure 8–2.

Representing Relations

An R:BASE database can contain up to 80 related database tables (relations), with a maximum of 800 columns for the whole database.
Every database table has the following characteristics:

- It consists of one or more rows of data (tuples), each of which is divided into one or more columns (attributes).
- The amount of data it can hold is dictated by the physical storage capacity or, in some cases, by the operating system.
- Any single row may contain up to 4,096 bytes of data.

Data Types

Each table contains one or more columns, which are defined by the type of data they contain. Figure 8–3 lists the data types.

Data Type	Description
DATE	A one-to-30-character date represented in a month, day, year format established with the SET DATE command.
TIME	A one-to-20-character time represented in an hour, minute, and second format established with the SET TIME command.
CURRENCY	An up to 23-character, 16-digit amount represented in the currency format established by the SET CURRENCY command.
REAL	Real number amounts in the approximate range $\pm 10 \pm 37$ with seven-digit precision.
DOUBLE	Double-precision real numbers in the range $\pm 10 \pm 37$ with 15-digit precision.
INTEGER	Whole numbers in the range $\pm 999,999,999$.
TEXT	Alphanumeric data, maximum of 1,500 characters.
NOTE	A descriptive text column that can hold a maximum of approximately 4,050 characters.
COMPUTED	A column that is computed from values in other columns. The column does not actually exist.

Fig 8-3   Column Data Types

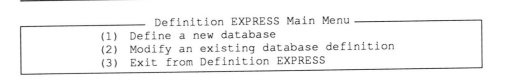

```
                 ─────── Definition EXPRESS Main Menu ───────
        (1)  Define a new database
        (2)  Modify an existing database definition
        (3)  Exit from Definition EXPRESS
```

```
[ENTER] Choose        [F10] Help
```

Fig 8-4   Database Definition or Modification Menu

Defining an R:BASE Database

There are several ways to define an R:BASE database. One method is to use the Definition EXPRESS mode, which is largely menu driven. Another method is to use the (original) R:BASE data-definition command language. The third is to use a SQL-like CREATE TABLE statement. All three methods are illustrated in the following sections.

Using Definition EXPRESS

First, start up R:BASE by entering the command RBASE at the DOS prompt level. You will be presented with a menu of nine options as shown in Figure 8–1. Select option 1: *Define or modify a database.* The next menu has four options, RBDEFINE, FORMS, REPORTS, and R:BASE commands. Select RBDEFINE—the "hand-holding" approach for definition of the GSL database using Definition EXPRESS.

Responding with a carriage return to the next two screens brings us to a menu of three choices, as shown in Figure 8–4. Select the first option, *Define a new database.* The next screen asks for a one-to-seven-character database name. After entering the name of the database, GSL in this example, a skeleton of a table is presented and Definition EXPRESS walks you through table and column naming, column type selection, and designation of indexed columns—the KEY option. Figure 8–5 shows a completed definition of the STUDENT table.

After defining the three tables, we could now begin data entry. First, however, we will describe the alternative database definition method using commands. For seasoned users, the Definition EXPRESS module proves a bit tedious.

Definition Using Command Mode

First, access to the COMMAND mode is by entering ESC (escape key) at the top menu level. You will then see a simple R> prompt—not a menu. You are now in the COMMAND mode.

There are three steps in defining a database with the DEFINE mode:

- Assigning a name to a database
- Defining the columns
- Grouping the columns into tables

```
Enter or change the column names

┌──────────────┐   An asterisk (*) identifies key columns
│  STUDENT     │   A plus sign (+) identifies computed columns
└──────────────┘

┌──────────────┬──────────────┬──────────────┬──────────────┬──────────────┐
│ *SID         │ NAME         │ SLEVEL       │ AGE          │ ZIP          │
├──────────────┼──────────────┼──────────────┼──────────────┼──────────────┤
│ INTEGER      │ TEXT 16      │ INTEGER      │ INTEGER      │ INTEGER      │
├──────────────┼──────────────┼──────────────┼──────────────┼──────────────┤
│              │              │              │              │              │
└──────────────┴──────────────┴──────────────┴──────────────┴──────────────┘

[F1] Insert  [F2] Delete  [ENTER] Change  [ESC] Done  [Shift-F10] More
Database GSL      --- Table STUDENT --- Column       6
```

Fig 8-5   Screen for Definition of the Student Table

Naming the Database

A database name consists of up to seven characters. The first character must be a letter, and there can be no embedded blanks or punctuation. (Drive and directory information is not included in the seven-character limit.) Syntax for the DEFINE command is:

    DEFINE [dbspec]

where dbspec is the name chosen for the database, along with any drive and directory information. For example:

    DEFINE C:\RECORDS\GSL

defines a database with the name GSL located in directory RECORDS, on drive C. After the DEFINE command has been given, the prompt will change to D>, signifying that the system is in the DEFINE mode and is now waiting for you to enter definitions for columns and tables.

Defining Data Items (Columns)

Each data item is defined by giving it a name, specifying its data type, and indicating whether it is a KEY or not:

- A column name consists of a letter followed by zero to seven characters, including letters and digits. A name cannot contain a blank.
- The column type is one of the eight data types described in Figure 8–3. If the data type is TEXT, a length of between one and 1,500 characters may be specified. The default length is eight characters.
- A column specified as KEY means that an index will be created. It has nothing to do with the relational meaning of KEY in the sense of *primary key*.

The entry of column definitions is initiated by typing COLUMNS at the D> prompt. The definition of each column is then entered by typing the name, data type, and optional KEY specification. A separate line is used to specify each column. The following example shows how to define the columns for the GSL:

```
                          Comment
R>DEFINE GSL
  Begin R:BASE Database Definition
D>COLUMNS                 Enter Column definition (sub)mode.
D>SID INTEGER KEY         SID is a nine-digit integer. SID will be indexed.
D>NAME TEXT 16            NAME is a 16-character field.
D>SLEVEL INTEGER
D>AGE INTEGER
D>ZIP INTEGER
D>BID TEXT 12 KEY
D>TYPE TEXT 4
D>LID INTEGER KEY
D>LDATE DATE              LDATE is of type date.
D>AMOUNT REAL             AMOUNT is a "single-precision" numeric value.
D>YEARS INTEGER
D>INT_RATE REAL
```

Defining a column as a key column can be beneficial if there will frequently be queries with predicates including the column and if the information it contains is "reasonably" unique. Examples of potentially good key choices for the GSL database are SID, LID, BID, NAME, LDATE, since most if not all rows have different values. The use of keyed columns containing unique information speeds up the process of locating information in those columns during relational select and join operations. It is not essential that each value in a keyed column be unique, but the more occurrences there are of any particular value within a column, the less advantage there is in designating it as a key column. For example, making SLEVEL a key column would be a poor choice because it has only five different values.

Defining Tables (Relations)

The TABLES command is used to initiate definition of tables. The definition of a table consists of a one-to-eight-character table name, followed by a list of the columns it contains. Columns must be defined before they can be included in a table definition. The name of one column is separated from the next by either a comma or a blank. The three tables for the GSL database are defined as follows:

```
D>TABLES
D>STUDENT WITH SID NAME SLEVEL AGE SZIP
D>BANK WITH BID, BZIP, TYPE
D>LOAN WITH LID LDATE YEARS INT_RATE AMOUNT, SID, BID
```

Errors made during the input are detected. For example, entering the last line as:

```
D>LOAN WITH LID DATE YEARS INT_RATE AMOUNT SID BID
```

results in the following error message:

```
-ERROR- DATE is an undefined column name
```

Leaving the DEFINE Mode

The END command is used to exit the DEFINE mode. At this time, any columns that have been defined but not placed in a table will be displayed. The user has the option of returning to the DEFINE mode and assigning the columns to tables, or of exiting, at which time all unused columns will be lost.

Once your database is defined, whether via the Definition EXPRESS or the command approach, you may safely leave R:BASE. The database definition will be saved. A defined database may be opened when you return to R:BASE either through appropriate menu choices (see Figure 8–1) or by the OPEN statement in the command mode. The OPEN statement has the form *OPEN database;* for example, OPEN GSL.

Database Definition using CREATE TABLE

The most compact method of database definition is to use the SQL-like CREATE TABLE command. Its syntax is:

```
CREATE TABLE tablename colname [= expression] datatype
[length] [NOT NULL] [UNIQUE]
```

Here is an example of the definition of the STUDENT table using this method:

```
R>CREATE TABLE STUDENT SID INTEGER UNIQUE, NAME TEXT 16 NOT NULL, +
+>SLEVEL INTEGER, AGE INTEGER NOT NULL, SZIP INTEGER
```

When a command entered at the R> prompt is longer than the single-line length of 75 characters, you can either type past the end of the line, or enter a plus (+) sign *as the last entry on the line* and continue the command on the next line. Do not enter a space after the plus sign. The following two examples are equivalent:

```
R>SELECT ALL FROM LOAN WHERE INT_RATE GE 7.0 AND AMOUNT GE 2000
```

```
R>SELECT ALL FROM LOAN WHERE INT_RATE GE 7.0 AND +
+>AMOUNT GE 2000
```

The second example uses the plus sign to extend the command line at the space between two words. When a line is extended, the prompt on the extension line is changed to +> instead of the R> prompt. The +> prompt also appears if a command line is typed past the end of a line or if a text string is split.

Displaying the Defined Database

The database definition may be displayed either via menu selections or commands. The appropriate menu choice is 6: *Query a database,* followed by *List structure* from the next menu. Then select the desired option from the menu shown in Figure 8–6. From the COMMAND mode, enter LIST, followed by one of these options:

ALL — Provides a complete overview of the database by displaying table structure, password status, and row counts, as well as the names, lengths, data types, and keys of the columns.

COLUMNS — Displays an alphabetically sorted list of all column definitions and shows which are keys.

TABLES — Displays information about all tables in the database.

tablename — Displays information about the specified table.

The command LIST without any option displays table names. The following example displays the structure of the STUDENT table.

```
┌─────────────────────────────────────────────────────────────────────┐
│  LIST  ...                                                            │
└─────────────────────────────────────────────────────────────────────┘

┌─────────────────────────────────────────────────────────────────────┐
│  LIST displays information about the structure of the open database.  │
│  LIST COLUMNS        Lists all columns in the database.               │
│  LIST DATABASES      Lists databases on the current directory.        │
│  LIST FORMS          Lists forms in the database.                     │
│  LIST REPORTS        Lists reports in the database.                   │
│  LIST RULES          Lists rules in the database.                     │
│  LIST TABLES         Lists all tables or, if you specify a table, the │
│                      columns in the table.                            │
│  LIST VIEWS          Lists all views or, if you specify a view, the   │
│                      tables and columns in the view                   │
└─────────────────────────────────────────────────────────────────────┘

┌───────────────────────── Choose an item to list ─────────────────────┐
│  COLUMNS  DATABASES  FORMS  REPORTS  RULES  TABLES  VIEWS             │
└─────────────────────────────────────────────────────────────────────┘
```

[ESC] Done   [F10] Help
Database: GSL

Fig 8-6   Menu Choices to Display Structure of a Database

```
R>LIST STUDENT

Table: STUDENT                     No lock(s)
Read Password: No
Modify Password: No

Column definitions
# Name            Type        Length           Key     Expression
1 SID             INTEGER                       yes
2 NAME            TEXT        16 characters
3 SLEVEL          INTEGER
4 AGE             INTEGER
5 SZIP            INTEGER

Current number of rows:              0
```

Loading Data

There are several ways to enter data to relations. Selecting the top menu option, 4: *Add data to a database,* produces the menu of Figure 8–7. Since no data yet exists in any of our tables, the APPEND option is clearly not applicable. ENTER can only be used if a form has been previously defined for data entry. For a production system, definition of a form would be the appropriate approach. The module, Forms EXPRESS, accessible from the top menu's

```
┌──────────────────────────────────────────────────────────────────┐
│ Add data to a database                                             │
└──────────────────────────────────────────────────────────────────┘

┌──────────────────────────────────────────────────────────────────┐
│ Several commands add data to a table in the database.              │
│ APPEND    Copies rows from one table to the end of another.        │
│ ENTER     Adds data to a table using a data entry form you create. │
│ INPUT     Changes the source for R:BASE command input.             │
│ INSERT    Adds a row of data to a table.                           │
│ LOAD      Adds data to a table, row by row, without a data entry form. │
│ OPEN      Opens a database. Use this command first if the database │
│           you want is not open.                                    │
└──────────────────────────────────────────────────────────────────┘

                         ─── Choose a command ───
┌──────────────────────────────────────────────────────────────────┐
│ APPEND   ENTER   INPUT   INSERT   LOAN   OPEN                      │
└──────────────────────────────────────────────────────────────────┘


[ESC] Done       [F10] Help
Database: GSL
```

Fig 8-7 *Alternatives for Loading Data to a Database*

Create or modify an existing database option, is where a form is defined. While it is easy to define an input form, we will use the more direct options.

The option INSERT essentially duplicates the SQL INSERT command but uses a menu approach to guide you through data entry. The LOAD command is used to enter new data directly without using a defined entry form. Optional system prompts supply the column name, data type, and order in the table. LOAD is accessed either through the menu or the COMMAND mode by keying *LOAD tablename.*

For example, the following enters two rows to the STUDENT table. Values must be listed in the same order as the corresponding column order in the table definition, in this case SID, NAME, SLEVEL, AGE, and SZIP. The prompt for the load mode is L>. User entries are underlined.

```
L> 2368, "JONES" 4, 23, 98155
L> 3749, "WATSON" 5, 29 98168
```

As illustrated, values are separated by either blanks or commas. Quote marks are required around any string that has embedded blanks or commas. R:BASE checks the type and length of all new input and prints an error message if either is incorrect. If there is an error the data is not added to the database and must be entered again.

An alternative mode of the LOAD is with prompts. In this mode R:BASE displays column name and data type as a prompt. The format of the command to LOAD data with prompts is as follows (user entries are underlined):

```
LOAD STUDENT WITH PROMPTS
Press {ESC} to end {ENTER} to continue
SID (INTEGER):8767
NAME (text):CABEEN
SLEVEL (INTEGER):5
AGE (INTEGER):24
SZIP (TEXT):98118
SID (INTEGER):[ESC]
R>
```

Pressing [ESC] at any time during the entry of a row causes it to be discarded. Pressing [ENTER] without any data loads null data into the column. Pressing [ESC] between rows returns the system to the R> prompt or to the menu depending on how you entered the LOAD mode.

Data Manipulation

R:BASE has two data manipulation languages: its own language which evolved from the earlier RIM product, and an adaptation of SQL. Since we have already covered SQL in earlier chapters, we will concentrate on the original R:BASE language. We will use the command approach, which is easier to illustrate in a textbook, but you should definitely try out the *prompt by example* menu approach.

SELECT Command

The SELECT command can be used to retrieve data from the database in several ways. The syntax for the command is:

```
SELECT ALL or col-list1 FROM tblname [SORTED BY col-list2] [WHERE condition]
```

SELECT ALL retrieves all of the data in a table or view. If there are too many columns to fit on the screen, R:BASE shows as many columns as possible beginning with the first column in the table. When the output is directed to a printer, the width can be set to a maximum of 256 characters.

For instance, to select all the columns from the STUDENT table, enter:

```
R>SELECT ALL FROM STUDENT
```

This results in:

SID	NAME	SLEVEL	AGE	ZIP
9735	ALLEN	1	21	98101
4494	ALTER	2	19	98112
8767	CABEEN	5	24	98118
2368	JONES	4	23	98155
6793	SANDS	1	17	98101
3749	WATSON	5	29	98168

SELECT col-list displays values for the columns listed in *col-list*. To display only the student name and age, enter:

```
R>SELECT NAME, AGE FROM STUDENT
```

A WHERE clause can be added to various R:BASE commands to specify restricting conditions. Only the rows that satisfy the conditions in the WHERE clause will be accessed. A column value may be compared to a constant or to the value of an expression using the operators EQ, GT, LT, GE, LE, NE, or the corresponding symbols, =, >, <, >=, <=, <>. And a column may be compared to another column using the operators EQA, NEA, GTA, LTA, GEA, LEA. For instance, to SELECT those students who are 23 years old:

```
R>SELECT ALL FROM STUDENT WHERE AGE EQ 23
```

When the comparison is being made to literal text, the comparison value must be enclosed in quotes if it contains embedded commas or blanks. For example:

```
R>SELECT ALL FROM STUDENT WHERE NAME EQ "LA VALLE"
```

Wildcard characters can be used with the WHERE clause to provide flexibility in text comparisons. The * and ? can be thought of as "don't care" characters that allow a range of text values to satisfy the conditions of a comparison. The ? can be used in place of any single character in a text comparison value to signify that any character is acceptable in that position. For example, the comparison value B?LL would accept comparisons with BILL or BALL but not CALL. The * is a wildcard for 0 or more characters. Here is an example of how the * is used:

```
R>SELECT ALL FROM STUDENT WHERE NAME EQ ?A*
```

returns all rows in which the second letter of the name is an A (CABEEN, SANDS, and WATSON).

To display data on "young" students, those whose age is less than 17 plus SLEVEL:

```
R>SELECT ALL FROM STUDENT WHERE AGE < (AGE+17)
```

In addition to the standard comparison operators, R:BASE also supports the following operators (among others):

CONTAINS	Determines if a column value contains a substring, for example, NAME CONTAINS "AB".
NOT CONTAINS	True if the column value does not contain the substring.
IS NULL or IS NOT NULL	True if the column value is null (not null).
BETWEEN or NOT BETWEEN	True if the column value falls between (not between) the indicated range; for example, AGE BETWEEN 19 AND 23.

Entering More than One Condition in a WHERE Clause

Multiple comparisons can be included in a where clause by connecting them with the logical operators AND, OR, NOT, AND NOT, OR NOT. Parentheses may be used to indicate order. To display all students with ages ranging from 22 to 25, the command is:

```
R>SELECT ALL FROM STUDENT WHERE AGE >= 22 AND AGE <= 25
SID       NAME              SLEVEL    AGE       ZIP
--------  ----------------  --------  --------  --------
    8767  CABEEN                   5        24     98118
    2368  JONES                    4        23     98155
```

The BETWEEN operator could also have been used in this case.

Rows containing values you do not want may be excluded by using the AND NOT operator. For example, the following WHERE clause will find undergraduates (that is, levels 1, 2, 3, or 4) who don't live in the 98101 ZIP code area.

```
R>SELECT ALL FROM STUDENT WHERE SLEVEL <= 4 AND NOT SZIP = 98101
SID          NAME            SLEVEL    AGE       ZIP
--------     ---------------  -------- --------  --------
    4494 ALTER                   2        19       98112
    2368 JONES                   4        23       98155
```

WHERE clauses containing multiple logical operators must be entered in the correct order if the desired result is to be obtained; otherwise parentheses must be used, which is the safer approach. The clause is always evaluated from left to right. For example:

```
R>SELECT ALL FROM STUDENT WHERE AGE >= 22 AND AGE <= 25 OR +
+>SLEVEL = 5

SID          NAME            SLEVEL    AGE       ZIP
--------     ---------------  -------- --------  --------
    8767 CABEEN                  5        24       98118
    2368 JONES                   4        23       98155
    3749 WATSON                  5        29       98168
```

Now look at what happens when the order of the AND and OR are changed:

```
R>SELECT ALL FROM STUDENT WHERE SLEVEL = 5 OR AGE >= 22 AND +
+>AGE < 25

SID          NAME            SLEVEL    AGE       ZIP
--------     ---------------  -------- --------  --------
    8767 CABEEN                  5        24       98118
```

The time R:BASE takes to process a WHERE clause can be reduced significantly by using keys, provided *all three* of these conditions are present:

- The last condition in the clause compares a keyed column.
- The last operator used in the condition is EQ, =, or EQA.
- The last condition is preceded by the logical operator AND if more than one condition is specified in the clause.

SELECT with Sorting

The SORTED BY clause may be added to some commands so that output rows are ordered. Columns can be sorted (except the NOTE type) in either ascending or descending order. The default is in ascending order. SORTED BY must precede the WHERE clause. When more than one column is specified, the column specified first is the major key for the sort. The syntax for the SORTED BY clause is:

```
SORTED BY col-list
```

where col-list is the list of columns on which to sort. Ascending order is designated by =A; descending order by =D.

The following example shows the LOAN file sorted by BANK for those loans of an amount greater than or equal to $2,000:

```
R>SELECT ALL FROM LOAN SORTED BY BID WHERE AMOUNT GE 2000
LID  LDATE      YEARS    INT_RATE AMOUNT          SID   BID
----  --------   --------  -------- --------------   ----  --------
    99 01/15/86      6        9.     $2,200.00      4494  FIDELITY
    92 01/12/85      6        7.5    $2,100.00      4494  FIDELITY
   493 06/24/85      7        7.5    $3,000.00      4494  PEOPLES
   490 05/07/84      6        6.     $2,500.00      3749  PEOPLES
    87 09/07/83      5        7.     $2,000.00      9735  SEAFIRST
```

Using Expressions

The SELECT command can be used to display temporary computed columns. An expression, enclosed in parentheses, may be included in a SELECT command in the same way as a column name. For example, the following command would display the LID, interest rate, amount, and total one-year interest (assuming no principal-reducing payments are made and no compounding occurs):

```
R>SELECT LID, INT_RATE, AMOUNT, (AMOUNT*INT_RATE/100) FROM LOAN
```

Computing Column Totals

There is an option in the SELECT command that computes column totals for CURRENCY, DOUBLE, INTEGER, and REAL data types. Column totals for other types of data cannot be calculated. The columns to be summed are indicated by entering =S immediately after the column name. The computed totals are shown immediately after the last row in the table.

Column widths can also be specified in the same command as column totals by including an =w specification before the =S, where w is the width of the column. The following SELECT command displays data for loans from PEOPLES bank and the total amount of money currently loaned. A column width of 10 is specified for AMOUNT:

```
R>SELECT LID, BID, AMOUNT=10=S FROM LOAN WHERE BID="PEOPLES"
LID        BID       AMOUNT
--------   --------   ----------
      78 PEOPLES     $1,000.00
     170 PEOPLES     $1,900.00
     490 PEOPLES     $2,500.00
     493 PEOPLES     $3,000.00
--------   --------   ----------
                     $8,400.00
```

Column totals can also be computed on "expression" columns :

```
R>SELECT LID, INT_RATE, AMOUNT=S, (AMOUNT*INT_RATE/100)=S FROM LOAN
LID        INT_RATE AMOUNT          COMPUTED
--------   -------- --------------  --------------
      27     8.5    $1,200.00          $102.00
      78     7.75   $1,000.00           $77.50
      87     7.     $2,000.00          $140.00
      92     7.5    $2,100.00          $157.50
      99     9.     $2,200.00          $198.00
     170     6.5    $1,900.00          $123.50
     490     6.     $2,500.00          $150.00
     493     7.5    $3,000.00          $225.00
--------   -------- --------------  --------------
                   $15,900.00        $1,173.50
```

Thus, the =S option provides a rudimentary report-generation capability.

Directing Output

Output results from the SELECT and from other commands described below can be sent to an output device (screen, printer, or file) as specified by the OUTPUT command. If saved to a disk file the data can be processed by other software such as a word processor or a spreadsheet. The alternative forms of the command are:

OUTPUT PRINTER	Directs output to the printer (no output to screen)
OUTPUT SCREEN	Output to screen (default)
OUTPUT filespec	Output to specified file
OUTPUT SCREEN WITH PRINTER	Output to both devices
OUTPUT filespec WITH PRINTER	Output to file and printer
OUTPUT filespec WITH SCREEN	Output to file and screen
OUTPUT filespec WITH BOTH	Output to file, screen, and printer

"Statistics" Commands

Aggregate statistics can be obtained by the use of the operators COMPUTE, TALLY, and CROSSTAB. Figure 8–8 shows these different operators.

A variety of arithmetic and statistical operations can be performed with the COMPUTE command. Operations include average, total, minimum, and maximum for CURRENCY, DOUBLE, INTEGER, REAL, DATE, and TIME columns. Minimum and maximum can also be calculated for TEXT types, and row counts can be determined on values for all data types. Standard deviations and variances can be calculated for CURRENCY, DOUBLE, INTEGER, and REAL types.

The syntax for the COMPUTE command is:

```
COMPUTE operation col-name FROM tblname
```

Available *operations* are listed in Figure 8–9 with explanations and any restrictions. Unless stated otherwise, the command works with all R:BASE data types. Null values are ignored by the COMPUTE command when it calculates averages, minimums, maximums, sums, and counts.

As an example of using an arithmetic command, the following command computes the average loan amount and then lists all loans that are greater than the average.

Operator	Explanation
COMPUTE	Displays calculated information about the values in a column or stores the results in a variable. Temporary computed columns can be created while calculations are being performed.
TALLY	Counts the number of occurrences of each unique column value in a table or view.
CROSSTAB	Counts the number of occurrences of each unique pair of values from two columns in a table or view.

Fig 8-8 Statistical Operators

Operator	Explanation
ALL	Computes values for all of the operations that apply to the data types of the column.
AVE	Computes the arithmetic average of CURRENCY, DOUBLE, INTEGER, REAL, DATE, and TIME.
COUNT	Counts the number of rows in the table.
MAX	Determines the maximum arithmetic or alphanumeric value in the column.
MIN	Determines the minimum arithmetic or alphanumeric value in the column.
ROWS	Determines how many rows there are in a specified table.
SUM	Computes the arithmetic sum of CURRENCY, DOUBLE, INTEGER, or REAL data types.
STD	Computes the standard deviation for CURRENCY, DOUBLE, INTEGER, or REAL data types.
VAR	Computes the variance for CURRENCY, DOUBLE, INTEGER, or REAL data types.

Fig 8-9   R:BASE Operators

```
R>COMPUTE AVE AMOUNT FROM LOAN
R>AMOUNT Average = $1,987.50

R>SELECT ALL FROM LOAN WHERE AMOUNT > 1987.50

LID  LDATE     YEARS     INT_RATE AMOUNT          SID   BID
---- --------- --------  -------- --------------  ----  --------
   87 09/07/83     5         7.    $2,000.00      9735  SEAFIRST
   92 01/12/85     6         7.5   $2,100.00      4494  FIDELITY
   99 01/15/86     6         9.    $2,200.00      4494  FIDELITY
  490 05/07/84     6         6.    $2,500.00      3749  PEOPLES
  493 06/24/85     7         7.5   $3,000.00      3749  PEOPLES
```

Note that the average value had to be entered manually in the SELECT command.

Saving Results in a Variable

The *COMPUTE varname* option is used to store the result of the computation in a so-called *global variable*. For example, the following command calculates the average loan amount and stores the value in the global variable AVEAMT.

```
R>COMPUTE AVEAMT AS AVE AMOUNT FROM LOAN
```

The variable AVEAMT can now be used to list all loans that are greater than the average without the need for manual entry of the average amount. Note that this R:BASE command violates the formal relational algebra characteristic that the output of every command is a relation. The global variable AVEAMT is not a relation.

To use a global variable in a SELECT, its name must be preceded with a period.

```
R>SELECT ALL FROM LOAN WHERE AMOUNT > .AVEAMT
```

You can display the values of global variables using the SHOW VARIABLES command. The values of system variables are also displayed as seen below.

```
R>SHOW VARIABLES

Variable = Value                             Type
-------- --------------------------          --------
#DATE    = 01/01/80                          DATE
#TIME    = 1:20:44                           TIME
#PI      = 3.14159265358979                  DOUBLE
AVEAMT   = $1,987.50                          CURRENCY
```

SELECT with Nesting

An important extension provided by the "for DOS" version of R:BASE over earlier versions is the ability to include a SELECT in the WHERE clause. This provides the ability to restrict results based on more than just a single table. To select all columns from STUDENT for all undergraduates with loans:

```
R>SELECT ALL FROM STUDENT WHERE SLEVEL <= 4 AND SID IN +
+>(SELECT SID FROM LOAN)

SID       NAME          SLEVEL    AGE      ZIP
--------- ------------- --------- -------- --------
     9735 ALLEN             1         21     98101
     4494 ALTER             2         19     98112
```

In fact, this looks very much like SQL. There are, however, differences and limitations. For example, only one sublevel of nesting is allowed. The following command, which appears to select all undergraduates with a loan from lenders of type BANK is not valid due to the second level of nesting:

```
R>SELECT ALL FROM STUDENT WHERE SLEVEL <= 4 AND SID IN +
+>(SELECT SID FROM LOAN WHERE BID IN +
+>(SELECT BID FROM BANK WHERE TYPE = "BANK" ) )
```

This query can be performed—but it requires a different approach.

SELECT DISTINCT

Duplicate rows may be eliminated from the output by using the DISTINCT keyword in the SELECT command.

```
R>SELECT DISTINCT SID FROM LOAN

SID
----
9735
4494
8767
3749
```

SELECT with GROUP BY

The R:BASE SELECT also has the GROUP BY option of SQL's SELECT, although with somewhat different syntax and several restrictions. The syntax is:

```
SELECT columns FROM tblname GROUP BY col-list [WHERE condition]
```

The *columns* in this definition may include column names, expressions, and the statistical functions SUM, AVE, MIN, MAX, and COUNT. To display the average loan amount and number of loans for each student:

```
R>SELECT SID, COUNT(SID), AVE(AMOUNT) FROM LOAN GROUP BY SID

SID        COUNT SID      AVERAGE AMOUNT
--------   -------------- --------------
   3749              2        $2,750.00
   4494              2        $2,150.00
   8767              1        $1,900.00
   9735              3        $1,400.00
```

As you can see from the syntax, the WHERE condition follows the GROUP BY and applies not to the group but to the table queried. If we want to find the average amount of loans for banks with a ZIP code greater than 98100 the command is:

```
R>SELECT BID, AVE(AMOUNT) FROM LOAN GROUP BY BID +
+>WHERE BID IN +
+>(SELECT BID FROM BANK WHERE BZIP >= 98100)

BID        AVERAGE AMOUNT
--------   ----------------
FIDELITY        $2,150.00
PEOPLES         $2,100.00
SEAFIRST        $2,000.00
```

Just when you are beginning to believe that R:BASE is on a par with most DBMSs that support SQL you learn the harsh truth. Here is an example. We would like to find the average loan amount by SLEVEL of student. But, try as we might, this cannot be written with a single SELECT on base tables. Why not? The problem is that the grouping variable, SLEVEL, and the variable on which we want to perform aggregation (AMOUNT) are from two different relations. Remember, the R:BASE SELECT cannot return columns from more than a single table. Again, there are approaches, several of them, to handle this problem but they involve learning additional commands.

Additional Relational Operations

As demonstrated above, the SELECT command of R:BASE implements the relational algebra operations of select and project—that is, row restriction and column projection. R:BASE provides six additional commands that more or less implement the remaining relational algebra operations. However, just as with the R:BASE SELECT, the name used in R:BASE is often not the same as the term used in the relational algebra.

Figure 8–10 lists the relational commands and their results. These commands, with the exception of APPEND, copy results to new tables without changing the operand tables. With the exception of the APPEND command, you can specify which columns each command will include (project) in its result.

Command	Result
PROJECT	Creates a new table that may be a row or column subset of an existing table. Thus, PROJECT implements the relational algebra select and project operation with the result assigned to a new relation.
APPEND	Adds rows of data from one table to another table. Does not form a new table.
UNION	Combines columns and rows from two tables into a new table using all of the rows. Differs somewhat from the relational algebra UNION in that union compatibility is not required.
INTERSECT	Implements the relational algebra natural join. Note that this command is quite unlike the relational algebra intersect operation.
JOIN	Implements a restricted version of the various joins of the relational algebra.
SUBTRACT	Implements a variation of the relational algebra difference operation.

Fig 8-10   Relational Commands

Project Command

This command is the same as the SELECT command except that the result is stored in a new relation instead of being displayed. The syntax is:

```
PROJECT newtable FROM oldtable USING col-list WHERE conditions
```

The USING clause must be included to indicate the subset of columns to project from the existing table. When projecting all columns, replace the column list with ALL. Optional clauses are SORTED BY and WHERE.

Project is useful to:

• Obtain a subset of a large table when the subset is needed for subsequent operations (typically for a join)
• Make a backup copy of a table
• Create a new table in which the order of columns differs
• Create a new table in which the order of rows differs

The following example creates a new table called UNDRGRAD, then uses a SELECT to display the results:

```
R>PROJECT UNDRGRAD FROM STUDENT USING SID NAME AGE WHERE SLEVEL <= 4
Successful project operation, 4 rows generated.

R>SELECT ALL FROM UNDRGRAD

SID        NAME           AGE
--------   -------------- --------
    9735   ALLEN             21
    4494   ALTER             19
    2368   JONES             23
    6793   SANDS             17
```

When a table is created, no columns are indexed in the new table; if you want to create the indexes, follow the PROJECT command with BUILD KEY commands:

```
R>BUILD KEY SID
```

The definition of a table created by a PROJECT (or by some other command) can be displayed by using the LIST tblname:

```
R>LIST UNDRGRAD

Table: UNDRGRAD              No lock(s)
Read Password: No
Modify Password: No

Column definitions
# Name        Type      Length          Key    Expression
1 SID         INTEGER
2 NAME        TEXT      16 characters
3 AGE         INTEGER

Current number of rows:          4
```

As with the SELECT, the WHERE clause of the PROJECT allows one level of nesting. To create a new table of student data for undergraduates with loans we write:

```
R>PROJECT UNDRLOAN FROM STUDENT WHERE SLEVEL <= 4 AND +
+>SID IN (SELECT SID FROM LOAN)
```

Natural Join: The INTERSECT Command

Except for the single level of nesting in the WHERE clause, the SELECT and PROJECT are limited to operations on a single table. The SELECT and PROJECT may not extract data from more than a single table. For example, suppose that we are interested in names and loan data for undergraduates. This involves output from more than a single table, thus it cannot be performed with SELECT or PROJECT. A natural join is required (INTERSECT in R:BASE terminology) of the STUDENT and the LOAN tables. The syntax is:

```
INTERSECT table1 WITH table2 FORMING newtable USING col-list
```

The rows of table1 and table2 are joined to form a new table if the two tables have at least one common column, that is, at least one column with the same name. For a row to be included in the new table, each set of values from the common columns of the two tables must match. If a USING clause is specified, only one or more of those columns listed in the clause must match. To display columns from both STUDENT and LOAN for undergraduates, the previously created UNDRGRAD table can be joined with LOAN:

```
R>INTERSECT LOAN WITH UNDRGRAD FORMING UNDRLOAN

Successful intersect operation, 5 rows generated
R>SELECT SID, LID, AMOUNT, BID FROM UNDRLOAN

SID        LID      AMOUNT         BID
--------  --------  --------------- --------
    9735        27    $1,200.00 HOME
    9735        78    $1,000.00 PEOPLES
    9735        87    $2,000.00 SEAFIRST
    4494        92    $2,100.00 FIDELITY
    4494        99    $2,200.00 FIDELITY
```

We return now to the problem posed at the end of our discussion of the SELECT: finding the average loan amount for each level of student. This query will use several of the commands described above. To answer the query, both the SLEVEL and AMOUNT columns are needed. Since these data are stored in different tables, they must be joined. The following is one approach—not necessarily the simplest or best. We first PROJECT the SID and SLEVEL from STUDENT and store them in a table, STLEV.

```
R>PROJECT STLEV FROM STUDENT USING SID SLEVEL
Successful project operation; 6 rows generated.
```

Next, the loan amount and SID are projected from LOAN. While this operation (and the previous project) are not necessary prior to the natural join (INTERSECT), they are done for efficiency to reduce the size of the relations to be joined.

```
R>PROJECT LOANAMT FROM LOAN USING AMOUNT SID
Successful project operation; 8 rows generated.
```

The two projections are then joined:

```
R>INTERSECT STLEV WITH LOANAMT FORMING LEVAMT
Successful intersect operation; 8 rows generated.
```

and the COMPUTE statement is used on LEVAMT for each value of SLEVEL:

```
R>COMPUTE AVE AMOUNT FROM LEVAMT WHERE SLEVEL=1
AMOUNT Average = $1,400.00

R>COMPUTE AVE AMOUNT FROM LEVAMT WHERE SLEVEL=2
AMOUNT Average = $2,150.00

R>COMPUTE AVE AMOUNT FROM LEVAMT WHERE SLEVEL=3
-WARNING- No rows satisfy the WHERE clause

R>COMPUTE AVE AMOUNT FROM LEVAMT WHERE SLEVEL=4
-WARNING- No rows satisfy the WHERE clause

R>COMPUTE AVE AMOUNT FROM LEVAMT WHERE SLEVEL=5
AMOUNT Average = $2,466.67
```

(Note: R:BASE provides a couple of editing capabilities so that we don't have to retype the entire command. This can prove very useful for situations such as the previous series of five almost-identical commands. The Page Up and Page Down cursor control keys cycle through the previous commands. Once a command is displayed, it may then be edited using the cursor arrow, INSERT, and DELETE keys.)

There must be an easier way! The SELECT with GROUP BY can be used once we have both the SLEVEL and AMOUNT columns in a single table. Table LEVAMT has these two columns. The averages can be displayed without the series of COMPUTEs by using the SELECT ... GROUP BY:

```
R>SELECT SLEVEL, AVE(AMOUNT) FROM LEVAMT GROUP BY SLEVEL
SLEVEL    AVERAGE AMOUNT
-------- ----------------
      1        $1,400.00
      2        $2,150.00
      5        $2,466.67
```

Ah—that's better. In fact, if we are not so concerned about efficiency, the STUDENT and LOAN tables may be joined in one step and the SELECT with GROUP BY applied to that table. A third approach is to define a view. Views are described later.

At this point, something should be bothering you. One of the objectives of the relational approach is to let the user describe *what* is wanted rather than *how* to obtain that output.

The simple query to find average loan amount by level can be solved in R:BASE by the two (plus) methods illustrated above and by another approach using a view yet to be illustrated. Which method is best? The user should not have to be concerned with that question. This illustrates another area where R:BASE and several other PC-based DBMSs violate the spirit of the relational model.

More Join Examples

As yet another example of a join, suppose that we want a listing of SID, name, and loan amount for undergraduate students from banks of type BANK. This query foiled us earlier because of the R:BASE limitation to one level of nesting and its inability to extract data from more than one table at a time with the SELECT and PROJECT. A messy approach is shown first. Begin by projecting bank IDs for banks of type BANK:

```
R>PROJECT BBANK FROM BANK USING BID WHERE TYPE=BANK
Successful project operation; 2 rows generated.
```

Next project student IDs and names for undergraduates:

```
R>PROJECT UG FROM STUDENT USING SID NAME WHERE SLEVEL <= 4
Successful project operation; 4 rows generated.
```

Next, the undegraduate projection and the LOAN relation are joined:

```
R>INTERSECT UG WITH LOAN FORMING UGL2 USING LID SID BID NAME AMOUNT
Successful intersect operation; 5 rows generated.
```

Next, the banks of type BANK are joined with the results of the last step:

```
R>INTERSECT UGL2 WITH BBANK FORMING BANKUGL2 USING SID NAME AMOUNT
-ERROR- Tables UGL2 and BBANK have no common column names
```

Note that this failed. The reason is that the join column, whether it is needed in the result or not, must be included in the *USING col-list*.

```
R>INTERSECT UGL2 WITH BBANK FORMING BANKUGL2 USING SID BID NAME AMOUNT
Successful intersect operation; 2 rows generated.
```

The last step is to display the result:

```
R>SELECT SID NAME AMOUNT FROM BANKUGL2
SID        NAME       AMOUNT
--------   --------   ----------
    9735   ALLEN      $1,000.00
    9735   ALLEN      $2,000.00
```

There are alternatives that require fewer separate commands. Using the commands described thus far, you can simplify this query by using nesting. This is left as an exercise.

Self-join Using INTERSECT and RENAME

As we have shown in earlier chapters, it is sometimes necessary to join a table to itself: a self-join. (Note: In SQL this can be done using SELECT with synonyms, which are not allowed in R:BASE.) In R:BASE this can be done with the INTERSECT command. For instance, to list all SIDs of students with more than one loan, the loan table is joined with itself over equal SIDs and unequal LIDs. First a new table, SIDLID, containing the LID and the SID, is projected from the LOAN table:

```
R>PROJECT SIDLID FROM LOAN USING SID LID
Successful project operation; 8 rows generated.
```

For efficiency, a copy of SIDLID, named SIDLID2, is made:

```
R>PROJECT SIDLID2 FROM SIDLID USING ALL
Successful project operation; 8 rows generated.
```

We now want to join these two identical tables (over equal SIDs, unequal LIDs). However, this causes a problem because unlike SQL, R:BASE does not allow the use of qualified column names to avoid ambiguity; that is, we cannot write WHERE SIDLID.SID = SIDLID2.SID AND SIDLID.LID <> SIDLID2.LID. R:BASE handles this problem by allowing column names to be renamed. The syntax of the RENAME command is:

RENAME oldname TO newname IN table

In our example, the LID in SIDLID2 is renamed:

```
R>RENAME LID TO LID2 IN SIDLID2
Column LID renamed to LID2 in table SIDLID2.
```

The join of the SIDLID and SIDLID2 tables can now be performed using INTERSECT. Note, however, that we cannot simultaneously restrict the join to unequal values of LID and LID2—the result will contain rows where LID equals LID2, rows that will subsequently be eliminated.

```
R>INTERSECT SIDLID WITH SIDLID2 FORMING SLL2
Successful intersect operation; 18 rows generated.
```

This creates a new table named SLL2 in which each loan a student has is matched with all of that student's loans. Even if a student has only one loan, that loan is matched with itself and appears in the table. The result of this query is:

```
R>SELECT ALL FROM SLL2
SID        LID        LID2
--------   --------   --------
    9735         27         27
    9735         27         78
    9735         27         87
    9735         78         27
    9735         78         78
    9735         78         87
    9735         87         27
    9735         87         78
    9735         87         87
    4494         92         92
    4494         92         99
    4494         99         92
    4494         99         99
    8767        170        170
    3749        490        490
    3749        490        493
    3749        493        490
    3749        493        493
```

To remove redundant rows, only those rows in which LID is less than LID2 are selected and only distinct SID values are displayed:

```
R>SELECT DISTINCT SID FROM SLL2 WHERE LID LTA LID2
SID
--------
    9735
    4494
    3749
```

Note that when the value of one attribute is compared to the value of another attribute, the operators are: EQA, LTA, LEA, GTA, GEA and NEA. Alternatively, the attribute on the right may be placed between ( ) and the standard operators used, for example, LID < (LID2).

You might wonder how you would identify students who have three or more loans. Recall that an SQL command for this uses GROUP BY and HAVING:

```
R>SELECT DISTINCT SID +
+>FROM LOAN +
+>GROUP BY SID HAVING COUNT(*) > 2
```

There is no HAVING clause in R:BASE's SELECT. Do you suppose you could use the PROJECT with GROUP BY to create a new relation that contained the counts, then apply SELECT to that? For example:

```
R>PROJECT SID_CT FROM LOAN USING SID, COUNT(LID) CT GROUP BY SID
R>SELECT SID, CT FROM SID_CT WHERE CT >= 3
```

We have invented some syntax here: the CT following COUNT(LID) is the column name for the count column. As you might guess, this doesn't work. Can you come up with a solution if we change the condition on the number of loans from two to some other value so that the only change is in a single parameter? This is left as an exercise.

SUBTRACT Command

The SUBTRACT command forms a new table from two existing tables. The new table is made up of rows from the second table that do not match those of the first. R:BASE looks in each table for columns that have the same name and compares each row of the first table with every row of the second table. Then each row of the second table that has no match in the first table is copied to the new table. This command is identical to the relational algebra difference operation *if* both tables have the same columns (in other words, if they are union compatible).

```
SUBTRACT table1 FROM table2 FORMING newtable USING col-list
```

The phrasing of the command is similar to that of arithmetic subtraction, such as "subtract 10 from 100 to get (to form) 90," in that the first table (table1) that you enter in the command is subtracted from the second. The new table (newtable) uses the rows from and follows the column order of the second table (table2) if you do not include a USING clause.

You can select one or more columns (col-list) for the new table from the second table with the optional USING clause. The order of the columns in the new table can also be arranged by using this clause. At least one column listed in the clause must exist in both tables. When the USING clause is not included, R:BASE checks all columns and places the rows from the second table into the new table when there is no match.

For example, to find all students with no loans we can subtract the LOAN table from the STUDENT table:

```
R>SUBTRACT LOAN FROM STUDENT FORMING NOLOAN USING SID NAME SZIP
Successful subtract operation; 2 rows generated.
```

This results in the following table:

```
R>SELECT ALL FROM NOLOAN

SID        NAME       SZIP
--------  --------  ---------
    2368 JONE          98155
    6793 SANDS         98101
```

Suppose that now we want to be able to send to banks the names of students within their general area as determined by ZIP code. To do this, we want to perform an intersection between the BANK and the NOLOAN tables over the ZIP columns:

```
R>INTERSECT BANK WITH NOLOAN FORMING STBANK
Successful intersection operation; 2 rows generated.
```

This results in:

```
R>SELECT ALL FROM STBANK

BID        BZIP      TYPE       SID        NAME
--------  --------  --------  --------  --------
FIDELITY   98101 MSB           6793 SANDS
SEAFIRST   98101 BANK          6793 SANDS
```

In this case, while there were two students without any loans, only one of them, SANDS, resides in an area with banks that provide this kind of loan.

Can this be done directly using the R:BASE SELECT? The answer is clearly *no*, because the result table has columns from more than one table. We can identify students with no loans using the SELECT and NOT IN operator:

```
R>SELECT SID, NAME, SZIP FROM STUDENT WHERE SID NOT IN
(SELECT SID FROM LOAN)
```

To be able to join this result with the BANK table we need to save it. But, unlike standard SQL, the result of a SELECT cannot be saved.

UNION Command

Suppose that we want to list every student who meets either or both of the following two conditions:

1. Has a loan from a bank with TYPE = "MSB"

2. Is a graduate student who has a loan

One approach is to use the UNION command, which combines columns and rows of two existing tables to form a new table. The two existing tables must contain at least one common column (that is, have identical names). R:BASE builds a new table containing all of the columns from the original two tables. Any common columns are combined into a single column. If the same values for the common column(s) are found in each table, R:BASE combines the two rows into one when it forms the new table. Nulls are used to fill out empty columns in rows that have no matching values.

The syntax for the UNION command is:

```
UNION table1 WITH table2 FORMING newtable [ USING col-list ]
```

Again, the command is similar, but not identical, to the relational algebra UNION. The primary difference is that R:BASE does not require union compatibility.

If a USING clause is specified, only the columns included in col-list must match. Col-list also specifies which columns are included in the new table. At least one of the columns in col-list must be common to both tables.

To answer the query given at the beginning of this section, first project from the LOAN table only those columns needed:

```
R>PROJECT LOAN2 FROM LOAN USING SID LID AMOUNT BID
Successful project operation; 8 rows generated.
```

Next, a new table, MSB, is created, with only those banks that are MSBs:

```
R>PROJECT MSB FROM BANK USING BID WHERE TYPE= "MSB"
Successful project operation; 1 row generated.
```

The intersection of these two new tables, LOAN2 and MSB, is then performed. This results in a table containing only those loans that are from banks with a type of MSB:

```
R>INTERSECT LOAN2 WITH MSB FORMING MSBLOANS
Successful intersect operation, 2 rows generated.
```

This successfully meets the requirements of the first part of the condition, namely, those loans from banks with a type of MSB. For the second part of the condition, we first create a table containing only graduate students:

```
R>PROJECT GRST FROM STUDENT USING SID WHERE SLEVEL=5
Successful project operation; 2 rows generated.
```

This new table is then intersected with the LOAN2 table created earlier to get the loan information for the graduate students:

```
R>INTERSECT LOAN2 WITH GRST FORMING GRLOAN
Successful intersect operation; 3 rows generated.
```

This creates a new table with the loan information for the graduate students. This new table, GRLOAN, can then be combined with MSBLOANS to meet the conditions set forth at the beginning of this section:

```
R>UNION MSBLOANS WITH GRLOAN FORMING GRMSBL
Successful union operation; 5 rows generated.
```

The result is:

```
R>SELECT ALL FROM GRMSBL
SID       LID  AMOUNT        BID        LDATE     YEARS
--------  ---- ------------- ---------- --------- ------
     449  492  $2,100.00     FIDELITY   -0-       -0-
    4494   99  $2,200.00     FIDELITY   -0-       -0-
    8767  170  $1,900.00     PEOPLES    04/30/83      6
    3749  490  $2,500.00     PEOPLES    05/07/84      6
    3749  493  $3,000.00     PEOPLES    06/24/85      7
```

This new table, GRMSBL, contains only those loans that are to graduate students or are from banks with a type of MSB. Should we also wish to display the student's name, we can perform the intersection of GRMSBL with STUDENT:

```
R>INTERSECT GRMSBL WITH STUDENT FORMING NMGRMSB
Successful intersect operation; 5 rows generated.

R>SELECT NAME, SID, LID, AMOUNT, BID FROM NMGRMSB
NAME       SID       LID       AMOUNT        BID
--------  --------  --------  ------------  --------
ALTER      4494        92     $2,100,00     FIDELITY
ALTER      4494        99     $2,200.00     FIDELITY
CABEEN     8767       170     $1,900.00     PEOPLES
WATSON     3749       490     $2,500.00     PEOPLES
WATSON     3749       493     $3,000.00     PEOPLES
```

Eliminating Unneeded Tables

The PROJECT, INTERSECT, UNION, and SUBTRACT operations create actual tables; they are not view tables. These tables take up space that should be reclaimed when the tables are no longer needed. The REMOVE TABLE command is used to remove a complete table (both the structure and the data) from a database. Its syntax is:

```
REMOVE TABLE tblname
```

For example, the following command would be entered to delete the table NOLOAN, created earlier in this chapter, from the GSL database:

```
R>REMOVE TABLE NOLOAN
Press [ENTER] to remove the table NOLOAN. Press [ESC] to stop the command.
R>[ENTER]
```

Exiting R:BASE

The EXIT command is used to leave R:BASE and return to the computer's operating system. To leave R:BASE, enter the following command at the R> prompt:

```
R>EXIT
```

R:BASE closes any open databases and returns to the system prompt, the system menu, or the calling batch file. EXIT must be used whenever R:BASE is shut down to ensure that all file buffers, internal counters, and pointers are properly stored. If they are not, the integrity of the database or the database as a whole can be destroyed.

Views

R:BASE allows an SQL-like view definition. As with the SELECT, view definition in R:BASE does not have the full flexibility of view definition in SQL, but it does allow for simpler solutions to many of the queries posed above. Views may be defined in Definition EXPRESS (under the *Define or modify a database* menu choice) or directly with an SQL-like CREATE VIEW command with syntax:

```
CREATE VIEW viewname AS SELECT col-list FROM table-list [ WHERE condition ]
```

The *col-list* may contain columns from several tables: those tables listed in *table-list*. Thus, the view feature will finally allow us to perform several of the queries illustrated above without the necessity of creating intermediate tables using the INTERSECT, UNION... operators. Unlike the SQL view definition, the WHERE clause does not specify join conditions for the tables in *table-list*. The tables are joined over their common columns. The WHERE clause is used to restrict the rows in the result. Several examples follow.

1. Create a view with SID and NAME for graduate students.

```
R>CREATE VIEW GRSTUD AS +
+>SELECT SID, NAME, SLEVEL FROM STUDENT WHERE SLEVEL = 5
```

Note that even though SLEVEL is constant, and thus not of much interest, any column referenced in a WHERE clause must be included in the view definition. The following view will be allowed but will not execute:

```
R>CREATE VIEW GRSTUD AS +
+>SELECT SID, NAME FROM STUDENT WHERE SLEVEL = 5
```

2. An earlier query wanted all undergraduate students with loans from banks of type MSB. This could not be performed with SELECT because only one level of nesting is allowed. A view can be defined that includes SLEVEL and TYPE and the WHERE condition can then test these two values:

```
R>CREATE VIEW UG_MSB AS SELECT SID, NAME, SLEVEL, TYPE, BID +
+>FROM STUDENT, LOAN, BANK +
+>WHERE SLEVEL <= 4 AND TYPE = "MSB"
```

Note the necessity of including in the view all columns that are required for the joins (SID and BID) or used in the WHERE (SLEVEL and TYPE).

3. Another troublesome query posed earlier was to find the average loan amount by level. Recall that the SELECT with GROUP BY cannot be used directly because it requires grouping on a column (SLEVEL) from a table (STUDENT) different from the table (LOAN) holding the column to be averaged (AMOUNT). Can the view be used? While it will help out, it cannot be used directly. For example, the following fails:

```
R>CREATE VIEW AVE_LEV AS +
+>SELECT SLEVEL, AVE(AMOUNT), SID+
+>FROM STUDENT, LOAN GROUP BY SLEVEL
```

The reason it fails is left as an exercise.

The view approach can help us by allowing the join of STUDENT and LOAN with projection of SID, SLEVEL, and AMOUNT. Then, a SELECT with GROUP BY can be applied to the view:

```
R>CREATE VIEW STLOAN AS +
+>SELECT SID, SLEVEL, AMOUNT FROM STUDENT, LOAN

R>SELECT SLEVEL, AVE(AMOUNT) FROM STLOAN GROUP BY SLEVEL
```

4. Another situation involving GROUP BY that foiled earlier, direct attempts is to identify all students who have more than a given number of loans. This couldn't be written directly because the R:BASE GROUP BY does not allow a HAVING clause. Can the problem be solved using a view? The answer is NO. The reason is left as an exercise.

Thus, the view does not solve all of our problems. For example, to find students with no loans and match them up with banks sharing the same ZIP, you might write the view definition:

```
R>CREATE VIEW NOL_STB AS +
+>SELECT BID, ZIP, TYPE, SID, NAME FROM STUDENT, BANK +
+>WHERE SID NOT IN (SELECT SID FROM LOAN)
```

Then, select everything from this view:

```
R>SELECT ALL FROM NOL_STB
```

But look at the R:BASE response:

```
-WARNING-No rows satisfy the WHERE clause.
```

How can that be? We don't know what the problem is. It appears that for some reason the IN and NOT IN operators do not work on a view.

Several other issues involving views are left as exercises, for example, can views be built upon views?

Updating

Methods for loading data to tables were described earlier. Deleting rows and changing values of data items can be done using the SQL-like commands DELETE and UPDATE or the native R:BASE command CHANGE. Command syntax and several examples follow.

To delete one or more rows from a table, the DELETE command is used:

```
R>DELETE ROWS FROM table WHERE condition
```

The command to drop all loans for student with SID 4494 would be:

```
R>DELETE ROWS FROM LOAN WHERE SID = 4494
```

The WHERE clause may contain a SELECT. For example, to drop all loans for graduate students:

```
R>DELETE ROWS FROM LOAN WHERE SID IN +
+>(SELECT SID FROM STUDENT WHERE SLEVEL = 5)
```

The syntax for the UPDATE command is:

```
UPDATE table SET column = constant or ( expression ) WHERE condition
```

To add $100 to all loans from PEOPLES bank:

```
R>UPDATE LOAN SET AMOUNT = (AMOUNT + 100) WHERE BID = "PEOPLES"
```

The CHANGE command is similar to the UPDATE except that it allows changes to more than a single table simultaneously. (*Multiple* table update would not be a very frequent operation in most databases.) Refer to the R:BASE help facility or the manual.

Conclusion

Our discussion has emphasized the basic database definition, query, and update commands and modules of R:BASE. As explained in the introduction, there are several other modules and many other features not described here. Over the years, the R:BASE product has been enhanced and new modules have been added. The full product provides an impressive range of capabilities. It is certainly suitable for most personal computer applications.

In the past, R:BASE and other PC-based systems such as dBASE led the mainframe-based systems in ease of use. (Note: We use PC in a very generic sense to include any personal computer model, not just IBM or IBM-compatible systems. "PC" includes, for example, the Macintosh.) Today, the two varieties of DBMSs are converging: the PC-based systems are adding SQL, can interface to host languages, and have multi-user features previously more or less limited to mainframe-based DBMSs. On the other hand, PC versions of main-frame systems have been developed and also offer friendly interfaces.

The proliferation of DBMSs for PCs makes the user's choice more difficult. Recently, prices of PC versions of several mainframe DBMSs have dropped dramatically, and at the time of writing are considerably lower than the original PC-based systems. We don't expect this price disparity to continue for long.

As noted, the R:BASE product has several problems. Many of these stem from the lack of a good initial design. The result is that while there is always some way to solve complex queries and report generations, there are almost always several ways to attack a problem. The difficulty, in part, is determining which of the several alternatives can solve the problem and then which is best. Some of the deficiencies of R:BASE follow:

- The results of some operations are not relations; that is, the R:BASE language is not closed.
- The poor implementation of the join operation. Two commands are available, one called JOIN which performs joins of the greater-than, not equal-to, ... variety over single columns, and INTERSECT, which allows a natural join over one or more columns (but is not a relational algebra intersect). The JOIN command has not been explained in the chapter since it is very rarely used. See the manual.)
- The curious implementation and naming of several relational operators. As noted above, the R:BASE operation INTERSECT is really a natural join.
- The general lack of coherent design. As often happens with systems that begin with deficiencies, attempts to overcome the fundamental design errors result in a hodgepodge. One measure of any system's design coherence is the size and organization of its manual. The R:BASE manual has grown like Topsy.

R:BASE is not the only PC-based DBMS that suffers from these problems. Even though most of the Macintosh DBMSs are new products and the designers should by now know better, most systems (ORACLE excluded) have similar fundamental design deficiencies. Macintosh developers have a preoccupation with clever graphics to the detriment of a solid database management design and manipulation language.

Questions and Problems

Questions

1. What are the major components of the R:BASE system? What does each do?

2. Describe the different operating modes used in R:BASE.

3. List and give examples of the different R:BASE data types.

4. When should an R:BASE column be defined as a key column? Must each occurrence within a column be unique?

5. Describe the R:BASE data output commands.

6. When are wildcard characters used? What does each wildcard character do?

7. What conditions are necessary to reduce processing time for a WHERE clause?

8. On which data types may a sort be performed?

9. List the R:BASE relational commands. Describe these commands and their common uses.

Problems

1. Define appropriate data types for the following items:

   a. An hourly pay-rate in dollars and cents with maximum value $99.99.

   b. Hours worked with precision to tenths of hours, maximum value 3000.

   c. Year-to-date gross earnings in dollars and cents with maximum value $9,999,999.99. (Indicate two possible types.)

   d. Part description of up to 25 characters.

   e. Quantity in inventory with maximum value 1 million.

   f. Value of inventory *computed* as the product of QTY and COST.

2. Use R:BASE and the GSL database as defined in this chapter to answer the problems indicated below from Chapter 5. If you have R:BASE and the ASCII files, you should first define and load the database. Some of the problems from Chapter 5 will require multiple R:BASE commands where the R:BASE version of SQL is not appropriate— that is, a sequence of PROJECT, INTERSECT, SELECT, ... may be required.

   a. Problem 4, a. to h.

   b. Problem 5, a. to d.

   c. Problem 6, a. to d. (Several of these will require multiple R:BASE commands.)

   d. Problem 7. (Translate the given SQL query into appropriate R:BASE commands.)

   e. Problem 9. (Show two different approaches—one using UNION.)

   f. Problem 12. (Translate the given relational algebra queries into R:BASE commands. Some may require multiple R:BASE statements.)

   g. Problem 13.

   h. Problem 14.

3. Use R:BASE and the GSL database to answer the problems indicated below from Chapter 6.

   a. Problem 1.

   b. Problem 2.

   c. Problem 3, a. to c.

   d. Problem 6.

   e. Problem 7.

   f. Problem 18.

   g. Problem 19.

4. The SQL command to list SIDs of students with more than n loans is:

```
SELECT DISTINCT SID FROM LOAN
        GROUP BY SID HAVING COUNT (*) > n;
```

a. Describe how to do this in R:BASE if n = 1.

b. Can you devise a general method for any value of n which does not change the set of commands? What is it?

5. Why is the following SQL command illegal in the R:BASE version of SQL?

```
CREATE VIEW AVE_LEV AS
        SELECT SLEVEL, AVE(AMOUNT) SID
        FROM STUDENT, LOAN
        GROUP BY SLEVEL;
```

6. In standard SQL, the following two commands are not equivalent—the presence of lack of a comma between two identifiers results in quite different meanings.

```
SELECT * FROM STUDENT, S        SELECT * FROM STUDENT S
    WHERE SLEVEL = 5                WHERE SLEVEL = 5
```

Discuss the meanings of the two commands in R:BASE.

7. Why does the following fail in R:BASE? How do you write an equivalent query using a sequence of operations?

```
CREATE VIEW TOT_BYA AS
        SELECT AGE, SUM(AMOUNT)
            FROM LOAN, STUDENT
            GROUP BY AGE
```

8. Can a view be defined on a view? For example, create a join-view called ST_LOAN of STUDENT and LOAN with columns SID, NAME, SLEVEL, and AMOUNT. Then try to create a view GR_STL which is a selection of rows from ST_LOAN where SLEVEL = 5.

9. Consider the Customer-Order-Part-Line database described in the problems of Chapter 4 and Figure 4–6 (Note: If you have access to R:BASE these exercises should be performed using the system and actual data. Data has been made available in the form of ASCII files with the instructor's manual for this text. Therefore, you will not need to manually key in the data.)

a. Define a database with these four relations using two different methods: Definition EXPRESS and the standard R:BASE command mode. Make reasonable assumptions for lengths of character columns. Assume that there are frequent queries to these relations on both primary and foreign keys. In addition, CUSTOMER is frequently queried by NAME.

b. Display the definition of the LINE ITEM relation.

c. Load the data shown in Figure 4–6. (If you do not have R:BASE and the ASCII files available, illustrate how to enter the first row of each table.)

d. Do the following problems from Chapter 4 using R:BASE:

(1) Problem 21

(2) Problem 22

(3) Problem 23

(4) Problem 24

(5) Problem 25

References

Microrim, Inc. *R:BASE for DOS—Learning Guide*. 1987.

Microrim, Inc. *R:BASE for DOS—User's Manual*. 1987.

Nonrelational Systems

9 CODASYL Network Systems

This chapter describes databases and database management systems based on the network model. Virtually all network-based DBMSs are of the so-called CODASYL variety. CODASYL is an acronym for Conference on Data System Languages, an organization of representatives from businesses, software vendors, government, and academia, who are devoted to the development and standardization of business programming.

The work of CODASYL is performed by special committees who develop "proposals" of software standards. One such committee, the Database Task Group (DBTG), developed a proposed set of network DBMS standards. It is important to note that the DBTG proposals were never formally adopted as standards but were accepted and implemented by many software vendors. Unfortunately, due to the evolution of the standard, and the need for vendors to freeze their DBMS designs at some point, there are differences from one implementation to the next. Our presentation emphasizes the major features that have been implemented by vendors, particularly the implementation called IDMS (Integrated Data Management System) by the Cullinet Software Corporation. However, we have also included what we believe are important features of the CODASYL standard that are not part of IDMS.

A CODASYL DBTG uses a host language for its data manipulation language (DML). Users communicate with the DBMS through a language such as COBOL, FORTRAN, or PL/I. The DBMS in a host-based system performs retrieval and update functions, transferring data to and from programs written in the host system language. There are also two data description languages, one for the definition of the conceptual schema and the other for the definition of subschemas, or the external level of the database. In fact, the schema DDL includes many specifications that more properly belong at the internal level. For example, definition of physical file structures such as hashing and indexing are part of this language.

Introduction to the Network Model

Even though the relational approach represents the state of the art in database management systems, there are several good reasons to be familiar with network models. Many existing databases are implemented in DBTG-based systems such as UNIVAC's DMS1100, IDMS from Cullinet, Honeywell's IDS-2, DEC's DBMS-11, Burrough's DMS-2, and Control Data's DMS-170. In addition, there are two widely used network DBMSs based on a restricted network model: Query/Image from Hewlett Packard and Cincom's TOTAL.

Network systems differ from relational systems in several significant ways. One difference is in the method used to represent associations between records. In the relational model, associations are represented implicitly by primary and foreign keys. In the network model the associations are very explicit—in fact, physical connections of some type (often linked lists) are established between related records. For example, all loan records for a given student (those with the same SID) might be on a linked list with the list head in the "parent" student record. While this does not present a particular problem for retrieval of a student record and one or more of the related loan records, it presents severe problems as soon as the query violates these established paths. For example, a query to identify all students with non-unique names, or a query to list all banks near a student are very difficult to handle. With the relational system, the desired connections are stated in the query itself, not in the definition of the database. Thus, as we saw in earlier chapters, virtually any associations between data items and records may be specified in a relational query.

Network DBMSs still exhibit a significant performance advantage over today's relational DBMSs for transaction-processing applications. This advantage is due in large part to the explicit connections that can be defined between records by the database designer. This allows the designer to optimize the database design for specific usage patterns. However, if we step outside the routine and predictable nature of transaction processing, network system performance takes a beating. The ad hoc environment, typical of decision-support applications, is where relational systems shine.

A further reason for the superior performance of a network system in routine applications is that network DBMS software is mature. Over the many years since the introduction of network systems they have undergone many revisions and refinements to improve their efficiency. Relational DBMSs are newcomers—they are at the adolescent stage of their devlopment. However, this performance advantage currently enjoyed by network systems is decreasing over time because each new release of a relational system implements improved methods of data access and better query optimization.

History of the CODASYL Standard

During the 1960s, the advantages of having a standardized database model and language were realized. The result was a series of language specifications and functional requirement proposals that described the network model. Most of these proposals were developed over the period from 1965 through the early 1980s. Much of the credit for network systems is due to Charles W. Bachman, a pioneer in the field of network models. In 1962 and 1963 he wrote papers that referred to an *integrated data store*, a term reflected in the commercial software product, IDS. Bachman originated many database diagramming techniques, file storage structures, and other computing concepts in common use today.

The first CODASYL proposal was published in 1969. This proposal met with considerable objection and resulted in a major revision that appeared in 1971. This was the last report of a subgroup of CODASYL called the Data Base Task Group (DBTG). Even though the group was disbanded, the DBTG acronym has stuck and many people will refer to a network system as a DBTG DBMS. Subsequent to the 1971 report, a new group called the Data Definition Language Committee (DDLC) was formed, and it made further revisions that were reported in 1973, 1978 and 1981. In 1984 the X3H2 committee of the American National Standards Institute (ANSI) took over the effort and developed a proposed standard for network data description and manipulation languages. This is the same standards committee that produced the SQL standard.

For a software developer, the almost continual revisions in proposed standards meant that it was not possible to build a DBMS to the current proposal. Thus, many developers froze their DBMS specifications in the early 1970s, choosing to implement a system that was, in most cases, close to the 1971 proposal: the final document of CODASYL's DBTG. It is for this reason that our emphasis is on those systems of 1971 vintage; indeed, except for an important extension to IDMS in the early 1980s, which added a relational-like front end, virtually all commercially available network sytems are DBTG-like.

One of the reasons for the continual revisions in the network proposals was the growing interest in the relational model. To put the CODASYL development into historical perspective, Codd's initial work on the relational model was reported in 1969–70. The relational model was attractive, since it had a formal basis. The network model, in contrast, was based more on practice and experience. The relational model quickly attracted a number of advocates who claimed that it represented a superior model to the network approach. Therefore, they argued, it was inappropriate to establish a database standard around the network model.

The network approach advocates argued the superiority of their model largely on the basis of its (at that time) vastly superior performance. For example, the author had the opportunity to use an early version of System R. A SQL query was written to identify all people in an employee relation who had non-unique names—a self-join query of which several examples are given in Chapters 4 and 5. While the relation had less than 100 rows, almost two minutes of mainframe processor time was required. (It would probably have taken no longer than that to perform the task manually.) A network system could probably have determined the answer in less than a second, although an hour or so of programming would probably have been required.

If this level of performance difference still existed, the network advocates would have been correct in their criticism. Most people realized, however, that criticisms of performance represented a weak argument, because there is nothing inherent in the relational model that precludes achieving performance comparable to levels realized by network-based systems.

DBMS Operation

The block diagram shown in Figure 9–1 depicts the general organization and operation of a network DBMS. The numbered lines between various software components, tables, and data show the flow of data and control, and the order in which it occurs when a program interacts with the database. (Note: This flow and its organization are essentially the same in a relational DBMS.)

1. A user's application program requests data from the database by issuing a call to the database control system (the actual DBMS software) using data manipulation language statements (commands). For example, a request might be made to retrieve the STUDENT record with SID equal to 9735.

2. The database control system analyzes the call and, using the schema and subschema, converts the command into lower-level file access operations.

3. The database control system then requests physical I/O operations from the operating system as required to execute the query.

4-5. The operating system retrieves information from the storage media containing the database *and* transfers it to the system buffers.

6. The database control system transfers data between the system buffers and the user's working area of memory. It also performs any data transformations specified in the subschema.

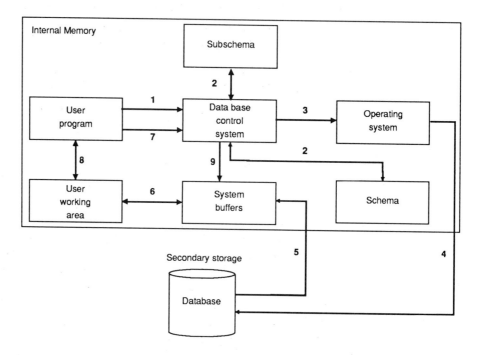

Fig 9-1 Architecture and Flow of Control and Data in a Network DBMS

7. Status information, such as codes indicating success or failure of the command (to retrieve a STUDENT record with SID = 9735), is sent to the program.

8. Data in the user's working memory area may then be manipulated as required by the host language.

9. The database control system manages the system buffers, which are shared by all of the run units serviced by the DBMS. The individual run units communicate with the system buffers entirely through the database control system.

Overview of Network Database Structure and Manipulation

The purpose of this section is to give an overview of both the structure of a network database and of its data manipulation language(DML). Subsequent sections then discuss the syntax and semantics of the data definition language (DDL) and DML and provide additional details.

The elements of a network database are data items, record types, and set types. Record types and data items are quite similar to the record types and fields of conventional files and to the relations and attributes of the relational model. For example, the record types of the GSL database would include STUDENT, LOAN, and BANK. Data items SID, NAME,

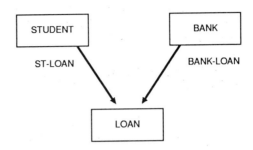

Fig 9-2 GSL Database Structure

LEVEL, AGE, and ZIP would be included in the STUDENT record type; LID, AMOUNT, DATE, INT_RATE, and so forth would be found in the LOAN record type.

A major difference in the network model and relational model is the *set* construct of network databases. A set provides the explicit connection between two record types that have a one-to-many relationship. For example, the STUDENT and LOAN record types would be connected by a set named (say) ST-LOAN. In every set, the record type on the *one* side of the relationship is designated as the *owner* and the record on the *many* side is the *member*. An occurrence of the ST-LOAN set is one owner (STUDENT) record and all of its associated member (LOAN) records. Likewise, the BANK and LOAN record types are connected by another set called BANK-LOAN as shown in Figure 9–2. BANK will be the owner of this set and LOAN the member.

Defining a set establishes a path from the owner record through all of its members. This path is used by the procedural language to "navigate" through the records. For example, to retrieve the student record with SID = 9735, all of the loans for that student and the ZIP for each associated bank, the following navigation takes place:

1. Get STUDENT with SID = 9735
2. Find first LOAN in the ST-LOAN set (i.e., the first loan for this student)
3. While LOANs exist (in this set)
   a. Get LOAN
   b. Get owner of LOAN in the BANK-LOAN set
      (i.e., retrieve the bank that "owns" this particular loan record)

From this example you can see that manipulation in a network system differs from manipulation in a relational system in several significant ways:

- The user (programmer) of a network DBMS must be aware of the access paths; access paths are transparent to the user of a relational DBMS.
- Network operations are record by record; relational systems operate on relations and return relations as results.
- The network access language is procedural; relational DMLs are specification oriented (you describe what you want, not how to get it). The relational DBMS translates the

retrieval specification of the, say, SQL command into the basic database access operations.

Network DBMS Architecture

A network DBMS has several languages and components for database definition and manipulation. They include:

- Schema data definition language: This DDL is used to define a database by coding its schema. The schema is a description of the logical structure of the database and includes the name and format of all record types, data items, and sets. A database has one schema.

- Subschema DDL: This language is used to define the external view of a database. It specifies those records, data items, and sets available to a particular application program. A network subschema corresponds to the view of a relational system. The subschema is used to provide customized views of the database for individual users or groups. Since some databases may be extremely large, subschemas provide for limiting the scope of access either for user convenience or security purposes.

- Data manipulation language: DML statements are a series of verbs such as GET, FIND, and UPDATE, written in a host language application program to manipulate data. As our example above illustrated, they are record-by-record commands that navigate through the database.

- Database Control System: This is the runtime database software, which carries out the operations specified by the DML statements.

- Device Media Control Language (DMCL): The DMCL describes the physical storage schema in terms of buffers, areas, database files, and journal files. This is a physical mapping language that provides the interface between the logical schema and system hardware such as disk drives. This language specifies the low-level physical aspects of the database—those not specified by the schema DDL.

Network Database Structure

The purpose of this section is to describe the structure of a network model: its records, data items, and set constructs. Particular emphasis is on the way that various relationships are modeled using sets. The specific syntax and semantics of the network (schema) DDL are described in a later section.

Records and Data Items

As noted above, there is nothing particularly surprising about the record structure of a network model. A record contains data items. Data item types include various numeric and character types. A record usually has a data item or group of data items defined as its key.

In addition to data items, it is also possible to have a data aggregate: a collection of data items within a record. A data aggregate may be a collection of data items that are referred to by a single name. For example, in the STUDENT record we might have an aggregate called ADDRESS, which is made up of two data items, LINE_1 and LINE_2, and a (lower-level) data item called CITY_ST, which itself is made up of CITY, STATE, and ZIP. In addition, an aggregate may repeat. For example, if student data included a history of addresses, then the ADDRESS aggregate would be a so-called repeating group. An ag-

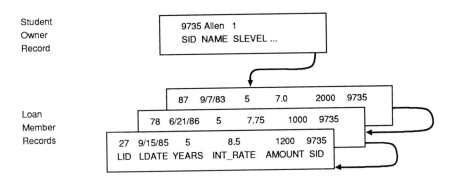

Student
Owner
Record

Loan
Member
Records

| 9735 Allen 1 |
| SID NAME SLEVEL ... |

87	9/7/83	5	7.0	2000	9735
78	6/21/86	5	7.75	1000	9735
27	9/15/85	5	8.5	1200	9735
LID	LDATE	YEARS	INT_RATE	AMOUNT	SID

Fig 9-3 Example Occurence of the ST-LOAN Set

gregate may also be a vector (or list) of same-type data items. If student data included a list of years during which the student was enrolled in a college or university, then these years might be stored as a data aggregate of the vector type. Note that the record in a network database need not be flat, as is required in a relational database. The repeating groups and vectors of a network record would have to be converted to separate relations if the record type were converted to relations.

A database record is the basic logical unit of access in a network DBMS. Retrieval and update statements always operate on individual records. That is, a larger unit (group of records) cannot be retrieved or updated as allowed in a relational system, nor is access to a subset of a record (for example, to an aggregate) allowed without access to its containing record.

Sets

A set type is a group of record types, one of which must be the owner and the rest members. In almost all cases, a set type is defined between two record types; that is, there is only a single member record type. As noted above, it is the set construct that defines the association between two record types. In the GSL database, one set type will be defined with STUDENT as owner, LOAN as member. Another set type will have BANK as owner, LOAN as member.

The occurrence of a set is the occurrence of one owner record and all of its associated member records. For example, the occurrence of the ST-LOAN set that contains the STUDENT record with SID=9735 would also contain all LOAN records with SID = 9735. While the method of connection between owner and member is not (properly) part of the set definition, the connection is often via linked list with the list head in the owner record as shown in Figure 9–3. In the sequel, we will usually just use the term *set* as opposed to *set type* or *set occurrence* unless the meaning is not clear from context.

The various ways sets are used to capture associations are described in the following sections.

Simple Hierarchical Sets

The simplest example of a set is a two-level hierarchy with a single owner-record type and single member-record type. The ST-LOAN set represents this situation. The BANK-LOAN set is another example. The network model is not limited to a two-level structure. For

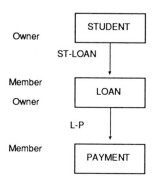

Fig 9-4 Example of a 3-Level Hierarchy—Three Record Types and Two Set Types

example, as shown in Figure 9–4, if PAYMENT records were included in the database, we would create a set named, say, L-P between LOAN and PAYMENT, with LOAN as owner, PAYMENT as member. An occurrence of an L-P set would be a single LOAN record with all of its related PAYMENT records.

We now have a three-level hierarchy. Also note that the LOAN record type serves as both a member of the ST-LOAN set and an owner of the L-P set. Of course, there is essentially no limit to the number of levels. If the database also had a SCHOOL record type, and students were assigned to a single school, there would be a set (say) SCHOOL-ST connecting SCHOOL as owner to STUDENT as member.

Keep in mind that the sets provide navigation paths. To find all payments a specific student has made we would, most likely, access the relevant student, move to the first LOAN of the ST-LOAN set, then access one by one the member PAYMENT records of that L-P set. When all PAYMENTS had been retrieved, we would access the next LOAN within this ST-LOAN set occurrence, then its payments (one at a time), etc. You should consider the ways in which this approach differs from the way it would be done using SQL.

There can also be so-called *empty sets* that are not really empty but contain only an owner with no members. A bank that had not made any loans would have an owner, the BANK record, but no member records.

Sets With Multiple Record Types

While it is uncommon in practice, a set may have more than a single member type. Such sets are called multiple-member sets. Figure 9–5 is an example in which the set L-PC contains two types of member records, PAYMENTs and CHARGEs (such as, interest charge, late payment charge, etc.). It should be mentioned, however, that this is generally not recommended as a good design practice. One reason is that as we navigate through the L-PC set, different record types are encountered. There is little reason not to establish two sets, L-P with LOAN as owner, PAYMENT as member, and L-C with LOAN as owner, CHARGE as member.

Multiple Sets Between the Same Owner/Member

Several set types, all with the same owner and member record types, may also be defined as shown in Figure 9–6. Three sets have been established between BANK and LOAN. A

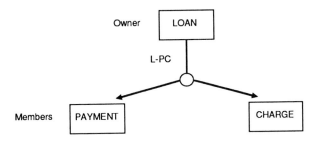

Fig 9-5 Multiple Set Types with the Same Owner and Member Types

given loan may be in one or more of the three sets depending on its status as "active," "closed," or "in default." With this approach, the specific set into which a loan falls tells us more than just which bank owns it. Now the set also tells us the status of the loan. (The reader should also consider how this same information would be represented in the relational model.) Setting up multiple set types between the same owner and member types is sometimes done to support faster access to specific groups of record occurrences. For example, to access all loans (for a specific bank) that are classified as "active," it is only necessary to access all loans for that bank which are in the ACTIVE set.

Network Structures

A set *occurrence* cannot have more than one owner-record occurrence. This also means that a given member record may not be associated with more than a single owner record in a given set type. This is equivalent to saying that only one-to-many relationships are supported (in most network DBMSs). In the GSL model this means that multiple banks cannot own a single loan. In this database, that is not a problem. We'll show later how to handle relationships that are many-to-many.

Figure 9-7 illustrates a variety of different set situations that can occur and be represented in the network model. As illustrated by the BANK record, a record type can be the owner of several sets: BANK is the owner of both the B-L and B-SUB sets. As seen here and by

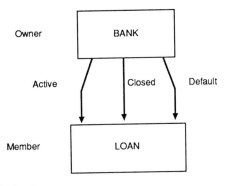

Fig 9-6 Multiple Member Sets

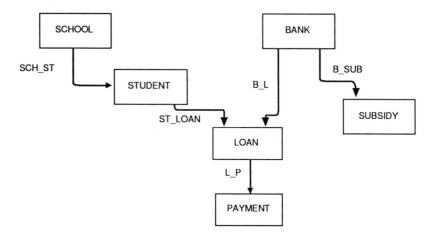

Fig 9-7 Extended GSL Database as a Network

other examples, a member can itself be a set owner: STUDENT is a member of the SCH-ST set and an owner of the ST-LOAN set.

The most important feature illustrated in Figure 9-7 is that a record may be a member of more than one set. For example, LOAN is a member of both the ST-LOAN and BANK-LOAN sets. It is this final feature, the ability of a given record to be a member of more than one set, that differentiates the network model from the hierarchical model.

Special Situations: Hierarchies of Homogeneous Records

There are situations in which a record type needs to be both an owner and a member of the same set. For example, suppose that certain banks in the GSL database are "home offices" to which other, "branch" banks are related. Thus, banks are related to other banks that might be represented as a set with BANK as owner and BANK as member. Most network DBMS implementations do not allow a record type to be both the owner and member of the same set. Thus, another record type that serves as a linkage is created. Figure 9–8 shows how this

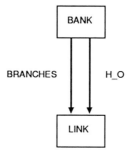

Fig 9-8 Method Used in a Network Model to Represent Information Structures in which a Second is Related to Other Records of the Same Type

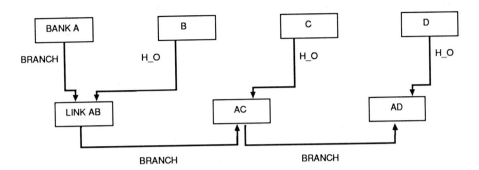

Fig 9-9 Example Occurences of the Network Model of Figure 9-8

is modeled. Two set types are created between BANK and LINK—one called BRANCHES and the other called H_O for "Home Office."

Figure 9–9 is an occurrence diagram for the model of Figure 9-8. It shows a situation in which Bank A is a home office and has branch banks B, C, and D. In this example, we assume that linked lists are used to represent set occurrences. Thus, an occurrence of the set BRANCHES with Bank A as owner includes all LINK records that connect (via the H_O set) to Banks B, C, and D. That is, the occurrence includes Bank A and link records AB, AC, and AD.

A program that wanted to list all of the branch banks with Bank A as home office would "navigate" as follows:

1. Access Bank A
2. Find first LINK record in the BRANCH set (i.e., record AB)
3. While records in the BRANCH set exist:
   a. Get LINK record
   b. Get owner of LINK record on the H_O set (that is, Banks B, C, and D on subsequent passes through the loop).
   c. Find next record in the BRANCH set

Special Situations: Cycles

In rare situations, relationships between records may create a cycle as shown in Figure 9–10, part a. Here the model is one of students taking courses that may also be taught by students (teaching assistants). Keep in mind that this example is a little farfetched. It says that each student may take only a single course. We will fix this error below, which will also eliminate the cycle.

When a cycle is allowed in the network model it gives rise to a chicken and egg problem: to enter a COURSE record into the database the student (who is the teacher) must already exist in the database. But that STUDENT record cannot enter the database until there is a COURSE record stored for that student to take. The solution is to allow, say, one of the relationships to be "optional." For example, we do not force a student to take a course so that the student teachers may first be entered, then the courses they teach, and finally the non-teacher students are entered and connected to the courses they take.

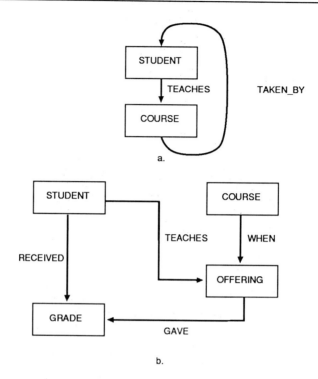

Fig 9-10 (a) Network Model of a Cycle. (b) Revised Model Using More Realistic Assumptions About Relationships

As noted above, the situation we pose as giving rise to the cycle is somewhat unrealistic since it allows a student to take only a single course. If students could take many offerings of courses, then the model would appear as shown in part b of Figure 9–10. Now no cycle exists, and the chicken and egg problem does not arise. Students and courses are entered to the database first. Then, to have an offering of a course, an OFFERING record is entered and connected to the proper COURSE record and its STUDENT (teacher) record. Students are enrolled in COURSES by creating GRADE records.

Representing Many-to-Many Relationships

There are numerous situations in which the relationship between two record types is "many-to-many." In our simple GSL model with STUDENT, BANK, and LOAN records, there is a many-to-many relationship between students and banks. A student may be a customer of many banks by virtue of having loans from more than one bank. And, of course a bank will have many students. But, it is not necessary to represent this relationship directly because it is captured through the two one-to-many relationships between BANK and LOAN and STUDENT and LOAN. This is the common situation in many-to-many relationships: there is so-called "intersection" data between the two record types that have a many-to-many relationship. Here the intersection data is LOAN—the loan data belongs, in some sense, to both the student and the bank. For example, the data item AMOUNT represents the amount owed by a student to a bank.

Another example of a many-to-many relationship exists in the aforementioned student-course model used to illustrate a cycle. The revised model in part b of Figure 9–10 has a many-to-many relationship between STUDENT and COURSE since a course over time may be taught by many different students and a student may teach more than a single course. This relationship is captured through the two one-to-many relationships: the TEACHES set between STUDENT and OFFERING and the WHEN set between COURSE and OFFER-ING. Thus, OFFERING, which contains the semester date, place and time the course meets, and so forth, is the intersection data. Another many-to-many relationship exists between STUDENT and OFFERING: a student may take more than one offering of a course and an offering is taken by many students. Here, the GRADE represents the intersection data and eliminates the need for a direct many-to-many relationship.

There are cases of no intersection data between two record types in a many-to-many relationship. For example, suppose a student audits a course, in which case no grade is given. A student may audit several courses, and a course may be audited by several students. Since there is no grade, no intersection data exists. What we would like to do is simply draw a line between STUDENT and OFFERING with an arrowhead at each end as shown in Figure 9–11. Most network DBMS implementations don't allow this.

Before describing how to get around this limitation of most network implementations, consider how a direct many-to-many relationship is represented in the relational model. A new relation is created with the primary keys of the two many-to-many related relationships. In the student-offering example, the relation would have the student identifier and the identifier of the offering, probably a course ID, section number, and date (for example, MIS301, B, Winter 1989).

The way to model this in a network DBMS that is limited to one-to-many relationships is to create a linking record, say AUDIT. Two sets are created, one with STUDENT as owner and AUDIT as member, the other with OFFERING as owner and AUDIT as member as shown in part b of Figure 9–11. As with the relational model, this link record could contain the primary keys of its owners. However, as we shall discuss later, the AUDIT record (in the network model) need not have any data items. It can be null, simply acting as the connection between the owners.

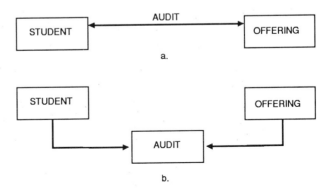

Fig 9-11 (a) Example of a Many-to-Many Relationship with No Intersection Data. (b) Representing a Many-to-Many Relationship by Introducing a Null-Linking Record (AUDIT).

Special Situations: Repeating Groups

One difference in the network and relational models is that a record in a network need not be flat: it may have repeating groups. This can be a handy feature, but it can also lead to trouble. We will illustrate with the GSL model concentrating on the STUDENT record. Suppose that a student attends one or more schools over time. It is tempting, and may be acceptable, to record the school name and attendance dates within the STUDENT record as a repeating group—for example, NYU, Sept. 82, June 87; Purdue, Sept. 88, Dec. 90. This saves us creating a new record type, such as ATTEND. Note that in the relational model, the proper solution is to create a new relation with the primary key of STUDENT and the school name (or ID) and attendance dates.

The use of a repeating group causes problems if we subsequently decide to create a SCHOOL record type that contains school location, type of institution, etc. Now, it would make sense to create a set between SCHOOL and STUDENT. But this is not possible, because a student may contain more than one occurrence of its attendance repeating group. It is also not possible because a member record (STUDENT) may not have more than one occurrence of an owner (SCHOOL) record. The proper approach is to remove the repeating group ATTEND from STUDENT and create two sets: one with SCHOOL as owner, ATTEND as member, and the other with STUDENT as owner, ATTEND as member.

If we persist in leaving the attendance data as a repeating group in STUDENT, then no navigation path exists that would allow us to retrieve all students who had attended a particular college. All we could do would be to scan the student records examining their (attend) repeating group for the identity of the desired college.

Another situation that causes trouble with repeating groups is one in which you would like to have an index built on a data item. If the data item repeats, the index cannot be constructed in most network DBMS implementations.

Special Situations: Singular Sets

As we shall see, the network set can force order on records. For example, we can specify that the loan records in the BANK-LOAN set be in descending order by date. Thus, the first member of a BANK-LOAN will be the loan with the most recent date. Suppose that we want to order the bank records on bank ID—possibly to facilitate a sequential file updating process. The problem is that BANK is not a member of any set. We could create a phony record called, say, ALL and a set called ALL-BANK with ALL as owner and BANK as member. We could then specify that BANK records be in ascending order in this set on bank ID. Note that there would be only a single occurrence of the ALL record, hence only a single occurrence of the ALL-BANK set.

Note that our record ALL could be used as the owner of other sets where order is desired across records. For example, we could create a set ALL-STUDENT with ALL as owner, STUDENT as member, ordered by student ID. We could also create a set with ALL as owner for records that are members of one or more sets but where we want an overall ordering. To order all loans by LID, the set ALL-LOAN could be defined with ALL as owner, LOAN as member, ordered by LID.

Rather than having to create the (empty) ALL record, network systems have already created such a record for us. It is called SYSTEM. Sets may be defined with SYSTEM as owner and any other record type as member. This creates a so-called singular, or system-owned, set. In addition to allowing order to be specified for members of a SYSTEM set, it is also the mechanism used to create an index. More on this later.

The remainder of this chapter is an overview of network DBMS statements, drawing heavily on IDMS and the 1971 DBTG proposal to show how the network structure and data manipulation are actually implemented. This is by no means a complete IDMS language reference. The vendor's set of manuals is several times the size of this book.

CODASYL (Schema) Data Definition Language

The DDL defines the records and their data items. It also defines the sets and their characteristics: owner, member, order of members in the set, and how inclusion of a member in a set is determined. The DDL also defines *areas*. Areas are groups of record types used to facilitate certain processing operations such as the following:

- Making runtime applications more efficient by allowing a program to open only those areas with relevant records.
- Improving the efficiency of serial processing operations by storing such data in contiguous areas.
- Providing for security and privacy by placing record types in different areas. Application programs can then be restricted from accessing certain groups of record types. The types of processing, such as read, write, and update, that an application program can perform against designated areas in the database can then be controlled through the subschema.
- Minimizing system interruptions caused by backup and recovery procedures by permitting unaffected application programs to run while other areas of the database are being recovered, banked-up, or reorganized.

Schema Overview

The first step in implementing a database is to define the logical structure and many of the physical aspects of the database by using the DDL to write the schema definition. Examples are not given for the storage portion of the schema, which is a required part of an actual database. In general, it defines lower-level physical aspects such as record blocking, load factors, and buffer sizes.

To describe the schema DDL, we will give an example definition in Figure 9–12 of a schema named GSL made up of the following records and attributes:

```
Student        (SID, Name, Level, Age, ZIP)
Bank           (BID, Type,ZIP )
Loan           (LID, Ldate, Int_Rate, Amount, SID, BID)
Agent          (A_ID, Name, Phone)
```

"Agent" is a collection agent assigned to track and attempt collection on loans declared in default.

The sets will include a STUDENT-LOAN set and a BANK-LOAN set. A set AGENT-LOAN will be defined with AGENT as owner, LOAN as an "optional" member. Several system sets will also be defined to provide ordering and indexed access to records.

Keep in mind when reading this example and the subsequent discussion that details have been suppressed. The example, as shown, will not actually work for any commercial network system because it is incomplete. Our feeling was that including all the details would

```
A        SCHEMA NAME IS GSL.

B        RECORD NAME IS STUDENT
         LOCATION MODE IS CALC USING SID DUPLICATES NOT ALLOWED

         02 SID  PICTURE 9(5).
         02 NAME PICTURE X(20).
         02 SLEVEL PICTURE 9.
         02 AGE PICTURE 99.
         02 ZIP PICTURE X(5).


C        RECORD NAME IS BANK
         LOCATION MODE IS CALC USING BID DUPLICATES NOT ALLOWED

         02 BID PICTURE 9(6).
         02 TYPE PICTURE X(4).
         02 ZIP PICTURE 9(5).


D        RECORD NAME IS LOAN
         LOCATION MODE IS VIA STUDENT-LOAN SET

         02 LID PICTURE 9(5).
         02 LDATE PICTURE 9(6).
         02 AMOUNT PICTURE 9(4).
         02 INT_RATE PICTURE 99V999.
         02 BID PICTURE 9(6).
         02 SID PICTURE 9(5).


E        RECORD NAME IS AGENT
         LOCATION MODE IS CALC USING A_ID DUPLICATES NOT ALLOWED

         02 A_ID PICTURE 9(6)
         02 NAME PICTURE X(20)
         02 PHONE PICTURE 9(10)


F        SET NAME IS BANK_LOAN
         ORDER IS SORTED
         OWNER IS BANK
         MEMBER IS LOAN
              AUTOMATIC MANDATORY
              ASCENDING KEY SID DUPLICATES ALLOWED
         MODE IS INDEXED
         OWNER LINKAGE.


G        SET NAME IS STUDENT_LOAN
         ORDER IS SORTED
         OWNER IS STUDENT
         MEMBER IS LOAN
              AUTO MANDATORY
              DESCENDING KEY LDATE DUPLICATES ALLOWED
         MODE IS CHAIN
         OWNER LINKAGE.
```

Fig 9-12 GSL Schema (Continued on next page)

```
H      SET NAME IS AGENT-LOAN
       ORDER IS FIRST
       OWNER IS AGENT
       MEMBER IS LOAN
            OPTIONAL MANUAL
       MODE IS CHAINED
       OWNER LINKAGE.


J      SET NAME IS SYS-LOAN
       OWNER IS SYSTEM
       ORDER IS SORTED
       MEMBER IS LOAN
            MANDATORY AUTOMATIC
            ASCENDING KEY LID DUPLICATES NOT ALLOWED
       MODE IS INDEX.


K      SET NAME IS SYS-STUDENT
       OWNER IS SYSTEM
       ORDER IS SORTED
       MEMBER IS STUDENT
            MANDATORY AUTOMATIC
            ASCENDING KEY NAME DUPLICATES ALLOWED
       MODE IS INDEX.
```

Fig 9-12 GSL Schema (Continued from previous page)

tend to obscure the important aspects. Furthermore, since there are minor but significant differences between implementations, a complete example would no doubt work for only one vendor's DBMS—most likely, not one you might have available.

The following sections explain these statements, keyed to the letters in the left margin.

Record Definition

The definition of a record type includes giving it a name and describing its attributes. In addition, the so-called "location mode" of the record is prescribed. The record is defined in the schema DDL by the statement:

```
RECORD NAME IS record name
```

The location mode specified in the schema determines the relative physical placement of a record occurrence. There are many considerations in choosing location modes for records. DBMS vendor's manuals include guidelines and decision trees to aid in determining the optimum location mode for a record. In general, record occurrences should be stored in a manner that minimizes the I/O operations required for anticipated usage patterns. The available modes are:

CALC. CALC is one of the two most commonly used location modes. It both identifies the primary key field of a record type and specifies that each record occurrence shall be located at an address determined by a system- or database administrator–defined hash function. This provides for (essentially) single-disk access to a record occurrence. The USING clause following the word CALC specifies the primary key (for example, SID), which is used by the hash function to compute the physical storage address.

CALC is a common location mode for records at the "top" of the logical structure—that is, those which are owners but not members of other than SYSTEM sets. In the GSL schema, STUDENT, BANK, and AGENT at B, C, and E all have location mode CALC. (LOAN, at D, uses a different location mode.)

The hashing in our example defaults to the DBMS hashing function. However, the database administrator can create a function and have it used for record placement. Here is an example of using a DBA-defined hash function called HASH_SID:

```
LOCATION MODE IS CALC HASH_SID USING SID
```

VIA SET. Another commonly used location mode places member record occurrences from a set occurrence close together. In order to do this, a set must be declared, specifying as a member the record type to be located VIA SET. In the GSL database, a set STUDENT_LOAN is declared naming STUDENT as owner and LOAN as member. The LOAN record type is defined using a location mode VIA STUDENT_LOAN SET (at D). This ensures that all of a student's loan records will be stored close to each other.

A VIA SET location mode is selected when groups of records, specifically all the members of a set, are frequently retrieved together. The choice of VIA SET STUDENT_LOAN for the LOAN records in the example would reflect frequent processes that require retrieval of all loans for one student. If, instead, all loans for a single bank were processed together, then VIA SET BANK_LOAN would have been the appropriate choice.

DIRECT. The DIRECT location mode allows an application program to specify data item values that are, in fact, physical storage locations (for example, relative page numbers within the area). In the other location modes, the DBMS determines an actual storage location based on criteria supplied by the database designer. A DIRECT location mode would be selected if there are specialized ways of locating and accessing a record that do not fall into the available options. For example, suppose that collection agents typically pursue loans that are in default for a specific bank. Then, it might be desirable to locate the AGENT record near this "most frequent" BANK record. But, since agents do not always pursue loans for one bank, it would not be appropriate to create a BANK-AGENT set, and thus not possible to use a location mode for AGENT of VIA SET.

SYSTEM. Finally, there is an overall placement option in which the DBMS implementor creates a procedure that determines record location. Note that this differs from the CALC mode, in which the procedure is specific to the record type.

As we will show below, these location modes do not determine all of the access paths to a record. For example, although a record occurrence is physically located using a hash function, it can also be accessed through any set of which it is a member including, of course, a SYSTEM set.

Following the location specification, the fields or data items are defined. As you can see from the example schema, the data item is named and its type and length are defined. A data item is of either fixed or variable length. If the length is variable, then some type of marking method is required to make known to the DBMS the actual length of a record instance. If a data item is a repeating group, then an additional data item is required to define the number of occurrences. There are many more options than we have shown for types, but details are beyond the scope of this introduction.

Set Definition

A set is defined in the schema with the DDL statement SET NAME IS set_name. The set name is frequently chosen as the owner record type, and one of the member record types, connected by an underscore character, as in STUDENT_LOAN at G. Following this statement are additional statements specifying the names of the OWNER and MEMBER record types and other characteristics of the set as shown at G, H, J, and K.

Set Order. The member records of a set will have an order. Set order determines the *logical* storage position of new record occurrences in the set. Thus, the set order will determine what the order in which records are returned when we navigate, one by one, through members of a set. There are five options:

1. Members are ordered (sorted) on some attribute of the record type. For example, the record occurrences of the loans for each student (that is, within each occurrence of a STUDENT_LOAN set) have been placed into descending order by LDATE by the statements at G:

```
ORDER IS SORTED
DESCENDING KEY LDATE DUPLICATES ALLOWED
```

This means that when we get the first loan for a student, we will retrieve that loan with most recent value for LDATE.

In the BANK_LOAN set, the loans have been placed in ascending order by SID. Note that the following would not make sense (why?):

```
SET NAME IS BANK_LOAN
    ORDER IS SORTED
    OWNER IS BANK
    MEMBER IS LOAN
    ASCENDING KEY BID
```

2. LAST. This is a first-in, first-out ordering that places new record occurrences last in the sequence; that is, at the end of a, say, linked list.

3. FIRST. This is a last-in, first-out ordering in which a new record occurrence is inserted first in the sequence. (Note: It is important to realize the distinction between *inserting* and *storing a record. Insert* means to place a record into a set. The record must already have been physically stored in the database. Thus, *store* means the physical addition of a record to the database while *insert* can be thought of as connecting a record to a set, as in adding the record to a linked list.)

4. PRIOR and NEXT. Here the programmer specifies that a new record occurrence is to be inserted before or after the "current" record. The details of "currency" are discussed in a subsequent section.

5. IMMATERIAL. Here it is left to the DBMS to determine where a new record occurrence will be inserted.

Storage and Retention Class. The MEMBER clause of set definition specifies not only the name of the member record type but also whether or not a member record must be in the set (the *retention* class) and by what mechanism, *automatic* or *manual*, a member is inserted into the set (the *storage* class). It makes sense, for example, that a loan could not be entered in the database without the associated student. In CODASYL terms this means that the MEMBER clause includes MANDATORY (see G). Similarly, the retention specification for the BANK_LOAN set at F is also MANDATORY. On the other hand, not all loans (we hope) are in default. Therefore, membership is OPTIONAL for the AGENT_LOAN set.

AUTOMATIC versus MANUAL defines which mechanism is used to store a member record into the set. AUTOMATIC means that when the record is added to the database, the DBMS will (automatically) connect it to the proper set occurrence. MANUAL means that an application program must execute a DML command (INSERT) that will add the record to the desired set.

MANDATORY means that a record must always be a member of some set occurrence, but it does allow for the record to be moved from one set occurrence to another (using the RECONNECT statement). Thus, if a bank sold a loan to another bank, an application program would issue a RECONNECT command to make that change in set membership. OPTIONAL means that a program may issue a REMOVE command to take a record out of a set.

Some network DBMS also include a retention option of FIXED. With a FIXED retention class, once a record is stored, it cannot be removed from a set without also being erased from the database. This means that the DML REMOVE statement cannot be issued against record occurrences in the set.

Owner-Member Physical Connection Method. These specifications establish the physical linkage between owner and member records in a set occurrence. There are four principal set linkage methods:

1. MODE IS CHAINED. This defines an owner-to-member chain (that is, a ring or linked list). A pointer in each record type points to the next member of the set, with the last member pointing to the owner.

2. OWNER LINKAGE. This implies a pointer directly from each member record to its owner. Since frequent retrievals in the GSL database require moving from LOAN to STUDENT, LOAN to BANK, and LOAN to AGENT, owner linkage is specified for these sets.

3. MODE IS CHAINED LINKED TO PRIOR means that a two-way linked list structure is used.

4. MODE IS INDEXED can be thought of as creating a set (or array) of pointers within the owner record that point to the members (as opposed to each member having a pointer to the next member). If the ORDER IS SORTED clause also appears, then an index is created that allows direct access from owner to member on the specified key.

The only set (other than SYSTEM sets) that uses the indexed mode is the BANK_LOAN set (see F). The combination of the clauses ORDER IS SORTED and MODE IS INDEXED create an index on SID within BANK. This means that loans for a specific student within a specific bank can be retrieved directly once the bank record is retrieved. For example, to retrieve all loans for SID = 9735 with bank SEAFIRST, the navigation would be:

1. Get BANK with BID = 'SEAFIRST'
2. Find first LOAN in BANK_LOAN set with SID = 9735
3. While LOANs exist:
   a. Get LOAN
   b. Find next LOAN with SID = 9735

No searching through the loans of the SEAFIRST BANK_LOAN set is required.

The other places where we have used MODE IS INDEXED are for the two SYSTEM sets, SYS_LOAN and SYS_STUDENT (at J and K). The reason for the SYS_STUDENT set is to create a direct path to STUDENT by NAME. The index on NAME is created by the following:

```
ORDER IS SORTED
KEY ASCENDING NAME DUPLICATES ALLOWED
MODE IS INDEX
```

Similar clauses in the definition of the SYS_LOAN set (at J) create an index to loans by their LID. There is also an interaction between the MODE IS INDEXED and LOCATION MODE of a record. If ORDER IS SORTED and MODE IS INDEXED are combined with a location mode of VIA SET, then not only is an index created on the specified key but the records are also stored in physical storage on that key (in IDMS). This creates a structure very much like a clustering index of DB2 or the cluster of ORACLE.

Figure 9-13 summarizes the design as a modified Bachman diagram showing both the logical and physical structure. As in a conventional Bachman diagram, record types are shown as rectangles and sets as lines between rectangles with an arrowhead at the many, or

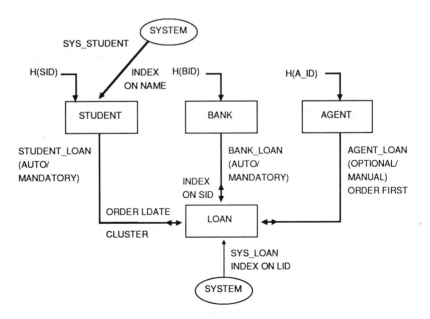

Fig 9-13 Summary of GSL Network Design as an Extended Bachman Diagram

member, end of the set. As per conventional practice, the rectangles and set lines are labeled with the name of the record type or set type, respectively. The following notations are used:

- H(*data item*) represents a hashed (CALC) location mode. For example, H(SID) indicates that the location mode for the STUDENT record is CALC on SID.
- The set lines show the storage and retention classes in ( ). For example, the set AGENT_LOAN shows (OPTIONAL/MANUAL).
- The set lines indicate the order of member records as ORDER *data item* or ORDER FIRST/LAST/PRIOR/NEXT as appropriate. For example, the STUDENT_LOAN set indicates ORDER LDATE.
- If the set mode is INDEXED, an entry INDEX ON *data item* is indicated. For example, the BANK_LOAN set shows INDEX ON SID. This also captures the ordering of members on this data item.
- If the location mode of a record is VIA SET, then the term CLUSTER appears on the set line. For example, since LOAN records are located via the STUDENT_LOAN set, that line is labeled CLUSTER.
- As in a conventional Bachman diagram, the many end of a set has an arrow pointing to the member record type. In addition, the presence of a reverse arrowhead—an arrowhead pointing towards the owner—at the many end indicates an owner pointer. All of the non-system sets were defined with OWNER LINKAGE, hence all have this reverse arrowhead.
- An oval labeled SYSTEM appears to denote system sets. SYSTEM appears twice for convenience in display.

Set Selection Clause

Our example schema has not shown one major clause of the definition of a set, the SELECTION clause. While this clause is part of the 1971 proposal and later CODASYL documents, it was omitted for two reasons: to avoid further "clutter" in the definition, and because while there is "set selection" in IDMS, there is only one choice, hence no specification is made.

SELECTION is a clause that tells the DBMS the criterion or method used to determine which set occurrence a member record belongs to. Usually the proper set is obvious or at least seems obvious. The STUDENT_LOAN set to which a loan belongs is determined by the value of SID in the loan. The BANK_LOAN set membership of a loan is determined by its BID value. But, suppose the LOAN record does not include the data items SID and/or BID. Then how is set membership determined? This is the role of the SELECTION criteria.

The different methods used to determine the proper set occurrence for a member record include the following:

1. SET SELECTION IS BY APPLICATION. This means that the application program must select the proper occurrence of a set prior to adding the record occurrence. (This is the only method available in IDMS.) If this method were used for, say, the STUDENT_LOAN set, it would mean that prior to storing a LOAN record the most recently (previously) accessed LOAN or STUDENT record must have been from the same set. Suppose that we want to add a loan for the student with SID = 4494. Then, the following steps would assure that the new loan appeared in the correct set:

    a. Input data for new LOAN (LID=333, LDATE=11/13/88,... SID=4494)

    b. Find STUDENT with SID = 4494

    c. Store the new LOAN record

We do not, however, have to access an owner record prior to storing the member. We could have also accessed any loan for this student at step b. Note that with this method of set selection, it is not necessary for the loan to contain the data item SID. The SID can always be determined from its owner.

2. SET SELECTION IS BY VALUE OF *data_item* IN *record*. Consider a specific example of this method used for the STUDENT_LOAN set:

```
SET SELECTION IS BY VALUE OF SID IN STUDENT
```

What this means is that rather than requiring access to a record prior to storing a new record, we simply establish the value of an attribute in the owner record type, for example, SID in STUDENT. The logic for a record addition would go something like this:

    a. Input data for new LOAN (LID=333, LDATE=11/13/88,... SID=4494).

    b. Move 4494 to SID in STUDENT.

    c. Store the new LOAN record.

Step b, setting the value of SID in STUDENT to 4494, is done internally—it does not create or update an SID value in STUDENT. Again, the SID does not need to be stored in LOAN.

3. SET SELECTION IS STRUCTURAL *data_item* IN *member* = *data_item* IN *owner*. Consider an example:

```
SET SELECTION IS STRUCTURAL SID IN LOAN = SID IN STUDENT
```

While this might sound a bit messy, it is the simplest method in terms of the logic for adding a record. All we must do is input data for, say, LOAN, then issue the DML STORE command. There is no need to access any records or even to move a data item into the user working area as with method 2. This method is also most similar to what we do in a relational DBMS—when a loan record is added, its relationship to both student and bank records is established through the values of the SID and BID attributes in the loan record.

In fact, the third method probably seems the most natural (especially after having studied the relational model). There are cases, however, in which the other methods have applicability. Consider, for example, the assignment of a collection agent to a loan deemed to be in default. There is no "natural" collection agent for a loan. To decide which agent to use we might look at the BID for the loan, then scan through agent records until we find one assigned loans from this bank. However, if that agent were already overloaded with work (that is, had a large number of loans assigned), we might continue looking until we found an agent assigned to loans from this bank who did not have an overload. By identifying the appropriate agent, we have also determined the appropriate occurrence of an AGENT_LOAN set for the loan in question. We would now execute an INSERT command that would place this loan in this agent's set.

Schema Summary

This concludes the discussion of the network schema definition. The important parts have been covered, but a tremendous amount of detail has been left out. Here are some of the additional capabilities and options that can be defined in the schema:

- **Data Privacy.** Privacy locks such as passwords may be established at the level of the database itself, in areas, records, data items, and sets. A privacy lock may be a password that is checked by the DBMS prior to allowing access, or it may be a procedure that is called. For example, access to a database could first require the user to respond to a series of questions put to the user by a database privacy procedure.
- **Data Integrity.** Specifications in the schema can control ranges of data item values and assure that owner records are not deleted while members remain (this is similar to referential integrity in the relational model).
- **Virtual Data Items.** Data items can be computed or derived from another record type. For example, a data item NAME could be defined for LOAN as coming from the (owner) STUDENT record. Thus, NAME would be stored only in STUDENT but would *appear* to also be stored in LOAN. This capability is similar to what can be done with views in relational DBMSs.
- **Search keys.** In addition to indexed sets, defining a search key for a set also constructs an index to members on that specified data item. The difference between an indexed set and a search key is subtle and beyond our scope.

The next section outlines the data manipulation language, and the final section returns to the data description language for external view or subschema definition.

Data Manipulation

The data manipulation language (DML), is the "steering wheel" of a DBMS. This is the language the programmer uses for queries and to modify the database. Retrieval commands include various FIND operations such as Find By Unique Key, Find First Occurrence Within a Set, Find Owner, etc. Updates consist of add, modify, and delete commands.

Before going into specifics of a network DML, we give a comparison of a network and a relational query. Recall that the network approach to data retrieval requires a record by record navigation through the structure. The DML of a relational DBMS by contrast, is a declarative language. For example, consider the following retrieval: "Get the names of students and bank identifiers for graduate students with loans from a bank of type, S&L." The DML for network and relational systems follows. The network DML does not follow the exact syntax but nonetheless captures the proper navigation.

- Network (Navigation) Retrieval

```
FIND FIRST STUDENT
    WHILE STUDENT EXISTS
        GET STUDENT
        IF SLEVEL = 5
            THEN FIND FIRST LOAN WITHIN STUDENT_LOAN SET
                WHILE LOAN EXISTS
                    GET LOAN
                    GET OWNER WITHIN BANK_LOAN SET
```

```
                           IF TYPE = 'S&L'
                               THEN PRINT NAME, BANK.BID
                           ENDIF
                           FIND NEXT LOAN WITHIN STUDENT_LOAN SET
                       ENDWHILE
            ENDIF
            FIND NEXT STUDENT
        ENDWHILE
```

· SQL (Relational) Retrieval

```
    SELECT NAME, BANK.BID
        FROM STUDENT, BANK, LOAN
        WHERE STUDENT.SID = LOAN.SID
            AND LOAN.BID = BANK.BID
            AND TYPE = 'S&L'
            AND SLEVEL = 5;
```

With a network DML, the user must tell the DBMS how to look for the desired data. This is typical of a procedural language. In the relational language example, the user states what he or she wants, as is typical of a non-procedural language. In the following subsections, several of the various forms of network DML statements are described and illustrated. We will begin, however, with the concept of currency.

Currency

The concept of currency is required to understand the operation of DML statements. The basic idea is that at any point in time there may be at most one occurrence of a record for each record type, set type, area, and the "run unit" or program. For example, if we just accessed the STUDENT record with SID = 9735, that record occurrence would be the *current of* STUDENT record type, the *current record* for the STUDENT_LOAN set, and the *current record* of the run unit. If the next access were to the first LOAN for that student then this loan would become *current of* LOAN record type, and would replace the STUDENT record as the *current of* run unit and *current of* STUDENT_LOAN set.

The following example illustrates the *current of* at each step of a series of database accesses using a GSL database with two bank records, five loan records, and three student records as shown in Figure 9–14b. For this example, bank IDs are capital letters (A, B), student IDs are digits (1, 2, 3) and loan IDs are identified by their bank ID, student ID, and lower-case letters (A1.a, A2.b, B1.a, B3.a, B3.b). The set names are abbreviated S_L for

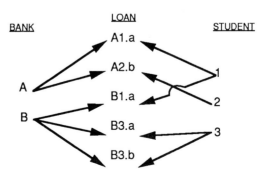

Fig 9-14a Sample Database with Record and Set Occurrences Shown

DML COMMAND	CURRENT RECORD OF.					
	Run Unit	STUDENT	LOAN	BANK	S_L Set	B_L Set
GET BANK						
With BID = A	BANK A	—	—	A	—	BANK A
GET FIRST LOAN						
IN B_L Set	LOAN A.1.a	—	A.1.a	A	LOAN A.1.a	LOAN A.1.a
GET STUDENT						
IN S_L Set	STUDENT 1	1	A.1.a	A	STUDENT 1	LOAN A.1.a
GET NEXT LOAN						
IN S_L Set	LOAN B.1.a	1	B.1.a	A	STUDENT 1	LOAN B.1.a

Fig 9-14b Currency Status Resulting from DML Statements

STUDENT_LOAN and B_L for BANK_LOAN. Again, for simplicity we use simplified DML statements.

FIND and GET

The first three GETs are straightforward: a bank is retrieved with BID = 'A', then its first loan is identified by 'A.1.a,' is retrieved. The STUDENT owner of this loan is retrieved next. Note how retrieval of either an owner or member of a set establishes the current record of that set. Now, look at the fourth GET, which retrieves the next loan within the STUDENT_LOAN set. Of course this changes the current record of the run unit and of the STUDENT_LOAN set. But it also changes the current of the BANK_LOAN set. At this point the current BANK and LOAN records are not from the same sets.

As you might imagine even from this simple example, keeping track of currency status when writing DML commands can get very complex. One way to visualize what is going on is to assume you have a token (marker) for each record type, set type, and run unit. Every time a database retrieval occurs, tokens will be moved. For example, when the fourth GET is executed in our example, the run unit token moves to loan B.1.a, the LOAN record token moves to LOAN B.1.a, the STUDENT_LOAN set token moves to LOAN B.1.a, and the BANK_LOAN token moves to LOAN B.1.a.

The physical disk locations of these token or currency indicators is available to the program. The physical disk location is required by one form of the DML FIND statement, described in the next section.

FIND Statement

There are several forms of the FIND statement to retrieve records that have location mode CALC or DIRECT, members of sets, records meeting specific conditions, and owners of sets. (Note: FIND identifies a record, and GET actually retrieves its values to the run unit. Thus, a FIND always precedes a GET.) Following are the more commonly used forms. For these examples we will use the specific record occurrences of Figure 9–15.

1. Access by hashing. If the LOCATION MODE of a record was declared CALC, then statements to retrieve the student with SID = 3749 would be:

```
SET STUDENT.SID = 3749
FIND CALC STUDENT
```

STUDENT Table

SID	NAME	SLEVEL	AGE	SZIP
9735	ALLEN	1	21	98101
4494	ALTER	2	19	98112
8767	CABEEN	5	24	98118
2368	JONES	4	23	98155
6793	SANDS	1	17	98101
3749	WATSON	5	29	98168

BANK Table

BID	BZIP	TYPE
FIDELITY	98101	MSB
SEAFIRST	98101	BANK
PEOPLES	98109	BANK
CAPITAL	98033	SL
HOME	98031	SL

LOAN Table

LID	LDATE	YEARS	INT_RATE	AMOUNT	SID	BID
27	15-SEP-85	5	8.5	1200	9735	HOME
78	21-JUN-86	5	7.75	1000	9735	PEOPLES
87	07-SEP-83	5	7.0	2000	9735	SEAFIRST
92	12-JAN-85	6	7.5	2100	4494	FIDELITY
99	15-JAN-86	6	9.0	2200	4494	FIDELITY
170	30-APR-83	6	6.5	1900	8767	PEOPLES
490	07-MAY-84	6	6.0	2500	3749	PEOPLES
493	24-JUN-85	7	7.5	3000	3749	PEOPLES

Fig 9-15 GSL Records

2. Finding the owner of the current record of a set.

```
FIND OWNER WITHIN STUDENT_LOAN
```

In this case, if the owner record is the current record of the set, nothing happens.

3. Finding the first and next members of a set.

```
FIND FIRST LOAN WITHIN STUDENT_LOAN
FIND NEXT LOAN WITHIN STUDENT_LOAN
```

These statements would usually be preceded by a statement to get the set's owner. For example, the sequence to retrieve all loans for the bank with BID = "PEOPLES" would be:

```
SET BANK.BID = "PEOPLES"
FIND CALC BANK
FIND FIRST LOAN WITHIN BANK_LOAN
WHILE LOAN EXISTS
      GET LOAN
      FIND NEXT LOAN WITHIN BANK_LOAN
ENDWHILE
```

In addition to being able to access the first and next members of a set, it is also possible to access the prior member, the last member, or the nth member. Note, however, that there are restrictions. For example, you can access the prior or last member of a set only if you have declared LINKED TO PRIOR in the schema. Again we see how the data definition and physical aspects of the database interact with the allowable retrieval statements.

4. FIND with condition. This is similar to FIND FIRST and FIND NEXT above, but screens the member record on one or more values.

```
FIND FIRST LOAN WITHIN STUDENT_LOAN USING BID IN LOAN
```

Suppose we want to retrieve all loans for "PEOPLES" but only for value of YEARS = 6.

```
SET BANK.BID = "PEOPLES"
FIND CALC BANK
SET LOAN.YEARS = 6
FIND FIRST LOAN WITHIN BANK_LOAN USING YEARS IN LOAN
WHILE LOAN EXISTS
      GET LOAN
      FIND NEXT LOAN WITHIN BANK_LOAN USING YEARS IN LOAN
ENDWHILE
```

5. FIND using database key. Every record has a unique database location called its *database key*. If you know the value of this key then it can be used in another form of the FIND. For example, suppose the variable ST_LOC stores the database key (the location) of a specific student record. Then that record may be retrieved using:

```
FIND STUDENT DB-KEY IS ST_LOC
```

You probably wonder how we would determine a record's database key. As noted in our discussion of currency, the storage locations of current records are available and the locations can be stored in a program variable. Here is an example that motivates the need for the database location of a record. Suppose we want to find all students who have loans at any of the banks with which student 9735 has a loan. If you look at the sample database, student 9735 has loans with HOME, PEOPLES, and SEAFIRST banks. The students who have loans at these banks include 8767 and 3749. Before we write the actual DML statements for this problem, consider the overall navigation required:

1. Retrieve student with SID 9735.
2. Find first loan for this student.
3. While loans in this set exist:
   a. Get owner bank.
   b. Find first loan for this bank.
   c. While loans in this set exist:
      1. Get STUDENT owner.
      2. Find next LOAN.
   d. Find next LOAN in the "9735" STUDENT_LOAN set.

The difficulty in this query is that when we perform step 3.b, retrieving the first loan for a specific bank, we lose track of our position in the set of loans for student 9735. Thus, step 3.d can't be executed. What we need to be able to do is to mark our position in two different occurrences of STUDENT_LOAN sets at the same time. This isn't possible. What we can do, however, is save our position in the "9735" set by storing the database key of that set's

LOAN record. Then we can restore our place prior to step 3.d. Here is the DML. Statements beginning with an exclamation point are comments.

```
SET STUDENT.SID = 9735
FIND STUDENT
FIND FIRST LOAN WITHIN STUDENT_LOAN
WHILE LOAN EXISTS
       !    Following stores the loan's database key in
                variable  LOAN_LOC
       ACCEPT LOAN_LOC FROM LOAN CURRENCY
       FIND OWNER WITHIN BANK_LOAN
       !   Note that the following statement is what loses
                our place within the loans for student 9735.
       FIND FIRST LOAN WITHIN BANK_LOAN
       WHILE LOAN EXISTS
             FIND OWNER WITHIN STUDENT_LOAN
             GET STUDENT
             !   (Display data from this student.)
             FIND NEXT LOAN WITHIN BANK_LOAN
       ENDWHILE
       !   Now we return to student 9735's loan and continue with
                the next Loan in that set.
       FIND LOAN DB-KEY IS LOAN_LOC
       FIND NEXT LOAN WITHIN STUDENT_LOAN
ENDWHILE
```

MODIFY, STORE, ERASE

The DML statements for record update, that is adding, deleting, and modifying data item values, are covered here. Record occurrences are added to the database by issuing a STORE statement. If the storage class was declared AUTOMATIC, the store command also links the record occurrence to the current owner of the set. The ERASE command is used to delete records from a database. The MODIFY statement is used to update data items within record occurrences.

MODIFY. Before data item values may be modified, the record must first be retrieved. For example, to change the age of student 9735 to 22:

```
SET STUDENT.SID = 9735
FIND CALC STUDENT
SET AGE = 22
MODIFY STUDENT
```

ERASE. Before a record may be erased, it must first be found. To delete the record for bank HOME:

```
SET BANK.BID = "HOME"
FIND CALC BANK
ERASE BANK
```

There are several alternative forms to ERASE that govern the impact on any records that are members of sets for which the identified record is the owner. For example, when bank HOME is deleted, what should become of any loan records in this bank's set? In fact, if any exist the ERASE will not succeed unless an alternative form of ERASE is used. If the form

ERASE...ALL is used, the owner, along with all members of its sets, is also erased. Furthermore, this deletion cascades: if a member is also an owner then its members will also be deleted. For example, if LOANs owned PAYMENT records, then deletion of a BANK record would delete not only all of its LOAN members but for each LOAN all of its PAYMENT records.

STORE. Record insertion is somewhat more involved because in addition to adding a record to the database, issues of connection to the appropriate set also arise. If the set selection clause simply specifies that set membership is determined by a value of a data item in the added record, or if the record is not a member of a set, then record addition is straightforward. To add a new LOAN record (LID = 888, LDATE = 11/29/88, ... SID = 2368, BID = "FIDELITY") we write:

```
!    Establish data item values for record; for example, by input
from terminal.
STORE LOAN
```

CONNECT, DISCONNECT, RECONNECT

The CONNECT and DISCONNECT statements provide a means of inserting record occurrences into as well as removing them from sets. This is accomplished by linking the current record type specified in the command to the set specified in the command as in:

```
CONNECT LOAN TO AGENT_LOAN
```

Disconnecting a record type removes the record from the set as in:

```
DISCONNECT LOAN FROM AGENT_LOAN
```

Before the CONNECT is issued, the appropriate set must be established as the current set. To assign a collection agent with A_ID = 8686 to a loan with LID 170 we write:

```
SET LOAN.LID = 170
!    Use the SYS_LOAN indexed set for direct access to
        the loan.
FIND FIRST LOAN IN SYS_LOAN SET USING LID
SET AGENT.A_ID = 8686
FIND CALC AGENT
CONNECT LOAN TO AGENT_LOAN
```

An important point to bear in mind here is that the effect, as well as the success or failure, of executing these commands is dependent upon specifications in the schema DDL MEMBER IS statement. You cannot, for example, DISCONNECT a record occurrence from a set if the retention clause is declared as MANDATORY in the schema.

To remove a record from a set occurrence, first find the record, then issue a DISCONNECT RECORD FROM SET command. To change a record from one set to another, the RECONNECT is used. Suppose that bank HOME sold loan 27 to bank FIDELITY. The following sequence will move the LOAN record from one bank's set to another.

```
SET LOAN.LID = 27
FIND FIRST LOAN WITHIN SYS_LOAN USING LID
SET BANK.BID = "FIDELITY"
FIND CALC BANK
RECONNECT LOAN WITHIN BANK_LOAN
```

The sequence above is important. If we first found bank FIDELITY, then found the loan, the current set would be that of the loan (i.e., HOME). The RECONNECT would have no impact on the loan's set membership.

DML Summary

A network DBMS data manipulation language represents a significant advance over the alternative of directly coding access and update statements at the file level. The DBMS automatically takes care of such things as linked list updates and index updates when records are added or deleted. Operations such as finding an owner record are also somewhat simpler than corresponding statements in most file level systems. (Note: We are not suggesting that a network DBMS represents only a small convenience to the programmer versus a file-level system. What we do claim is that for retrievals, in particular, the network DML itself is only somewhat simpler than file-level access statements. The advantages of a DBMS over a file approach in terms of data sharing, data independence, and relieving the programmer of many tasks, such as concurrency control, rollback/recovery, and so forth, are considerable.) Still, the network DML is quite complex. With its use, the problem remains of translating a statement of what is desired into specific record-by-record operations. Some situations require the user to maintain pointers (physical record locations) as illustrated by the FIND DB-KEY statement.

To add to the complexity of writing DML, there are often alternative ways to satisfy a particular query. There are at least two ways to navigate to find all loans for a particular student (say, 9735) with a particular bank (say, Peoples). These obvious alternatives are:

1. Access STUDENT with SID = 9735. Then, set BID = "PEOPLES" and execute FIND ... WITHIN STUDENT_LOAN USING BID statements to retrieve loans within the STUDENT-LOAN set that have the desired BID value.

2. Access BANK with BID = "PEOPLES". Then, set SID = 9735 and execute FIND ... WITHIN BANK_LOAN USING SID statements to retrieve loans within the BANK-LOAN set that have the desired SID.

Which method is better? Given our schema, the first method is probably better since it will result in searching through a relatively small set of loans. Furthermore, since we have clustering of LOANs by STUDENT, due to the VIA SET STUDENT_LOAN location mode of LOANs, the loans for a student can be expected to be in a single page. On the other hand, LOANs in the BANK-LOAN set are indexed on SID. Thus, the second method will only access those loans that meet both criteria (SID = 9735, BID = "PEOPLES").

The problem with the network approach is that the user, an application programmer, must decide which method is best. There is no query optimizer to make this decision. The programmer must be extremely familiar with the schema and the implications of such choices as MODE IS INDEX, LOCATION VIA SET, and so forth to make the choice. He or she must also have knowledge of the number of occurrences of records and selectivity of indexes in order to make an intelligent choice between DML alternatives. A good programmer may be able to write very efficient DML code. A poor programmer may make very expensive choices. Even the good programmer will take longer to write correct, efficient code using a network DML than using a language such as SQL.

The arguments over the relative merits of record-level procedural code and the specification-oriented relational DML are not unlike arguments that once raged over the merits of programming in the, at the time, new high-level languages such as FORTRAN or COBOL versus machine-level languages. If you know what you are doing, and take enough time at it, you can always write more efficient machine-level code. The question, of course, is whether the human time, and hence cost, is worth the savings in computer time. Today, it is a rare situation in which the hardware cost savings of coding in machine language compensate for the added people costs.

Most network DBMSs currently provide higher-level retrieval and report writer interfaces to their systems in order to make their databases more accessible to end-users. An important example of such extensions is described in a subsequent section on IDMS/R.

Subschema

A subschema may specify a subset of the database schema to be used by an application program. Thus, it may omit or restrict access to:

- Areas
- Sets
- Records
- Data items

Subschemas are defined for several reasons. As with views in relational systems, they simplify the user's logical image by eliminating unnecessary records, sets, and data items. They also provide a degree of security similar to that afforded by views. Network subschemas are, however, much more limited than relational views. They cannot, for example, generate perspectives that require the equivalent of SQL joins or "group-by" operations.

In some network implementations, a subschema may also make the following changes:

- Sets, records, and data items may be given different names.
- Data item types may be changed. This can be very useful for situations in which the programming language does not support a data type used by the database.
- The order of data items within a record may be altered.

Here is an example subschema explained below:

```
ADD SUBSCHEMA NAME IS BANK&LOAN
    OF SCHEMA NAME GSL.
ADD RECORD BANK
    ELEMENT BID
    ELEMENT TYPE.
ADD RECORD LOAN
    ELEMENT LID
    ELEMENT AMOUNT
    ELEMENT INT_RATE.

ADD SET BANK_LOAN.
ADD SET SYS_LOAN.
```

This subschema includes only the BANK and LOAN records, and only the specified data items (elements) of those records. The set between the two records, BANK_LOAN, is also included, as is the SYS_LOAN set, which provides an index to loans on SID.

Extensions: OnLine Query and IDMS/R

With the advent of relational DBMs, some vendors have attempted to breathe new life into existing network products by adding relational features. Considering the commercial entrenchment of network systems, this is helpful for existing customers as well as vendors. The IDMS product provides an ad hoc query language with limited relational-like features called OnLine Query, or OLQ. There is also a batch-oriented report writer called CULPRIT. Furthermore, the IDMS product has evolved into IDMS/R or IDMS Relational with the addition of two features called the Logical Record Facility (LRF) and the Automatic System Facility (ASF). These two extensions provide an additional degree of relational-like capabilities to the underlying network database. Overviews of OLQ, LRF, and ASF follow.

OnLine Query

This retrieval language has a syntax similar to SQL but is limited to operations on a single file (record type). Joins are not possible. We will not describe this language in detail. The following retrieval example will give you its flavor. We want all loans of AMOUNT >= 2000 for banks with type = "BANK". The following steps are performed:

1. Retrieve the first BANK record with TYPE >= "BANK."

   ```
   GET FIRST SEQUENTIAL BANK RECORD WHERE TYPE = "BANK"
   ```

2. Retrieve all loans for this bank with AMOUNT >= 2000. We will assume that the previous GET FIRST statement has just been executed, which establishes a value for BID.

   ```
   GET ALL LOAN RECORDS BELONGING TO THIS BANK
       WHERE AMOUNT >= 2000
   ```

3. Retrieve the next bank with TYPE = "BANK."

   ```
   GET NEXT SEQUENTIAL BANK RECORD WHERE TYPE = "BANK"
   ```

Step 2 may now be repeated for each entry of step 3.

Logical Record Facility

The LRF creates an interface between the IDMS network database and the user, which provides a relation-like view to the user. A specific view is defined by the database administrator, by writing what is essentially standard network DML statements to define the view. The user, actually an applications programmer, employs a "friendlier" DML to access and manipulate the database. For example, suppose a given program needs a view of the GSL database called LOAN_BY_SID, which includes only the LOAN records. The program retrieves LOAN records by SID which meets certain conditions such as AMOUNT greater than some value.

Once the view is defined (see below), the programmer accesses records by using the LRF data manipulation language. To retrieve all loans for a student with SID = 4494 where YEARS = 6, the programmer would write LRF/DML statements such as:

```
OBTAIN FIRST LOAN WHERE SID = 4494 AND YEARS = 6
WHILE LOAN EXISTS
    OBTAIN NEXT LOAN WHERE SID = 4494 AND YEARS = 6
ENDWHILE
```

This DML would be translated into record-by-record navigation, based on code written by the DBA for this particular view, to generate the desired (external level) records. The view definition code specifies the navigation necessary to generate the view record. For this example, the navigation requires first accessing the STUDENT record with given SID, then one by one accessing LOAN records using the FIND ... USING AMOUNT version of the FIND statement.

While this provides a degree of simplification for the programmer, the burden is shifted to the DBA to write the supporting definition. Furthermore, the options available to the user in terms of the form of LRF/DML statements are limited by the allowable options written into the view definition. Our example above was for access to loans by SID and YEARS. If the user also wanted to be able to access all loans with given values for BID and YEARS, different code would be required in the view definition, since different access paths would be used. In defining the view the DBA establishes determines the alternative LRF/DML options open to the user.

The LRF does not allow the DBA to create views that include all equivalents of relational operations. While joins can be coded by the DBA, a view that requires a self-join is not allowed. Union and difference operations are also not possible. Records cannot be reordered, and duplicates cannot be eliminated in the view definition.

The user's LRF/DML is even more limited. Essentially, all the user may do is operate on what appears to be a single file. That is, a user cannot perform a join—the join must have been coded into the view definition by the DBA. Most important, the user is constrained to those operations for which DML navigation has been explicitly created by the DBA. By contrast, given a relational view the user is able to treat it more or less like a base table—almost any form of SQL *retrieval* statement is permissable on a base table is also permissable on a view.

Automatic System Facility

The ASF permits the definition and manipulation of new databases that look something like relational databases. The ASF also allows existing CODASYL databases to be redefined and manipulated as if, to some degree, they were relational databases. ASF sits on top of the base IDMS software. Unlike the Logical Record Facility, databases defined in ASF do not require the DBA to code procedures for the translation of the underlying network structure into relations. Rather, ASF *automatically* generates these procedures based on the database definition.

Three types of tables can be defined using ASF: basic stored tables that are essentially like base tables in relational systems; derived stored tables; and views that are similar to relational views. A derived stored table is quite similar to a view except that it exists physically and must have data stored into it by issuing a POPULATE command and be updated by issuing a REPOPULATE command.

Query and report generation for ASF-created relations are supported by using either LRF/DML commands, the OnLine Query system, or the CULPRIT report writer. In all cases, since these "languages" are limited to record-at-a-time operations (LRF) and to operations on a single table, joins must have been predefined as views.

When ASF is used to define a basic stored table, a forms-based language is used to define the table name, its data items, and their types. Indexes can also be specified for data items. The definition is then translated by ASF to create a record-type definition and indexed-set definitions. ASF also automatically generates an LRF view with access procedures that make use of the indexes. Thus, the LRF data manipulation commands may be used against an ASF-defined relation.

ASF view definitions can now be written referencing the basic stored tables. Allowable operations include selection, projection, and (most) join operations. The ASF translates the view into an LRF view, generating access procedures. The user may now operate on the view using LRF/DML commands, OLQ, or CULPRIT.

Conclusion

A good way to summarize the network approach is by comparison to the relational approach. The following table evaluates and summarizes the two alternatives on a number of features.

Feature	Network	Relational
Structure	Records with explicit connection paths.	Flat files with implicit connections.
Logical/physical interdependence	Many physical aspects included in conceptual (logical) schema.	Quite independent.
Data Manipulation and DML characteristics	Record-by-record "navigation." Procedurally oriented. Not closed. Embedded language only.	Relation at a time. Specification oriented. "Closed"; result of operation always a relation. Embedded and UFI languages very similar.
Independence of programs to database design changes	Low to moderate; many changes require recoding, recompilation.	High; most database redefinitions result in automatic recompilation (if needed).
Suitability for:		
Transaction proccessing	Very good — excellent performance	Good—improving. Performance not up to network level.
Ad hoc queries & report writing	Poor; add-on query & reporting languages help somewhat.	Excellent.
Time/cost for database design	High; changes are expensive to incorporate (require recoding).	Moderate; subsequent alterations have minimal impact.
Application development time/cost	Lower than file approach.	Low; even lower with 4GLs. Easy to prototype.
Miscellaneous	Developed largely without theoretical underpinnings; or — "evolved."	Based on mathematical theory of relations.
Future	Virtually no new DBMS since late 70s.	SQL standard being adopted by DBMS vendors for micro-to mainframe-level systems.

Keep in mind that compared to our discussion of relational systems, many more details of network systems have been omitted. The approach for network systems did not have the objective of providing you with enough information to be able to use a vendor's system to design and manipulate a database. Rather, the goal was to provide a "generic" introduction to the characteristics and features of these systems. To be able to use a network system you will probably need to refer to the vendor's manuals or to specially prepared training documents. Vendors' manuals also provide excellent detailed design advice since the software vendor has a vested interest in user-satisfaction with his product.

While it is evident that we are not enamored of network systems, you should not be led to believe that they will soon disappear. There are two good reasons why they will be around for some time. One, of course, is the significant performance advantage they currently enjoy over relational systems. For high transaction-rate applications, a relational system may simply not be a viable alternative. The other reason for their persistence is the enormous number of application programs that use network DBMSs.

Organizations with an investment in network databases are taking one of three approaches to the relational approach: (1) do nothing, at least for the present; (2) use both network and relational DBMSs, bringing up new databases as relational (if the DBMS performance is satisfactory), but continuing to operate existing network-oriented applications, possibly with gradual conversion; (3) wholesale conversion of existing databases and application code to relational systems. Many organizations that are taking approaches 2 and 3 are, however, installing relational DBMSs for decision support. Data is periodically extracted from their network databases and loaded into relational databases to support nonroutine query and reporting activities. Obviously, this incurs considerable additional expense in terms of DBMS software purchase or license fees and in storage costs. But it does capitalize on the relative advantages of both types of systems: network for routine transaction processing, relational for ad hoc information needs.

Questions and Problems

Questions

1. What is the meaning of each of the following acronyms: CODASYL, DBTG, ANSI? What role did each of these organizations have in the development of the network standard?

2. What version (or vintage) of the standard has typically been implemented?

3. Why have subsequent improvements to the network standard been largely "academic" efforts? For example, why haven't software developers implemented the recent ANSI standard?

4. On what types of systems (mainframe, mini, PC) are network DBMSs usually found?

5. What is the logical construct for representing relationships between record types?

6. Describe two physical methods commonly used by network DBMSs for "connecting" related records.

7. What are two reasons why the performance of network DBMSs is better than relational systems?

8. What are the differences in the purpose of schema and subschema DDLs?

9. What are the major differences in the data manipulation languages of network and relational systems?

10. Describe and give an example or two of a data aggregate.

11. What is the difference between a set type and a set occurrence? Give examples.

12. What distinguishes a hierarchy from a network structure?

13. How are many-to-many relationships modeled in a network DBMS that is limited to sets with only a single owner record?

14. Suppose there were no such thing as a SYSTEM set. How could you achieve the same effect?

15. What are the most commonly used location modes?

16. What location mode is typically used for a record type that is a member of a set in which a common query retrieves an occurrence of that set?

17. Which location mode(s) assures essentially single-disk access to a record of a given unique key?

18. Describe, by example, the difference between adding a record to the database and inserting a record into a set.

19. How do you create a physical organization for (say) student records that is more or less like a primary B-tree in that records are physically ordered on SID and indexed?

20. Describe the concept of *currency*, using an example.

21. Where does the FIND using a database key come in handy?

Problems

1. A network version of the GSL database has three set types defined between STUDENT and LOAN. They are LOAN_APPL, which contains loans a student has applied for but not received; ACTIVE_LOAN, which contains loans on which there is a balance due; and CLOSED_LOAN, which contains those loans that have been paid off. How would this classification of loans be represented in a relational model?

2. Consider an employee database represented as relations with attributes EMP# and MGR#. EMP# is the employee's unique identifier and MGR# is the employee number of his manager. An example of several rows from this relation appears below. The null entry for employee 10 indicates that this person has no manager (that is, he or she is the president).

EMP#	MGR#
10	—
12	10
13	10
15	10
18	13
20	13

Define record(s) and set(s) to represent this data and give an occurrence diagram (that is, show all record occurrences and links between records).

3. Refer to the GSL schema defined in this chapter to answer the following questions:

a. Suppose that there is frequent access to AGENT by NAME. What changes/additions should be made to the schema?

b. Data on schools is added with school name, an identifier, location, type (for example, two-year, four-year, university, trade-technical), enrollment, accreditation, etc. In addition, an indication is made for each student of that school in which he or she is enrolled. Assume that a student may be enrolled in at most one school at a time. Make the appropriate additions and changes to the schema.

c. Suppose that a student may be enrolled in more than one school at a time and that, in addition, if enrollment changes we want to keep a historical record of all schools in which the student was enrolled, including the beginning and ending dates of enrollment. Modify your answer to part b accordingly.

d. A DEGREE record type is added with data items SID, DEGREE TYPE (for example, BA, BS, MBA, ...), YEAR AWARDED, MAJOR, and SCHOOL. A set called ST_DEG is created with STUDENT as owner, DEGREE as member. Would "owner linkage" be needed for this set? Why or why not?

e. Suppose we have identified a relatively small group of students (for example, 1 percent of the database) who we feel are apt to default on one or more of their loans. What database structure would be appropriate so that we could quickly access students in this set? Describe added record and set types and all relevant characteristics of these records and sets.

f. Write DML for the following queries:

   (1) Retrieve all STUDENT records for the person with NAME = "JOHNSON, MARY"

   (2) Retrieve the student with SID = 4494 and all of his or her loans.

   (3) Retrieve all students with LEVEL = 5 and loans they have with BID = "FIRST BANK".

   (4) Agent 007 wants a report that lists each student who holds a loan on which this agent is trying to collect. Write the DML to generate this report.

g. Write the DML to reduce the amount of every loan with SID = 9735 by $100.

h. Write the DML to assign all loans with SID = 3749 to agent 816.

i. A student has an average of three loans. Estimate the number of accesses to retrieve all loans for a given SID value.

j. Describe the alternative navigation paths to find all loans for students with LEVEL = 1 from banks with TYPE = "MSB." Which of the alternatives do you feel would be best and why?

k. Is it possible for a loan with SID = 4494 to be current of the STUDENT_LOAN set while the student with SID = 9735 is current of the STUDENT record type? Why or why not?

l. Consider the IDMS/R Logical Record Facility. Outline what would be required by the DBA to create a "view" of all students who have one or more loans that have been assigned to an agent.

4. This problem requires a network database design for a personnel/project application. The company performs specialized engineering design for large aerospace firms. Data on each employee and on an employee's education, positions held, and salary (over time) can be described by the following:

   a. Employee "master" record data with employee name, SSN, birthdate, employee number, address, marital status.

   b. Degree (such as B.A., M.S., Ph.D., ...), date, school, major. An employee may have several degrees.

   c. Position data: Each person is assigned to a single position in one department of the company at any point in time. Historical records on positions held are to be maintained. Specific data includes the identity of the department (such as design, engineering, drafting, data processing) in which the person works, the name of the position (such as clerk A, typist B, ad. asst., sr. engineer, systems analyst, personnel director), and the start and end dates for the position and department. If a person changes either position or department (or both), a new record is generated.

   d. Salary data gives the salary amount and the effective dates (start and end) of the salary. Each change in salary (or a hire) generates a new record.

   The other major set of data relates to projects. A project contains a project ID, a brief description (for example, A27 nose-gear brake design), budgeted project amounts for labor and material, and the start and (estimated) end dates of the project. In addition, each project has an employee who is assigned responsibility for the project: the "project manager."

   Finally, for cost accounting purposes, data is collected and aggregated to show the total dollar charge by each employee to each project for each day. An employee may work on several projects on a given day, and a project will (typically) have several employees making charges to it each day.

   a. Draw Bachman diagrams to illustrate the record and set types. Then write a network schema defining record types and set types. At this point, do not include location modes, set order, or set linking methods.

   b. Accesses to employee master data is by employee number. Access to employee degree, salary, position, and department information is first through the employee master, then to the desired data. For salary, position, and department data, the current status information is usually what is wanted (for example, an employee's present or last salary). Indicate location modes and set orders for your records containing this data.

   c. All of the charge data for one project is frequently accessed to determine the "to-date" labor charges. What location mode does this suggest for your record containing charges?

   d. If there are frequent accesses to employee data by employee name, what should be created?

   e. Based on your design, create an extended Bachman diagram such as is shown in Figure 9–13.

   f. Write DML code for the following assuming a location mode of CALC on project ID for project and the location modes you chose above.

(1) Retrieve employee master and degree data for employee #8731.

(2) Retrieve all employees with the name "BAKER,THOMAS."

(3) Retrieve employee master data and all charge records for employee # 7632 for charges made to the project with ID = "CD490."

(4) Retrieve master and degree data for all employees who have made charges to project with ID = "HDY88."

(5) Identify all projects for which total labor charges exceed the budgeted amount for labor (tough).

(6) Consider the problem of identifying all charges made by employees who hold an MBA on projects begun in 1988. Describe two (or more) alternative navigation paths. You do not need to code the DML.

References

American National Standard Institute Database Committee. *Draft Proposed Network Database Language NDL.* Document X3H2-1984-100. New York: ANSI Inc.

Bradley, J. *Introduction to Data Base Management in Business.* 2d ed. New York: Holt, Rinehart and Winston, 1987.

Cardenas, Alfonso. *Data Base Management Systems.* 2d ed. Boston: Allyn and Bacon, Inc., 1985.

CODASYL, 1971. *Data Base Task Group Report.* Assoc. for Computing Machinery, New York.

Cohen, Leo J. *Data Base Management Systems.* Performance Development Corp. and Q.E.D. Information Sciences, Inc., 1973.

Cullinet Software Inc. IDMS/R Database Design, Revision 0.0, Release 10.0. August, 1986.

Date, C. J. *An Introduction to Database Systems.* 3d ed. Reading, Mass.: Addison-Wesley Publishing Co., 1981.

_____. *An Introduction to Database Systems.* Vol. 1. 4th ed. Reading, Mass.: Addison-Wesley Publishing Co., 1985.

McFadden, Fred, and Hoffer, Jeffery. *Database Management.* 2d ed. Menlo Park, Calif.: The Benjamin/Cummings Publishing Co., Inc., 1988.

Teorey, T., and Fry, James P. *Design of Database Structures.* Englewood Cliffs, N. J.: Prentice-Hall, 1982.

U.S. Department of Commerce, National Bureau of Standards. *CODASYL Data Description Language, Journal of Development.* June 1973.

Wiederhold, Gio. *Database Design.* 2d ed. New York: McGraw-Hill, 1983.

10 A Hierarchical System: IMS

Introduction to Hierarchical Systems and IMS

A hierarchy is defined as a database model in which each and every record type has only one parent (that is, only one owner type in CODASYL). Of course, the record type at the top of the hierarchy, the "root" of the tree, has no owner. The three record types—STUDENT, LOAN, and PAYMENT—of the GSL model form a hierarchy. STUDENT is the parent (owner) of LOAN, and LOAN is the parent of PAYMENT. A given record occurrence, say LOAN with LID = 87, has only a single occurrence of a single parent record type, specifically the STUDENT record with SID = 9735. A STUDENT record has no parent; it is the root record type. A hierarchical database is made up of many trees. In this example, each tree has a STUDENT record as the root. A given student with all of his of her LOAN records and all of the PAYMENT records for these loans is a single occurrence of a tree of records. (Peek ahead at Figure 10–1 for an example.)

In contrast to relational and CODASYL models, hierarchies specify the conceptual and storage models in a single schema. Another difference is that there are no accepted design standards such as those that have been developed for network and relational systems. Since there are few hierarchical DBMSs, this is not a real problem.

Hierarchical models are simple to understand if the underlying data structure is hierarchical. But as the complexity of the structure increases it becomes increasingly difficult to map into a hierarchical model. Understanding hierarchical systems and becoming proficient at designing databases for them is significantly more difficult than achieving the same level of skill with relational systems.

At present, there are few hierarchical DBMSs, due mainly to the inherent limitations of this data model. The most widely used hierarchical DBMS is IBM's IMS, Information Management System, which is the system described in this chapter. IMS was introduced in the late 1960s, having been initially developed to assist North American Aviation in its management of the massive amounts of data needed for the Apollo moon program. IMS runs on medium-to-large IBM machines such as the earlier System 360/370 series and, later, the 303x, 308x and 3090 computers, under operating systems such as OS/MFT, OS/MVT, OS/VIS, OS/VS2, or OS/MVS. The basic IMS version, called "DB," is a database-only version, designed to operate in a batch-processing environment. A data communications feature, "DC," is available to support online multiuser processing from local or remote terminals.

As you will see, IMS is not limited to representing data that has a strict hierarchical structure. It is able to represent somewhat more complex structures (for example, most network structures) by allowing multiple physical hierarchical databases to be combined through a logical database definition. This gives IMS a partial network capability.

The reason for studying the hierarchical model is its prevalence. The dominance of IBM in the computer marketplace and the long history of IMS have resulted in the existence of

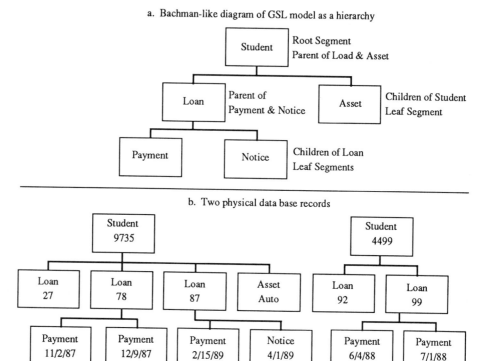

Fig 10-1   GSL as Tree

many IMS databases. And due to the massive investment in software using IMS databases, we can expect to see IMS around for many years to come. After rumors several years ago that IBM would discontinue support for the product, they subsequently introduced enhancements, including the ability to query IMS through SQL.

While we feel it is important to introduce IMS, our treatment of this system is much less ambitious than for relational and network systems. IMS is easily the most complex DBMS in existence. Its documentation runs to several thousand pages. We will be content in this book with outlining the main features, capabilities, and limitations of IMS. The presentation will stop considerably short of providing the details needed to design and use an IMS database, leaving that to subsequent courses or on-the-job training.

The Hierarchical Data Model

A hierarchical data model is a tree structure in which nodes representing record types, in CODASYL terminology, are arranged in a hierarchy. In the IMS model, the proper term for a node is *segment*. The term *record* has a different meaning as is seen below. The top segment of a tree is called the *root*. Figure 10–1 is a Bachman-type diagram of a hierarchical database using the GSL as an example. The model has been enhanced with two added segment types. NOTICE contains data that notifies a student of some deficiency or problem with a loan, such as notice of payment past due. ASSET describes a physical asset such as an automobile that the student owns. The IMS term for a hierarchical structure is *physical database* (PDB).

As seen from part a of the figure, the root segment may be related to one or more segments at a lower level. In our example, STUDENT is the root segment. The root is called the "parent" of the lower level segments, which are called "children." LOAN and ASSET are children of STUDENT. Parents and children are connected by "branches." LOAN in turn is a parent to PAYMENT. The lowest-level segments, those with no children, are called "leaves"—PAYMENT and ASSET in the example.

Part b of the figure shows occurrences of two trees: one with the root segment SID = 9735, the other with the root segment SID = 4494. All of the children, grandchildren, and so on of a parent segment are called its "descendants," or "dependent segments." Similarly, the parents, grandparents, and so forth of a parent are referred as its "ancestors." Multiple children of a parent are called "siblings." The occurrence of a root segment and all of its dependent segments is called a *physical database record*, or PDBR, in IMS terminology. Thus, an IMS segment type is comparable to a network DBMS record type or a base table in a relational DBMS. The IMS physical database record has no comparable unit in a network or relational data model.

You will have noted that there is no BANK segment in the example. Since BANK is a parent to LOAN, but not a parent to STUDENT, nor is STUDENT a parent to BANK, the BANK segment cannot be added to the hierarchy without introducing redundancy. That is, we have a situation in which the natural data structure is a network: one record type (or segment), LOAN, has two parent types, STUDENT and BANK. There are two ways to handle the addition of BANK data to the model. One is to allow redundancy; the other is to define two physical databases and link them as a logical database. The first method is described here; multiple physical databases are discussed in a later section.

There are several ways in which BANK data can be added and still maintain a pure hierarchy, although all of these methods will result in redundant storage. Figure 10–2 shows one alternative (which illustrates only the STUDENT, BANK, and LOAN segments for simplicity). This first method inserts BANK between STUDENT and LOAN. This means that data for BANK must be redundantly stored, as seen from the two physical database records. Data for PEOPLES occurs twice: once under STUDENT 9735 and again under student 3749. Of course, this redundant storage is not only expensive in terms of space costs, but also leads to potential inconsistencies and requires extra disk accesses to update BANK records.

Another way to include BANK is to place it above STUDENT as shown in Figure 10–3. Again, redundancy occurs, this time in storage of student segments. This is probably better because it will result in less redundancy—many students will have only a single loan or will have all of their loans with one bank.

A third approach is to include STUDENT data in each occurrence of a LOAN—join the STUDENT and LOAN segments. The hierarchy then has only two segments, BANK and STUDENT_LOAN. This of course, results in considerable redundancy. Clearly, another approach is to include BANK data in each LOAN, creating a BANK_LOAN segment hierarchically under STUDENT. Obviously, none of these methods is very satisfying.

Similar to a network, the access paths in a hierarchy are implied by the data structure itself. The data manipulation language navigates through the tree following the paths

a. BANK segment added to GSL model resulting in redundant storage of BANK data.

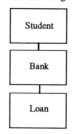

b. Example physical data base records illustrating redundant occurrences of BANK segments.

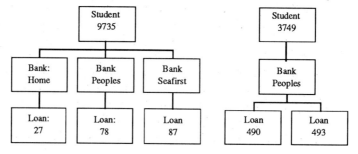

Fig 10-2   Redundant BANK

a. BANK segment added to GSL model resulting in redundant storage of STUDENT segment.

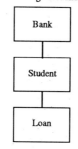

b. Example physical data base records illustrating redundant occurrences of STUDENT segment.

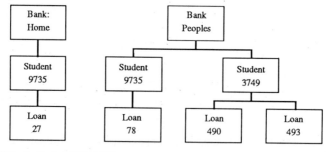

Fig 10-3   Redundant STUDENT

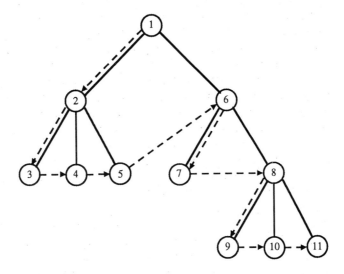

Fig 10-4 Order of segments in a hierarchy is top to bottom, left to right. The dashed lines show the hierarchical sequence linked list which captures both the hierarchical relationships and the segment ordering. Note that the solid lines do not exist as pointers.

between nodes. The order of the segments is called the hierarchical sequence and is illustrated in Figure 10-4. However, other paths can be defined, including child-to-parent paths, and secondary indexes that allow direct entry to a child record without access to the parent.

Data Definition Language

The *database description* (DBD) specifies the logical and physical schema of a hierarchical database. This is done by naming each segment in the database and then naming the parent of each segment. In addition, the fields of each segment are also defined. The statements in a DBD describe the hierarchical arrangement of segment types.

The following statement types are used to define an IMS database:

- DBD   Names the database
- ACCESS   Identifies the file access method used (see section "Physical Structure")
- SEGM   Names a physical segment type
- FIELD   Names and defines the fields of a segment type

Example Database Definition

Figure 10–5 defines the GSL database as shown in Figure 10–1—that is, with segments STUDENT, LOAN, ASSET, PAYMENT, and NOTICE.

The first line of the DBD names the database:

```
DBD  NAME=GSL
```

```
DBD      NAME=GSL
SEGM     NAME=STUDENT, BYTES=196
FIELD    NAME=(SID, SEQ), BYTES=4, TYPE=P, START=1
FIELD    NAME=SNAME, BYTES=30, START=5
FIELD    NAME=SLEVEL, BYTES=1, START =35
FIELD    NAME=ADDRESS, BYTES=50, START=36
FIELD    NAME=STREET, BYTES=25, START=36
FIELD    NAME=CITY_ST, BYTES=20, START=61
FIELD    NAME=ZIP, BYTES=5, START=81
. . .
SEGM     NAME=LOAN, PARENT=STUDENT, BYTES=64
FIELD    NAME=(LID,SEQ), TYPE=P, BYTES=4, START=1
FIELD    NAME=L_DATE, TYPE=P, BYTES=3, START=5
FIELD    NAME=INT_RATE, TYPE =P, BYTES=5, START=8
. . .
SEGM     NAME=ASSET, PARENT=STUDENT, BYTES=90
FIELD    NAME=(A_ID,SEQ), TYPE=P, BYTES=2, START=1
FIELD    NAME=A_DESCR, BYTES=40, START=3
. . .
SEGM     NAME=PAYMENT, PARENT=LOAN, BYTES=45
FIELD    NAME=(P_DATE,SEQ), TYPE=P, BYTES=3, START=1
FIELD    NAME=P_AMOUNT, TYPE=P, BYTES=6, START=4
FIELD    NAME=P_TYPE, BYTES=8, START=10
. . .
SEGM     NAME=NOTICE, PARENT=LOAN, BYTES=103
FIELD    NAME=(N_DATE,SEQ), TYPE=P, BYTES=3, START=1
FIELD    NAME=MESG, BYTES=100, START=4
```

Fig 10-5   GSL DBD. Definition of the physical database for the GSL model of Figure 10–1.

Succeeding lines describe either segments (records) or fields. Each segment except the first must specify a parent using the PARENT= clause. Since STUDENT is the root segment, no PARENT clause appears. Subsequent segments such as LOAN include parent definition (PARENT=STUDENT) to indicate its position in the hierarchy. Each segment also specifies the number of bytes in the segment using the BYTES= clause. (We have chosen realistic segment sizes, which are considerably longer than those required by our example GSL segments.) While variable segment lengths are possible, fixed-length segments are generally used. Up to fifteen hierarchical levels are allowed and a maximum of 255 segment types. Segment declarations are listed in hierarchical sequence, that is, from top to bottom and left to right.

Field definitions specify the number of bytes in the field using the BYTES= clause, the starting location of the field within the record using the START= clause, and field type with the TYPE= clause. Valid types and code include character (C), which is the default and packed decimal (P). For example, the SID field in STUDENT is defined as a four-byte packed-decimal field starting at the first byte position. SNAME is defined as starting in the next byte position, 5, with length 30. Since no TYPE specification is given, it is a character string.

A unique sequence field for each segment is also specified by adding a comma and the SEQ clause following a field name. For STUDENT, this is the SID field. Sequence fields determine the ordering of segment occurrences within one occurrence of a parent. This field is sometimes referred to as the *key field,* or *primary field,* of a segment type.

It is not necessary to describe all of the fields of a segment in the DBD. Only those fields that will be accessed using the data manipulation language search statement need to be described, although the remaining bytes need to be accounted for in some way. Note also that field descriptions may overlap. In the STUDENT segment we have defined a field ADDRESS of 50 bytes, beginning at 36. Within this field there are three *subfields*: STREET, of 25 bytes beginning at 36; CITY_ST, of 20 bytes, starting at byte 61; and ZIP, of 5 bytes, starting at 81. This is similar to the data aggregate of CODASYL.

External Logical Database Definition

The concept and definition of the external level will be addressed from two perspectives. First, an *external view* (not an IMS term) can be defined on a single physical database. This is the simpler situation and will be described first. It is also possible to define a logical database that combines two or more physical databases. This is a more complex situation and is discussed in the subsequent section.

External View on a Single PDB

The programmer's or user's view of a physical database is defined in what is called the *program communication block,* or PCB. The PCB defines the subset of segments, called *sensitive segments,* known to the application. The subset of segments can include any sub-tree of segments in the hierarchy—that is, if a segment is included, all of its ancestor segments (parent, grandparent, and so on) are also included. In addition, the PCB may specify a subset of the fields of the sensitive segments.

Here is an example. Suppose a program needs to deal with only the STUDENT and PAYMENT segments and with only a subset of the fields within each of these segments. The PCB would therefore need to specify that STUDENT, LOAN, and PAYMENT were sensitive, and indicate those fields that were required. The LOAN segment must be specified because it falls between STUDENT and PAYMENT in the hierarchy. However, aside from its inclusion in the PCB,the user is able to more or less ignore its presence. This defines the user's logical database: segment types STUDENT and PAYMENT. An occurrence of a STUDENT segment and all of its PAYMENT segments constitutes the view's logical record.

The statements used in a PCB are similar to those used in the definition of the physical database:

- · PCB   Names the DBD (database description, which defines the relevant physical database) on which the LDB is defined
- · SENSEG   Names a sensitive segment and its parent, and indicates processing options
- · SENFLD   Names the sensitive fields
- · PSBGEN   Names the PSB (explained below) and indicates the language used in processing the PCB

A database subset defined by a PCB must share the same root segment as the underlying DBD and be hierarchical. This is accomplished by specifying sensitive segments in hierarchical order, just as in the DBD. In addition, the types of processing allowed for a segment type are defined in the SENSEG statement. Processing options include G (Get), I (Insert), R (Replace, or modify), and D (Delete). For a segment that falls between two sensitive segments in the hierarchy but is not needed by the applications, processing option K is used.

The following PCB is for an application that processes STUDENT and PAYMENT segments but has no knowledge of ASSET or NOTICE segments and only "passing" knowledge of LOAN. Assume that the application needs to get and modify STUDENT records, hence processing options are G and R. Read-only access is required to PAYMENT.

```
PCB      TYPE=DB, DBDNAME=GSL, KEYLEN=11
SENSEG   NAME=STUDENT, PROCOPT=GR
SENSEG   NAME=LOAN, PARENT=STUDENT, PROCOPT=K
SENSEG   NAME=PAYMENT, PARENT=LOAN, PROCOPT=G
SENFLD   NAME=P_DATE, START=1
SENFLD   NAME=P_TYPE, START=4
PSBGEN   LANG=COBOL, PSBNAME=ST_PAY
```

The PCB clause TYPE=DB specifies that the database is of type DB, as opposed to DB/DC (database/data communication). The KEYLEN=11 clause requires a little explanation. The application program must provide space for the fully concatenated key of the segments in the LDB. The key of STUDENT (SID) requires 4 bytes, LID requires 4 bytes, and P_DATE requires 3 bytes for a total key length of 11 bytes. This concatenated key is available to the application program and identifies exactly where the DML navigation has taken it. For example, if the key value (translated from packed decimal into characters with / inserted between keys from different segments) is 4494/99/880604, we know that the current PAYMENT record has a P_DATE of 6/4/88 and that PAYMENT has a LOAN parent with LID=99, which in turn has a STUDENT parent with SID=4494.

The first SENSEG statement in this PCB names the root segment and indicates processing of retrievals (G for get) and update (R for replace or modify). Since no specifications of sensitive fields follow, all STUDENT fields are sensitive. The SENSEG for LOAN indicates a processing option of K, which means that while LOAN is in the hierarchy, it has "key sensitivity" only—no fields are needed from LOAN. The user may search on LOAN (for example, to specify a value of LID) but field values from LOAN will not be passed to the program.

The SENSEG statement for PAYMENT indicates retrieval-only processing. The immediately following SENFLD statements indicate that only these two fields are relevant. Note that the start position of P_TYPE has been changed from the database description (where it was defined to start in byte 8). The *order* of fields within segments may also be altered.

An application program may access more than one physical database (or logical database—see the following section). This is accomplished by defining several separate PCBs. A collection of all the PCBs required for an application is called a *program specification block* (PSB). The PSBGEN statement in the above example indicates that the language using the PCB is COBOL and that the PCB will be part of the PSB called ST_PAY.

Both the DBD and PCB are statically created by executing an IMS utility. This contrasts sharply with most relational systems, in which tables and views can be created dynamically at runtime.

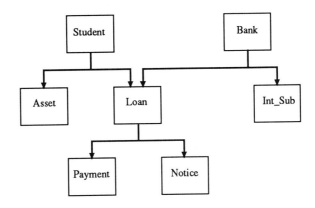

Fig 10-6   GSL Network

External Views over Multiple Physical Databases

IMS provides for the definition of an external database comprising more than one physical database, called a *logical database* (LDB). A logical database is defined with a *logical database description* (LDBD) and may include segments from two or more physical databases. The user external view is then defined using the PCB, but reference is to the logical, rather than a physical, database. What the user sees appears to be a hierarchical database. In fact, the underlying structures may have a degree of network structure to them due to links between segments of different physical databases.

The ability to define a logical database is what takes IMS out of the strictly hierarchical world. It allows us to satisfactorily address (real) information structures of the network variety without resorting to redundancy (in some cases). LDBs are quite complex. We will content ourselves with an overview of their capabilities and limitations. Our intention is that you grasp the significantly added power afforded to IMS by logical databases, without getting you bogged down in the details.

Consider the GSL database as a network, as shown in Figure 10–6. With a single physical database it is not possible to represent this data model as a hierarchy without redundancy. Its representation as multiple, interlinked, physical databases that form a logical database is realized as follows:

Two physical databases are created as shown in Figure 10–7. The physical database ST_A_L consists of the segment hierarchy STUDENT, ASSET, LOAN, PAYMENT, and NOTICE. The PDB B_IS consists of segments BANK and INT_SUB. The logical database is realized by a link (pointer) from LOAN to BANK. The LOAN is called the "logical child" of BANK; BANK is the "logical parent" of LOAN. To distinguish between logical and physical relationships, LOAN is called the "physical child" of STUDENT; STUDENT is the "physical parent" of LOAN. All segments within one physical database are, therefore, physical children of one physical parent (unless the segment is the root) and are physical parents to zero or more physical children.

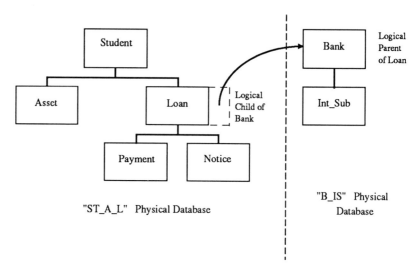

Fig 10-7 Representation of GSL Network of Figure 10-6 as Two Physical (Hierarchical) Databases

The user view of the logical database is not as shown in Figure 10–7. Rather, the user sees the hierarchy shown in Figure 10–8. This LDB *appears* to have redundancy. The segment LOAN:BANK appears to replicate BANK data for each occurrence of LOAN. This is not the case. Each LOAN segment belonging to a given BANK segment will point to that BANK segment. The fields of BANK are not physically replicated for each LOAN.

Pointers used to implement a logical relation may be actual address pointers or a symbolic key. The method used is dependent on the access method used (see section "Physical Structure"). For example, LOAN will include either the key of BANK (BID) or a pointer to the BANK segment, depending on the access method.

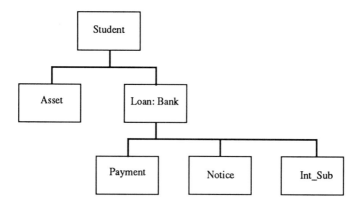

Fig 10-8 GSL Logical Database Defined Using the Two PDBs of Figure 10-7

The logical database provides the user with a convenient view for retrievals. But update operations may require that the user be aware of the underlying physical database. This is one example of how IMS is not able to capture the full capabilities of network DBMSs. Another problem arises in the types of access supported. The logical database defined in Figure 10–8 is fine for retrievals that start with the STUDENT segment. It does not support retrievals that start with the BANK segment. To support queries such as "obtain all LOAN segments for a given BANK" would require definition of another logical database. The approach would be to add a segment, such as BL as a physical child of BANK. There would be one such segment for each LOAN occurrence. The BL segment would then be defined as a logical child of STUDENT and STUDENT the logical parent of BL. Details are, however, beyond the scope of this text.

Since the logical database is implemented by storing pointers in segments, it is not possible to create a logical database without impact on the physical databases. First, a logical database description is written that defines the logical segments and pointers. Furthermore, since the pointers are physically stored, the physical DBD is affected by the logical DBDs in which it participates. If the logical database was not anticipated when the physical DBD was written, it will be necessary to unload the PDB, modify its definition, and then reload it. This is an expensive operation. You should contrast this approach to the impact of defining a view for a relational database.

This overview of the logical database capability of IMS shows that it is possible to represent a limited network in a logical hierarchical database, but not without some difficulty and complexity when compared to DBMSs designed for network structures. There are several additional constraints on the types of logical structures that can be defined. These are illustrated in Figure 10–9 and can be summarized as follows:

1. A logical database must have a root segment that is a root segment of a physical database. This would preclude us from defining a LDB that, for example, had LOAN as the root, with the children PAYMENT and NOTICE.

2. A logical child must have a single logical parent and a single physical parent. This requirement precludes several types of relationships. Assume a physical database, SCH, containing SCHOOL as the root segment, and another PDB, ST_L, with segments STUDENT and LOAN. STUDENT could not be a logical child of SCHOOL because STUDENT has no physical parent. This "illegal" LDB is illustrated in part a of Figure 10–9.

3. Since a segment may be a logical child to only one logical parent, ternary and higher-order relationships are precluded. For example, assume the physical database SCH, with the single segment SCHOOL; the PDB ST_L, with STUDENT and LOAN; and the PDB LENDER, with the segment BANK. If a loan is from a given bank and is used by a student for costs at a given school, then a ternary relationship exists between SCHOOL, STUDENT, and BANK, with the intersection data LOAN. This structure, illustrated in part b of Figure 10–9, cannot be represented in IMS.

Data Manipulation

The data manipulation language of a hierarchical system allows operators to process data arranged in the form of trees. The six basic types of operations are:

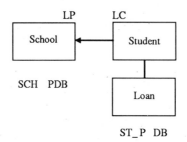

a. A logical child must have a physical parent.
Thus, a root segment may not be a logical child.

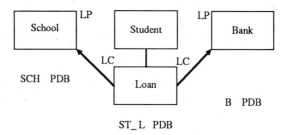

b. A logical child may have only a single logical parent.
Thus, Ternery and higher order relationship cannot be represented.

Fig 10-9 Examples of Logical Databases that Violate IMS Restrictions

1. Locate a specific tree, that is, a root segment.

2. Move from one segment to another in the hierarchical sequence.

3. Move from a parent segment to a child segment within a tree.

4. Move from a segment to a twin or sibling segment in the hierarchical sequence.

5. Insert a new segment in a tree.

6. Update a specific segment.

7. Delete a specific segment.

These operators allow an IMS application programmer to "traverse the tree." This is the CODASYL equivalent of "navigating a network." IMS data manipulation operations are initiated by calling DL/1 subroutines from an application program written in a host language. The host language could be PL/1, COBOL, or assembler.

The particular IMS operations to retrieve and update data are supported by the following DL/1 statements:

• GET UNIQUE (GU). Direct retrieval of a specific segment.

• GET NEXT (GN). Retrieval of the next record in hierarchical sequence, independent of the parent.

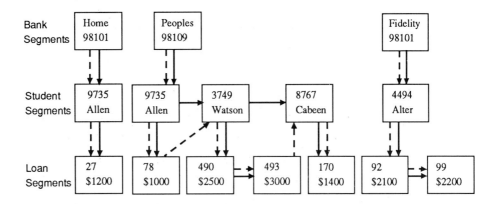

Fig 10-10   GSL Segments

- GET NEXT WITHIN PARENT (GNP). Provides for sequential retrieval within the same parent occurrence.
- GET HOLD (GH). Used in conjunction with the insert, delete, and replace statements. Following are variations of the GET HOLD statement:
  - –GET HOLD UNIQUE (GHU)
  - –GET HOLD NEXT (GHN)
  - –GET HOLD NEXT WITHIN PARENT (GHNP)
- ISRT. Insert a new segment occurrence.
- DLET. Delete a segment occurrence.
- REPL. Modify segment by replacing a segment occurrence with an updated version.

In addition to the above statements, a statement may include *segment search arguments* (SSA) to find specific segment occurrences, such as a student named ALLEN. An SSA may be a reasonably general predicate on the fields of a segment. It may use the various comparison operators (= < > ≥ ≤) and the Boolean operators AND and OR. The syntax shown here for the commands is not the full syntax required in a COBOL or PL/I program. It is an abbreviated syntax that captures the essence of the commands. The syntax is similar to that used by other writers such as C. J. Date and A. F. Cardenas.

The following examples illustrate the usage of these statements on the GSL database with the segment occurrences shown in Figure 10–10. Note that this database has redundant storage of STUDENT segments.

Two types of pointers are shown in the figure. The dashed lines link the segments within a root in their hierarchic sequence. The solid lines are so-called "physical child" and "physical twin" pointers that allow movement through segments of one type without the necessity of traversing to lower-level segments. Note in particular, the difference in the hierarchic (dashed line) pointers and child/twin pointers for PEOPLES bank. If the hierarchic pointers are used to find STUDENT 8767, the path would be through the following segments (keys indicated): SID=9735, LID=78, SID=3749, LID=490, LID=493, SID=8767. If child/twin pointers are followed, the sequence is SID=9735, SID=3749, SID=8767. These pointers, and other possibilities, are described in the section, "Physical Structure."

IMS Retrieval Examples

1. Retrieve the BANK segment with key HOME:

```
GU BANK (BID="HOME")
```

2. Retrieve the first occurrence of a STUDENT segment with key 3749:

```
GU BANK
    STUDENT (SID=3749)
```

This search starts at the first BANK segment in the database (HOME) and searches its STUDENT segments using the physical child and twin pointers. Since no STUDENT segment under HOME has SID=3749, the next BANK (PEOPLES) is accessed and its STUDENT segments searched until SID = 3749 is found.

3. Retrieve all students with SID = 9735.

```
GU BANK
    WHILE STATUS = "OK"
        GN STUDENT (SID=9735)
    ENDWHILE
```

IMS will begin with the first BANK segment, then proceed to search each STUDENT segment within that BANK segment (with BID=HOME) for SID=9735. When the STUDENT segments under HOME are exhausted, search will continue with the next BANK segment and its STUDENT segments. When IMS retrieves the last STUDENT, a status indicator will be returned to the calling program, which will indicate that no more segments exist to be searched.

4. Retrieve all students within parent (BANK) PEOPLES.

```
GU BANK (BID="PEOPLES")
    WHILE STATUS = "OK"
        GNP STUDENT
    ENDWHILE
```

The status indicator value will be other than OK after the last student within BANK PEOPLES is accessed. If the command GN (get next) instead of GNP (get next within parent) were used, accesses would continue with the next BANK segment. We would, therefore, need to check the current BID key and stop when it was no longer PEOPLES.

5. Segment search arguments can be defined for more than one segment. For example, to retrieve all LOAN segments with AMOUNT > $2000 within BANK PEOPLES we write:

```
GU BANK (BID="PEOPLES")
    WHILE STATUS = "OK"
        GNP LOAN (AMOUNT > 1000)
    GOTO LOOP
```

This search will move from one STUDENT segment to another, but only within the specified parent BANK, PEOPLES.

IMS Update Examples

Segment insertion and deletion operations are similar to search operations.

1. To add a LOAN for BANK="HOME" and STUDENT with SID 9735:

```
(Place loan segment in working storage; assume LID=30.)
ISRT BANK (NAME="HOME")
     STUDENT (SID=9735)
     LOAN
```

2. To update the LOAN inserted above, a GETHOLD operation is performed first, the information is changed, and then the segment is replaced:

```
GHU BANK (NAME="HOME")
    STUDENT (SID=9735)
    LOAN (LID=30)
    (Change LOAN segment in working storage.)
    REPL
```

3. To delete the LOAN inserted above, a GETHOLD operation is performed first, and then the DELETE:

```
GHU BANK (NAME="HOME")
    STUDENT (SID=9735)
    LOAN (LID=30)
    DLET
```

Physical Structure

In addition to defining segments and their hierarchical sequence in the PDB, the physical structure of an IMS database involves selecting the access path, indexes, and partitions. Probably the most important design choice facing the DBA is the choice of IMS "access method." Two additional physical features—secondary indexes and "data set groups"—are also outlined. The example GSL database of Figure 10–10 will be used to illustrate the physical structures.

Access Method

IMS supports four types of physical storage structures or access methods. Each of these structures has advantages and disadvantages for different types of database organizations and usage patterns. Each physical database description will specify one, and exactly one, access method. The alternatives are:

- Hierarchical Sequential Access Method (HSAM)
- Hierarchical Indexed Sequential Access Method (HISAM)
- Hierarchical Direct Access Method (HDAM)
- Hierarchical Indexed Direct Access Method (HIDAM)

HSAM. In an HSAM database, segments are stored in physically contiguous areas. Segment occurrences are written to the storage media one by one in hierarchical sequence to fixed-length blocks. Figure 10–11 illustrates storage of the example GSL segments in an

Block

Bank Home	Student 9735	Loan 27	Bank Peoples	Student 9735	/////

1

Loan 78	Student 3749	Loan 490	Loan 493	Student 8767	Loan 170	/////

2

Bank Fidelity	Student 4494	Loan 92	Loan 99	/////

3

Fig 10-11 HSAM

HSAM database. As seen in the figure, there is usually some space wasted at the end of a block because a segment cannot span block boundaries. Unused space is indicated by /////.

HSAM is tapelike. Access to both root and lower-level segments is strictly sequential. Furthermore, HSAM databases can only be updated by sequential file-processing methods that is, updates are made by reading in data, modifying it, and then writing it back out to a new (HSAM) file. Thus, only the DL/I get operations GU, GN, and GNP are valid.

HSAM is parsimonious with storage. It is appropriate for databases that do not require online access, particularly those that are periodically updated in batch mode by sequential methods.

HISAM. In the HISAM structure, both *indexed sequential access method* (ISAM) and *virtual sequential access method* (VSAM) files may be used. We will describe the (modern, B-tree based) VSAM structure.

With VSAM, root segments are stored in the B-tree indexed file—that is, a standard VSAM file using the key of the root segment. Subordinate segments are stored in separate, so-called "entry-sequenced" VSAM file, with a pointer from the root segment to its first child segment. Space occupied by segments that are not part of the example data are marked by a bullet (•). Unused space is again indicated by /////.

With HISAM the DBMS uses indexed access to root segments with a pointer from the root to the first subordinate segment in the separate (entry-sequenced) VSAM file. Segments are stored with pointers across blocks if necessary, as shown in Figure 10–12.

HISAM supports online processing as well as a fast sequential scan of the database in key order. Additional root segments use standard B-tree block splitting when overflow occurs. This access method is one of the most widely used because of its ability to support sequential-access processing as well as direct access. Furthermore, the VSAM file's dynamic reorganization capability minimizes the necessity of reorganizing the key-sequenced (root segment) database as it grows. Over time, however, the dependent segments will become scattered as added segments can no longer be located near their siblings. This may necessitate reorganization of the entry sequenced file to re-cluster the dependent segments.

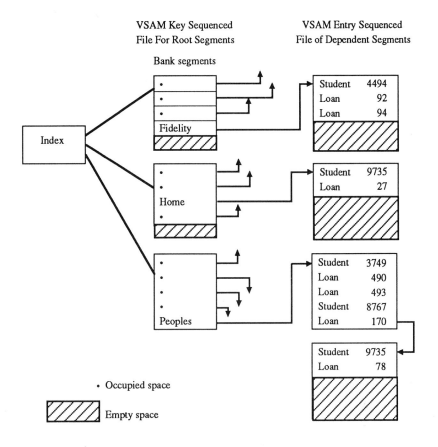

VSAM Key Sequenced
File For Root Segments

VSAM Entry Sequenced
File of Dependent Segments

Bank segments

Index

Fidelity

Student	4494
Loan	92
Loan	94

Home

| Student | 9735 |
| Loan | 27 |

Peoples

Student	3749
Loan	490
Loan	493
Student	8767
Loan	170

| Student | 9735 |
| Loan | 78 |

• Occupied space

/// Empty space

Fig 10-12   File Access Methods

HDAM. The *hierarchical direct access method* provides hashed access to root segments and then uses a pointer system for access to dependent segments. An attempt is made to place each dependent segment close to the root segment occurrence, in the same block if possible. Thus, HDAM provides the fastest possible access method for an IMS database. However, with file growth, reorganization will be necessary to avoid deterioration in performance (as occurs with all conventional hashing schemes).

Figure 10–13 illustrates the example segments stored as an HDAM database. To make the example somewhat more interesting, the symbol • (bullet) is used to indicate space occupied by a record that is not part of our example data. The notation ///// is used to show empty space.

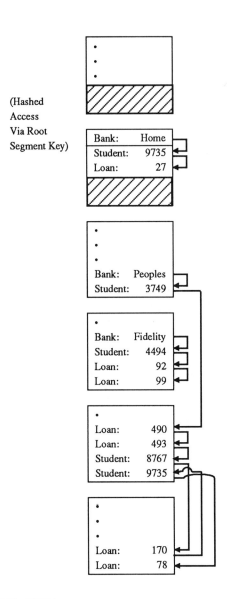

(Hashed
Access
Via Root
Segment Key)

Fig 10-13   HDAM

The segments are shown connected by hierarchical pointers. (Hierarchical pointers were illustrated in Figure 10–10.) These pointers connect the segments in hierarchical sequence: top to bottom, left to right. An alternative pointer scheme is to have linkage by physical child/twin pointers. With child/twin pointers, there is a linked-list head in each parent to its first child. Children of one segment type are then stored on a linked list. (Figure 10–10 also illustrates child/twin pointers.)

HDAM provides very fast access to both root and dependent segments. The number of accesses is comparable to that required by the network model using the location mode CALC for an owner record type and the location mode VIA SET for members. (In the hierarchical model, all dependents are "automatically" clustered since there is only a single owner record.)

Retrieval will be fast until a large number of additions have been made. With additions, the hashed file will require more and more use of linking to find both root and dependent segments. Thus, reorganization will eventually be required for HDAM files that experience growth.

HIDAM. The *hierarchical indexed direct access method* is, as its name suggests, a blend of the HDAM and HISAM organizations. As with HISAM, the storage organization comprises two files. One file is a VSAM key-sequenced file that contains only root-segments with pointers to first child segments. The other file contains the dependent segments that may be linked using either hierarchic pointers or child/twin pointers. We have not illustrated this organization because it can be viewed as the HDAM organization with "hashed access on the root segment key" replaced by a "dense B-tree index on the root segment key."

This organization provides access that is almost as fast as HDAM: traversing an index is required as opposed to hashing. But it has the advantage over HIDAM of supporting sequential processing. Another advantage over HIDAM is that reorganization is less frequent because the physical location of a root segment is not dictated by its hashed address. The HIDAM advantage over HISAM is that since pointers are used to link segments, space occupied by deleted segments can be recovered. Furthermore, if physical child/twin pointers are used, the amount of time needed to locate a segment may be less because it is not necessary to scan through the dependents in hierarchic sequence.

A disadvantage of HIDAM (and HDAM) is that in practice, descendant segments of a root segment can become widely scattered over a large storage area. This can cause excessive I/O operations to be performed for both serial and random access operations.

Additional IMS Physical Storage Features and Options

Three additional IMS options for physical structures are outlined in this section:

- Physical database partitioning
- Secondary indexing
- Fast path

PDB Partitioning. IMS allows the PDB to be partitioned into *data set groups* (DSG). There is one primary DSG for the root segment and one or more secondary DSGs that contain one or more subtrees of the database. The creation of data set groups allows a database to be physically spread over several storage devices and allows direct access to the newly created "root" node in each secondary DSG.

For example, consider the GSL model with the PAYMENT segment added. If it were important to provide very fast access directly to a LOAN segment and its payments, the database could be partitioned between the STUDENT and LOAN segments. It would now be possible to directly access a LOAN segment without accessing its STUDENT parent.

Another benefit of a DSG is that storage fragmentation is reduced. A DSG defined as a single segment type allows the DBMS to keep all segments of a given type, and therefore of a given length, in their own DSG so that holes created by deletions are always the same length as added segments. DSGs may be assigned to separate devices to afford a degree of parallel searching of disks or to reduce conflict between two applications that access different segment types from the same physical database.

Secondary Indexes. Secondary indexes can be defined to provide direct access to a root or dependent segment based on any field of the segment or of a dependent segment. Indexes on dependent segments thus provide for entry at points other than the root of a tree.

A secondary index to the root segment is used to access the tree by other than its sequence field. For example, with the GSL model and hierarchy BANK/STUDENT/LOAN, a secondary index to BANK on ZIP might be established. An index may also be constructed to the root segment on fields of dependent segments. To support direct access to BANK segments by SID value of STUDENT, a secondary index could be defined.

Secondary indexes are also used to provide fast access to frequently retrieved dependent segments. An example would be to index on student name. By creating a secondary index for a dependent segment in a subtree of the hierarchy, and accessing by index, the segment becomes a "root" segment with its ancestors as dependents. A secondary index to STU-DENT on SID would reorganize the hierarchy with STUDENT as a root node, BANK as a first child segment, and LOAN as a second child segment:

                    STUDENT
        BANK   LOAN

IMS indexes provide two additional capabilities: the ability to index only on the selected value of a field—a so-called sparse index—and the ability to include fields in the index itself. A sparse index points only to segments whose values satisfy the selection predicate of the index. For example, suppose the LOAN segment contains a field STATUS that indicates whether the loan was in good standing (OK), behind in payments, in default, or closed. A secondary index could be created that would point only to those loans where the STATUS value was other than OK.

The secondary index is a file itself and this is what affords the capability to place data other than the indexed value into the index. Suppose, for example, that a frequent query were to determine the name of a student given the SID value. An index to STUDENT on SID can have the name field stored in the index. This will provide very fast access for queries that only need to retrieve name given SID.

Clearly, the creation and use of secondary indexes can result in dramatic reductions in the time and cost of a search. This is even more true in an IMS database than in a relational DBMS, because to search a segment at a low level of the hierarchy, IMS may need to scan all ancestor segments. (Obviously the scanning necessary depends on the access method, whether hierarchical or child/twin pointers are used, and whether any DSGs have been created.) In a relational DBMS, the scan will be limited to the tuples of the relevant relation.

The secondary indexing capability has a number of deficiencies, particularly in the area of data independence. The DL/I statements must explicitly reference an index in order for IMS to use the index in a retrieval. For example, if an index named ST_SIDX is created to STUDENT on SID and the get statement is GN STUDENT (SID = 4494), then access will be by sequential scan of the segments. To use the index, the DL/I statement must name the index: GN STUDENT(ST_SIDX = 4494). Clearly, this creates a high degree of *data dependence*. The deletion of an index will require modification of any program that used the index. To reap the benefits of a newly added index, programs that access by the index's key must be modified.

Fast Path. IMS supports two special types of databases for applications in which very high performance is required. One type of database is a called a *main storage database* (MSDB) and resides in central memory. It is limited to root-only segments. The other is called a *data entry database* (DEDB) and, while stored on external devices, is designed for fast access and rapid data entry.

The availability of massive amounts of central memory, at a continually lower cost over time, has encouraged DBMS designers to consider central memory as a repository for frequently referenced data that requires fast access. MSDBs are used for such data as small tables. For example, suppose that the GSL system stores a *code* for a student's college, but data input is a college name. A table relating college name to code might be stored in main memory to minimize translation cost.

The data entry database is similar to the HDAM organization in that it has hashed access to root nodes, but is limited to a 15-level hierarchy and 127 segment types (for most databases these are not serious restrictions). The first dependent segment may be designated as the *sequential dependent*. This segment can be read and written, but not updated. The intention is that the sequential segment be used for rapid collection of detailed data—possibly for subsequent batch update processes.

The DEDB can be divided into *areas*. The DBA is given considerable control over physical characteristics of each area, including placement on storage devices. This gives the DBA yet another tool to fine-tune a database for optimum performance in transaction-processing environments in which the data access characteristics are highly predictable.

Summary

IMS is a very mature product. It is highly refined and "tuned." This means that it makes quite efficient use of computer resources, especially when compared to the newer relational systems. IBM has invested, at the very least, hundreds of thousands of hours in the development, enhancement, and refinement of IMS. As noted earlier, for very predictable, routine applications, it is hard to beat an IMS database from a performance standpoint. For example, at the time of this writing users report that it is roughly twice as efficient as IBM's relational products.

The large number of options available in IMS in terms of physical file structures, choices of pointers, secondary indexes, PDB partitioning, fast-path databases, and other features provides the database designer with a wide array of choices. This allows the DBA to tailor and tune each database to its particular applications. The ability to define logical databases takes IMS out of the strict hierarchical world, so that many real-world databases can be satisfactorily modeled with little or no redundancy.

However, the large number of options adds to the complexity of IMS and to the difficulty of understanding the system. Relational systems provide fewer options and make many choices for the user. In particular, many relational systems use only a single file structure: B+ tree dense indexes. Most relational systems allow the creation of a database without the necessity of defining indexes, clustering, and so on. While performance may suffer if no indexes are defined, a user can define and load a database very rapidly and with relatively little training. By contrast, it takes considerable training to create and manipulate even a simple IMS database. Furthermore, while relational system queries (as in SQL) can be written independently of the choice of indexes, IMS DL/1 queries are not independent of the physical structure. Thus, IMS forces the user to know more about the organization of the database, and may require changes in the DML if changes are made in the database structure.

This does not mean that IMS will disappear or even fade away, at least not in the next 10 or more years. Many companies have a considerable investment in IMS databases and the programs that access them. IBM has created interfaces between relational query languages and IMS databases that provide a means for handling ad hoc queries. (Note, however, that this adds yet another option and thus more complexity to IMS.) But we would expect, and indeed are witnessing, a shift by many formerly entrenched IMS users to RDBMSs. Some companies use both systems, an approach once advocated by IBM. But others are biting the bullet and converting IMS databases to an RDBMS to take advantage of the dramatically lower application-system development costs and the attractiveness of SQL (and similar languages) for the less-routine applications required for management decision support.

Questions and Problems

Questions

1. What is the essential difference between the hierarchical and network data models?

2. How are the hierarchical and network models similar, especially compared to the relational model?

3. Relate the following network terms to corresponding terms in IMS: *record type, record occurrence, data item, key.*

4. Give a definition of a *physical database record*. Why is there no corresponding element in either the network or relational models?

5. What are the elements of a physical database definition? That is, exactly what must be defined and/or described?

6. Which fields must be included in the definition of a *segment?*

7. What are the meanings of the following statements?

   a. FIELD NAME=AMOUNT, TYPE =P, BYTES=4, START=12

   b. FIELD NAME=(ACCNT,SEQ), TYPE=C, BYTES=6, START=10

8. Define the following acronyms: DBD, PDBR, PCB, LDBD, PSB.

9. A PCB is comparable to a network database's _____and a relational _____.

10. To define a user view over more than one physical database, a _____ must be defined.

11. Should DL/1 be classified as a "result oriented," or a "procedural oriented" DML?

12. What is the difference between the GN and GNP commands?

13. Why doesn't IMS need a "get parent" command comparable to the "get owner" of network systems?

14. Outline the essential differences between the four access methods of IMS: HSAM, HISAM, HDAM, HIDAM.

15. Which of the access methods would be appropriate for processing that involves both random access to a root node and sequential processing of root nodes in sequence field order?

16. Which access method provides fastest access to a root node?

17. What are two different ways to provide direct access to a dependent segment (that is, without accessing the root node)?

18. What is the difference between hierarchical pointers and child/twin pointers?

19. In what physical storage device is a fast path database stored?

20. What are the typical characteristics of databases that are designated as FP (fast path)?

21. Discuss some of the deficiencies of IMS in terms of data independence. For example, you should address secondary indexes.

Problems

1. Consider the GSL model with three record types: STUDENT, LOAN, BANK. Assume that one physical database is to be defined to contain the three.

   a. Describe the alternative hierarchies that might be created. In your answer, consider alternatives that join segments.

   b. Consider the two possible hierarchies described in the text:

   ```
   STUDENT          BANK
      |               |
   BANK            STUDENT
      |               |
   LOAN             LOAN
   ```

   There are 1 million students, 10,000 banks, and 4 million loans. Assume that each student has exactly four loans, and that the four loans are from two different banks. For each of the above PDB designs, determine the number of redundant BANK and STUDENT segments respectively.

2. Write down the segment types of the PDB "ST_A_L" of Figure 10–7 in their hierarchical sequence.

3. Write down the segment occurrences of part b of Figure 10–1 in their hierarchical sequence.

4. The following questions are based on the GSL model defined below as GSL_BSL. Figure 10–10 illustrates the hierarchy and segment occurrences.

   ```
   DBD      NAME=GSL_BSL

   SEGM     NAME=BANK, BYTES=143
   FIELD    NAME=(BID,SEQ), BYTES=12, START=1
   FIELD    NAME=BANK_NAM,BYTES=20, START=13
   FIELD    NAME=TYPE, BYTES=4, START=33
   FIELD    NAME=ZIP,BYTES=3,TYPE=P,START=37
   ```

```
SEGM      NAME=STUDENT, PARENT=BANK, BYTES=196
FIELD     NAME=(SID, SEQ), BYTES=4, TYPE=P, START=1
FIELD     NAME=SNAME, BYTES=30, START=5
FIELD     NAME=SLEVEL, BYTES=1, START =35
FIELD     NAME=ZIP, BYTES=5, START=81

SEGM      NAME=LOAN, PARENT=STUDENT, BYTES=64
FIELD     NAME=(LID,SEQ), TYPE=P, BYTES=4, START=1
FIELD     NAME=L_DATE, TYPE=P, BYTES=3, START=5
FIELD     NAME=INT_RATE, TYPE =P, BYTES=5, START=8
FIELD     NAME=AMOUNT, TYPE=P, BYTES=6,START=13
```

a. Extend the DBD to add a new segment type PAYMENT with key PAY_NO and other fields PAY_AMT and DATE.

b. Write a PCB for an application that requires read access to LOAN segments and the ability to add new PAYMENT segments. (Ignore the PSBGEN statement.)

The following problems involve writing DL/1 queries and updates for the GSL_BSL database using the abbreviated DL/1 syntax described in the text.

c. Find the bank with BID = PEOPLES.

d. Find all student segments with the name ALLEN.

e. List data for all BANK segments which have a STUDENT segment with name = ALLEN.

f. Modify the LOAN with LID 490, changing its amount to $3,000.

g. Insert a new loan for student 9735 with bank PEOPLES. The new loan has LID 498.

5. Consider the following DBD for a physical database named CUST_ORD.

```
DBD       NAME=CUST_ORD
SEGM      NAME=CUSTOMER, BYTES=80
FIELD     NAME=(ACNT_NO, SEQ), BYTES=4, TYPE=P, START=1
FIELD     NAME=CST_NAME, BYTES=25, START=5
SEGM      NAME=CREDIT, PARENT=CUSTOMER,BYTES=120
FIELD     NAME=(DATE, SEQ), BYTES=6, START=1
SEGM      NAME=INVOICE, PARENT=CUSTOMER,BYTES=60
FIELD     NAME=(ORD_NO,SEQ), BYTES=3, TYPE=P, START=6
SEGM      NAME=LINE_ITM, PARENT=ORDER, BYTES=46
FIELD     NAME=(LINE_NO, SEQ), BYTES=1, TYPE=P, START=1
```

a. Translate this DBD into a Bachman-like diagram that shows the hierarchical relationship of the segments.

b. What is the key of the segment CREDIT?

c. What is the fully concatenated key of LINE_NO?

d. Write a statement to define a field in CUSTOMER, which contains the telephone number. Telephone numbers may be up to 10 digits and are to be stored in a packed decimal form. The telephone number immediately follows the customer name.

e. Write statements to add another segment to the database. This segment contains payment data. Payments are made against specific invoices. The key of the payment is a date, stored in packed decimal at the start of the segment. Following the date is an amount field with values up to $9,999.99, to be stored as packed decimal.

Beginning in byte 45 is space to store the customer's check number or other notation indicating method of payment. This field is 10 characters long. Clearly indicate where these statements belong in the DBD.

   f. An application program needs to access CUSTOMER and LINE_ITM segments. Write a PCB for this application. For simplicity, assume that all fields in these segments are relevant. (Ignore the PSBGEN statement.)

6. Consider the Customer, Order, Line, Part (Inventory) database used for questions 17 through 26 of Chapter 4. (See Figure 4-6.)

   a. Can this database be organized as a hierarchy without introducing redundancy? Discuss.

   b. Describe a logical database for this data using Bachman-like diagrams and two physical databases. Indicate the logical child/parent segments.

   c. Provide an alternative structure to the one you suggested in part b.

   d. Write a DBD for a physical database that includes the INVENTORY and LINE ITEM segments from this database. (Make up reasonable field definitions.) Is it necessary to include the PART# field in LINE ITEM?

   e. Suppose data on personnel is added to this database. Each employee is assigned an employee number. Other data includes name, job, date of birth, sex, and company phone number. How would you incorporate this data into your physical and logical design?

   f. Returning to the original, four-segment model, describe two alternative ways to provide direct access to the ORDER segment by SALESPERSON name.

   g. Suppose that IMS did not support secondary indexes or DSGs. How could you design a database that would provide direct access to ORDER by SALESPERSON name? (An objective of this question is to point out the similarity between a secondary index and physical databases that have logical parent/child links.)

   h. What database structure should be used to provide direct access to customers with a rating of C or lower?

References

Cardenas, Alfonso. *Data Base Management Systems*. 2d ed. Boston: Allyn and Bacon, Inc., 1985.

Date, C.J. *An Introduction to Database Systems*. 3d ed. Reading, Mass.: Addison-Wesley Publishing Co, 1981.

_____. *An Introduction to Database Systems*. Vol. 1. 4th ed. Reading, Mass.: Addison-Wesley Publishing Co, 1985.

IBM Reference Manual Gh20-1260. *Information Management System Virtual Storage (IMS/VS), General Information Manual*.

Loomis, Mary E.S. *The Database Book*. New York: Macmillan Publishing Co., 1987.

Database Design and Administration

11 The Database Design Process and Logical Data Modeling

Overview of the Database Design Process

This chapter and the two following chapters are devoted to the database design process. Chapter 11 deals with the determination of the information needs of an organization and culminates with the specification of a data model in the form of a so-called extended entity relationship model (E-ERM). Chapter 12 deals with the refinement of the model—specifically, the normalization of the relations developed by the E-ERM. The mapping of these relations into the specific form supported by the DBMS to be used is the topic of Chapter 13. The result of this mapping is the conceptual schema. Chapter 13 also deals with the physical database definition: the definition of the internal schema.

Figure 11–1 outlines the overall process of database design, from the highest levels of defining organizational objectives to the final implementation and testing of a database. In this design process, step one is based on the first three stages of IBM's business system planning (BSP) method. These stages are: identifying the environment, business planning,

Chapter 11:	**Step 1:** Who are we and what are our goals? Identifying the business environment, developing a business plan, and performing a system analysis.
	Step 2: What data do weneed to realize our goals? Analyzing data requirements and performing formal modeling using the extended entity relationship model (E-ERM).
	Step 3: How should the data be organized? Development of the conceptual data model, transformation of the E-ERM to relations.
Chapter 12:	Normalization.
Chapter 13:	**Step 4:** How can this be implemented? Mapping to a relational, network, or hierarchical DBMS schema.
	Step 5: What is the most cost effective way of organizing this data? Physical design of relational, network, and hierarchical database systems.

Fig 11-1 Design Process/Major Steps in Database Analysis and Design and Corresponding Chapters in This Text

and business analysis. The second step is based on the final phase of the BSP method, database analysis. The E-ERM can be used as a tool for database analysis.

In the past, there were few formal methods to assist the database designer. Today that situation has improved, and there are a number of commonly used tools and techniques. While there is no single universal design method, the techniques we describe are representative of those used by successful organizations.

Planning a Database

A critical element for a successful database is planning. Experience has shown that planning is usually best performed by a team of four to eight people, made up of both users and data-processing personnel. It is essential for the design team to have in-depth knowledge of the structure and operating procedures of the organization and to be supported by the organization's top management. The primary objective of the planning team is to produce a database plan that specifies the data needs of the organization and the ways in which they are to be met now and in the future. Planning involves the development of a preliminary conceptual data model called the *data enterprise model,* which defines the important entities and the relationships between them. The plan also sets out a schedule for the overall design and implementation of the database.

In practice, the design of a database is a combination of top-down and bottom-up planning and analysis, with the trend towards increased emphasis on the top-down approach. The top-down thrust begins with the corporate business plan, a document that provides an overall statement of the goals, objectives, policies, and constraints of an enterprise. The design proceeds to determine the entities, functions, processes, activities, and events of the enterprise. Working down from the business plan ensures that the database will support the goals and objectives of the enterprise, both now and in the future.

While the top-down approach is attractive in theory and as a philosophy, it is not always a realistic approach since virtually all companies already have existing database systems, data files, and applications. Such existing data and applications cannot be ignored. Thus, the design process must intergate the top-down approach with the consideration and examination of existing systems, or the bottom-up portion of the design.

We caution the reader that no company of any significant size translates the enterprise data model into a single database to serve all the information needs of the entire company. Even moderate-sized companies will have several databases; large companies may have literally hundreds of databases. Separate databases often exist to support various functional and support areas such as personnel/payroll, marketing, accounting/finance, production, engineering, legal counsel, purchasing, etc. To attempt a full integration of all data needs into a single database is a recipe for failure. Nevertheless, the importance of generating a corporate business plan is not to be minimized. This plan will serve as the guiding document for the design of the enterprise model, which in turn will guide the development and refinement of these many databases.

Importance of Database Planning

Failure to carefully plan a database all too often results in a database that has been designed to meet the immediate needs of an organization but may not be able to accommodate the changing needs of the organization or changes brought about through the introduction of new hardware or software. This lack of flexibility in traditional information systems often results when databases are developed in connection with the data handling *procedures* used by an organization. While this approach usually satisfies the immediate needs of an organization, it has proven to be inadequate for handling new requirements brought on by the growth of an organization, increased competition, and advances in technology.

Current design techniques concentrate on the *data* and treat it as a resource that must be managed in the same way as any other resource such as capital, material, or personnel. This produces a database design that is much more likely to satisfy the information needs of the organization, because an organization's data changes more slowly than the procedures used to process it.

The database structure developed by the design team must be relatively independent of the languages and programs that will be used to update and use the database. If properly carried out, the planning of a database will result in a comprehensive plan for the design and implementation of a database that meets the short-term and long-term needs of the enterprise.

Organizational Environment

A *strategic data model* is used to show the present and anticipated data needs for the organization. This projection should encompass at least the next five years. It is imperative that this overall data model be understood and supported by each functional area of the organization. The following four functional areas are typical of most organizations: (1) *management*, which directs and plans for the organization; (2) *production and operations*, which provide the products and services; (3) *marketing*, which creates the demand for products and services; and (4) *support services*, which provide engineering, accounting, personnel, and maintenance services.

Clearly it is unlikely that all of these various units will require the same data. Each unit has its own specific data requirements to meet its responsibilities. There will also be overlapping data needs: in a manufacturing firm, for example, the sales and production functions are clearly interrelated. So too is there an overlap of engineering and manufacturing. Personnel overlaps with all of these functional areas since each area has employees on which data is maintained. In the federal government, it would be nonsensical to speak of a single integrated database. (The idea of increased integration of the data maintained by the feds is attractive to some from a standpoint of efficiency or effectiveness. Tracking down students who default on guaranteed student loans would be much easier if the records of the IRS, Social Security Administration, and all various government payroll systems were integrated. But many of us are willing to sacrifice a degree of efficiency and effectiveness to minimize the probability of more serious problems, such as lack of privacy and encroachment of individual liberties.)

Thus database planners are faced with the fundamental and important task of determining the extent to which the data needs of the entire enterprise data are to be integrated. Should a single database be designed and implemented? This is impractical if not virtually impossible. Should each functional and support area have its own independent database? That alternative is also fraught with pitfalls. Independent databases lead to the replication of data items and incompatibilities. For example, the payroll department will clearly need employee pay rates in order to issue paychecks. But engineering and manufacturing will also need pay rates in order to estimate production costs. If pay rates are stored separately, there is a risk that inconsistencies will develop, such as two different values stored for the same individual. Worse, the several data items may not even share the same definition: payroll might store an hourly rate, engineering and manufacturing a monthly rate.

Is there a solution to the problem? The appropriate answer seems to lie between fully integrated and the completely independent databases. Separate databases are probably the best answer, with high-level control and coordination to assure a commonality of data item definitions and to maintain inconsistencies at an acceptable level. The operational level (that is, the day-to-day responsibility) of control and coordination is the job of the database administrator. It is the repsonsibility of higher management to establish policies to assure that the DBA has the authority to do his or her job, that is, to exercise control over the development of a new database.

The existence of separate databases with potentially overlapping data items means that data will need to be transferred between them. The ideal situation is for the creation and update of a data item value to be the responsibility of a single database. For example, all pay rates are first entered into the personnel/payroll database. Then, to meet the cost estimation needs of engineering and manufacturing, pay rate values are periodically transferred from the payroll database to the engineering and manufacturing databases. This will result in some degree of temporary inconsistency. If the transfer is made each Friday at midnight, a salary increase that is made (and becomes effective) on Tuesday will not be immediately reflected in all databases. Usually, this is not a severe problem.

Even a single federal government program area (such as GSL, Direct Student Loans, Medicare, AFDC, farm subsidies) typically requires multiple databases. In the GSL system, a separate database is created for those students with loans determined to be in default. The reason for the creation of a separate database is that the data needs of the collection area of the GSL and the level of online interaction with the data differs from the normal requirements of the GSL system. To minimize inconsistencies across several databases, when a student is declared in default, his or her data is not rekeyed into the "collection" database but rather is extracted from the primary GSL database.

Strategic, Tactical, and Operational Level Needs

In addition to the obvious differences in data needs across the various functional and service units of an organization, data needs also differ by management level within and across these units. To illustrate our point, take a couple of extreme examples. The president of the United States should not be bothered by the particulars of a single student's loan default (unless, of course, the situation somehow involves very high-level policy setting or there is political hay to be made by becoming familiar with the situation). But, the overall benefits of the program *should* be of considerable interest to the president. By contrast, the particulars of a single default are of relevance to the collection agent. The overall costs and benefits would normally not be relevant—or at least, not relevant to the discharge of the collection agent's job.

In an automobile manufacturing company, the board of directors will have considerable interest in the profitability of each line of automobiles and the costs and prospects for planned models. These executives should also be concerned about facts that are external to the company: how well did the competition perform, what are the competitor's plans, what is the state of the company, what are the propects for once again reducing the Department of Transportation's minimum corporate average fuel economy limit? As an assembly line manager, most of this data might make interesting coffee-break reading but would hardly be relevant to job responsibilities. The line manager needs to have data on his or her worker resources (such as the number of employees of various skills who are available for work that day), planned production levels, component availability and expected delivery times, and the status of machines and other systems (such as robots that are on strike).

Data needs are often categorized by the three levels of management: strategic, tactical, and operational. While there are not clear divisions between each level, it is useful to describe some of the primary responsibilities of management at these levels.

Strategic management is concerned with the overall performance of an enterprise. This is the process of deciding an organization's goals and objectives, determining the resources that will be needed, and deciding on the policies governing the acquisition, use, and disposition of these resources. Managers responsible for strategic planning require highly summarized data and make frequent use of ad hoc inquiries. They need a great deal of data from outside the organization, such as business forecasts, economic data, and competitor data. They also require historical data to facilitate planning.

Tactical management ensures that resources are obtained and used effectively to meet the objectives of the organization. Management at this level is concerned with balancing the use of resources, monitoring progress against plans, and taking corrective action where necessary. It requires information in the form of summarized operational data, management reports, budget summaries, and so on.

Operational management focuses on the execution of specific tasks and activities such as scheduling and controlling individual jobs, procuring materials, assigning personnel, and so on. The data required by operational-level management is more detailed and must be suitable for making immediate operational decisions.

At the lowest level of the hierarchy are the nonmanagerial employees who require data to perform their tasks. In the GSL program operational level employees include loan approval staff and collection agents. In a manufacturing firm these employees include line workers who interact with terminals or receive hard-copy reports which direct their activity or are used to indicate the completion of tasks. In an airline or travel agency, operational level staff include the reservation agents.

Thus we see that there are significant differences in data needs at these levels in terms of three dimensions: (1) the degree of detail versus aggregation (summarization); (2) the source of data (external vs. internal); (3) the need for historical data. Figure 11–2 presents the situation in graphical form. At the top of the pyramid sits top (strategic) management with a need for highly summarized data of both current and historical nature from both internal and external sources. The middle levels rely less heavily on external and historical data and require greater levels of detail. Operational levels rely almost solely on internal data of a current nature.

These efforts frustrate any effort to create a single database. Even if we focus on a single functional area, such as manufacturing, it is likely that the best approach will be to develop two or three databases oriented towards the differing needs at each level. The typical approach to meeting data needs from internal sources is to concentrate on the needs of lower levels and develop the necessary databases for operational support. Then needs at higher levels are met by the extraction and aggregation of data from the operational level database in the decision-support database(s) for middle and upper levels of management. While noncurrent data may be purged from online operational-level databases, historical/aggregated data will be maintained in higher-level databases to support planning and control responsibilities at these levels.

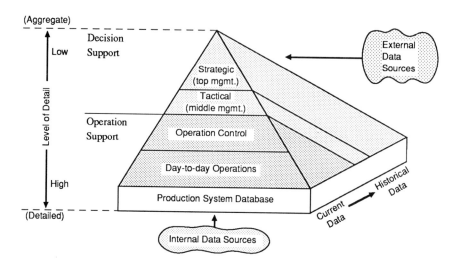

Fig 11-2 *Information Sources, Level of Detail, and Historical vs. Current Data Needs by Level of Management*

The decision-support databases will also be designed to incorporate data from external sources. Or separate databases may be established to house external data. In some cases, external data may be acquired, as needed, from various national data banks maintained by government agencies and private organizations.

Database Planning Process

Database planning should result in a long-term plan for the organization, supporting both the present and anticipated needs of the organization. Ideally, the database plan is an important part of the information systems plan, and the information systems plan is an important part of the corporate plan.

IBM developed the business system planning (BSP) method as a top-down method to assist organizations in establishing a system architecture plan. BSP assumes that "an information system plan for a business must be integrated with the business plan and should be developed from the point of view of top management and with their participation" (*Business System Planning*, IBM Corporation, 1975). This section provides a model based on the integration of the BSP approach and the approaches of other writers. The planning of a database can be broken down into several major tasks. While these tasks are carried out in a more or less sequential order, constant refinements occur as the data requirements of the organization become better understood.

There are four top-level stages in this process: identifying the business environment, business planning, business systems analysis, and database analysis. These stages are similar to the four stages of the BSP process. However, we have expanded these stages to include some sub-stages not originally included.

Identifying the Business Environment

The first step in the BSP approach is to define the environment within which a business must operate and to identify all the factors that influence the environment, for both the present and the foreseeable future. This step can be subdivided into two steps: identifying the external environment and identifying the internal environment. In the GSL system, the external environment could include students, schools, banks, government bureaucracy, technology, and local, national, and global economies. The internal environment includes departmental policies, practices, and employees.

Business Planning

The business plan is used by an organization to direct present and future business development. This plan defines goals, objectives, competitive strategies, resource requirements, policies, and constraints for the organization within the identified business environment. This plan should also include the goals and objectives for the implementation of the database, and should be related to the goals and objectives of the organization as a whole. If another information system is already in use, its limitations should be identified, and the anticipated benefits of a database approach should be considered. Due to the changing nature of most businesses, this plan will need to be updated to reflect changes within the business.

Business System Analysis

A comprehensive database plan can be developed from a *business systems analysis*. The business system analysis identifies the functions and subfunctions of an organization, both in the present and in the future. The information required by these functions can then be identified.

When analyzing the structure of an organization, major functions are first defined in a top-down approach. The processes included in each major function are then defined, and these are broken down into sets of activities. Through this process, the business functions, processes, and activities can be identified and documented.

In the GSL, business functions might include granting loans, tracking lender banks, and lobbying Congress for increased monetary support. Business functions are groups of similar activities that perform an important corporate service or provide a major corporate product. The size of an organization influences the number of functions, with small organizations having fewer functions than large organizations.

The business function of granting loans mentioned in the previous paragraph could include the business processes of loan applications, tracking loan payments, and collecting on loans that are past due. Business processes are made up of activities that are related to the management of resources such as people, materials, and information.

In the GSL system, business activities that contribute to the process of applying for a loan include entering student details, entering loan details, checking bank balances, and issuing a check. Business activities are those actions necessary to actually complete a business process. In general, these activities will have an immediate affect upon a database, requiring the entering, updating, or deletion of data.

The results of a business systems analysis are displayed in the form of a simple chart, called a *business chart* (see Figure 11–3). The functions, processes, and activities of the

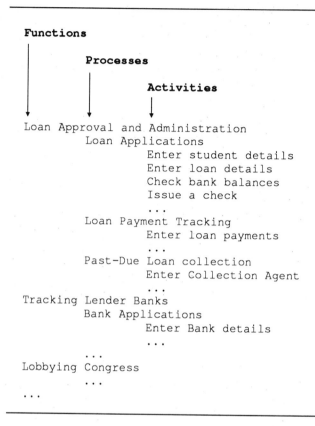

```
Functions

        Processes

                Activities

Loan Approval and Administration
        Loan Applications
                Enter student details
                Enter loan details
                Check bank balances
                Issue a check
                . . .
        Loan Payment Tracking
                Enter loan payments
                . . .
        Past-Due Loan collection
                Enter Collection Agent
                . . .
Tracking Lender Banks
        Bank Applications
                Enter Bank details
                . . .
        . . .
Lobbying Congress
        . . .
. . .
```

*Fig 11-3 A **Business Chart** Resulting from a Business Systems Analysis, Showing Functions, Processing, and Activities*

GSL system are represented. The business chart is then used in the database analysis phase to identify the entities and relationships in the organization.

Database Analysis

Database analysis is the fourth and last phase. Its purpose is to develop an enterprise data model, a data distribution plan, and an implementation plan. Because this is not a business planning text, but rather a database textbook, we will concentrate on this section. The reader desiring more information on the previous phases should consult a business planning textbook.

The first part of the database analysis phase, the *enterprise data model*, is developed by determining business entities (persons, objects, or events about which data is recorded in the database) and the relationships between these entities using the business chart developed in the business systems phase. Development of the enterprise model is a major step in the development of a database plan.

The enterprise model has three important functions in the development of the database: (1) It provides an overall, integrated view of the corporate entities and data; (2) it can be analyzed to show whether it will be necessary to divide the corporate data requirements among several databases and, if this is the case, how these divisions should be made; and (3) it provides a cross-check of data structures developed during subsequent detailed design phases. It is not the purpose of the enterprise model to show details such as data structures or data views. These are developed as part of the implementation phase.

The second part of the database analysis phase is to develop a *data distribution plan*. In most organizations it is necessary to distribute the data over several databases. The data distribution plan describes how the data will be distributed over these databases. This plan is based upon information in the enterprise model.

The third part of the database analysis phase is to develop an *implementation plan*. Priorities are established and a timetable generated for the implementation of the various stages of the database plan.

Determining the Data Needs

As mentioned previously, *user views* are one source of information describing the data needs. A user view is a subset of data required by a particular user to make a decision or carry out some action. The type of user, whether concerned with operational, tactical, or strategic management, determines the type of data required. Determining exactly what this data is is part of the planning process. Information contained in forms submitted to or submitted by these users can be an important source of this data. Reports and other documents can be another.

A data dictionary should be used to contain the results of this analysis. The dictionary should include the data item name, a description of the item, type of data (character, numeric, Boolean, etc.), allowable range if applicable, and the size of the field. The tables that make up a database will be indicated as well.

The data dictionary for the files STUDENT and BANK might look like:

TABLENAME	FIELDNAME	FIELDTYPE	FLDRANGE	FLDLENGTH
STUDENT	SID	CHARACTER		6
STUDENT	NAME	CHARACTER		20
STUDENT	AGE	INTEGER	<150	3
STUDENT	SLEVEL	INTEGER	1<= AND <=5	1
STUDENT	ZIP	CHARACTER		6
BANK	BID	CHARACTER		6
BANK	TYPE	CHARACTER	BANK/S&L	4
BANK	ZIP	CHARACTER		6

The data dictionary can then be carefully examined to be sure that there are no multiple entries for the same data item under different names, or a common name for two or more different data items.

The process we have just described is called a *top-down* process because it begins with the overall organization goals and objectives and works downward to determine the best way of organizing a database system that will meet those goals and objectives. The outcome of these activities includes the enterprise model, which shows the major entities of the organization and the associations between these entities: the data distribution plan, which shows the distribution of data across databases at possibly several physical locations; and an implementation plan.

As we noted in the introduction, a top-down approach is usually supplemented by a bottom-up analysis. Bottom-up planning deals with integration of data from existing files and databases. Current management reports are analyzed to determine if their content is relevant and then to determine if the data needed to generate them is included in the planned database. If not, that data is added.

Summary of Database Planning

Database planning is accomplished using the enterprise model to identify entities and relationships. In addition, a data distribution plan and an implementation plan should be developed. These plans will organize and simplify the designing of an effective database that will meet both the present and future needs of the corporation.

Introduction to Entity-Relationship Modeling and Constructs

Entity-relationship modeling (ERM) is the formal expression of the enterprise data model developed in step 4 above. The ERM approach, developed by Peter Chen, defines database information in terms of entities, their attributes, and the connections between entities, which are called relationships. This approach has been modified and extended by others. An advantage of the entity-relationship approach is that it is easy to understand. For complex databases the entity-relationship approach provides an overview of the entities and relations within the database without overwhelming the designers with low-level details.

It should be noted that the ERM is intended to facilitate the design of a single database, rather than an entire set of databases. As mentioned previously, corporations rarely have a single massive database. Rather, corporate information is typically spread across many smaller databases. The ERM is not intended to encompass the entire set of databases that an organization may need.

In the following section, we will provide a brief overview and example database design for the GSL using fundamental entity relationship modeling techniques. The form of an entity relationship model is a graph with rectangles for entities, diamonds for relationships, and lines connecting these objects. Information about attributes is suppressed from this graphical model to keep it from becoming so detailed that the primary objects (entities and relationships) are obscured. In subsequent sections various extensions and enhancements to the original ERM are presented and illustrated with examples.

Basic ERM Constructs: Entities, Attributes, and Relationships

An *entity* is an object about which information is being collected. This object can be a person, place, thing, or event. In the GSL database, obvious entities include students, loans, and banks. But it is not always easy to identify all the relevant entities, especially those based on events. For example, suppose that a student address changes. Is that event a relevant entity? Certainly the fact that the student has a new address is of interest and calls for an update of the address for the student. But is the *move* itself a relevant event/entity? It is if a historical record of addresses is needed. In this case an entity *move* should be established. However, if all that is needed is the current address, then the event of changing addresses becomes only transient input data.

It is important to distinguish between entity occurrences and entity types, or sets. The student *entity type* is a definition of the student entity. It does not have values. An *entity occurrence* is an instance of an entity and, in the database, is represented as a set of values—usually a record or tuple. In general, we will refer to an entity type as an entity, unless it is not clear from the context whether we are referring to an entity type or an entity occurrence.

Entities have properties. For example, a student has an age, name, sex, race, residence location, and school. In the ERM, properties are termed *attributes*—the same term used for the columns/data items in the relational model. In the GSL, attributes of the student entities include the properties listed above. Loan attributes include the loan identifier, the amount, the interest rate, and the repayment terms. Attributes are of two types: identifiers and descriptors. In the GSL, identifiers are the student number, the bank identifier, and the loan number. An entity may have more than a single identifier, and some identifiers may be composite (multiple attributes). For example, the student entity might have both a social security number and a composite attribute, such as a school identifier and a school-assigned student number. Attributes such as date of birth, race, address, and amount of loan are clearly descriptor atrributes.

There are attributes that are sometimes tempting to classify as identifiers. Consider the student name. Is this a descriptor or an identifier? The key is to ask whether if given a value of an attribute you can always uniquely identify a single entity. Could there be more than one student with the same name? Do you know a James Smith? What a coincidence—so do I!

Note that attributes are not represented in the graphical ERM of the database. Attributes must, of course, be described somewhere in a conceptual database model. In the ERM they are expressed separately from the graph; a tabular form or a linear form may be used that is similar to the form we have used to describe relations. For example, the attributes of STUDENT, and the fact that STUDENT is the containing entity can be written as: STUDENT (SID, SLEVEL, DATE_OF_BIRTH,...).

While you may disagree at first, it is sometimes difficult to distinguish between attributes and entities. Are data about a student's parents attributes of the student or attributes of another entity called *parent*? Mull this around for a while—we'll adddress this issue later.

The final element of the ERM is *relationships*. These are descriptions of the associations between entities. Relationships can be one-to-one, one-to-many, or many-to-many. As an example of a one-to-one relationship, suppose that each student has a single financial statement (an entity). Then the relationship between the student and the financial statement is one-to-one. A case of a one-to-many relationship is between the student and the loans received by that student. Another example is the relationship between banks and loans. Relationships are represented on the graph by diamonds with lines connecting the related entities. On a "many" side of a relationship, the diamond is blackened, while on a "one" side it is left open.

Figure 11–4 shows the ERM for the GSL database. The students, banks, and loans are represented by boxes. The relationships between them are represented by connecting lines, with triangles to indicate whether the relationship is one-to-one, one-to-many, or many-to-many.

An example of a many-to-many relationship is the relationship between students and banks. However, this many-to-many relationship is captured by the two one-to-many relationships beween students and loans, and banks and loans.

There are situations of many-to-many relationships that are not captured by several one-to-many relationships. Assume that another entity, *school,* also exists and that a student

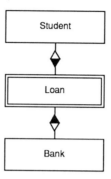

Fig 11-4 Initial ERM for the GSL Database. The double-lined rectangle around LOAN indicates it is a weak entity—its existence depends on BANK and LOAN (see figure 11-7).

may over time, or even simultaneously, be enrolled in more than one school. Since a student may attend several schools, and clearly each school has many students, the relationship between entities of these types is many-to-many. Therefore, we would add a *school* (entity) rectangle to the graph with a fully blackened *student-school* (relationship) diamond between *school* and *student*.

Additional ERM Features and Extensions

In this section we present several of the important extensions that have been developed by various researchers and practitioners over the almost 15 years since the publication of the first ERM paper by Chen. Our discussion draws heavily from an excellent article by Teorey, Yang, and Fry.

The extended entity relationship model (E-ERM) adds the enhancements *subset hierarchy* and *generalized hierarchy*. If every occurrence of an entity A is also an occurrence of an entity B, then the entity type A is a subset of the entity type B. This is known as a subset hierarchy. Substituting actual entity types for A and B helps decipher the definition: every occurrence of an entity type *engineering student* is also an occurrence of an entity type *student*. The subsets may overlap. For example, the entity type *graduate student* is also a subset of *student* but clearly overlaps *engineering student*. This is also called an overlapping subset. For example, if A designates students, then B could be students who are applying for a loan, students who have a loan, or students who are behind in their loan payments. Note that any single A can be related to more than one B. This could also be called an inclusive relationship.

In a generalized hierarchy, the entity B can be related to only one of several As. For example, a student can be either male or female, not both. A loan can be either paid in full or not.

Degree of Relationship

The E-ERM describes the degree of relationship, which consists of the number of entities associated with the relationship. For example, if the degree is one, two, or three, then the terms unary, binary, or ternary are used. An n-ary relationship is of degree *n*. If the relationship is with one other entity, then the degree is binary. For example, the relationship between a student and a loan is binary. If there is a relationship to two other entities, then

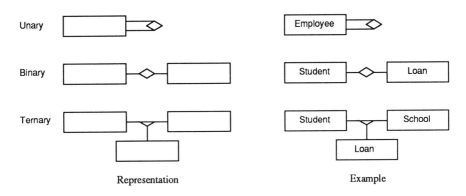

Fig 11-5 *ERM Method of Representation of Degree of Relationship—Unary, Binary, Ternary.*

the degree is ternary. Suppose in this case that there is also an entity called *school* in the database. If each loan is for a particular student at a particular school, then the degree is ternary. (However, if the loan is not specified for a particular school, then the degree would only be binary.)

Unary relationships occur when an entity is related to another entity (or entities) of the same type. A common situation in which this occurs is in a personnel database with the *employee* entity type. Each employee has a single manager. Thus, each employee is related to another employee entity: his manager. (In a relational model, this relationship is indicated by storing the identifier of the manager record in the employee record.) Another situation in which the unary relationship occurs is in a "bill of materials" database. There is often just a single entity type, *part,* in a bill of materials database. Parts are combined into *assemblies,* which are also of the same entity type, *part.* Parts, which are assemblies, can themselves be combined into higher-level assemblies, and so forth. In the bill of materials example, a part is often used in several assemblies. For example, a specific electronic chip may be used in several different circuit boards in a computer. This unary relationship is many-to-many: a part is used in many parts (assemblies) and a part (assembly) is made up of many parts. The employee example is a unary, one-to-many relationship: each manager has many employees.

Figure 11–5 shows the represention of unary, binary, and ternary relationships. For illustration purposes, we have labeled the entity boxes with names used in these examples.

Connectivity of Relationship

The connectivity of the relationship specifies the number of occurrences of two or more related entities. Entities may occur once or many times. The numeric value of "many" is known as the *cardinality* of the connectivity. Limits may be placed on the cardinality. For example, if a student is limited to a minimum of zero and a maximum of 10 loans, then this range is expressed by entering (0,10) on the line between the entity rectangle and the relationship diamond.

Figure 11–6 shows how to represent one-to-one, one-to-many, and many-to-many relationships.

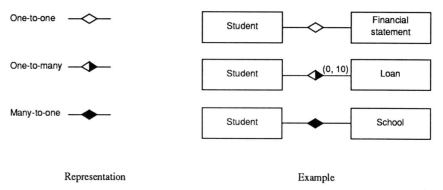

Representation   Example

*Fig 11-6 ERM Representation of **Connectivity** of Relationships—One-To-One, One-To-Many, and Many-To-Many. Entry (low, high) indicates lower and upper limits on number of occurences on the entity.*

Membership Class

The "one" or "many" side of a relationship can be mandatory or optional. If an entity on the "one" side must always exist, then it has a membership class of mandatory. If a one-sided entity's existence is not required, its membership class is optional. In the same way, if an entity is on the "many" side of a relationship and it must exist, its membership class is mandatory. If its existence is not required, its membership class is optional.

An independent (strong) entity associated with a dependent (weak) entity cannot be optional. An example of a relationship between strong and weak entities is given by a loan and its payment. The payment (a weak entity) cannot exist without the loan (a strong entity); see Figure 11–7. However, the entity on the weak side of the relationship can be optional. For example, a loan may exist without any payments. In this case, the weak side of the relationship, *payment,* can be optional.

Figure 11–8 shows how to represent mandatory and optional relationships.

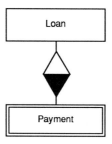

*Fig 11-7 Representation of **Strong** (Independent) Entities by Single-Lined Rectangle and **Weak** (Dependent) Entities by Double-Lined Rectangle*

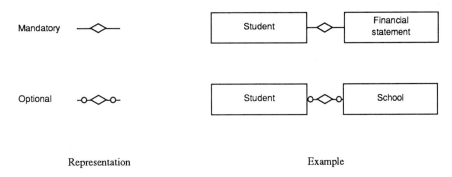

Fig 11-8 Representation of Mandatory and Optional Membership on Entity

Identifing Entities and Attributes

As noted earlier, it is not always easy to distinguish between entities, attributes, and relationships. This process is made much easier by using the E-ERM described earlier in this chapter to identify and classify entities vs. attributes.

Distinguishing Entities and Attributes

If an object is accompanied by descriptive information (a descriptor), it is an entity; otherwise, it is an attribute. Thus STUDENT, BANK, and LOAN are entities. STUDENT has the descriptive information NAME, SLEVEL, AGE, and ZIP. NAME, TYPE, and LDATE are attributes of STUDENT, BANK, and LOAN respectively.

As an example of an object that might or might not be represented as an enitity, consider *school*. If the school a student is attending is an important fact, then clearly the school's name or ID must be part of the database. If this is the only attribute of the school that is needed, then the school is not treated as an entity. However, if other properties of the school are relevant, such as its address, type (junior college, trade school, university, etc.) then the school becomes an entity with these attributes and has a relationship to the student.

Multivalued Attributes As Entities

If more than one value of the descriptive information (descriptor) is associated with a given entity occurrence, then the descriptor should be classified as an entity rather than an attribute. For example, if we had the relationship STUDENT with the descriptor LID in the GSL database, then LID should be classified as an entity because a single student could have more than one loan, even though LID might only have a loan identification number as its descriptor. The same is true if we wish to keep track of a student's dependents. DEPENDENT would be classified as an entity, because once again a student could have more than one dependent, even though, once again, DEPENDENT might only have a dependent name as its descriptor.

A Many-to-One Descriptor As an Entity

If a descriptor has a many-to-one relationship with an object it should be classified as an entity. Because there is a many-to-one relationship between BANKID and TYPE in the

GSL database example (several of the bank names could be savings and loan types), BANKID should be classified as an entity.

Tying Attributes to the Object Most Directly Described

A student's ZIP code should be an attribute of STUDENT, not LOAN, because the ZIP code is information more directly about a student than about a loan. However, this is not always easy to determine. For instance, where does CITY belong? To STUDENT or ZIP? A student lives in a particular city, but a ZIP code belongs to a particular city, or part of a city. (As we will see in following chapters, CITY should be part of ZIP; however, to reduce processing costs and time delays it may instead be part of STUDENT.) As another example, does COLLECTION AGENT belong to LOAN or STUDENT? A collection agent is attempting to collect on a particular loan, but he or she is also trying to collect from a particular person. However, if COLLECTION_AGENT belonged to STUDENT, and a student had more than one loan, it would imply that the collection agent was trying to collect on *all* the loans, even though all but one loan might be up to date on the payments. Because of this ambiguity, it is better to include COLLECTION_AGENT in LOAN rather than STUDENT.

Avoiding Identifiers Composed of Multiple Attributes

If two entities with the same identifiers include the same attributes you can eliminate one of the entities, later replacing it with a relationship to the other entity that had the same identifiers or included those identifiers. For instance, if the education department wanted to track those students who were doing student teaching (because as a teaching incentive they are not required to make loan payments immediately), a STUDENT_TEACHER entity might be added to the database. In this case there exist the entities STUDENT_TEACHER, with identifiers SID and TEACHER_ID; STUDENT with identifier SID; and TEACHER with identifier TEACHER_ID. However, the entity STUDENT_TEACHER can be dropped. Instead, it can later be replaced with the relationship STUDENT_TEACHER between the entities STUDENT and TEACHER.

Should an entity's composite identifier's attributes not be repeated as described above, you can convert the several attributes to entities and later relate the original entity to these new entities. If any of the attributes do not lend themselves to conversion to an entity you should leave the original relationship unchanged. For example, if in the GSL database you had an entity ATTENDANCE with the attributes STUDENT and CLASS, you could drop the ATTENDANCE entity and make STUDENT and CLASS entities. Later you could make ATTENDANCE a relationship between STUDENT and CLASS.

Identifying Generalization and Subset Hierarchies

Reattach attributes if a generalization or subset hierarchy is found. Tie the identifier and generic descriptors to the generic descriptors, and the specific identifiers and descriptors to the subset entities. As an example, consider the GSL database with the addition of an entity DEFAULT_LOANS with identifier LID and descriptors LOAN_AMNT, LDATE, SID, and COLLECTION_AGENT. We also have the entities ACTIVE_LOAN with identifier LID and descriptors LOAN_AMNT, LDATE, SID, and CURRENT_BALANCE; the entity CLOSED_LOAN with the identifier LID; and the descriptors LOAN_AMNT, LDATE, SID, and FINAL_PAYMENT_DATE.

Noting that we have a generalization hierarchy, we can provide the entity LOAN with the generic identifier LID and the generic descriptors LOAN_AMNT, LDATE, and SID.

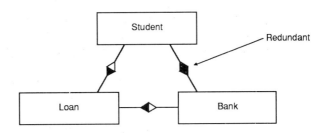

Fig 11-9 Example of a Many-To-Many Relationship That Is Redundant Due to the Existence of Two One-To-Many Relationships

The entity DEFAULT_LOAN is then assigned the identifier LID and the specific descriptor COLLECTION_AGENT; ACTIVE_LOAN is assigned the identifier LID and the descriptors LOAN_BALANCE; and CLOSED_LOAN is assigned the identifier LID and the descriptor FINAL_PAYMENT_DATE. Now we can tie the generic LOAN entity to any of the loan types (default, active, closed) via the common identifier (primary key), LID.

Defining Relationships

If an object has not yet been classified as an entity or an attribute we must define it as a relationship. A relationship requires a definition consisting of its degree, connectivity, membership class, and attributes.

Determine if a relationship is redundant. In the preceding example we could have three relationships. LOAN (many) could be related to STUDENT (one) and also BANK (one). STUDENT (many) could be related to BANK (many). See Figure 11–9. The redundancy can be eliminated by dropping the relationship between BANK and STUDENT. We can still discover the student's bank through the BID identifier in the loan.

An additional point to remember is that relations are between entities, not the entities' identifiers.

Transformations to Relations

The basic transformations lead to the following three basic types of relations:

- An entity relation with the same content as the original entity
- An entity relation with the embedded foreign key of the parent entity
- A relationship relation with the foreign keys of all the related entities

Foreign Keys and Null Values

In a one-to-one relation, when both entities are mandatory, each entity becomes a relation, and the key of either may appear as a foreign key in the other.

If the relationship is one-to-many, both sides can be either mandatory or optional. The foreign key must appear on the "many" side: the child entity. If the "one" side is optional, the foreign key can be null. For example, suppose we add a "collection agent" to the model, as in Figure 11–10. A loan is assigned a collection agent if the loan is declared in default.

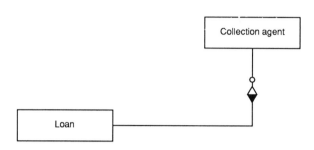

Fig 11-10 Example of a One-To-Many Relationship with Optional Entity on the One (COLLECTION_AGENT) Side. That is, a LOAN does not necessarily have a collection agent assigned.

Loans not in default are not assigned a collection agent; therefore, COLLECTION AGENT is optional. A loan relation with no collection agent would have a null value for the (foreign key) collection agent identifier.

In the many-to-many relationship, with both sides either mandatory or optional, only primary keys are permitted; embedded foreign keys are not possible. For instance, suppose that a school entity exists and that a student may be registered, possibly at different times, in more than one school (see Figure 11–11). In this case the relationship entity will have the foreign keys of both school and student.

A single entity with a one-to-one relationship with itself requires that both sides be completely mandatory or completely optional. In the resulting relation, the pairing entity key appears as a foreign key. For example, suppose that each collection agent may have a backup agent, but that each agent can back up only one other agent (see Figure 11–12). The collection agent relation will have a primary key, which will be the collection agent ID, and a foreign key, which will be the collection agent backup. The foreign key can be null if it is not mandatory that an agent have a backup.

In any ternary or higher order relationship, a relation must be created with the primary keys of the related entities. For example, if a loan must be used by a student while enrolled

Fig 11-11 Example of a Many-To-Many Relationship. A student may be enrolled at more than one school.

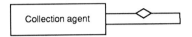

Fig 11-12 Example of a One-To-One Unary Relationship. Each collection agent has a single backup agent.

at a specific school, then a ternary relationship exists and a relation with SID, LID, and school identifier is created.

After these additions, the GSL database E-ERM might now look like Figure 11–13.

Summary of E-ERM

The E-ERM provides a means for modeling the data requirements of an organization without becoming bogged down in the details. Using the E-ERM, entities are identified and the relationships between them are defined. In addition, generalization and subset hierarchies can be identified. Through this process, the E-ERM provides a way of integrating different user views into one coherent data model.

The E-ERM can then be transformed into relations. Every entity is transformed into one relation, using the key and non-key attributes of the entity. Binary many-to-many relationships are then transformed into a *relationship* relation. Ternary and n-ary relationships are also transformed into relationship relations.

The E-ERM simplifies the database analysis phase of the BSP by providing a thorough and efficient means for analyzing and organizing corporate data needs. This information can be used to build the relations discussed in the next chapter.

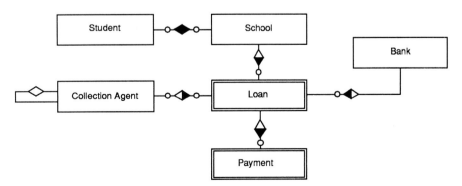

Fig 11-13 Full E-ERM of the Extended GSL Database

Questions and Problems

Questions

1. Describe the most critical element for a successful database.

2. How does a database design proceed in both a top-down and bottom-up manner?

3. Describe the four functional areas typical of most organizations.

4. What are the three levels of management, and how do their data needs differ?

5. Describe the three important functions that the enterprise model accomplishes in database planning. What does the enterprise model not encompass?

6. List and describe the four steps in the business system planning process.

7. What is the difference between entities and attributes? When should attributes be entities?

8. Define *identifiers, descriptors,* and *relationships.*

9. What are the basic types of relations in the E-R model?

10. Describe a *subset hierarchy* and a *generalized hierarchy.* Give examples of each.

11. How are E-ERM constructs classified?

Problems

1. The federal government operates several student loan and grant programs. Each of these programs requires a considerable amount of data on students such as name, address, SSN, date of birth, etc. Due to historical, organizational, and funding reasons, each loan/grant program has its own database. In addition, the different databases are stored on several completely independent computers. Clearly, this leads to a significant amount of redundancy and inconsistency. The separation of data leads to problems ranging from small annoyances, such as the necessity for students to submit multiple address changes if they have loans/grants from more than a single program, to fraud—students may obtain grants and loans in excess of legislated limits if they use a little care to disguise their identity. (For example, use slightly different social security numbers via, say, a transposition error for different loan/grant applications.)

   Suggest what might be done to reduce redundancy and inconsistency and the concomitant problems. But, keep in mind that your suggestions have severe constraints: each program will continue to operate more or less independently, obtaining funding to operate an "umbrella" database might be difficult, there are civil rights concerns about building large shared databases, etc.

   The following two problems represent extensions to the basic GSL model of Students, Loans, and Banks.

2. A loan can be sold by one bank to another. Of course, there must always be some bank that holds a loan—it cannot disappear into the ether. Assume that we need to be able to track the bank ownership of a loan, so that we can determine which bank owned a loan on any given date. Describe this process using the E-ERM and show the resulting relations.

3. Banks are usually branches of a parent institution. For example, there are hundreds of "Bank of Americas" in the database, each with its own identifier. Information is also maintained on the parent institution—the "corporate headquarters." However, not all financial institutions (for which we use the generic term "bank") have a parent. Many small savings and loans and credit unions have only a single office; thus, the office and the corporate headquarters are one in the same. Show how this is modeled in the E-ERM. Also show the resulting mapping to relations.

The following two problems are database design exercises that require you to develop an E-ERM diagram and translate that into relations. In Chapter 12 you will be asked to perform further refinements to the designs and, in Chapter 13, to deal with implementation and physical design issues.

4. This problem involves a database design for a personnel/project application. The organization is a manufacturer that develops and builds electronic components under contract to large aerospace firms. Data on each employee and on an employee's education, positions held and salary (over time) can be described by the following:

a. Employee Name, SSN, Birthdate, Employee number

b. Degree (for example, BA, MS, PhD), Date, School, Major. An employee may have up to five degrees represented in the database. If the individual actually earned more than five degrees, only the most recent five are actually stored.

c. Position data: Each person is assigned to a single position in one department of the company at any point in time. Historical records on positions held are to be maintained.

Specific data includes the identity of the department (design, engineering, drafting, data processing, etc.,) in which the person works, the name of the position (such as Clerk A, Typist B, Ad. Asst., Sr. Engineer, Systems Analyst, Personnel Director), and the start and end dates for the position and department. If a person changes either position or department (or both), a new record is generated. Every employee is assigned to a position and department.

d. Salary data gives the salary amount and the effective dates (start and end) of the salary. Each change in salary (or a hire) generates a new record. Of course, since most people like to be paid, every employee must have at least one salary record. And, since the company thinks that a single salary for each person is sufficient, only one salary per person exists at any point in time.

The other major set of data relates to the contracts. A contract contains a Contract ID, a brief description (for example, avionics module for B808), contract amount, and the start and end dates of the contract. In addition, each contract has an employee who is assigned responsibility for the contract—the "contract manager." Note that contract manager is not a position. While a contract manager is typically a mid-level manager, on occasion a senior, non-managing, engineer may be assigned the responsiblity of managing a small contract.

Finally, for cost accounting purposes, data is collected and aggregated to show the total dollar charge by each employee to each contract for each day. An employee may work on several contracts on a given day and a contract will (typically) have several employees making charges to it each day.

If you need to make assumptions about the data semantics, state them as part of your design. Express your design in the form of an E-ERM. Indicate entities and whether they are strong or weak; indicate relationships, their degree, connectivity, and the cardinality limits on connectivity, if any. Then, translate the model to relations.

5. A property management firm maintains a set of files on the apartment houses they manage including data on the property owners and the tenants. The file design was done some time ago, and the company now realizes that good design practices were not followed. They have asked you to provide a database design which will subsequently be mapped into a relational DBMS. The design is to be in the form of an E-ERM and a set of preliminary relations.

There are currently several files in the system. You are to focus on the following four: Property, Unit, Receipt, and Expense. Each file and the meaning of its attributes are described below.

a. **Property** (ID, Street Address, City, State, ZIP, Number of units, (Owner's) Name, Street Address, City, State, ZIP, Phone)

This file includes data on each apartment house and its owner. The ID is a unique identifier assigned by the company to each apartment house. The first set of address data items are for the property; the second group is for the owner. In some cases a property is owned by more than one person, that is, there are partners in the ownership. In this case a record is entered with ID and data for each owner but without the address data for the property. In addition, an individual may own more than a single piece of property. When this occurs, data about the owner is simply entered into each property record. Of course, every property has an owner.

b. **Unit** (Unit #, ID, Monthly rental, Deposit, Tenant name, Reference, Phone, No. of bedrooms & bathrooms, Lease start date & end date, Rent due date)

This file describes an individual unit in an apartment and the rental terms. The unit has a number which is usually just the number of the individual unit (such as #304). A unit number is assigned by the company if one does not exist. The ID is the property ID. "Reference" is the name of a reference for the tenant. When a unit is rented to a new tenant, data for that tenant and the lease replace the current data. If the unit is vacant, the data that relates to the tenant (deposit, name, reference, phone and lease data) is erased, but the record is kept in the file so that data on the unit itself (such as Unit #, No. of bedrooms) is available.

c. **Receipt** (ID, Unit#, Pay_Date, For, Amount, Tenant name, Method of Payment)

This file records rental and other payments. The ID and Unit # identify the particular rental unit. Pay_Date is the date of payment; Due_Date is the date the payment was due. The item "For" indicates what the payment is for, by using a code: R = rent, D = payment for repairs (for example, tenant breaks a window), U = payment for utilities (for example, when they are paid by the tenant), etc. The method of payment indicates cash, money order, or check (with check number).

d. **Expense** (ID, Unit#, Date, Amount, Type, Description)

This relation records expenses incurred by the company in the management of a unit. Type is a code for the expense to indicate cleaning, painting, utilities (if not paid by the tenant), etc. If the expense relates to the apartment building itself and not a particular unit, Unit # = 0 is entered.

Develop an E-ERM diagram for this data and translate it into relations.

References

Blaha, M. R.; Premerlani W. J.; and Rumbaugh J.E. "Relational Database Design Using an Object-Oriented Methodology." *Communications ACM,* vol. 31, no. 4 (April 1988), pp. 414–427.

Chatfield, A. T., and Rajkumar, T. R. "Comparison of Analysis Techniques for Information Requirement Determination." *Communications ACM,* vol. 31, no. 9 (September 1988), pp. 1090–1097.

Chen, P. "The Entity-Relationship Model—Toward a Unified View of Data." *ACM TODS,* vol. 1, no. 1 (March 1976), pp. 9–36.

IBM Corporation. *Business System Planning: Information System Planning Guide.* 1975. Pub. no. GE20-0527-1. White Plains, N. Y.

Martin, J. *Managing the Date-Base Environment..* Englewood Cliffs, N.J.: Prentice-Hall, 1983.

_____. *Strategic Data-Planning Methodologies.* Englewood Cliffs, N.J.: Prentice-Hall, 1982.

Peckham, J., and Maryanski, F. "Semantic Data Models." *ACM Computing Surveys,* vol. 20, no. 3 (September 1988), pp. 153–190.

Shuey, S., and Wiederhold, G. "Data Engineering and Information Systems." *Computer,* vol. 19, no. 1 (January 1986), pp. 18–33.

Smith, J., and Smith, D. "Database Abstraction: Aggregation and Generalization." *ACM TODS,* vol. 2, no. 2 (June 1977), pp. 105–133.

Teorey, T.; Yang, D.; and Fry, J. "A Logical Design Methodology for Relational Databases Using the Extended Entity-Relationship Model." *ACM Computing Surveys,* vol. 18, no. 2 (June 1, 1986), pp. 197–222.

12 *Normalization*

Introduction

Normalization is a database design activity that occurs after the entities and relationships of an entity relationship modeling design have been mapped into relations. Normalization is performed to further refine the relations, with the primary goal being to design relations that minimize the possibility of data inconsistencies. Of course, normalization can be applied to relations derived through any process. They don't have to be the result of an ERM approach.

What Are Normal Forms?

A *normal form* is a set of rules that a relation must obey in order to be classified at that level of normal form. There are six normal forms, designated as 1NF, 2NF, 3NF, BCNF, 4NF, and 5NF. BCNF (Boyce/Codd normal form) is a refined version of the third normal form. These forms are used to help the database designer eliminate redundant information in the database and reduce the possibility of inconsistencies. Before launching into definitions of the various forms, we will give an example to illustrate how failure to properly normalize a database results in both redundancy and in the potential for so-called "update anomalies," that is, inconsistencies in the database.

As an example of a poorly normalized database consider the GSL database with revised relations LOAN_NOT3 and BANK1. These tables differ from the original design in having the bank's ZIP code moved into the LOAN table. The following results:

BANK1 Table

BID	TYPE
FIDELITY	MSB
SEAFIRST	BANK
PEOPLES	BANK
CAPITAL	SL
HOME	SL

LOAN_NOT3 Table

LID	LDATE	YEARS	INT_RATE	AMOUNT	SID	BID	BZIP
27	15-SEP-85	5	8.5	1200	9735	HOME	98031
78	21-JUN-86	5	7.75	1000	9735	PEOPLES	98109
87	07-SEP-83	5	7.0	2000	9735	SEAFIRST	98101
92	12-JAN-85	6	7.5	2100	4494	FIDELITY	98101
99	15-JAN-86	6	9.0	2200	4494	FIDELITY	98101
170	30-APR-83	6	6.5	1900	8767	PEOPLES	98109
490	07-MAY-84	6	6.0	2500	3749	PEOPLES	98109
493	24-JUN-85	7	7.5	3000	3749	PEOPLES	98109

Clearly, this is a change for the worse. Instead of five occurrences of BZIP we now have eight. In a real database, with thousands of banks but millions of loans, the increased number of BZIP occurrences would result in a serious increase in database size. One could argue that the gains in processing efficiency might offset the added storage cost. For example, suppose (for some curious reason) that we frequently want the bank's ZIP code, but not other bank data, when loans are retrieved. In the revised design, the BZIP value is available without joining BANK and LOAN.

But, there is another, more severe problem introduced by this design. That is the potential inconsistency problem and the fact that, despite the increase in number of BZIPs stored, we have lost information with this design. Every time we add a loan to the database we have to supply the bank's ZIP code. Suppose FIDELITY had a change in BZIP value. Then every loan tuple with a BID of FIDELITY will have to have its BZIP changed. This not only increases the update cost (versus a single update of BZIP in the BANK relation), but it also opens the possibility of inconsistency. It is now possible that some loan tuples with BID = FIDELITY will have one BZIP value while others will have a different BZIP value.

As noted, the revised design also results in a loss of information. With the original design, we had the ZIP for every bank. With the revised design, any bank with no loans has no ZIP. Since CAPITAL has no loans, we can't determine its ZIP code.

It should be obvious that BZIP doesn't belong in LOAN_NOT3. Fortunately, we have more than just intuition to rely on to identify the revised design as deficient. The rules for normalization will prevent this type of situation.

A relation is in one of the designated normal forms if it meets specific conditions. The rules for the first normal form are trivial: All relations that contain only atomic values and a primary key are in first normal form (1NF). In most relational DBMSs, relations must be in 1NF.

There is a hierarchical ordering to the normal forms so that a relation that is in a given normal form is also in all the lower forms. For example, a relation in 4NF is also in BCNF, 3NF, 2NF, and 1NF. A lower form may be in a higher form, so that a relation in 2NF might also be in 3NF, BCNF, and so on; however, this is not guaranteed. Usually the higher the normal form of the relation, the better the database design—but not always, as we shall see.

Note that while normal forms are defined in terms of relations (not record types, sets, segments, etc.), the process of normalization is also an important part of database design for all data models including network and hierarchical.

Functional Dependence

The concept of functional dependence (FD) is fundamental to normalization. An attribute, Y, is said to be *functionally dependent* on another attribute, X, if the value of Y is determined by the value of the attribute X. A simple way of saying this is that knowing the value of X uniquely determines the value of Y. It is important to note that the attribute X may be a composite.

As examples of functional dependency, consider the GSL STUDENT relation, reproduced below. Since SID determines NAME, NAME is said to be functionally dependent on SID. This means that given a value for SID, say 8767, we can determine, without ambiguity, the value of NAME (CABEEN in this case). AGE, LEVEL, and SZIP are also functionally dependent on SID. But, clearly, several of the attributes of STUDENT do not determine the values of other attributes. For example, given LEVEL = 1, there are two possible values for other attributes: SID could be either 9735 or 6793; NAME could be either ALLEN or SANDS. SID, NAME, AGE, and SZIP are not functionally dependent on LEVEL.

STUDENT Table

SID	NAME	LEVEL	AGE	SZIP
9735	ALLEN	1	21	98101
4494	ALTER	2	19	98112
8767	CABEEN	5	24	98118
2368	JONES	4	23	98155
6793	SANDS	1	17	98101
3749	WATSON	5	29	98168

But, what about NAME? Does it determine, for example, SID? Given NAME = JONES, we know that SID = 2368 from the example data. In fact, SID is not functionally dependent on NAME because for functional dependency to hold it must be true that for all time and for all possible data situations we can determine SID given NAME. While NAME determines SID for the example data, it is clearly possible to have two or more people with the same name. While the uniqueness of SID is assured, the uniqueness of NAME is not. Therefore, the only functional dependencies that exist in the student relation are the dependencies of NAME, LEVEL, AGE, and SZIP on SID.

The functional dependencies in BANK are BZIP on BID and TYPE on BID. To make this statement we assume, of course, that BID is a unique identifier of BANK. For the entire population of banks that might be represented in our database, there is no duplication of BID values. In the LOAN relation, every attribute is functionally dependent on the LID attribute. Given a value for LID, values for LDATE, YEARS, INT_RATE, AMOUNT, SID, and BID are uniquely determined. Again, while a couple of these attributes happen also to be unique (LDATE, INT_RATE, and AMOUNT), no attributes are functionally dependent on them because clearly there is no constraint that limits the database to having only one loan with a given LDATE value, one loan of a given AMOUNT, etc.

Another definition, that of *full functional dependence,* is needed before the second normal form can be defined. *An attribute B has full functional dependence on a composite attribute A if B is functionally dependent on A and not functionally dependent on any subset of A.* To illustrate this concept, an alternative LOAN table called LOAN_NOT2 is defined with its key made up of the pair of attributes SID and SEQ. SEQ numbers loans within students; thus, the loans held by a particular student have SEQ values 1, 2, etc. Furthermore, the student's name is included in LOAN_NOT2. The LOAN_NOT2 relation now looks like the following, with INT_RATE, AMOUNT, and BID suppressed for simplicity:

LOAN_NOT2 Table

SEQ	LDATE	YEARS	SID	NAME	BID
1	15-SEP-85	5	9735	ALLEN	HOME
2	21-JUN-86	5	9735	ALLEN	PEOPLES
3	07-SEP-83	5	9735	ALLEN	SEAFIRST
1	12-JAN-85	6	4494	ALTER	FIDELITY
2	15-JAN-86	6	4494	ALTER	FIDELITY
1	30-APR-83	6	8767	CABEEN	PEOPLES
1	07-MAY-84	6	3749	WATSON	PEOPLES
2	24-JUN-85	7	3749	WATSON	PEOPLES

Now all attributes in this relation are functionally dependent on the composite attribute SID, SEQ. But NAME is not fully functionally dependent on the pair because it is functionally dependent on SID alone. That is, to determine NAME it is sufficient to know SID alone—SEQ is extra baggage. With the definition of full functional dependence, FFD, in hand we are ready to define second, third, and BCNF normal forms.

Second, Third, and Boyce/Codd Normal Forms

Even before defining second normal form, you can see that there are clear problems with the LOAN_NOT2 relation. Changes in student name, for example, must be changed in multiple rows—an undesirable situation that can lead to inconsistencies. As we will see, the problem stems from the fact that LOAN_NOT2 is not in second normal form.

Second Normal Form

A relation is in second normal form if all of its attributes are fully functionally dependent on its primary key. As demonstrated above, LOAN_NOT2 is not in 2NF because NAME is not FFD on the composite, SID:SEQ. As with the introductory example, this non-2NF table creates a variety of problems:

1. Two (or more) rows with identical SID values may have different values for NAME.

2. We cannot add data for a student who does not yet have a loan. It is not "legal" to add the SID and NAME values alone, making other attributes null, because this would result in a null value for SEQ; SEQ cannot be null because it is part of the primary key.

3. To avoid losing track of the student name when loans are deleted, we cannot delete the last loan for a given student.

The relation is converted to 2NF and these update problems eliminated by making the following changes: remove NAME from LOAN_NOT2, renaming it LOAN2, and create a new relation, such as ST, which contains SID and NAME. Now the attributes in LOAN2 are all FFD on the primary key, SID:SEQ. The new relation ST has key SID and its attribute, NAME, is FFD on SID. Of course, if we already have the STUDENT table, then the ST table is redundant and should be eliminated.

The modification of a table that is not in 2NF and the creation of new table(s) is performed using the steps below: Assume that the non-2NF table is called NOT2; its key is the composite attribute K1:K2:....Km. Attributes Y1, Y2, ...Yn are FFD on the key. Attributes Z1, Z2, ...Zp are not FFD on the key; each attribute Zi (i=1,2,...,p) is FFD on some subset of the key. For purposes of illustration, assume Z1, Z2, and Z3 are FFD on K1; Z4 and Z5 are FFD on the composite K1:K2; Z6 and Z7 FFD on K1:K3.

1. Project the key (K1:K2:...Km) and all attributes, say, Y1,Y2,...Yn that are FFD on the key into a new table. The new table will contain K1,K2, ... , Km, Y1, Y2, ..., Yn.

2. For each subset of the key on which attributes are FFD, create a new table projecting that subset and the FFD attributes. For the example, the resulting three tables would contain the following attributes (with keys underlined):

```
K1, Z1, Z2, Z3
K1, K2, Z4, Z5
K1, K3, Z6, Z7
```

Note that the new tables are created by relational algebra projections—thus, any duplicate rows will be eliminated. For example, the projection of LOAN_NOT2 over SID and NAME creates:

ST Table

SID	NAME
9735	ALLEN
4494	ALTER
8767	CABEEN
3749	WATSON

As noted above, we should always check a projected table to see if it is a subset of an existing table, in which case it should not be created. The original, non-2NF table can always be recreated by appropriate joins, and therefore no information is lost.

The conversion of LOAN_NOT2 to LOAN2 and ST has eliminated many possible inconsistencies. With the new tables it is not possible to have two rows with identical SID values but different NAME values. We can add a new student to the database even if that student does not have a loan.

At first blush it might appear that the projected 2NF tables could have inconsistencies that are not possible in the original 1NF table. As an example, inconsistency would be caused by the addition of a loan with an SID value that does not exist in the ST table. But this is ruled out by referential integrity—SID in LOAN2 is a foreign key and all values of SID in LOAN2 must exist as SID values in ST. Similarly, referential integrity prevents dropping a tuple from ST if its SID value exists in LOAN2. Keep in mind that most RDBMS implementations do not directly support referential integrity. Thus care must be exercised by application programs to prevent these anomalies.

Unfortunately, conversion to second normal form is not sufficient to eliminate all potential inconsistencies. The table called LOAN_NOT3, illustrated at the beginning of the chapter and reproduced below, is a 2NF table but has the same types of inconsistency problems that LOAN_NOT2 exhibited. The problems exist because LOAN_NOT3 is not in third normal form and, of course, also not in higher normal forms such as BCNF.

LOAN_NOT3 Table

LID	DAY	YEARS	INT_RATE	AMOUNT	SID	BID	BZIP
27	15-SEP-85	5	8.5	1200	9735	HOME	98031
78	21-JUN-86	5	7.75	1000	9735	PEOPLES	98109
87	07-SEP-83	5	7.0	2000	9735	SEAFIRST	98101
92	12-JAN-85	6	7.5	2100	4494	FIDELITY	98101
99	15-JAN-86	6	9.0	2200	4494	FIDELITY	98101
170	30-APR-83	6	6.5	1900	8767	PEOPLES	98109
490	07-MAY-84	6	6.0	2500	3749	PEOPLES	98109
493	24-JUN-85	7	7.5	3000	3749	PEOPLES	98109

Before preceding with the definition of BCNF, note that it is very easy to show that LOAN_NOT3 is 2NF—any relation that has an atomic (noncomposite) primary key must be 2NF. Since all attributes of a relation are functionally dependent on its primary key, they must also be FFD on the primary key if it is atomic.

Third and Boyce-Codd Normal Forms

The definition of *third normal form* is, in a sense, flawed. The definition was intended to eliminate a broad class of potential update problems, but after its definition was published flaws were found. They were corrected by Boyce and Codd, in a definition termed BCNF. Therefore, we will skip the 3NF definition for now. Not only is it flawed, but it is also more difficult to precisely define than BCNF. After explaining BCNF, the 3NF definition and its flaw will be explained.

The definition of BCNF relies on the definition of a *determinant*. An attribute A, possibly composite, is a determinant if some other attribute B is FFD on A. In fact, we have been using the term *determines* in our discussion of functional dependence. In the GSL database, NAME is FFD on SID, hence SID is a determinant. Other determinants in that database include LID, BID, and the composite SID:SEQ if the relation LOAN_NOT2 is used.

The *definition of BCNF* simply says that *all determinants in a relation must be candidate keys*. In terms of full functional dependency (that is, skipping the definition of determinate), *BCNF requires that if an attribute B is FFD on A then A must be a candidate key.*

The relation LOAN_NOT3 contains LID, DATE, YEARS, INT_RATE, AMOUNT, SID, BID and BZIP. It is easy to see that this relation is not BCNF. (Later we will address the question of whether it could be 3NF.) The problem is that BID is a determinant in LOAN_NOT3—BZIP is FFD on BID. But BID is not a candidate key of that relation. The decomposition of LOAN_NOT3 to BCNF relations is simple: BZIP and its determinant, BID, are projected to form a new relation (say) BK. And all attributes of LOAN_NOT3 that are FFD on its primary key (LID) are projected into a new relation, LOAN. Again, we check to see if these new relations are either subsets of existing relations or have a one-to-one relationship with existing relations. In this case, the BK and BANK1 (BANK1 is BANK without BZIP) relations have a one-to-one relationship and should be joined. (Strictly speaking, BANK1 and BANK are not one-to-one since BANK1 may be missing one or more rows for banks that do not yet have any loans. Of course, this is corrected by adding ZIPs for those banks without loans.)

The example relation LOAN_NOT3 is intuitively inappropriate. The problem arises because LOAN_NOT3 has facts about two different entities, *loans* and *banks*. The BZIP attribute is, at best, a very indirect fact about a loan. Since we have the bank entity represented in the database, attributes such as BZIP should be stored in BANK, not with loan data. This gives us a "quick and dirty" test for BCNF: *If a relation contains attributes that relate to more than a single entity, that relation is usually not BCNF.*

This intuitive test for BCNF does not always work. Suppose that we add the name of (one) parent to the STUDENT table. Now, does STUDENT contain facts about two entities, the student and his or her parent? The answer depends in part on what other data is in the database. If there is a table, PARENT, with data on parents (such as social security numbers, names, addresses, etc.), then our design is flawed. We should have the parent's SSN in STUDENT and the parent name should not be in STUDENT. But if other data on parents is not maintained, then having the parent name in STUDENT is appropriate. In this case a parent is not an entity, it is an attribute of STUDENT, just as birthdate, address, etc., are attributes even though some of them are associated with entities (for example, ADDRESS is a fact about a physical location).

There are situations of non-BCNF relations in which the intuitive definition of BCNF may fail us. Suppose that student data includes CITY, STATE, and ZIP in a new relation,

ST_NOT3. It seems that this relation contains facts about only a single entity. However, each ZIP code value is associated with a single value of city and state; thus, the attributes CITY and STATE are functionally dependent on ZIP, and ZIP is a determinant. But ZIP is clearly not a candidate key. Hence, new relations should be created. ST_NOT3 will be decomposed into STUDENT with ZIP, but excluding CITY and STATE. The other table will be called ZIP_TABLE and will contain ZIP, CITY, and STATE. The only determinant in STUDENT is SID, which is the primary key. The only determinant in ZIP_TABLE is ZIP, and it is the primary key.

Before outlining the steps for decomposition to BCNF, another example is given. The student data is extended to include data on parents—specifically, the SSN, name, ZIP, city, and state for one parent. The resulting relation can be described as:

ST_PAR (SID, NAME, SLEVEL, AGE, ZIP, PAR_SSN, PAR_NAME, PAR_ZIP, PAR_CITY, PAR_ST)

ST_PAR clearly has data on more than one entity and is therefore (probably) not BCNF. What are its determinants? SID is a determinant of all attributes in the relation (SID is the key). PAR_SSN is also a determinant—of PAR_NAME, PAR_ZIP, PAR_CITY, and PAR_ST. PAR_SSN is not a candidate key because a person could be a parent to more than one student. PAR_ZIP is also a determinant of PAR_CITY and PAR_ST. The appropriate decomposition creates the following BCNF relations:

```
STUDENT3 (SID, NAME, SLEVEL, AGE, ZIP, PAR_SSN)
PARENT (PAR_SSN, PAR_NAME, PAR_ZIP)
ZIP_TAB (ZIP, CITY, ST)
```

Note that PAR_ZIP, PAR_CITY, and PAR_ST attribute names have been changed.

The rules for decomposition to BCNF can be described more generally by the following example. Suppose we have a relation with determinants D1, and the composite D2:D3. Assume that the following FFDs exist: A1, A2, and A3 are FFD on D1. D1, A4 and A5 are FFD on the composite D2:D3. Of course, since D1 is FFD on the composite D2:D3, this also means that attributes A1, A2, and A3 are also FFD on the composite D2:D3. However, they are not directly FFD on D2:D3. Rather, attributes that are FFD on some attribute (D1 in this example), which is in turn FFD on some other attribute (D2:D3 in this case), are said to be *transitively FFD* (on D2:D3) and directly dependent only on D1. The appropriate relations will have attributes that are determinants and those attributes that are directly FFD on these determinants. For this example, the appropriate relations are (with keys underlined):

```
X (D1, A1, A2, A3)
Y (D2, D3, D1, A4, A5)
```

We may have situations in which the decomposition creates relations with more than one candidate key. Extending the above example, suppose that an attribute D4 is a determinant with attributes D1, A1, A2, and A3 directly FFD on D4. However, D1 is also a determinant of D4. The only change would be the addition of attribute D4 to relation X. D4 would be, of course, a candidate key of relation X.

BCNF vs. 3NF

There are situations in which this decomposition approach can lead to improper results. This occurs when determinants are composite and overlap—a somewhat rare situation but nonetheless an important one to know about. We will see that this is also a situation in which a relation may be in 3NF but not BCNF. We will use the following example.

First, in addition to SID in the STUDENT relation there is also SSN (social security number). SSN and SID are functionally dependent on each other—each is a determinant. STUDENT is still BCNF. The LOAN relation is redefined as follows:

```
LOAN3_NOTBCNF (SSN, SEQ, LDATE, YEARS, INT_RATE, AMOUNT, SID, BID)
```

The definition of SEQ is as before: Loans are assigned numbers within each student. Thus, SID:SEQ is the loan identifier. Since SID and SSN are both identifiers of STUDENT, SSN:SEQ is also the identifier of LOAN. The determinants of this relation are SID:SEQ and SSN:SEQ, which determine LDATE, AMOUNT, and so forth. But there is another pair of determinants: SSN, which determines SID; and SID, which determines SSN. Clearly they are not candidate keys—the relation is not BCNF. Here is the relation with example data to make clear the potential inconsistencies. For simplicity SSNs are given as letters.

LOAN3_NOTBCNF Table

SSN	SEQ	LDATE	YEARS	INT_RATE	AMOUNT	SID	BID
A	1	15-SEP-85	5	8.5	1200	9735	HOME
A	2	21-JUN-86	5	7.75	1000	9735	PEOPLES
A	3	07-SEP-83	5	7.0	2000	9735	SEAFIRST
B	1	12-JAN-85	6	7.5	2100	4494	FIDELITY
B	2	15-JAN-86	6	9.0	2200	4494	FIDELITY
C	1	30-APR-83	6	6.5	1900	8767	PEOPLES
D	1	07-MAY-84	6	6.0	2500	3749	PEOPLES
D	2	24-JUN-85	7	7.5	3000	3749	PEOPLES

Consider the potential update problems. Suppose we add a new LOAN for SID 8767. We must take care that the proper SSN value, C, is used to avoid inconsistency. Any change in SID or SSN may be required in multiple tuples to avoid inconsistency. The proper decomposition removes either SSN or SID (but not both) from the relation. Assuming that the STUDENT relation exists, we might add SSN to STUDENT, dropping it from LOAN3_NOTBCNF. The new LOAN relation (without SSN) will be BCNF.

The relation LOAN3_NOTBCNF is in 3NF. The *definition of 3NF says that all non-key attributes must be directly dependent on the primary key*. LOAN3_NOTBCNF satisfies the 3NF definition. This points out the flaw in 3NF: in situations of overlapping candidate keys, the 3NF definition may allow for inconsistencies that are not allowed by BCNF.

A relation can be in 3NF but not BCNF only if all three of the following conditions hold true:

• There are multiple candidate keys.
• The keys are composite.
• The keys overlap; that is,

• they have one or more attributes in common.

Note that these three conditions are *necessary* conditions for a relation to be 3NF but not BCNF. They are not *sufficient* conditions; that is, a relation may be 3NF, meet all of the conditions, and also be BCNF. An example follows.

Suppose data on students' enrollment at schools is stored in a relation ST_SC, with attributes school identifier (SCHOOL#), student identifier *within* the school (ST#), SSN, and GPA (the grade point average earned at the school). The candidate keys of this relation are the composites SCHOOL#:ST# and SCHOOL#:SSN. Since different schools may use the same student numbering scheme, ST# by itself is not a key. Since students may attend multiple schools, SSN alone is also not a key. Here is some example data for this relation.

```
ST_SC Table
SCHOOL#   ST#   SSN   GPA
-------   ---   ---   ---
UCLA       21    A    2.7
UCLA       30    C    3.8
UVA        30    A    3.1
PURDUE     21    B    2.5
```

In this case, the three necessary conditions for a relation to be 3NF but not BCNF are satisfied. However, the non-overlapping parts of the two candidate keys, SSN and ST#, are not determinants. Therefore, the relation is BCNF.

Here is an easy-to-remember statement that defines BCNF. "Every attribute must depend on the key, the whole key, and nothing but the key." *Key* must be interpreted to mean "candidate key." (Note: Recently one of my students suggested the addition "so help me Codd." He received an A in the class.)

We conclude this section with a few more examples of transforming relations to BCNF.

Examples

1. A university maintains information about classrooms in a relation ROOM with attributes BLDG# (identifier of a building), ROOM# (room number within the building), room capacity (CAP), and number of floors in the building (FLOORS). This relation clearly has information on more than one entity—it contains data on the rooms, such as capacity, and on the building, such as FLOORS. The determinants are the composite BLDG#:ROOM#, which determines CAP, and BLDG#, which determines FLOORS. The relation should be decomposed into ROOM3 (BLDG#, ROOM#, CAP) and BUILDING (BLDG#, FLOORS).

   The original relation, ROOM, is not even 2NF—the attribute FLOORS is not FFD on it's composite key BLDG#:ROOM#.

2. A record of a sale of a product to a customer is stored in the relation SALE with attributes INV (invoice number), CID (customer identifier), PRICE, item identifier (PART#), and quantity sold (QTY). INV is a determinant and the only candidate key. An open question is whether PART# determines price. This depends on whether there is a fixed price for each part or whether prices can differ for, say, each sale. If PRICE is determined by PART#, then the relation is clearly not BCNF. PRICE should be stored with PART# and not in SALE. No doubt, there is a relation that maintains other data on parts, such as number in stock, description, supplier, etc. The price should be stored only in that relation.

   As another example, suppose that the price for a part differs for each customer (but for multiple sales of a given part to a given customer there is a single price). PRICE is now determined by the composite PART#:CID, and a separate relation will need to be created with the three attributes PART#, CID, and PRICE.

3. A taxicab company keeps track of the location of its cabs as they report in. The data is stored in a relation PLACE, with attributes CAR#, DRIVER_ID, DATE, TIME, and LOCATION. First, we will assume that a driver may be assigned to more than one car on a given day. In this case, determinants are the composites DRIVER_ID:DATE:TIME and CAR#:DATE:TIME. While it might be unlikely that two taxis would be in the same location at the same time, we cannot rule that possibility out. Thus, LOCATION:DATE:TIME is not a determinant.

The determinants are candidate keys. This is a case of multiple, composite, over-lapping keys. But the relation is both 3NF and BCNF.

Now if we change the situation so that a driver is assigned to only a single vehicle for a day, the composite DRIVER#:DATE is a determinant of CAR#: DATE. Since several drivers may be assigned to a given car on the same day (for example, one person for the day shift, one for the night shift), CAR#:DATE is not a determinant of DRIVER#. Because DRIVER#:DATE is a determinant and not a candidate key, the relation is not BCNF. CAR# must be removed and a new relation created with DRIVER#, DATE, and CAR#. Both relations are now BCNF.

Multivalued Dependencies and Fourth Normal Form

Normalizing to the BCNF level is usually sufficient to keep potential inconsistencies to a minimum. And, in most situations, BCNF relations also satisfy the definitions for the higher-level forms 4NF and 5NF.

Relations that are BCNF but not 4NF result when so-called *multivalued dependencies* exist. Before defining multivalued dependencies, the following data is given as an example. Students may have multiple addresses—indicated, for simplicity, as a city name. Further-more, schools that students are attending or have attended are also recorded in the relation SCH_CITY. Here is some example data:

```
SCH_CITY Table
SID         SCHOOL          CITY
--------    -------------   ---------
4494        U MICH          ANN ARBOR
4494        U CHICAGO       ANN ARBOR
4494        U MICH          CHICAGO
4494        U CHICAGO       CHICAGO
4494        U MICH          SAN JOSE
4494        U CHICAGO       SAN JOSE
9735        U AZ            TUCSON
9735        U AZ            DENVER
```

The semantics of this data need a little explanation. There is no association between SCHOOL and CITY—they simply represent the cities where the student has lived and the schools attended. Therefore, all possible combinations of schools and cities are recorded for each student. There is something unsatisfying about this method of representing the data since it seems to suggest that the student lived in the given city while attending the given school; for example, that student 4494 lived in Ann Arbor while attending the University of Chicago. At best, that would be a long commute. The sensible representation of this data is as two relations: one with SID and CITY, the other with SID and SCHOOL. This gives:

ST_SCH Table

SID	SCHOOL
4494	U MICH
4494	U CHICAGO
9735	U AZ

ST_CITY Table

SID	CITY
4494	ANN ARBOR
4494	CHICAGO
4494	SAN JOSE
9735	TUCSON
9735	DENVER

This makes better sense. But note that the original SCH_CITY table was BCNF. In fact, SCH_CITY is a pure key table: all of the attributes are part of a single candidate key. Thus, it is trivially BCNF. Nevertheless, the SCH_CITY table is odd. It also gives rise to inconsistencies. Consider adding the fact that student 4494 now lives in Dallas. The appropriate update requires adding two rows: (4494, U MICH, DALLAS) and (4494, U CHICAGO, DALLAS).

The intuitive explanation as to why the SCH_CITY table is unsatisfactory is that the city and school facts are independent. Therefore, they should not be included in the same table. If the city and school were dependent, that is, if we recorded the city or cities where a student lived while attending a given school, then the SCH_CITY table would be appropriate. But it would not have the same rows as the original example.

The formal reason why the SCH_CITY table is not appropriate (when school and city are unrelated) is that SID *multidetermines* CITY and SID *multidetermines* SCHOOL. The dependence of CITY on SID is called a *multivalued dependency*, or *MVD*. Consider three attributes: X, Y, and Z. *The attribute X is said to multidetermine the attribute Y if the set of values associated with a given value of X and Z is independent of the value of Z.* Mapping this definition into our example, the attribute SID multidetermines CITY because the values of CITY for one student (one value of SID) do not depend on the value of SCHOOL. For the given data, the SID value 4494 is associated with CITY values of Ann Arbor, Chicago, and San Jose; furthermore, this is independent of the value of SCHOOL.

The definition of *fourth normal form* uses the concept of MVD as follows: *A relation is in 4NF if and only if any dependencies in the relation are simple dependencies (i.e., not MVDs).* To see that the relations ST_SCH and ST_CITY are 4NF we note that no dependencies remain (other than the trivial dependencies of the keys on themselves, i.e., SID:SCHOOL determines SID:SCHOOL and SID:CITY determines SID:CITY)."

Before concluding this section, note what happens if SCHOOL and CITY are not multidetermined by SID. That is, the value of CITY depends on both SID and SCHOOL as shown by the following data in SCH_CITY2:

SCH_CITY2 Table

SID	SCHOOL	CITY
4494	U MICH	ANN ARBOR
4494	U CHICAGO	CHICAGO
4494	NORTHWESTERN	CHICAGO
9735	U AZ	TUCSON
9735	U AZ	PHOENIX
9735	U CHICAGO	CHICAGO

Again, the table is pure key and hence is BCNF. Since a set (possibly of size 1) of CITY values for a given SID value now depends on the SCHOOL value, there is no MVD of CITY on SID. Neither does SID multidetermine SCHOOL. But suppose the relation is decomposed into ST_SCH2 and ST_CITY2. Here is what results:

```
ST_CITY2 Table
SID        CITY
--------   ----------
4494       ANN ARBOR
4494       CHICAGO
9735       TUCSON
9735       PHOENIX
9735       CHICAGO

ST_SCH2 Table
SID        SCHOOL
--------   -------------
4494       U MICH
4494       U CHICAGO
4494       NORTHWESTERN
9735       U AZ
9735       U CHICAGO
```

Both relations are still pure key, hence BCNF. And they are also 4NF, since there are no (trivial) dependencies in the data. But is this a good decomposition? In fact, we have created a problem by this decomposition. Suppose someone poses the query, "In which cities did student 9735 live while attending the University of Arizona?" From the original SCH_CITY2 table, the answer is Tucson and Phoenix. Tables ST_SCH2 and ST_CITY2 might lead you to believe that this student lived in three cities, Tucson, Phoenix, and Chicago. In fact, by decomposing SCH_CITY2, information has been lost (spurious information has been generated). This problem is dealt with in the next section.

Nonloss and Independent Decompositions

The example decomposition of SCH_CITY2 into ST_SCH2 and ST_CITY2 is unsatisfactory: it resulted in a loss of the fact that the city, or set of cities, in which a student lived is associated with the school attended and vice versa. Information was lost through this redesign of the relations. A characteristic of any decomposition performed in normalizing a relation is whether or not it is a so-called *nonloss decomposition*. There are rules to test a decomposition to determine if it is nonloss. Generally, a decomposition of the relation R into R1 and R2 is nonloss if the join of R1 and R2 over the common attribute(s) (a natural join) does not introduce any spurious information (tuples). Let's test the decomposition of SCH_CITY2 to determine if it is nonloss.

The join of ST_SCH2 and ST_CITY2 results in the following relation:

```
ST_SCH2_CITY2 Table
SID        SCHOOL          CITY
--------   -------------   ---------
4494       U MICH          ANN ARBOR
4494       U CHICAGO       CHICAGO
4494       NORTHWESTERN    CHICAGO
4494       U MICH          CHICAGO
4494       U CHICAGO       ANN ARBOR
4494       NORTHWESTERN    ANN ARBOR
9735       U AZ            TUCSON
9735       U AZ            PHOENIX
9735       U CHICAGO       CHICAGO
9735       U AZ            CHICAGO
9735       U CHICAGO       TUCSON
9735       U CHICAGO       PHOENIX
```

This is hardly the original table, SCH_CITY2. Six new tuples have been created, those in italics, which represent spurious information. Student 9735 did not, for example, live in Chicago while attending the University of Arizona. Thus, the decomposition was not a nonloss decomposition and should not have been performed.

As another example of a bad decomposition, consider the following LOANX table.

LOANX Table

LID	AMOUNT	SID	BID	BZIP
27	1200	9735	HOME	98031
78	1000	9735	PEOPLES	98109
87	2000	9735	SEAFIRST	98101
92	2100	4494	FIDELITY	98101
99	2200	4494	FIDELITY	98101
170	1900	8767	PEOPLES	98031
490	2500	3749	PEOPLES	98109
493	3000	3749	PEOPLES	98109

This table is not BCNF because one of its determinants, BID, is not a candidate key. The relation should therefore be decomposed. But suppose we fail to follow the decomposition rule that the determinants should become candidate keys in the resulting relations, and instead create new relations LOANY and SZ as follows:

LOANY Table

LID	AMOUNT	SID	BID
27	1200	9735	HOME
78	1000	9735	PEOPLES
87	2000	9735	SEAFIRST
92	2100	4494	FIDELITY
99	2200	4494	FIDELITY
170	1900	8767	PEOPLES
490	2500	3749	PEOPLES
493	3000	3749	PEOPLES

SZ Table

SID	BZIP
9735	98031
9735	98109
9735	98101
4494	98101
8767	98031
3749	98109

You might argue that a person would have to be half asleep to perform this decomposition, and we would agree. Nevertheless, understanding why this is a bad decomposition should reinforce your understanding of the proper approach to decomposition and of how to detect a poor decomposition.

It should be obvious without joining LOANY and SZ that the result would certainly introduce many spurious tuples. For example, one spurious row will be (27, 1200, 9735, HOME, 98109). The only way that spurious rows would not be introduced would be if, perchance, each student had only a single loan. Then the SID value would be one-to-one with BID values and using either SID or BID in the SZ relation would give equivalent join results.

It is possible to perform a decomposition that gives BCNF results and is nonloss yet is still improper. A further test for decompositions is that they be *independent projections*. The two criteria for independence are as follows:

1. The common attribute of the projections forms a candidate key for at least one of the projections.

2. Every functional dependency in the original relation can be deduced from those in the projections.

An example of nonindependent projects of the LOANX table is in the same LOANY table given above and a table LZ containing LID and BZIP attributes:

```
LZ Table
LID        BZIP
--------  --------
27        98031
78        98109
87        98101
92        98101
99        98101
170       98031
490       98109
493       98109
```

LZ is BCNF, and the join of LZ and LOANY recreates the original, LOANX, table. Nevertheless, our intuition is troubled by the LZ table, because while LID is a determinant of BZIP it is not a direct determinant: LID determines BID, which in turn determines BZIP. The rules for an independent projection provide a formal way of showing that the LZ table is inappropriate.

The first test of independence is satisfied by the LOANY and LX projections—the common attribute of the projections, LID, is a candidate key in at least one of the relations. In fact, it is a candidate key in both of them. But the second condition is not satisfied. The functional dependency of BZIP on BID cannot be deduced from these projections. Thus, they are not independent.

Returning to the projection of LOANX into LOANY and SZ (with attributes SID and BZIP), we see that in addition to those projections being lossy, they also fail both conditions for independence. The common attribute of the projections, SID, is not a candidate key for either relation, and the functional dependence of BZIP on BID cannot be deduced.

Fifth Normal Form

You might wonder how high normal forms go. Are there sixth and seventh normal forms? Fortunately, 5NF is the highest normal form that can be generated by projections with the original relation recreated by joins. Thus, it is sometimes referred to as a *projection-join normal form*.

In fact, we are not going to give you more than an overview of fifth normal for two reasons. It is a rare situation, almost a pathological case, in which a relation that is 4NF is not also 5NF. Furthermore, even if the situation exists, it is very hard to recognize. Fifth normal form arises in cases in which it is not possible to nonloss decompose a relation into a pair of relations. The only way a nonloss decomposition can be achieved is by decomposition into three or more relations at once. If you are interested in examples and methods for creating 5NF relations, refer to a text such as *An Introduction to Database Systems* by C. J. Date.

Conclusion

There are (at least) two alternative approaches to database design. The approach we recommend, and the approach that is most prevalent in practice, is to deal with data needs first in terms of entities, then identify the relevant properties of those entities and the relationships between entities. The entities are mapped into relations, which are then analyzed to determine if further decomposition is justified to minimize the possibility of inconsistencies. This approach is based on a philosophy of aggregation—a divide and conquer philosophy. By focusing on entities and relationships between entities, the number of elements that must be dealt with is manageable—almost always much less than 100 and typically on the order of 10 to 25. While the attributes must still be determined, they are determined for each entity and relationship more or less independently. Normalization then can deal with each entity and the relationship more or less in isolation of the others.

The alternative approach deals with the attributes and relationships between them—the functional and multivalued dependencies directly. Given all the attributes, FDs, and MVDs, it is now possible to construct 4NF relationships directly. The problem is that the number of attributes is usually an order of magnitude or two greater than the number of entities. Thus, while an entity approach might involve 20 entities, an attribute approach might involve 1,000 attributes. Identifying all of the attributes is difficult enough; identifying all the relationships between them is usually overwhelming.

Given a good entity relationship model, most relations will already be in BCNF. This is simply because if we are careful to create entities that contain facts only about a single thing, the attributes of each entity will be functionally dependent only on its identifier. Nevertheless, as examples in this chapter have shown, decompositions may still be required, for example, to create ZIP code tables.

The approach we recommend for creating BCNF relations is to decompose directly to that form. That is, there is no point in successive decompositions that first create 2NF, then 3NF, and finally BCNF relations. This approach requires identifying the determinants and checking to see if they are all candidate keys. If not, the relation is projected so that the determinants become candidate keys in the resulting relation.

Eliminating multivalued dependencies that are not also simple functional dependencies can be done next. Alternatively, elimination of MVDs can be done as a first step. In fact, a good entity relationship design will usually reflect the independence of certain attributes through its entities and relationships. For example, the fact that a person has attended certain schools, lived in particular cities, and worked at particular jobs will usually be reflected in several entities that will be directly mapped to relations that, after possible decomposition to handle normal functional dependencies, will have also taken care of MVDs.

It is also important to keep in mind that not all potential inconsistencies and violations of the information semantics can be eliminated by database design. A real information system will have many conditions on the data that should be true but that cannot be assured simply through good definition of relations. Some DBMSs provide mechanisms for adding such rules to the database definition, but they are still rather limited. Future DBMSs can be expected to include more of the information semantics in the definition. In fact, the term *semantic data model* is being used to describe such extensions and alternatives to the relational model.

Finally, there are often good reasons for not decomposing a relation. An example is given by relations that contain data about a person or place and in addition contain the attributes ZIP, CITY, and STATE. When we decompose such a relation the result is two relations that will, most likely, be stored in physically separate disk blocks. To retrieve CITY and STATE attributes for an individual means that a join must be performed with the ZIP tables that means extra disk accesses. Therefore, the price that is sometimes paid to reduce the possibility of inconsistency is a degradation in performance. These tradeoffs are addressed in the chapter on physical database design, following.

Questions and Problems

Questions

1. What are the reasons for transforming relations into higher normal forms?

2. A relation that is in BCNF is also in which of the following: 1NF, 2NF, 3NF, 4NF, 5NF?

3. If a relation has an atomic key it must be in which one of the following: 1NF, 2NF, 3NF, 4NF, 5NF?

4. What is the relationship between functional dependence and determinants?

5. True or false: If an attribute T is functionally dependent on an atomic attribute V, then T is fully functionally dependent on V.

6. The following intuitive definition applies to which normal form: "Every non-key attribute must depend on the key, the whole key"?

7. Suppose that you are assured that relation R is 3NF. R has two candidate keys, a composite key of attributes A:B and an atomic key C. Is the relation R in BCNF? Why or why not?

8. A relation R has two composite candidate keys, A:B and B:C. The relation is in 3NF. Is it also BCNF? Why or why not?

9. Give a definition of multivalued dependency and an example of it that differs from those given in the text.

10. If a relation is pure key, then it must also be which one of the following: 1NF, 2NF, 3NF, BCNF, 4NF, 5NF?

11. Construct a simple example of a lossy decomposition and show the spurious tuples that result from a join of the projections.

12. Give an example of information semantics that cannot be reflected through normalization.

13. What are some of the factors that can discourage the database designer from projecting relations into higher normal forms?

Problems

A number of the following problems have been marked with an arrow; they are "mind stretchers," intended to make you think and be creative. The material in the chapter may not be sufficient to answer the problem. Suggested answers have been provided in the instructor's manual.

1. The following problems relate to the basic GSL model with STUDENT, LOAN, and BANK relations: STUDENT (SID, NAME, SLEVEL, AGE, SZIP); LOAN (LID, LDATE, YEARS, INT_RATE, AMOUNT, SID, BID); BANK (BID, BZIP, TYPE).

   a. A new relation, ST_L, contains data about a student and a loan. The attributes in ST_L are SID, LID, AMOUNT, NAME, and LDATE. What is the highest normal form that this relation is in? What is the proper decomposition?

   b. The database is extended to add a table, SC_ST, which shows the school each student has attended and his or her grade point average at that school. This table contains both the student's social security number and a unique student number, SID. (That is, SID is not a number assigned by the school.) The SCHOOL attribute is the name of the school and may not be unique but the SCHOOL_ID is.

```
ST_SC Table
SCHOOL    SID  SSN  GPA  SCHOOL_ID
--------  ---- ---- ---- ---------
UCLA      191  A    2.7  CA21
UCLA      108  C    3.8  CA21
U VA      191  A    3.1  VA02
PURDUE    21   B    2.5  IN07
```

   (1) What is the highest normal form that this relation is in?

   (2) Illustrate the types of update anomalies that can occur with this table.

   (3) How should ST_SC be decomposed? Look out—the proper decomposition may result in more than two relations.

➡ c. A PAYMENT relation is added with attributes LID, SID, AMT, and PDATE, where AMT is the amount of payment and PDATE is the payment date. Assume that for a given loan there is at most one payment each day. Assume also that a student never makes a payment on someone else's loan. Thus, the SID value in PAYMENT must be the same as the SID value in the loan with same LID value. Clearly, the presence of SID in PAYMENT creates a potential inconsistency. For example, we could have a LOAN row (LID=27, 15-SEP-85, 5, 8.5, 1200, SID=9735, HOME) and a PAYMENT row (LID=27, SID=4494, $100, 30-MAR-88).

   Discuss which rules/considerations of normalization theory would indicate that it is improper to have SID in PAYMENT.

➡ d. Suppose that TOT_AMT is added to the STUDENT relation. TOT_AMT is the total of the AMOUNT attribute of the student's loans. Is this a good idea? Does normalization theory provide any guidance in answering this question?

2. Consider a university database of faculty, course, and grade information that contains the following relations and attributes:

```
FACULTY (F#, FNAME, RANK, DEPT, DEPTCHAIR)
COURSE (ID, TITLE, CREDITS, YR, QTR, F#)
GRADE (ID, YR, QTR, S#, SNAME, GRD)
```

in which:

> FACULTY is an individual faculty person.
> F# is the faculty person's identifier.
> FNAME is the faculty person's name.
> RANK is his or her rank, such as ASST PROF, INSTR.
> DEPT is the department the person is in, such as Finance, Math, History. Assume that a person can be in only a single department.
> DEPTCHAIR is the faculty number of the person who is the chair of DEPT.
> COURSE is the description of a course and its offering.
> ID is the course identifier, such as IS 403, ENGR 141.
> TITLE is the course title, such as INTRO. TO COBOL.
> CREDITS is the number of credits for the course.
> QTR and YR indicate the quarter and year in which the course is offered, such as W, 83.
> F# is the faculty number of the course offering's instructor. There is only one instructor per course offering.
> GRADE is the record of the grade a student received in a course.
> S# is the student identifier.
> SNAME is the student's name.
> GRD is the grade itself (A, B, C, D, F)

  a. The COURSE relation is in which normal form?

  b. How should COURSE be decomposed to create BCNF relations?

  c. Since FACULTY has an atomic key it must be in 2NF. But it is clearly not BCNF. Decompose FACULTY to BCNF.

  d. Assume for this part that SNAME is unique. With this assumption, what normal form is the relation GRADE in? If SNAME is not unique does it change the normal form of the relation? Discuss.

  e. Assuming SNAME is not unique, how should GRADE be decomposed to create BCNF relations?

3. The employee/contract database design problem of Chapter 11 has resulted in the following relations:

```
EMP (SSN, EMP#, BIRTHDATE, NAME, DEGREE, DATE, SCHOOL, MAJOR)
POS (SSN, EMP#, STARTDATE, ENDDATE, POSITION)
DEPT (SSN, EMP#, STARTDATE, ENDDATE, DEPTCODE)
SALARY (EMP#, STARTDATE, ENDDATE, SAL)
CONTRACT (C_ID, DESCRIPTION, AMOUNT, STARTDATE, ENDDATE, MANAGER)
CHARGE (C_ID, EMP#, DATE, AMOUNT)
```

An explanation of several of these attributes follows: DEGREE, DATE, SCHOOL, and MAJOR (in EMP) record data about college degrees the employee has earned. An employee may hold several degrees. The DEPT relation contains DEPTCODE which is the code number of the department in which an employee works during the period STARTDATE through ENDDATE. SAL is the employee's annual salary. MANAGER in CONTRACT is the employee number of the contract manager. A contract may have only a single manager but an individual may manage more than one contract.

a. What is the proper normalization of the EMP relation?

b. Suppose that only the highest degree an employee has received is recorded in EMP.

   (1) What is the normal form of EMP with this assumption?

   ➡ (2) Would it still be appropriate to decompose EMP? Why or why not?

c. The POS and DEPT relations are 3NF. They are not BCNF. Why? What changes should be made so that they are BCNF?

d. If CHARGE and CONTRACT are not in BCNF make the appropriate decompositions.

➡ e. As stated, an employee can hold only a single position and be in a single department on any given date. Furthermore, the start and end dates in POS, DEPT, and SALARY should be consistent. For example, it would not make sense for an employee (who is in continuous employment) to have a STARTDATE in POS that is earlier than the earliest STARTDATE in SALARY.

   (1) Do these relations enforce these restrictions?

   (2) Is there a way to redesign the database so that these restrictions are enforced?

4. Refer to the database design problem for the property management firm described in Chapter 11. Suppose that the following relations have been created.

   PROPERTY (ID, street address, city, state, ZIP, number of units, owner's name, street address, city, state, ZIP, phone)
   UNIT (Unit #, ID, monthly rental, deposit, tenant name, reference, phone, no. of bedrooms and bathrooms, lease start date and end date, rent due date)
   RECEIPT (ID, unit no., payment date, for, amount, tenant name, method of payment)
   EXPENSE (ID, unit no., date, amount, type, description)

   Generate BCNF relations by decomposing these relations.

References

Codd, E. F. "Recent Investigations into Relational Database Systems." *Proceedings IFIP Congress,* 1974. (Includes definition of Boyce/Codd Normal Form.)

Date, C. J. *An Introduction to Database Systems.* Vol. 1. 4th ed. Reading, Mass.: Addison-Wesley Publishing Co., 1985.

Fagin, R. "Multivalued Dependencies and a New Normal Form for Relational Databases." *ACM TODS,* vol. 1, no. 3 (September 1977), pp. 75–116.

Kent, W. "A Simple Guide to Five Normal Forms in Relational Database Theory." *Communications ACM,* vol. 26, no. 2 (February 1983), pp. 120–125.

Loomis, Mary E. S. *The Database Book.* New York: Macmillan Publishing Co., 1987.

13 Database Implementation and Physical Design

This chapter discusses the implementation of a database on the different varieties of database systems: relational, network, and hierarchical. The design is assumed to begin with a conceptual model in the form of normalized logical relations. These relations are first mapped to the logical structure that is appropriate to the DBMS, then mapped to the physical structure. There are always several alternatives for the physical implementation of a logical database design. The major choices available to the database designer include the horizontal and vertical partitioning of relations, the clustering of records, the selection of indexes, and the "prejoining" of records from several tables. For all types of database systems, these choices will ultimately affect the performance and cost of the database.

Unfortunately, the logical and physical design are not independent in any current DBMS. The database designer cannot perform the logical implementation and then turn to physical structure issues. The extent of interaction between the two will become apparent in our subsequent discussion. In particular, for the designer of a hierarchical database, the logical and physical design choices are considerable, complex, and highly interactive.

Mapping to a Relational DBMS

Mapping relations to a relational model is straightforward, at least at first glance. Each normalized relation from the conceptual data model becomes a relation (or base table) in ORACLE, DB/2, INGRES, R:BASE, or other relational DBMS implementation. Thus, the logical mapping process involves writing statements in the data definition language to define the base tables. For SQL-based systems this means writing CREATE TABLE statements.

The logical-physical interaction results because a logical base table may not, for example, be physically represented as, say, two linked physical tables without having some impact on users' logical views. Before getting into physical design details, here is an example of the interaction—a situation in which subsequent physical design choices may require redefinition of the base tables.

Suppose we decide that the GSL LOAN relation should be divided into two sets of tuples—one set for all loans that are closed, the other set for active loans, those still in repayment. The desirable situation is that a single, logical LOAN table be defined. Then, the physical design specifies two files, say CLOSED_LOAN and OPEN_LOAN. The user would see the tuples as all belonging to the single LOAN table.

To some extent we can achieve this end by creating two tables, then writing a view that is the union of the two—for example:

```
CREATE VIEW LOAN AS
SELECT * FROM CLOSED_LOAN
UNION
SELECT * FROM OPEN_LOAN;
```

But with the view approach, the ability to update LOAN is lost. While queries can be written against LOAN, updates must be directed to the appropriate underlying table, CLOSED_LOAN or OPEN_LOAN. The logical and physical independence is not complete.

In such situations the physical design dictates changes in the logical design—they may not be done independently (at least not with today's technology). This type of interaction, by the way, is not limited to the relational model. The logical-physical design interdependence is stronger in the network and hierarchical models.

While the logical-physical designs are not entirely independent, any decent relational DBMS will shield the user from many of the physical database aspects. As we saw in the SQL and R:BASE languages, given that the user operates on base tables or on simple select/project views of base tables, he or she requires minimal knowledge of the underlying physical storage structures used for these tables. For example, the user is unaware of which attributes are indexed, of tuple clustering, and of lower-level details such as page sizes.

Physical Design for Relational DBMS

While this section uses relational terminology, most concepts and design choices apply equally to network and hierarchical DBMSs. The subsequent sections that discuss physical design for these systems will assume knowledge of this material.

When mapping the database's logical design onto its physical design, the designer usually implements each relation in the logical design as a base table. Sometimes, however, performance can be improved or cost can be reduced for a given relation by splitting the *attributes* appropriately between several tables. This is called *vertical partitioning*. In other cases performance can be improved by apportioning the original relation's *tuples* into several new tables. This is called *horizontal partitioning*. A third physical design choice that interacts with the logical design is to create a base table that is the join of two or more tables from the conceptual model. This is called a *prejoin*.

Let's look at these alternatives and their implementation in more detail.

Vertical Partitioning

In the GSL database, the STUDENT relation (in the real system) has hundreds of attributes. These include several addresses for the student (local, permanent, parents'), attributes that characterize the student's financial status, data on school attended, degree objective, etc. A considerable number of these attributes are seldom used. For example, only a relatively few queries ever involve display of the parent's address. (Note: *query* is used here in a very general sense to include both retrievals and updates of tuples, not just retrievals.) Placing all of these attributes in a single relation may significantly increase retrieval time.

To improve performance, attributes may be divided into two or more groups. Such a partition is called a *vertical partition,* since we view the relation as a table, with attributes as columns and tuples as rows. Figure 13–1 illustrates this type of partition graphically.

A vertical partition has several benefits: it will reduce the processing time required to transform a stored record into its external view. It will also reduce data transfer time, especially for sequential-processing applications. For example, suppose the STUDENT relation includes the following attributes:

```
SID, NAME, BIRTHDATE, SLEVEL, ADDRESS, GPA, HIGH SCHOOL, HIGH SCHOOL GPA
```

Relation

Relation

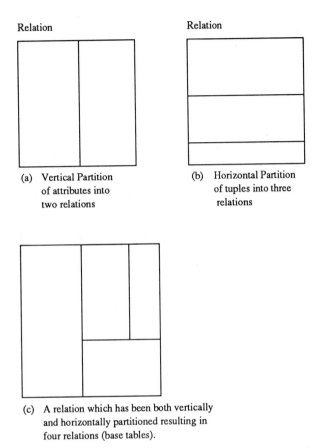

(a) Vertical Partition
of attributes into
two relations

(b) Horizontal Partition
of tuples into three
relations

(c) A relation which has been both vertically
and horizontally partitioned resulting in
four relations (base tables).

Fig 13-1 V-H

Further assume that the high school and high school GPA are rarely used with the other student information. Since only a portion of the attributes are frequently needed, the attributes of the original STUDENT table can be vertically partitioned into two new tables, STUDENT1 and STUDENT2, with SID included in both tables:

```
STUDENT1 (SID, NAME, BIRTHDATE, SLEVEL, LOCAL ADDRESS, GPA)

STUDENT2 (SID, HIGH SCHOOL, HIGH SCHOOL GPA)
```

When a student's name, high school, and high school GPA are all required, a join can be used to retrieve the original table's data.

Even when all (or most) attributes in a relation are frequently involved in queries, it may be the case that the queries "induce a partition" on the attributes. This is a fancy way of

Query			Attributes			
	SID	Name	Birthdate	SLevel	Address	GPA
1	X			X		X
2	X					X
3	X	X				
4	X	X	X		X	
5	X	X			X	

Fig 13-2 *STUDENT1 Table Showing Incidence of Attributes and Queries*

saying that one group of queries uses one group of attributes while another group of queries uses another (non-overlapping) group of attributes. Figure 13–2 shows the columns from the STUDENT1 relation. Each row of this display shows an X under those attributes that are required by that query.

This situation suggests that the relation should be implemented as two (physical) tables. One table would include the attributes SID, SLevel, and GPA; the other table would include the attributes SID, name, birthdate, and address. Each query now requires attributes from only a single table.

When a table is partitioned, provision must be made so that the parts can be reconnected. In RDBMSs this is done by placing the original relation's primary key in each vertical subset. Thus, there is a cost to vertical partitioning—extra storage cost for the replicated key. With typical relations (that is, those in which the space required by the key is a small proportion of the total space), this is a small cost. The larger cost occurs when it is necessary to join a partitioned table to satisfy a query that requires attributes from two or more of the partitions. For example, suppose that a report containing a student's GPA, name, and address is required. Because this query requires information from both tables, the tables must be joined. These extra costs of storage and disk accesses (for joining) must be compared to the performance gains realized for queries that do not require joins.

Another situation suggesting vertical partitioning occurs when only a subset of the attributes in the original table is accessed at one geographical location, while a separate subset is most often used at another location. If there are computers at each location, consideration should be given to partitioning the table and geographically distributing the new tables. Managing a database that is distributed across several computers requires a so-called "distributed" DBMS, or DDBMS. Such systems are just now becoming commercially available and are described in Chapter 15. Distributed database design issues are, however, beyond the scope of this text.

Another reason for vertical partitioning is to keep attributes containing sensitive data out of tables accessible to users who have no need to know that data. Even though we can write views and make use of other methods to help assure data privacy, security is increased if sensitive data is maintained in a separate file. For instance, if a student's name and address were available to several user groups, but his or her financial data were available only to the loan approval office, the table might be appropriately partitioned.

Horizontal Partitioning

Another means of reducing costs and increasing performance is through horizontal partitioning. Horizontal partitioning is similar to vertical partitioning, except that rather than partitioning attributes, partitioning is done on the rows. Figure 13–1, part b is a graphical representation of a relation that has been horizontally partitioned into three relations. Many of the same situations that give rise to vertical partitioning also suggest that horizontal partitioning be considered.

One situation in which horizontal partitioning should be considered is when records fall into active and inactive sets. For example, once a student in the GSL loses eligibility for loans (for example, by graduating from a university), the accesses to that student will be greatly reduced. When all of his of her loans are paid off, the activity will be even lower. Physical separation of active and inactive tuples will speed processing of active tuples, especially for queries that involve sequential processes (such as report generation). When queries require tuples from both sets, a *union* of the two tables may be performed.

Horizontal partitioning can also reduce random access time (for example, by reducing index size). We may also reduce storage costs if fewer indexes are required on the inactive file than on the active file. For example, an inactive student table might have an index only on student ID, while the active table might have several indexes (SID, name, school).

When students fall into the inactive set, the level of update to their attributes will fall to virtually zero, and their data becomes essentially static. A relation with static data never needs backup. By contrast, a relation with a high update level should be backed up (that is, a complete dump of the relation should be copied to tape) quite frequently. If we have a single table of, say, 1 million active and inactive entries, which is backed up daily, we will spend a considerable amount of both processing and I/O time for this backup. If the relation is partitioned into two tables of, say, 200,000 active and 800,000 inactive records that are backed up daily and monthly respectively, the backup cost will be reduced by almost 80 percent.

Horizontal partitioning can also decrease the cost of file reorganization. Reorganization is often needed for hashed files in which record additions occur. While there is less need to reorganize B-tree indexed files, reorganization may be indicated to restore physical record clustering. With active records in one file and inactive records in another, it is likely that only the active file will require reorganization.

With the advent of alternative secondary storage media such as optical disks, we can also reduce storage costs by moving inactive records to the lower-cost (albeit slower and not erasable) optical media. In situations in which the inactive records are maintained only for archival purposes, or only for very infrequent batch processes, the inactive file may be stored off-line on tape media.

As with a vertical partition, the cost savings must be compared to the added costs when tuples are required from more than one horizontal partition (more than one base table). The union operation is inexpensive as long as there is no requirement to eliminate duplicates. If checking for duplicates is not performed, a union of a horizontally partitioned table will generally be much less expensive than a join of a vertically partitioned table.

We must also consider the costs of added complexity: it is usually easier to deal with a single table than with the union of two or more tables. As noted in the introduction, processes such as updates may require direct access to the underlying base table; they cannot be performed on tuples defined by a view that is the union of several tables.

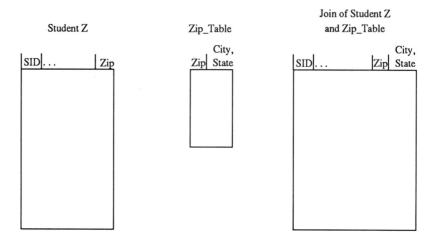

Fig 13-3 Prejoin

Maintaining (updating) a horizontally partitioned table may prove problematic. Consider the situation of horizontally partitioning students into active and inactive sets. When a student changes status, it will be necessary to delete the record from the active base table and add it to the inactive base table. This, in fact, results in updates to the inactive file (the file itself is not static). Movement of a student record from one table to another would, most likely, not be done at the instant of status change but rather as a periodic batch process; for example, at the end of each month students who had become inactive would be moved.

It is possible, of course, to partition a relation both horizontally and vertically into several base tables. Figure 13–1 also graphically illustrates this situation.

Prejoins

Consider the STUDENT relation in which CITY, STATE, and ZIP are stored. Because ZIP determines CITY and STATE, this relation should be decomposed into two tables: one, STUDENTZ, with ZIP only (along with, of course, other attributes); and a second table, ZIP_TABLE, with attributes ZIP, CITY, and STATE. In order to, say, print mailing labels, the two tables would have to be joined. This would be expensive if done frequently. Therefore, it might be better to store the two relations as their join, that is, as a single "prejoined" table. While this will eliminate the cost of dynamically joining the tables, there are other costs to consider.

Prejoining will (almost always) increase storage cost. For example, suppose we have 1 million STUDENT tuples but only 10,000 different ZIP codes. Suppose further that the average storage space for ZIP, CITY, STATE is 15 bytes (with ZIP requiring 3 bytes). Storing the two tables separately will require 3*1 million + 15*10,000 bytes = 3.15 million bytes for these three attributes. Storing the join will require 15*1 million = 15 million bytes. A graphical representation of the prejoin appears in Figure 13–3 and illustrates how the resulting join table has the same length as the table on the "many" side of the join

(STUDENTZ), and a number of columns equal to the sum of the columns in the two tables less the common join column(s).

Balancing storage costs against access costs is not simple. A reasonable estimate of storage cost is on the order of $1.50 per megabyte per month. Thus, the added storage cost of the prejoin is on the order of $18 per month. (Note: This is based on a disk cost of $25,000 per gigabyte with full maintenance factor of .03, that is, a monthly cost of $750. In addition, it is not reasonable to figure 100 percent use of disk space; a factor of 75 percent is used, resulting in a cost of $1.00 per megabyte per month. To this must be added operating costs for file backup and other costs, which will add probably 30 to 60 percent to the cost.)

Determining access cost is more difficult. First we analyze the case of a join of the full STUDENTZ table with the ZIP_TABLE. Assuming that the ZIP_TABLE is loaded to central memory so that the join does not require substantial additional disk accesses (beyond those required to read the STUDENTZ and ZIP_TABLE base tables), we estimate the join cost to be $5 per million records. Thus, if the join of the full STUDENTZ and ZIP_TABLE files were required more often than 18/5 (about three to four) times per month, prejoining would be less expensive. (Note: This cost is based on a CPU/central memory cost of 1 million dollars, a 0.03 monthly lease factor, 300 effective processing hours per month, and 2,000 CPU seconds per hour. The CPU time to perform an internal join is estimated at 0.1 milliseconds.)

A join of a single STUDENTZ tuple and a ZIP_TABLE tuple will be more expensive per tuple since it involves external disk accesses. The cost is estimated at $75 per million random joins. If over 18/75 million (240,000) joins are required per month, prejoining would be less expensive.

Two other considerations, in addition to the storage and access costs, should be considered in any partitioning or prejoining. One of these costs is due to the potential error resulting from storing relations in non-BCNF form. If the tables are prejoined, it is highly likely that updates to CITY, STATE, and ZIP will create inconsistencies. The other cost relates to the affect on response time of the system. Designs that increase response time should be analyzed to determine if they reduce user productivity.

Other "Denormalization"

There are alternatives that fall between storing the join of two tables and maintaining the two tables separately. It can prove efficient to store one or more attributes redundantly in a relation. For example, suppose that loan data and student name are often specified in a query. With fully normalized relations, this will require a join of STUDENT and LOAN. An alternative is to store the student name in both STUDENT and LOAN tables. Of course, LOAN is now not BCNF (it is 2NF). Cost savings are in reduced disk accesses and response time. Added costs are for extra storage and in the increased probability of inconsistency.

Another question involves storage versus the calculation of data items. Suppose we frequently need to know loan balance. Should the balance be calculated every time it is needed by subtracting payments and adding interest charges to the initial loan amount, or should the balance (as of a specified date) be stored in the LOAN relation? The "correct" answer from a theoretical standpoint is that the balance should be defined in terms of a view—thus, recalculated whenever needed. But this can be very expensive. Storing the balance requires space but saves recomputation. Storing also runs the risk of inconsistency—if a payment amount is updated for some reason, such as a bounced check, we must remember to recompute the current balance. Again, the choices involve tradeoffs of space, efficiency (reduced computer time and faster response), and potential for error.

File Structure and Selecting Attributes to Index

Once base tables have been defined, the next physical design step is to determine the physical file structure and which attributes should have physical access paths. In general, physical file structure alternatives are those described in Chapter 2: sequential, hashed, and indexed (usually by some form of B-tree). After determining the file structure, there may be additional attributes for which direct access paths are desired. These may take the form of additional indexes or be implemented as linked lists with a list head (usually) in the parent record.

In most relational systems, the range of choices is limited, and there is not a clear distinction between what is usually termed the "primary" file key and the "secondary" access paths. To our knowledge, no relational system makes use of linked lists. Only a very few, among them INGRES, provide a hashed-file alternative. The decisions that must be made when using most RDBMSs essentially boil down to the following two:

1. Which attributes should be indexed (using the system's dense B-tree indexing scheme).

2. If more than one index is selected for a table, which one should be the "clustering" index.

These two possibilities will be analyzed here. As noted, INGRES provides additional choices. Systems such as R:BASE and dBASE provide fewer alternatives, as they have no clustering index.

You might want to reread the sections in Chapter 7 that describe the physical structures for typical RDBMSs (ORACLE, DB2, SQL/DS) and the statements (such as CREATE INDEX) used to specify the indexes. To review, all indexes are dense; that is, every attribute value and pointer appear in the index. There is no "primary index." If a clustering index is defined, the DBMS will attempt to store new records in proximity to other records with same values as the clustering index attributes. For example, if the LOAN relation has a clustering index on SID, then we would expect to find all loans for a given student on the same physical page. But there is no assurance that this will be the case.

The attributes chosen for indexing are those that require fast access. These usually include the various keys: primary, foreign, and alternate. An index is constructed on a primary key because most updates and, typically, most retrievals will be by this attribute. In the GSL, primary indexes would most likely be on the following attributes: SID for STUDENT, BID for BANK, and LID for LOAN. When a table has an alternate key, it is also a prime candidate for an index. A discussion of considerations in the selection of additional attributes to index appears in this section under, "Selecting Additional Indexes."

An index is constructed on a foreign key because most joins are over a primary and a foreign key. In the GSL, a join of LOAN and STUDENT will virtually always be over SID; a join of LOAN and BANK will be over BID. For the LOAN relation, in addition to the index on LID, indexes would probably be specified for SID and BID.

Not all foreign keys should be indexed. Consider the STUDENT table with attribute ZIP and the ZIP_TABLE with attributes ZIP, CITY, STATE. ZIP is a primary key in ZIP_TABLE and would most certainly be indexed. But we would index the foreign key ZIP in STUDENT only if joins of STUDENT and ZIP_TABLE were required due to retrievals that involved selections (restrictions) on ZIP_TABLE. An example will clarify this and show why the foreign keys SID and BID in LOAN would be indexed while ZIP in STUDENT would not.

A join of STUDENT and ZIP_TABLE will, most likely, be performed to supply the CITY and STATE for a given student. Thus, the restricting condition applies to the STUDENT table, rather than the ZIP_TABLE. Once the STUDENT tuple is accessed, using the SID index to STUDENT, the ZIP_TABLE is accessed, using the value of ZIP obtained from STUDENT. This type of query could not take advantage of a ZIP index to STUDENT. Now if the restriction were over ZIP_TABLE, the situation would differ. Suppose we want all students who live in Laramie, WY. The appropriate way to process this query is to search ZIP_TABLE (using an index on CITY, ST if available) to determine all ZIP values for this city. Then the STUDENT table would be accessed for all tuples with these ZIP values. If this were a frequent type of query, building an index to ZIP on STUDENT would be appropriate.

The foreign keys SID and BID in LOAN are appropriate for indexing because joins of LOAN and STUDENT or LOAN and BANK will probably involve restriction over the table containing the corresponding primary key. The most common need for joins will be to retrieve all loans for a given student or all loans for a given bank.

Composite Key Indexes. Indexes may, of course, be created over composite attributes. Suppose that the primary key of LOAN is not LID but rather the composite SID:LID. The LID is a sequence number which is unique only within SID. An index would probably be created on the pair SID, LID in that order. That is, SID is the major attribute, LID the minor attribute. (The index would not be created on LID, SID.) As shown in Figure 13–4, this index serves equally well as an index on the foreign key SID. It is not necessary, indeed it would be wasteful, to create another index on the atomic attribute SID.

There are other situations in which indexes on composite keys are appropriate. If STUDENT contained the attributes SLEVEL and MAJOR and frequent queries included restrictions such as SLEVEL = 5 AND MAJOR = "BUSADM," it might be appropriate to construct an index on the composites of SLEVEL and MAJOR. In this case the order of the attributes is not obvious. If there were other queries with a restriction only on MAJOR, then the index should be on MAJOR, SLEVEL as opposed to SLEVEL, MAJOR.

Clustering Indexes

An important aspect of file design is record or tuple clustering. The objective of clustering is to store those records that are frequently retrieved together in physical proximity. Physical data clustering is an extremely important factor in performance, as can be seen from the following example: Refer again to Figure 13–4. Suppose the stored record just accessed is for the LOAN with SID=8767, LID=1, and the next loan record required has SID=3749, LID=1. The loan with identifier 8767/1 is stored on page *p1;* the loan with identifier 3749/2 is stored on page *p2*.

1. If *p1* and *p2* are one and the same, the access to the second loan will not require any physical I/O at all, because the desired page *p2* will already be in a buffer in main storage.

2. If *p1* and *p2* are distinct but physically close together—in particular, if they are

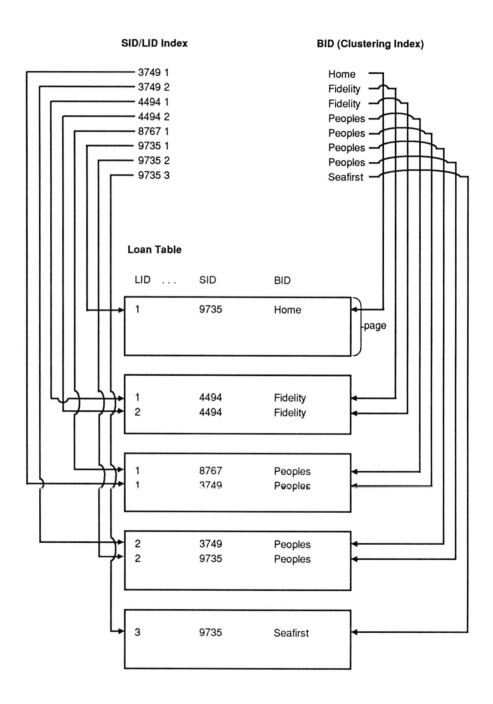

Fig 13-4 Example of a Composite Index on Attribute SID:LID and a Clustering Index on BID to the LOAN Table

adjacent—then the access to the second loan will require a physical I/O, but the seek time involved in that I/O will be small (it will be zero if *p1* and *p2* are in the same cylinder), because the read/write heads will already be close to (or at) the desired cylinder.

3. If *p1* and *p2* are not close, a disk access will be required to retrieve the second loan. This access will probably involve a disk arm movement.

How do we "encourage" the two loans to be stored in physical proximity? These two loans are, in fact, for the same bank, BID = PEOPLES. All loans for a given bank will tend to be stored in physical proximity if a clustering index to LOAN is defined on BID. Figure 13–4 illustrates a clustering index to LOAN on BID. Note how records with common BID value are in proximity. This is an example of *intra-file* clustering: the clustering is over tuples from a single table.

A clustering index tells the DBMS to try and store records in a physical order that is close to their logical order on the index's attribute. When a relation has a clustering index on a unique attribute, the DBMS will try to store tuples in a physical order that corresponds to the logical order of that attribute. For example, given a clustering index to BANK on BID, when a new BANK tuple is added the DBMS will attempt to store it close to the existing BANK tuple that has a "nearby" BID value. (Since BID is unique within BANK, the DBMS will not be able to find another BANK tuple with an identical BID.) A clustering index on BID to BANK would facilitate sequential processing of updates by BID.

If access to some specific bank *together* with all loans for that bank is a frequent requirement, then the BANK and LOAN records should be stored interleaved, with the LOAN records for BANK B1 in physical proximity to the BANK B1 record itself, the LOAN records for BANK B2 close to the BANK B2 record, and so on. This is an example of *inter-file* clustering.

Different RDBMSs have different mechanisms for supporting inter-file clustering. In DB2, clustering indexes on BID to both BANK and LOAN should be defined. Records should then be loaded in an intermixed fashion. ORACLE provides for the definition of a cluster and subsequent definition of which tuples should be stored in the cluster. For details, see the appropriate DBMS system manuals.

Of course, a relation can have only a single clustering index. The choice of an index on which to cluster may be non-trivial. For many relations, a foreign key is the proper choice for a clustering index. Consider the GSL database, whose PAYMENT relation has the attributes LID, DATE, PAY_AMT, PAY_METHOD, etc. It is likely that a frequent process would require retrieval of all payments for a given loan. Thus, the foreign key LID would be a likely choice for a clustering index.

When a relation has multiple foreign keys, the choice of a clustering index is usually more difficult. Candidates for a clustering index for the LOAN relation include LID, SID, or BID. The choice between these three depends on access patterns. If sequential processes are performed by LID, such as updates to loans batched and sorted on LID, then a clustering index on LID would reduce processing costs. If there is a reasonable percentage of retrievals of all loans for a given student, a clustering index on SID is attractive. And if there is a reasonable percentage of retrievals of all loans for a specific bank, a clustering index on BID is attractive.

To simplify the problem somewhat, assume that while updates are by LID, they are done either online or in small batches so that physical ordering of LOAN records by LID is of marginal value. Therefore, the important alternatives are a clustering index on SID versus one on BID. It is important to consider more than just the percentage of retrievals on each attribute (BID vs. SID) to decide which to use as a clustering index (and which to make a standard index). Assume that of all retrievals by SID or BID, the breakdown is as follows:

Attribute	Percentage Retrievals
SID	90
BID	10

Now, at first blush this might seem to suggest that a clustering index on SID would be appropriate. The error in this reasoning is that it ignores the number of records that are retrieved by each type of query. Suppose that the average student has four loans and the average bank has 100 loans. To analyze the two alternatives, the following assumptions are made:

1. All indexes have three levels, with the top level in internal memory and direct page pointers (direct page pointers are used in DB2, SQL/DS, and ORACLE). To retrieve the first record of a given SID or BID requires three accesses. To retrieve additional records of the same SID or BID requires one additional access for each record *if* the index is non-clustering.

2. There are 25 records per page. If records are clustered on the retrieval attribute, retrieval of the first record of a given attribute value will also retrieve up to 24 additional records from that same page with the same attribute value. If the clustering index is on SID, retrieval of all LOAN records of a given SID will probably take three accesses. If the clustering index is on BID, the first loan will be accompanied with (on the average) about 12 more loans of the same BID. Four more accesses will be required to retrieve the remaining 87 loans, for a total of seven accesses.

The following table estimates the expected number of disk accesses for each choice (between SID and BID) of a clustering index:

	Cluster on:	
	SID-------------------	BID-----------------
Retrieval by:	(Accesses times percent of occurrences)	
SID	3*90% = 2.7	(3+3)*90% = 5.4
BID	(3+99)*10% = 10.2	7*10% = .7
Expected Accesses	12.9	6.1

The results show that, everything else being equal, the best choice is to use a clustering index on BID. Everything else being equal means that we have the same need for rapid online response by each of these attributes. Of course, if the retrievals by SID require fast response but the retrievals by BID can be batched, then the choice might be to cluster on SID.

Every base table should have a clustering index. There is little incentive not to have a clustering index unless the table is very small so that, for example, it occupies only a single page and will essentially end up being held in central memory.

Selecting Additional Indexes

While primary and foreign keys should always be considered for indexing, access patterns should be studied to determine if indexes on other attributes are appropriate. It is important to avoid becoming "index happy"—creating an index for any attribute that might ever be used in a restricting condition. There is a significant space overhead to a secondary index. For example, assume that our student records are 200 bytes long. An index on name will probably require about 15 bytes (name value plus pointer). This will add about 7 percent to the space required by the file. It is easy to see how a file with several secondary indexes could require 50 or more additional spaces for these indexes.

We can provide some general guidelines for the selection of additional indexes. First, a parameter is defined called the "activity level" which is the proportion of records that are relevant to a query. For example, if the query "retrieve all freshmen" (SLEVEL = 1) could be expected to retrieve about 15 percent of the records, the activity level is 15 percent. The indexing guidelines follow:

1. A frequent retrieval with an activity level below 1 percent is a good candidate for an index. There is no point in building a secondary index for a data item that is seldom used in retrievals unless the data item is more or less unique.

2. A frequent retrieval with an activity level of from 1 to 5 percent should be *considered* for an index. As the activity approaches 5 percent, the attractiveness of the index depends on the value of rapid response and the level of update activity. The more static a file, the lower will be the index maintenance costs and the more attractive the index.

3. For a data item *occasionally* used for retrieval and an activity level of over 2 percent, an index should probably not be constructed. What this implies is that the improvement in retrieval efficiency (versus full file access) for queries that retrieve 2 percent or more of the records is not enough to offset the added cost of index space and index maintenance.

Figure 13–5 represents the "to index or not to index" decision in terms of the frequency of access, the activity level, and the importance of rapid retrieval. Two other factors that should be taken into account in the decision are the record size and the frequency of update. Other things being equal, the larger the record the greater the value of indexing. As the frequency of update increases, the value of indexes decreases due to the costs of index maintenance. If an indexed attribute value is changed, that index will need to be updated. The addition or deletion of a record requires updating every index in most RDBMSs.

As examples of index selection, consider the STUDENT records in the GSL table and the following situations:

1. If retrievals on student name have even low frequency, an index should be constructed because the activity level is very low (a query on a single name will have an activity level approaching 1/N, that is, a single, or very close to a single, record).

2. If frequent retrievals are made for all students of a specific major, then an index is probably recommended as long as there are (about) 200 or more different majors. With 200 different majors the average activity level is 0.5 percent.

3. Even if there were frequent processes on student level (freshman, sophomore, etc.) it would not pay to construct an index on this item. The reason is that over 10 percent of the records will satisfy the average query. A full sequential scan will be cheaper.

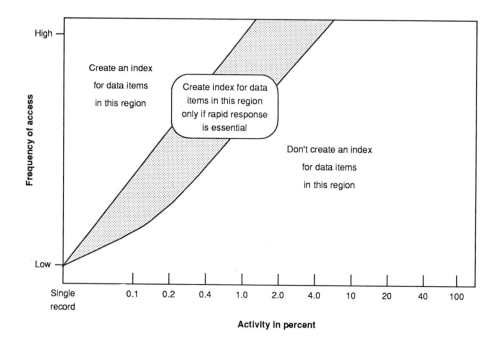

Fig 13-5 Indexing Guide

4. A gray area would be an attribute such as year of birth, which would have an activity level on the order of 2 to 3 percent. An index should be constructed if:

   a. Retrievals by year of birth are frequent.

   b. Retrievals are performed online, and therefore rapid response time is desired.

   c. The level of file update activity is low to moderate—in particular, if the number of record additions and deletions is low. (Of course, the year of birth will not change. Therefore, the only updates required of the index will be for adds and deletes.)

As we have shown, the choice of attributes for indexing is not an easy one. However, with careful consideration, system performance can be enhanced and system cost reduced through the judicious use of clustering and indexing. Fortunately, addition and deletion of indexes in a relational system does not require costly database "dump and restore" operations. Therefore, it is possible to modify the design over time, based on actual experience.

Relational Database Design Summary

The following is a summary of the steps and considerations in the implementation of a database in a relational DBMS.

A. Mapping Relations to Record Types and Selecting Primary File Structure

The following transformations of records that either combine two or more record types or partition a single record type into two or more types usually affect storage space, query processing costs, response time, and the potential for inconsistency. There is also a potential impact on the user, since not all partitions and joins may be made transparent through the use of views. These costs must be considered before record types are transformed.

1. Determine if records should be partitioned.

   a. Consider vertical partitioning if either of the following statements is true:

      (1) Certain data items are very infrequently used.

      (2) Applications induce a partition on the data items.

   b. Consider horizontal partitioning if either of the following statements is true:

      (1) Records can be classified as frequently and infrequently used.

      (2) Applications induce a partition on the records.

2. Consider prejoining two record types that are frequently accessed together if either of the following statements is true:

   a. The relationship between the two is one-to-one or one-to-n where n is small.

   b. The record on the "one" side is small (thus, the amount of redundancy in storage will be small).

   (Note: Keep in mind that inter-record clustering achieves essentially the same result as physically joining the records. With inter-record clustering, the records to be joined are often on the same page, or on nearby pages, thus the join time is very small. Clustering does not involve redundancy.)

3. Consider replication of data items if the following conditions exist:

   a. Items from two different records are frequently specified in a query.

   b. The two different record types are not clustered.

   c. The total size of the replicated data items is not large.

4. Determine the physical structure of the relation.

   a. If no other file organizations are available, select a clustering index that minimizes accesses over the anticipated queries.

   b. If other organizations are available, compare costs of the alternatives (such as hashing) versus a clustering index.

B. Determining Additional Indexes

Use the indexing guidelines to define additional indexes on atomic and/or composite attributes. The activity level, frequency of query, and response time requirements should be determined and Figure 13-5 used as the first guideline in index selection. Then, if the choice remains vague, the update frequency should also be taken into account.

These sections have addressed most of the major decisions that should be made in the design of a database for a relational system. Other aspects of the design, however, have been ignored. For example, we have not delved into lower-level physical design issues such as the definition of physical areas to which base tables are assigned, the definition of page size, the determination of how much free space to allocate to pages when the database is loaded, and so forth. Many of these choices are simply beyond the scope of this text. Some of them can safely be left to default values. Others are quite dependent on the specific DBMS being used.

What we have discussed will enable you to start on the road to being a good database designer. Practice and guidance under the tutelage of an experienced DBA are essential to achieving journeyperson status.

Mapping to a Network DBMS

Virtually all of the choices faced by the designer of a relational database are also faced by the designer of a database for a network DBMS. Therefore, this section assumes that the reader understands the preceding sections. Furthermore, the discussion here will be briefer, with emphasis on those areas of design that differ.

Mapping Relations to a Network Model

Mapping relations that are in BCNF to a network DBMS implementation is straightforward in most cases: each relation simply becomes a record type. A set is then created for each pair of relations, R1 and R2, when the following conditions exist:

1. R1 contains a primary key, and R2 contains a foreign key that is R1's primary key;

2. There are no "intervening" relations between R1 and R2 that capture the relationship between R1 and R2.

To illustrate what is meant by "intervening" relations, consider the GSL model with STUDENT, BANK, LOAN, and PAYMENT relations.

```
STUDENT (SID, NAME, SLEVEL, AGE, SZIP)
BANK (BID, BZIP, TYPE)
LOAN (LID, LDATE, YEARS, INT_RATE, AMOUNT, SID, BID)
PAYMENT (SID, LID, PDATE, PAMOUNT, METHOD)
```

The keys for STUDENT and BANK are as described before. The key of LOAN is the composite SID, LID—that is, loans are identified within STUDENT. The key of PAYMENT is the composite SID, LID, PDATE (implying that only one payment for a given loan is made per day). The foreign keys in PAYMENT are SID and the composite SID, LID. Therefore, sets are created as follows:

Set Name	Owner	Member
STUDENT_LOAN	STUDENT	LOAN
BANK_LOAN	BANK	LOAN
LOAN_PYMT	LOAN	PAYMENT

Even though SID is a foreign key in PAYMENT, no set is constructed between STUDENT and PAYMENT because the relationship is captured through the intervening relation, LOAN. A set between STUDENT and PAYMENT would not add any new information—it would be redundant.

There are, however, several situations in which the mapping from relations to record and set types is more complex. Descriptions of these situations follow.

One-to-Zero and One-to-One Relationships. When a potential owner record has either zero or one member-record occurrences, consideration should be given to collapsing the two record types into a single record. An example of this situation is when a student may have a financial statement—that is, the STUDENT to FINANCIAL_STATEMENT relationship is either one-to-zero or one-to-one. If the potential member record has a relationship to another record type, then a set should be created. For example, if the financial statement includes checking account data, so that the checking account is related to BANK, then a set should be created with STUDENT as owner, FINANCIAL_STATEMENT as member.

If the potential member record has no other relationships, then it may be incorporated into the owner. Considerations include size of the member record and retrieval patterns. Also see the discussion of repeating groups below—the design guidelines there are applicable to this situation.

Unary Relation. Most network DBMSs will not allow a set with the same owner and member record type. Several examples of unary relationships were described in Chapter 11, and Chapter 9 described how to represent them in network systems. To review, a common example of a unary relationship occurs in personnel systems in which each person's EMPLOYEE record contains not only his or her own employee ID as the primary key but also the key of his or her manager. The manager ID is a foreign key. The representation requires creating another record type, say MBMO, with (at least conceptually) the identifiers of the employee and manager. Since MBMO contains two foreign keys, employee ID and manager ID, the following two sets are defined:

Set Name	Owner	Member
MNG_BY	EMPLOYEE	MBMO
MGR_OF	EMPLOYEE	MBMO

Many-to-Many Relationships. If we are working from normalized relations, many-to-many relationships will already have been resolved into relations that can be mapped directly to record types and then appropriate sets added. For example, suppose a student attends more than a single school (and that a SCHOOL relation exists). The normalized relations will include a relation (say, ST_SCH) with attributes student ID and school ID. The relation ST_SCH has two foreign keys, thus two sets are created:

Set Name	Owner	Member
ATTEND	STUDENT	ST_SCH
ST_BODY	SCHOOL	ST_SCH

Ternary and Higher-Order Relationships. Again, such relationships should have been mapped into BCNF relations so that the definition of record types and set types is automatic. Here is an example that has been used before. Loans are for use by a student at a given school. Thus, a relation, say, ST_SC_LOAN with attributes student ID, school ID, and loan ID is created. The appropriate sets are:

Set Name	Owner	Member
SC_ST_LOAN	SCHOOL	ST_SC_LOAN
ST_SC_LOAN	STUDENT	ST_SC_LOAN
LOAN_ST_SC	LOAN	ST_SC_LOAN

Set Order

The logical order of records in a relation is unspecified; that is, to retrieve records in some order the DML must specify the order, such as SELECT ALL FROM STUDENT *ORDER BY SID*. In the network model, the order of member records is specified as part of the set definition. The order options include first-in, first-out; last-in, last out; order by specified data item; and default ordering. Two additional options, PRIOR and NEXT, were discussed in Chapter 9 and you are referred there for details.

The order of member records spans both physical and logical design. If we want to retrieve records in a particular sequence, such as loans for a given bank in ascending order of student ID, then we are speaking of a logical aspect. But our incentive for ordering can also be to speed processing. If most retrievals of PAYMENT are for the most recent payment on a loan, then it would make sense to order the PAYMENT records descending on PDATE. Depending on the type of association mechanism used for members of a set, this ordering could greatly speed retrieval.

Set Retention

Definition of sets requires definition of the SET RETENTION rule. If the foreign key value can be null, then the retention should be defined as OPTIONAL. The more typical case is a non-null foreign key value, in which case the retention is MANDATORY (or FIXED). An example of a null foreign key value occurs when we add a collection agent (relation AGENT) to the GSL model. The key of AGENT is added to LOAN as a foreign key. When a loan is declared in default, a collection agent is assigned to the loan, resulting in a non-null foreign key value. When we map these relations to the network model, a set will be created with owner AGENT, member LOAN. The set retention will be OPTIONAL because the agent ID in LOAN can be null.

Determining Data Elements

One issue that arises in the mapping of relations to record types is whether or not to explicitly include foreign keys. Since a set will be defined between the owner and member, it is not necessary to store the owner key in the member record. For example, in the LOAN relation, neither SID nor BID are required. There is a space savings if the foreign key is not stored. There are two disadvantages:

1. If the owner-to-member connection is ever broken (if, for example, a linked-list pointer connecting LOAN records for one student is somehow lost) it will not be possible to identify which student owns the loans that follow the broken link.

2. If the member record is accessed via other than its owner, the owner identity cannot be determined without access to the member. For example, suppose LOAN is stored without SID and BID. When a LOAN is accessed via its STUDENT owner, it is not possible to determine the BID value without access to the owner BANK record. When a record has only one owner, and access is always through that owner, there is less incentive to store the foreign key. This is probably the situation with the PAYMENT record, which would, most likely, always be accessed through its LOAN owner.

Repeating Groups

Another option available to us in a network DBMS but not in a relational system is the use of a repeating group. The use of a repeating group creates a record type that is not flat—not even in first normal form. Therefore, some designers believe that repeating groups should simply not be considered. Nevertheless, the use of a repeating group can provide savings in space and reductions in disk accesses.

First of all, if the repeating data are members of several sets and/or the repeating data is itself the owner of a set, it should, in almost all situations, be stored as a separate record type. An example from the GSL is the LOAN record, which is owned by both STUDENT and BANK and is itself an owner of PAYMENT records. Since it is a member of two sets and is itself an owner, LOAN data should clearly not be a repeating group.

A situation in which a repeating group should be considered occurs when the repeating data is not voluminous and is also frequently retrieved with its owner data. By "not voluminous" we mean that the average number of occurrences times the size of an occurrence is small relative to the owner record: not over 20 to 50 percent of its size. Suppose that we have data on student majors, but that a student may have declared from zero to a maximum of five majors. Most students will have only a single major, a few will not yet have declared a major, and a few more will have two; a very few may have even more. To create properly normalized relations (and record types), a record type, say, ST_MAJOR should be defined with data items SID and MAJOR. A set will be defined with STUDENT as owner, ST_MAJOR as member. The repeating group alternative is to embed the possible multiple occurrences of MAJOR in the STUDENT record. The use of a repeating group is quite attractive for this example.

Note that this discussion of repeating groups also applies to relationships that are one-to-zero or one-to-one, except for the fact that if the limit on the number of replications is one, the group may be included in the owner and the owner will still be in (at least) first normal form. It is only when two or more replications are possible that inclusion will result in a non-flat file.

Physical Design of Network Databases

The physical design of a network database allows more choices than the design of a relational database for most RDBMSs. This is due to the wider range of physical file structures supported by most network DBMSs. First, we will review two of the choices that were extensively covered in the discussion of physical design of relational databases: partitioning and prejoining.

Partitioning

The same reasons for using *vertical* partitioning in a relational DBMS hold for a network DBMS. If a record is partitioned into two records, it will be necessary to define a set between the two new record types with either record type as owner. (Note that the two record types will have a one-to-one relationship.) Alternatively, each record type may include the primary key and have the location mode CALC on that key. Unlike the relational model, the partition cannot be obscured from the user by a view defined as a join.

A logical record type should be partitioned *horizontally* in a network for the same reasons that horizontal partitions are indicated in relational systems—namely that records that are logically retrieved as a group will be in physical proximity. Horizontal partitioning is often called for when records can be classified as active versus inactive, or "high probability of access" versus "low probability of access." The horizontal partition is usually implemented by defining two different record types.

Prejoins

Owner and member records within a set are candidates for prejoining, for the purpose of creating a single record type. In the network model, we have the added option of embedding the member records in their owner record as a repeating group. But, as described above, repeating groups should be considered only if the member has a single owner type and is not itself an owner type for a set.

As with a relational implementation, we also have the choice of replicating data items from the owner record into the member. An example includes storing BANK data items (redundantly) in the LOAN record. This should be done only if the member record is frequently accessed by some other path than through its owner. There would be no point in storing, say, the BANK ZIP code in the LOAN record if the LOAN record is almost always accessed through BANK_LOAN. If, however, LOAN access is frequently via the STU- DENT_LOAN set, and data item values from BANK are needed, consideration should be given to storing those items in the LOAN record. As with the relational model, added costs of storage and increased probability for inconsistency must be balanced against improved performance.

Physical File Structure: Primary Access Path

The issue here is the physical placement of a record. Network systems generally give us four choices, which are specified in the design by the location mode for the record. The alternatives are:

1. Hashing: location mode CALC

2. Clustered: location mode VIA SET

3. Indexed sequential: location mode VIA SET combined with an ordered and indexed system set

4. Sequential: location mode VIA SET combined with an ordered, but not indexed, system set

Records that are set owners, but not members, are typically organized by hashing to provide essentially one access retrieval. If it is also desirable to sequentially process the records or to process records over a range of key values, the third choice (indexed sequential) is appropriate.

Record clustering is usually chosen for records that are members of a set and accessed along with their owner. The GSL LOAN record would be a candidate for clustering via its STUDENT_LOAN set or via its BANK_LOAN set. Calculations similar to those illustrated for the relational model and the choice of a clustering index need to be made to determine which set should be selected for clustering. If a member record is frequently accessed directly, such as a LOAN record retrieved by its primary key, then a location mode of CALC should also be considered.

Keep in mind that this choice determines the (relative) physical location of the record but still allows the definition of additional access paths through its owners, including the system owner.

Physical Representation of Owner-Member Relations

Network DBMSs usually support two alternative methods of representing owner-member relationships in the database. These are linked lists and some form of pointer array or index.

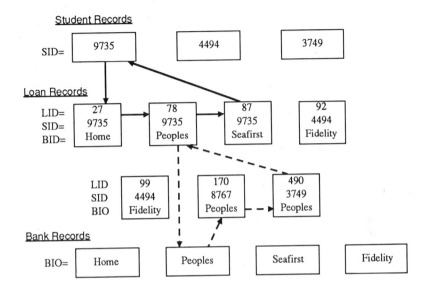

Fig 13-6 Owner-Mem

Linked Lists: MODE IS CHAIN; PRIOR LINKAGE; OWNER LINKAGE

If a linked list is used, the owner record of a specific set occurrence contains a pointer to its first member record. Figure 13–6 shows a subset of GSL records and a few linked-list pointers. For example, STUDENT with SID = 9735 contains a list-head pointer to its first LOAN record with, say, LID = 27. That member record, in turn, has a pointer to the next LOAN record (LID = 78) for this student. Typically, as shown in the example, the last LOAN record (LID = 87) in the set will point to the owner, which is the STUDENT record. This provides a mechanism by which no matter where you enter the member chain, it is always possible to determine the owner. This organization is specified by MODE IS CHAIN in the set definition.

This figure also illustrates a linked-list structure to capture the BANK-LOAN owner-member set. Again, for simplicity only the linked list originating in one bank, PEOPLES, is shown.

There are usually two additional options for linked lists: two directional pointers, specified by PRIOR LINKAGE, and a pointer from member to owner, specified by OWNER LINKAGE. Two-way linked lists are illustrated in Figure 13–7 by placing arrowheads at both ends of the links. The use of two-way pointers is recommended in three situations: (1) to navigate backward through the member records; (2) to facilitate adding

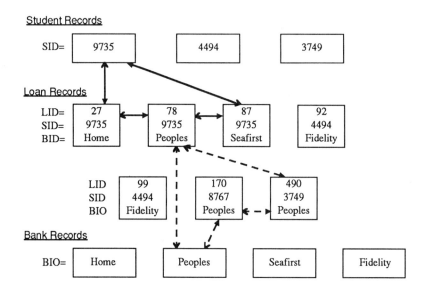

Fig 13-7 Owner-Mem2

records logically; that is, when ORDER LAST is specified, a new record is added logically at the end of the set; or (3) to facilitate record deletion when access is not through the member's owner or when it has more than one owner.

The justification for a two-way linked list in the first two cases should be obvious. The third situation is somewhat more subtle. Suppose that we want to delete a LOAN record and access it via its BANK owner. It is a simple matter for the DBMS to remove the LOAN from the BANK_LOAN set by adjusting the pointer of the previous LOAN record to bridge around the deleted LOAN. It is easy because to find the deleted LOAN the system traversed the linked list (beginning with the BANK owner record), hence saving the location of the previous set member. (Note that the previous record could be either a LOAN or the BANK owner record.) The problem occurs when the system tries to remove the LOAN from its STUDENT_LOAN set. Since access was via the BANK_LOAN set, the DBMS has no easy way of knowing the location of the previous record in the STUDENT_LOAN set. No easy way, that is, unless the STUDENT_LOAN set has two-way pointers.

The difficulty with member-record deletion can be seen from the example in Figure 13–6. Suppose a LOAN with LID 78 is to be deleted and access is via its BANK owner, PEOPLES. The appropriate update of BANK_LOAN pointers is to change the pointer in LOAN 490 to point to the BANK (PEOPLES) record rather than to the deleted LOAN (78). The

STUDENT_LOAN set pointer from LOAN 27 must also be changed to point to LOAN 87, thus skipping around LOAN 78. While it is easy to see what must be done from the simple example, it is not so easy to see, or do, in situations where the number of members is large. It is easy if two-way pointers are used, as can be seen from Figure 13–7.

Owner pointers facilitate quick navigation from member to owner. If access to a record is always through a specific owner, then there is no point in having an owner pointer. For example, suppose the PAYMENT record is always accessed via its LOAN owner. Then, including an owner pointer would be of no value.

When access to a member is possible through more than one owner (that is, when the record is a member of more than one set), or if direct access to the member is possible (for example, its location mode is CALC), then the owner pointer can prove very valuable. The LOAN record has multiple owners and is very apt to be accessed through either of these owners. When an access occurs through the STUDENT owner, access to the BANK owner will be very slow unless LOAN includes an owner pointer. The analogous statement holds for access to LOAN via BANK: it will be expensive to access its STUDENT owner (though less expensive than in the previous case—why?).

Additional pointers add storage space. Added pointers will increase costs of adding a record since more pointers are modified—especially in the case of two-way pointers. If both the STUDENT_LOAN and BANK_LOAN sets use two-way pointers, then the addition of a LOAN record will require the modification of pointers in two other records in the STUDENT_LOAN set and two other records in the BANK_LOAN set. These "other" records that need modification are those that point forward to and backward to the newly added record.

Pointer Arrays and Indexes

A pointer array is a set of pointers to the member records. In fact, a pointer array is equivalent to removing linked-list pointers from the members and storing them in the owner. While the set of pointers may not actually be stored in the owner, they are stored in a contiguous area—they are no longer embedded in the member records. With a pointer array several types of finds and updates are faster than with linked lists. For example, to find the last record of a set the DBMS simply refers to the last pointer in the array. To add a new member record to a set does not require any traversal of member records if the set order is LAST or FIRST—the new record is added and a pointer added to the array in the appropriate location. In the IDMS network system, a pointer array is specified by MODE IS INDEX combined with a set order of FIRST, LAST, PRIOR, or NEXT.

If the specification is MODE IS INDEX combined with ORDER IS SORTED on a specified data item, then the pointer array becomes an index on this data item. Now it is not only possible to quickly access the first, last, or nth member of a set but it is also possible to quickly access a member by the specified data-item value. Consider the example shown in Figure 13–8.

The BANK_LOAN set is defined with ORDER IS SORTED, ASCENDING KEY SID, and MODE IS INDEX. This creates one B- tree index for each BANK record on data item SID to the BANK's LOAN records. This choice would be appropriate when specific members of a set are desired, and when they can be identified by some data item value. The creation of an indexed set should depend on the guidelines given for the creation of indexes for relational databases. An index will be of value only if the following conditions exist:

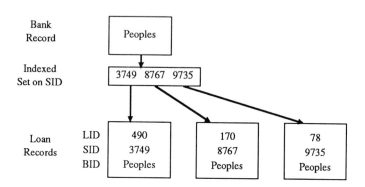

Fig 13-8 *Indexed Set*

1. There are enough member records in a set so that a sequential search of the set would be relatively expensive when compared to access via an index. Since BANK_LOAN sets are large, this justification for indexing the set is met. In contrast, the STUDENT_LOAN sets are probably small, hence there would be no reason to index that set.

2. The activity level is low; that is, the number of records that have a common value of the indexed data item is small relative to set size. It might make sense to create an indexed BANK_LOAN set on SID. It would not make sense to create an index on YEARS (which probably only has five to 10 distinct values).

3. There are frequent retrievals by the indexed data item.

4. Rapid response time is needed.

Keep in mind that the index is within a set occurrence. If an index that spans sets is desired, then an indexed *system* set must be defined.

Defining System Sets

System sets are used to provide access paths or ordering that cuts across all records of a given type. A primary reason for constructing a system set is to create an index on all records of a given type. This is virtually identical to the type of index generated by the CREATE INDEX specification of SQL-based RDBMS. And the same guidelines for creating an index hold for both types of DBMS.

In the GSL database, it is likely that a system set would be defined for STUDENT records and that it would be indexed on NAME. (We are assuming that the location mode of STUDENT is CALC on SID.) This would provide direct (indexed) access to students by name. If the unique identifier of LOAN is LID (as opposed to the composite SID:LID), an indexed system set with LOAN as member, ordered on LID, would probably be advisable. This would afford direct access to LOANs by LID.

It does not make sense to create an indexed system set on a data item for which there is an alternative direct-access path. The STUDENT_LOAN set provides a means to directly access LOANs by SID (assuming the location mode for STUDENT is CALC on SID). Therefore, a system set with LOAN as member, indexed on SID, would be redundant.

Network Database Design Summary

The following is a summary of the steps and considerations involved in mapping a set of normalized relations to a network database. You will note that while there are many similarities between these steps and the summary for mapping to a relational DBMS, there are more choices and steps in the design of a network database.

A. Mapping Relations to Record Types and Selecting a Primary File Structure

1. Add record types as necessary to capture relationships.

   a. Add linking records for unary relationships.

   b. Add linking records for many-to-many relationships.

   c. Add linking records for ternary and higher-order relationships.

   The same considerations of costs as outlined for relational database design are relevant to the following design steps: storage space, query processing costs, response time, and potential for inconsistency.

2. Determine if records should be partitioned.

   a. Consider vertical partitioning if either of the following statements is true:

      (1) Certain data items are very infrequently used.

      (2) Applications induce a partition on the data items.

   b. Consider horizontal partitioning if either of the following statements is true:

      (1) Records can be classified as frequently or infrequently used.

      (2) Applications induce a partition on the records.

3. Consider prejoining two record types that are frequently accessed together. A prejoin is practical only if the member record type is not an owner of a set or a member of some other set. The prejoin may be attractive if all (or most of) the following conditions exist:

   a. The relationship between the two is one-to-zero, one-to-one, or (in general) one-to-n where n is small.

   b. The record on the owner side is small (thus, the amount of redundancy in storage will be small when the owner record is replicated).

   c. The record on the many side is small, in which case you should consider absorbing the record type into its owner as a repeating group.

4. Consider the replication of data items if the following conditions exist:

   a. Items from two different records are frequently specified in a query.

   b. The two different record types are not clustered.

    c. The total size of the replicated data items is not large.

5. Consider eliminating foreign keys for records that have only one owner and to which access will always be through that owner.

6. Select location mode.

    a. Use CALC for fastest direct access, typically for records that have no owner (other than the system).

    b. Use VIA SET and create an indexed system set for records to be directly accessed and sequentially processed by a given attribute. (See Part C: "Defining System Sets.")

    c. For member records with only one owner, consider VIA SET if access is often along with the owner.

    d. For member records with multiple owners, compare access costs that result from the different VIA SET choices for clustering.

B. Defining (Standard) Sets

1. Create a set for each foreign key with a record containing the corresponding primary key as owner, and a record containing the foreign key as member.

    a. Define RETENTION OPTIONAL if the foreign key can be null.

    b. Define RETENTION MANDATORY if the foreign key cannot be null.

2. Select SET ORDER.

    a. Use FIRST (LIFO) for fastest insertion, if none of the following alternatives are more attractive.

    b. Use LAST if member records are often accessed in chronological order of insertion.

    c. Order by data item if access requires sorting on that attribute, if access is frequently to a specific extreme value of a data item (such as the most recent date), or if an indexed set is to be created.

3. Define the method of associating members of a set.

    a. Use the simplest method—one-way linked list—if other considerations are not important.

    b. Use a two-way linked list if navigation in two ways is important, online deletion is frequent, and access may be via other than owner, or ORDER LAST is specified.

    b. Define an indexed set if access to a member record by a specific data item value is frequent and guidelines for creating an index are satisfied.

C. Defining System Sets

1. For records needing direct access and sequential processing by a given data item, create an indexed system set on that data item and locate the record via that system set.

2. Follow guidelines for establishing additional (secondary) indexes and create an indexed system set for each cost-effective index.

Database design for a network system provides more options than design for current relational systems. With the added options comes the opportunity to fine-tune the database to provide excellent performance. But the range of alternatives and the complexity inherent whenever there are many choices also allow for a very poor design. Mapping the conceptual design to a logical network database and determining the physical structures requires careful study. Greater diligence is required for a network design because it is more difficult to make subsequent changes if the design proves deficient. In particular, a change in design can have a significant impact on the data manipulation language, meaning that source code modification will be necessary.

Mapping Relations to a Hierarchical DBMS: IMS

A conceptual database is rarely a simple hierarchy. Therefore, the database designer for a hierarchical DBMS is faced with the problem of how to translate a set of normalized relations (which if first mapped into a graphical structure will inevitably have a network structure) into a hierarchy. Unfortunately, there is no "standard" way of mapping a nonhierarchical logical design to a physical hierarchical data design. Furthermore, given a network, there are usually many alternative hierarchical designs possible. Choosing the best is not easy.

We can provide some guidelines and insight. But as we warned the reader in Chapter 10, systems such as IMS are complex, and achieving proficiency in designing and using hierarchical databases will require considerable training and experience beyond the coverage of this text.

With a hierarchical DBMS, it is difficult to separate the physical and logical design—they are very interdependent. The first part of the design, which we will term the *logical* portion, involves the definition of the physical databases (you might feel that there is a bit of a contradiction here). It will also define the logical database. The *physical* design will address the choice of access method, the partitioning of physical databases into data set groups (DSGs), and the selecting of secondary indexes.

IMS Logical Database Design

The initial steps of a hierarchical database design are quite similar to those of a network design. These steps are essentially the same as Steps A.1 through A.4 for the network design. Of course, some of the terminology must be changed; in particular, *record type* becomes *segment type*. Furthermore, the repeating group of a network is really just the segment type of a hierarchy. Thus, the possibility of collapsing a segment type into its parent as a repeating group (Step A.3.c) does not exist.

The design process results in a network structure that must then be translated into multiple, hierarchical physical databases with appropriate "logical" interconnections. Our approach will be to begin with a model in the form of a network, then discuss the process of mapping to a hierarchical model.

The logical model to be used for illustration is a variation of the GSL model. It is shown in Figure 13–9 as a network. Because two of the segments, ATTEND and LOAN, have

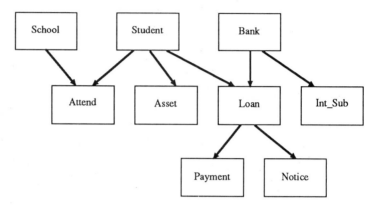

Fig 13-9 Net for IMS

multiple owners, it is not possible to structure the database as a single hierarchy without redundancy. At least three physical databases will be required. It is clear what the root segments of these three databases will be and also clear what several of the physical dependent segments should be. We will call the three physical databases (PDBs) SCH, ST, and LENDER. Their root and dependent segments (at this point) are:

PDB Name	Root Segment	Dependent Segments
SCH	SCHOOL	
ST	STUDENT	ASSET
LENDER	BANK	INT_SUB

We must now decide where to place the remaining segments: ATTEND, LOAN, PAYMENT, and NOTICE. Logical parent/child relationships will then be established to define the connections between the three PDBs and thus define the logical database.

Consider first the ATTEND segment. There are two choices:

1. Place ATTEND in SCH as a dependent segment (parent SCHOOL) and define it as a logical child to the logical parent STUDENT.

2. Place ATTEND in ST as a dependent segment (parent STUDENT) and define it as a logical child to the logical parent SCHOOL.

When a segment has two parent segments, these symmetric alternatives will always be available. Which should be chosen? The choice is really a physical design choice—it depends on the types of processing done and response time considerations. The access time to a physical child is generally faster than the access time to a logical child. Therefore, if it is more common to access ATTEND segments from STUDENT than from SCHOOL, ATTEND should be made a physical child of STUDENT and a logical child of SCHOOL. We will assume that is the situation and add ATTEND as a physical child of STUDENT.

This decision of which physical parent to select for a child segment is comparable to the choice of a clustering set in a network model for a record type with two parents. If we were

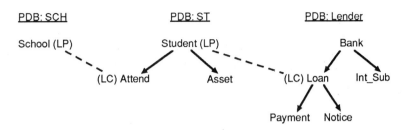

Fig 13-10 Physical and Logical Design of an IMS Database for the GSL Model of Figure 13-9

mapping this conceptual model into a network, and the assumed prevalence of STUDENT to ATTEND access holds, we would probably choose a location mode of VIA SET using the STUDENT_ATTEND set for ATTEND.

A similar decision is faced with the segments LOAN, PAYMENT, and NOTICE. First of all, whichever physical database is selected for LOAN will also be the PDB for PAYMENT and NOTICE. Should LOAN be the physical child of STUDENT or BANK? Again, access patterns and response requirements will influence, if not dictate, the choice. We will assume that a study of applications shows that the number of disk accesses will be lower if LOAN is made a physical child of BANK (that is, if LOAN segments are clustered by BANK). LOAN will therefore be a logical child of STUDENT.

The resulting physical databases and logical database are shown in Figure 13–10, with solid lines connecting physical parent to physical child, and dashed lines connecting logical parent/logical child segments.

Physical Design of the IMS Database

The primary issues addressed in this section are the selection of access method, including the choice of parent-child pointers; the hierarchical ordering of segments; secondary index selection; and physical database partitioning into DSGs.

Access Methods

The four access methods of IMS were described in Chapter 10. To review, they are:

- HSAM. "Tapelike." Segments are stored physically in hierarchical sequence. Sequential-only access. Update is by sequential file-processing methods.
- HISAM. Indexed access to root segment using a keyed VSAM (B-tree) file. Dependent segments are stored in hierarchical sequence in an entry sequenced file.
- HIDAM. Indexed access to root segment. Dependent segments are linked in hierarchical order by hierarchical pointers or by child/twin pointers.
- HDAM. Hashed access to root segment. Dependent segments are linked in hierarchical order by hierarchical pointers or by child/twin pointers.

For any online database, HSAM is clearly ruled out. HSAM is used primarily for backup storage of a database or for those rare databases that are processed only with sequential methods. HIDAM is the most "robust" scheme; that is, you cannot make a truly bad design choice if you select HIDAM as the access method. However, depending on processing characteristics, HISAM and HDAM can prove advantageous. Considerations for each of the directly accessible methods follow.

After describing the pros and cons of each access method, we will use the three physical databases SCH, ST, and LENDER, along with hypothetical access patterns, to further illustrate design decisions.

HISAM. HISAM is an excellent choice for applications that are retrieval intensive, especially where the retrieval requires only the root segment or requires the root and all or most of its dependent segments. This is because HISAM provides relatively fast indexed access to the root; in this case access time is essentially equivalent to that of HIDAM. But access to dependent segments requires a sequential scan through the segments. If only a few segments are desired, especially if they are at a low level of the hierarchy and the physical record size is large, access time can be high.

HISAM is also not the best choice if there will be a large number of updates, particularly the addition of dependent segments. This is because IMS must scan the dependents to find the proper location for insertion, then shift subsequent segments to provide space for the added segment. HISAM is, however, a reasonable choice if root segments are added, since the VSAM file that supports the root can split to accommodate additions.

HIDAM. HIDAM uses essentially the same storage mechanism for root segments: a VSAM keyed file. Therefore, its performance for root segment retrieval and additions is essentially the same as HISAM. But HIDAM overcomes some of the problems that HISAM has in dealing with dependent segments, by using pointers instead of storing dependents in physical sequence. The designer has a choice of two types of pointers (both illustrated in Chapter 10): either hierarchical sequence pointers that link segments in hierarchical order, or child/twin pointers that link all segments of one type together with a list head in their parent segment. (Note that child/twin pointers are identical to the MODE IS CHAIN option of the network model.)

With pointers, adding dependent segments does not require the physical shifting of segments. More important, if child/twin pointers are used, access to segments that are at low levels of a large hierarchy will not require chaining through all hierarchically preceding segments.

Pointers solve some problems but create others. There is the obvious problem of added space. But there is also the problem of developing long chains of pointers that traverse back and forth across disk page boundaries. Since segments are added in hierarchical sequence, it is easily possible for a chain of twin pointers to begin at, say, block A, jump to block B, back to block A, to block C, to B, and so on. One design trick is to provide extra space in pages so that added segments may be physically stored similar to their logical order.

HDAM. HDAM uses essentially the same mechanism for storage of dependent segments as HIDAM, thus the same considerations for dependents hold. The difference is that access to the root is via hashing, with chaining to overflow pages for synonyms that overflow the home page. In fact, depending on how the database is loaded, dependent segments may either be stored in pages with the root or in a separate file. (Details are beyond the scope of this text.)

The advantage over HIDAM is the more rapid access to root segments afforded by hashing, compared to indexing. A disadvantage is that with the addition of root segments, a considerable number of them may end up in overflow, increasing access time and eventually necessitating reorganization.

Examples of Access Method Selection

Figure 13–10 will be used in this section to illustrate the choice of access methods.

The PDB SCH is a root-only database with the segment SCHOOL. Any of the direct-access methods, HISAM, HIDAM, or HDAM, are candidates. If there are few additions of new SCHOOL segments to the database, which is probably the case, the HDAM access method would afford very fast access with practically no necessity to reorganize. HDAM is our choice for SCH.

The PDB ST, containing the STUDENT root segment and the dependents ATTEND and ASSET, presents a somewhat more difficult design problem. Again, any of the three direct-access methods are reasonable. Several of the relevant characteristics of this physical database include:

1. The physical record sizes will tend to be small. Most students will have only a few ASSET segments and only a very few ATTEND segments. These characteristics do not preclude any of the direct-access methods; HISAM is still an attractive choice because the number of dependent segments is small, and the addition of new segments will not require either an extensive search for an insertion point or shifting to allow insertion.

2. There will probably be a moderate level of added root segments. We could expect 5 to 15 percent growth per year in the number of STUDENT segments. This moderate level of growth would necessitate periodic reorganization if HDAM were selected. However, we would not expect that reorganization would be required any more frequently than a couple of times per year.

3. We would expect that updates could be done in a batch mode, with transactions sorted prior to processing. This encourages the use of HISAM or HIDAM so that conventional sequential file processing could be used.

Analysis of this file neither eliminates any access method nor makes a particular method stand out as clearly superior. The choice would hinge on access frequency and response time considerations. If the STUDENT segment is frequently part of online retrievals and rapid response time is important, the HDAM method emerges as the preferred alternative. If access frequency and/or response time requirements are less severe, the acceptable performance of HISAM and its simplicity make it an attractive choice.

The best (or worst, depending on your viewpoint) has been saved for last. The LENDOR database has several characteristics not found in the other two PDBs:

1. The physical record will be quite large. A typical bank might have hundreds to thousands of LOAN segments. The number of payment segments would run to an order of magnitude greater than the number of LOAN segments.

2. The level of segment addition activity will be very high. With, say, 4 million loans

and monthly loan payments, there will be over 4 million segment additions per month. (Additions will be primarily PAYMENT segments, plus a not insignificant number of new LOAN segments and a moderate number of NOTICE segments.)

The large size and high level of segment additions rule out HISAM for this PDB. Since the number of root segment additions will be small (because very few new banks will be entering the program), an HDAM organization would not require frequent reorganization. (Note that if we somehow organized the PDBs so that PAYMENT were a root segment, HDAM would not be a good choice due to its high level of segment adds.) HIDAM is also viable, especially if updates are performed in batch mode and transactions include the BID in their key.

Note that while access patterns to the root BANK should be considered, the number of BANKS is not large. This means that the difference in performance between HIDAM and HDAM would be small. Frequent access to LOAN and/or PAYMENT segments would not influence the choice of access method for this file. What frequent access to these dependent segments *will* influence is the choice of database partitioning or the selection of secondary indexes, both of which are discussed below.

Order of Dependent Segments

With HISAM organization, or HDAM/HIDAM organizations using hierarchical pointers, access time to the segments at the bottom right of the tree is greater than access time to the first dependent segment occurrence. Therefore performance can be affected by the order specified for segments at a given level. In the example ST PDB, if ASSET segments were retrieved more frequently than ATTEND segments, the ASSET segment should be listed first in the DBD. Since we expect very few segment occurrences of either of these, performance would not be very dependent on the order.

With a large LENDER, PDB performance could vary sharply based on dependent segment order if hierarchical pointers are used. If there were frequent access to NOTICE segments, and NOTICE followed LOAN as suggested in Figure 13–10, retrieval would be slowed by the necessity of traversing all PAYMENT segments before reaching the first NOTICE segment for a LOAN. If NOTICE and LOAN are reversed in ordering, then NOTICE segments would appear before LOAN segments on the hierarchical chain. If parent/twin pointers are used for HIDAM or HDAM, segment ordering has no impact on performance.

Secondary Indexes

You will recall from the discussion in Chapter 10 that secondary indexes can be constructed on any field to provide either alternative access paths to the root segment or direct access to dependent segments. (Note that it would not make sense to index on the sequence field value of a root segment.)

The guidelines for the selection of secondary indexes are essentially the same as the guidelines for index selection for the relational model and the creation of indexed sets and indexed system sets for the network model. The considerations are, however, a bit more complex for IMS, due to the impact of secondary indexes on allowable types of updates— another example of lack of data independence. These details are beyond the scope of this text.

For the example physical databases of Figure 13–10, secondary indexes should be considered for the root segments SCHOOL, STUDENT, and BANK, depending on the types of retrievals. If any online retrieval of, say, STUDENT by name is to be supported, then a secondary index on name is mandatory.

Other prime candidates for secondary indexes are dependent segments for which direct retrieval (that is, without retrieval of parent segment) is desired. Since we would expect a reasonable level of direct retrieval of LOAN segments without retrieval of the BANK parent, a secondary index to LOAN on LID should be established. However, there is an interaction between secondary indexes and database partitioning, and decisions on creating secondary data set groups and secondary index selection need to be made jointly.

Database Partitioning: Secondary Data Set Groups

Partitioning a physical hierarchy into multiple data sets (physical files) allows direct access to the root of each DSG. Partitioning is also an attractive means of creating files with homogeneous segments. Separate DSGs may also be separately reorganized.

For the PDBs of Figure 13–10, there appears to be little reason to partition either the SCH or ST databases. In contrast, there are several reasons to partition LENDER. First, partitioning LENDER into primary DSG with BANK and INT_SUB records would create a file with a low growth rate (few added BANK segments; one INT_SUB segment added every three months per BANK).

A larger gain will be realized by having LOAN as the root of a secondary DSG so that direct access to LOAN by LID would be possible. Assuming an HDAM file organization with a single data set group, access to a specific LOAN segment (via its BANK root segment) could be expected to require on the order of 20 to 100 disk accesses depending on the number of LOAN segments for the bank and the degree of clustering. As LOAN segments are added, clustering will worsen (that is, the number of pointers that traverse back and forth between pages will increase). This will increase the frequency of reorganization.

With LOAN as the root of a secondary DSG and an HDAM organization, retrieval of a specific LOAN could be expected to require only a single access, or slightly more due to overflow. Reorganization would still be required, just as any conventional hashed file requires reorganization with growth, but the frequency of reorganization can be controlled by the choice of load factor.

Hierarchical Database Design Summary

As we warned the reader, while no database design activity is trivial, the design of hierarchical databases is particularly problematic. Just to provide an overview takes considerable space because of the many options. And our presentation has oversimplified the situation because we have not considered the interaction between database design and update processing.

The complexity of database design for IMS can be attributed to three factors:

- The hierarchical model is deficient because real information structures are inherently network structures. This means that the database designer must "force fit" the conceptual design into one of a myriad of possible IMS databases, none of which are obvious.
- Initial development of IMS began at a time when the field of databases and even of file structures was in its infancy. Thus, fundamental design mistakes were made, which had to be patched up and compensated for in later versions of the software.

• IMS is a mature product; that is, many of the alternative structures were added to provide real improvements in performance (such as fast-path databases). We can expect such enhancements to be added to relational systems, which will increase their performance but will also increase their complexity, making the designer's job more difficult.

The following is a summary of design steps for IMS databases. It might have been appropriate to make the first step: "Enroll in an IBM course on IMS database design."

A. Mapping Relations to Segment Types

1. Add segment types as necessary to capture relationships.

   a. Add linking segments for unary relationships.

   b. Add linking segments for many-to-many relationships.

   The same cost considerations outlined for relational database design are relevant to the following design steps: storage space, query processing costs, response time, and the potential for inconsistency.

2. Determine if segments should be partitioned.

   a. Consider vertical partitioning if either of the following statements is true:

      (1) Certain fields are very infrequently used.

      (2) Applications induce a partition on the fields.

   b. Consider horizontal partitioning if either of the following statements is true:

      (1) Segments can be classified as frequently or infrequently used.

      (2) Applications induce a partition on the segments.

3. Consider prejoining two segment types that are frequently accessed together. A prejoin is practical only if the dependent segment is not a parent of a segment or a child of some other segment. The prejoin may be attractive if all (or most of) the following conditions exist:

   a. The relationship between the two is one-to-zero, one-to-one, or (in general) one-to-n where n is small.

   b. The parent segment is small.

4. Consider replication of fields if the following conditions exist:

   a. Fields from two different segments are frequently specified in a query.

   b. The two different segment types will not be in the same physical database.

   c. The total size of the replicated fields is not large.

B. Designing Physical and Logical Databases

1. Create "obvious" physical databases made up of a root and sub-tree of dependent segments that have only one parent.

2. For the remaining segments, base the choice of physical versus logical child relationships on access patterns. This is the same as the clustering decision required in relational and network database design.

C. Selecting an Access Method

1. Consider physical record size, access patterns, and update characteristics in selecting between HISAM, HDAM, HIDAM. Keep in mind that subsequent PDB partitioning may influence the decision.

2. Use HDAM or HIDAM with child/twin pointers to provide fast access to dependent segments and to manage large physical database records (PDBR).

3. Use HDAM for fastest access to root segments, recognizing the necessity to reorganize with high volume of root segment additions.

4. Use HISAM if PDBR is small to moderate in size and the volume of dependent segment additions is small to moderate. HISAM is good for applications requiring the retrieval of all dependents or of roots only, and not so good for the retrieval of a specific dependent segment, especially if PDBR is large.

5. Consider HISAM and HIDAM for applications with considerable sequential updating.

D. Partitioning Databases and Selecting Secondary Indexes

1. Consider access patterns, response time requirements, and update characteristics to determine the need for the creation of multiple dataset groups and secondary indexes.

2. Use multiple DSGs to provide direct access to dependent segments, especially when update of ancestor segments is not needed.

3. Use multiple DSGs to create files of homogeneous segments (in terms of update characteristics).

4. Follow guidelines for establishing secondary indexes to root segments. Use secondary indexes to dependent segments as opposed to separate DSGs, especially when ancestor segments are also retrieved.

Questions and Problems

Questions

Many of the following questions apply equally to all three DBMS models. However, if you did not study all three, try to answer for those systems which you did study.

1. Discuss how the logical model and physical model interact in RDBMSs.

2. Describe *vertical partitioning*. Describe the circumstances under which it is appropriate.

3. How can a vertically partitioned relation be made transparent to the user in an RDBMS? To what extent can the user be shielded from the vertical partition? (Or to put it another way, under what conditions must the user be aware of the vertical partition?)

4. Describe *horizontal partitioning*. Describe the circumstances under which it is appropriate, and explain how a horizontally partitioned relation may be transparent to the user of an RDBMS.

5. For the network (hierarchical) model, can a vertically partitioned record type (segment type) be transparent to the user? Discuss.

6. Under what considerations should attributes (data items, fields) be replicated? What are the advantages and disadvantages of replication?

7. For each DBMS model (relational, network, hierarchical), outline the available file organizations of the following types:

  a. Hashing

  b. B-tree (or similar) "primary" index

  c. B-tree secondary index

8. Which network location mode is most comparable to IMS's HDAM organization?

9. Describe the differences between intra- and inter-record clustering.

10. Explain how inter-record clustering achieves much the same result as prejoining.

11. A clustering index in a relational DBMS is comparable to _____ in a network system and _____ in IMS.

12. What potential problems arise in a network DBMS if a system set is created with MODE CHAIN and ORDER on some attribute? How are these problems alleviated if MODE INDEX is specified instead?

13. What are the advantages and disadvantages of defining a network set with PRIOR LINKAGE?

14. Discuss how the size of a set (that is, the number of member records in a set) has an influence on choices such as ORDER IS SORTED, PRIOR LINKAGE, MODE IS INDEX.

15. Describe the differences in the following set specifications, both in terms of the structures created and their impact on processing efficiency:

     (1) MODE IS INDEX, ORDER IS SORTED on ...
     (2) MODE IS INDEX, ORDER IS LAST
     (3) MODE IS CHAIN, ORDER IS SORTED on ...
     (4) MODE IS CHAIN, ORDER LAST

16. What are the conditions that make the use of a repeating group in a network DBMS attractive? Under what circumstances should a repeating group be avoided?

17. Why is there no repeating group construct in IMS?

18. What are the conditions that make mapping relations to a hierarchical model easy?

19. A segment is on the "many" side of two one-to-many relationships. What considerations should be made when deciding which parent segment should be the logical parent and which the physical parent?

20. A file structure uses a non-dense index to a "master" record on its primary key. Each master record contains a list head to a linked list of its "detail" records. The detail records are stored in a separate file. Which organizations in the network and IMS database systems are most similar to this scheme?

21. For each of the following statements, indicate the IMS access method or methods that best fit each statement:

   a. Indexed access

   b. Sequential-only access

   c. Indexed access to root segment, sequential access to dependent segments.

   d. Hashed access.

   e. Ideal for situations in which each physical database record is small, and there is considerable sequential processing but some online processing is also performed.

   f. Fastest access to root segment.

22. What are the similarities and differences between IMS secondary indexes and DSGs?

Problems

In the following, if the problem relates to a specific type or types of DBMS, an indication is made as follows: RM = relational model, NET=network model, IMS = hierarchical model as implemented in IMS.

1. (NET). A relation RA contains primary key A. A relation RB contains attribute A, which is a foreign key because it is from the same domain as the primary key A in RA. Should a set be defined between RA and RB? Discuss.

2. (RM, IMS). An IMS database has a segment named B in the physical database ABC, which is the physical child of segment A. B is also the logical child of logical parent segment X in the PDB XYZ. If A, B, and X are relations (that is, they have attributes corresponding to the fields of segments A, B, and X with the possible additions of key attributes), what can you say about the attributes in A, B, and X?

3. A table named STUDENT with attributes SID, NAME, STREET, ZIP, BIRTH_DATE, PHONE, PARENT_ST, PARENT_ZIP, MAJOR, has been vertically partitioned into the following three tables with some replication of data items:

   ST1 (SID, NAME, MAJOR, SCHOOL)
   ST2 (SID, NAME, STREET, ZIP, BIRTH_DATE, PHONE)
   ST_PAR (SID, PARENT_ST, PARENT_ZIP)

   a. Describe how to provide the user with a database for retrieval that appears to be the original STUDENT table.

   b. Does the partitioning create any potential for inconsistencies? Explain.

   c. For each of the following queries, indicate whether the original STUDENT table or the three "sub-tables" would involve lower access costs. Assume that all tables have indexes on SID and that the STUDENT, ST1, and ST2 tables have indexes on NAME. Assume that the three sub-tables are stored in separate areas of the database (that is, they are not inter-clustered on SID).

      (1) NAME and MAJOR for given SID value.

      (2) NAME, STREET, and ZIP for given SID value

      (3) NAME, MAJOR, and BIRTH_DATE for given SID

(4) SIDs of all students who live with or near parents, defined as PARENT_ZIP equal to ZIP.

(5) NAMEs of all students with MAJOR = 'ENGL' born before Jan. 1, 1970.

4. Given the STUDENT table (record type, segment) of the previous question and the following retrieval patterns, suggest a partitioning of the table, with replication of attributes into two or more subtables that could be expected to reduce access times.

Query ----------------------------------Attributes Needed for Query----------------------------------

Query	SID	NAME	STREET	ZIP	BIRTH_DATE	PHONE	PARENT_ST	PARENT_ZIP	MAJOR
1	X	X				X			
2		X	X	X	X				
3	X			X					X
4	X	X		X					
5							X	X	
6	X	X				X			X
7	X			X		X			

5. Suppose that the application programs that deal with the STUDENT table tend to deal separately with graduate and undergraduate students. What logical/physical design approaches might be used to improve efficiency due to this fact?

6. Consider the following queries against the STUDENT table of Question 3. Assume that each query occurs with a frequency indicated in { } on a scale from 1 to 9, with 1 being very low frequency, 5 moderate frequency, and 9 high frequency. Assume that rapid response time is desired. There are 100 different values for MAJOR. What indexes should be defined? (Note that even though the queries are expressed in SQL, the answers are not dependent on the type of DBMS.)

```
{3}    SELECT NAME, STREET, ZIP FROM STUDENT
       WHERE ZIP BETWEEN 10000 AND 11000;

{6}    SELECT SID, NAME, MAJOR FROM STUDENT
       WHERE BIRTH_DATE BETWEEN 1/1/70 AND 1/31/70;

{1}    SELECT SID, NAME FROM STUDENT
       WHERE NAME LIKE 'JOHNS%';

{2}    SELECT SID, NAME, STREET, ZIP FROM STUDENT
       WHERE MAJOR = 'ACCTG';
```

7. A division of the GSL administrative offices performs extensive statistical analyses on the data. The data needed includes attributes (data items, fields) from the STUDENT and LOAN tables (records, segments). The analysts are not particularly interested in having completely up-to-date data—as long as the data is current within the last month they are satisfied. What approach do you suggest to meet their needs?

8. Consider Problems 4 and 5 of Chapter 11, which ask for the definition of conceptual models using the E-ERM, and Problems 2 and 3 of Chapter 12, which result in normalized relations. Carry those problems through to logical and physical designs in one or more of the DBMS models. Obviously, this is rather open-ended; you will need to make assumptions about processing characteristics in order to develop a good logical and physical design.

References

Finkelstein, S.; Schkolnick, M.; and Tiberio, P. "Physical Database Design for Relational Databases." *ACM TODS,* vol. 13, no. 1 (March 1988), pp. 91–128.

Gillenson, M. L. "The Duality of Database Structures and Design Techniques." *Communications ACM,* vol. 30, no. 12 (December 1987), pp. 1056–1065.

Loomis, M. E. S. *The Database Book.* New York: Macmillan Publishing Co., 1987.

McFadden, Fred, and Hoffer, Jeffrey. *Data Base Management.* 2d ed. Menlo Park, Calif..: The Benjamin/Cummings Publishing Co., 1988.

Teorey, T., and Fry J. *Design of Database Structures.* Englewood Cliffs, N.J.: Prentice-Hall, 1982.

14 Database Administration and the Database Environment

Database Administration

Introduction

It is clearly critical that data be managed correctly. We use management here in the broad sense of managing a resource. Some examples of poor management include inconsistent representation of the same data across several databases, missing key data, incorrect data, and poor documentation of data. As an answer to these problems, many companies have appointed a database administrator (DBA) to manage the data resource.

The DBA should be a senior-level middle manager, reporting to top management, not a computer technical person. The DBA is in charge of the data resource, much as a head librarian is in charge of a library's resources. The data resource, however, belongs to the entire organization, not to the DBA and not to a specific department such as Data Processing. (Note that "Data Processing" is a bit old-fashioned; the term conjures up images of punched cards, wired-board machines, etc.—the good old days.)

Among the DBA's responsibilities are:

- Database planning
- Database design
- Database implementation
- Database maintenance
- Database protection
- Improving database performance
- User education
- User training
- User consulting

The DBA must also interact with top management and the computer applications specialists.

Some of the tools used by the DBA will be discussed later in this chapter.

The Roles of Data Administrator and Database Administrator

The DBA responsibilities are often divided among several people with different titles. If this is the case, the possible positions include the following:

- Data Administrator. A high-level manager responsible for all the organization's data needs. This person sets *policy* concerning data utilization, protection, database performance, and so forth.

- Database Administration. A group (or person) assigned the task of managing the organization's databases. The group is part of the information systems department. It is frequently a technical group and is responsible for the system software and hardware employed by the data resources.
- Data Steward. A person who manages a single logical entity, such as customers, products, etc. The data steward is usually a manager from the department that provides that data or is most interested in that entity. The data steward is responsible for that entity's data definitions, access authorization, and planning, among other things.

Database Administrator

The DBA's responsibilities are listed below. Most of them are described in detail elsewhere in the book.

- Database Planning. Includes developing entity charts, data standards, and the implementation plan, analyzing costs and benefits, and selecting software and hardware.
- Requirements Formulation and Analysis. Includes defining user requirements and developing data definitions and a data dictionary.
- Database Design. Includes conceptual, external, internal, and integrity control design.
- Database Implementation. Includes specifying data access rights; developing application program standards; establishing backup, recovery, and security procedures; training users; and supervising the initial loading of the database.
- Operation. Includes user support.
- Maintenance. Includes "tuning" the database for peak performance.
- Growth and Change. Includes anticipating change in the size of the database, the structure of the database, and the way the database is used.

Interaction with Management, Users, and System Personnel

The DBA must deal with three diverse groups—management, users, and data processing personnel—who may have conflicting objectives. Therefore the DBA frequently must exercise diplomatic skills. Earlier it was suggested that the DBA be a senior-level middle manager, reporting to a top manager, which would assist in the political ramifications of the position. Often, the DBA is a top manager, which is even better.

There must be two-way communication between the DBA and each of these groups:

- Management to DBA: Budget support and notice of changes in the business plan's goals, priorities, and constraints.
- DBA to Management: Budget requirements, database plans, schedules, and status reports on current database projects.
- User to DBA: Data requirements, future database requirements, and changes in usage that require changes in database relationships.
- DBA to User: Applicable portions of the data dictionary, training, education, new applications, and methods for performance improvement.
- Data Processing to DBA: Reports on database usage, performance, errors, and problems.
- DBA to Data Processing: Update, backup, and archiving schedules, security procedures, and error recovery.

Data Dictionary/Directory

Objectives of the Data Dictionary/Directory System

A data dictionary/directory system is a system separate from the database with which it is associated. The data dictionary/directory system is itself a database containing *metadata*, which is data describing or about other data. The metadata describes the data in the database.

A typical data dictionary/directory system also includes the physical database and file structures, activity reports, and user list. As an example, here are just a few of the items found in an ORACLE dictionary. Note that the information concerning a specific user is different for each user who accesses the dictionary.

- An audit trail of accesses to the user's tables.
- An audit trail of the user's log-ons/log-offs.
- A profile of tables accessible to the user.
- Specifications of columns in tables created by the user.
- Indexes created by the user and indexes on tables created by the user.
- Private synonyms created by the user.
- A record of log-on sessions for the user.
- Data and index storage allocation for the user's own tables.
- A profile of tables and views accessible to the user.
- A directory of column-level update grants by or to the user.
- A directory of access authorization granted by or to the user.
- A list of ORACLE users.

The DBA has access to much additional information.

Functions

The data dictionary/directory system has three primary functions: the glossary, the catalog, and the controller. All the features described below may not be found in every data dictionary/directory system.

Glossary

The glossary portion of the dictionary provides the maintenance facilities. It loads the dictionary when you begin using the software; it updates the dictionary as your database changes; it keeps track of database usage; and it issues reports on the dictionary's (database's) contents. It also analyzes and documents the effect of any changes, such as a change of field size, and reports any changes required in other tables to support this change.

Catalog

The catalog portion of the dictionary is used to provide common definitions across the database. Once you describe a specific entity, the description will be used in every new table in the database. You can also use the catalog to get a report that provides you with a list of all that database's tables in which some specific entity appears.

Controller

The controller portion of the data dictionary/directory system directs the execution of the program. Programs and transactions are directed to the correct workstation or physical location, and any required translation of the incoming or outgoing data is performed.

Controllers are especially useful when a network and several databases are used. The controller can divide a complex request into queries to several databases, if required, and convert the outputs of the several databases into a single response. The controller can work with any combination of the relational, network, and hierarchical models.

Database Security

Most database software has built-in security measures; in other cases the user must rely on the security provided by the network software or the computer operating system, if these in fact include such provisions. In some cases a separate security software system is required.

The details of the security measures vary considerably. The software might permit users to access only specific databases, tables, or fields. A more flexible system might allow a user to read a table but not permit the records to be updated. An option might be to permit the user to read only some of the fields in a table and perhaps to update only some of those fields. Many combinations are possible. The user's privileges are generally indicated in the data dictionary/directory system.

Typically the user must enter an account number or name and a password when the database software is started. The DBA sets the restrictions, if any, imposed on each user. Of course, the DBA has unlimited access to all the databases.

Introduction: Security vs. Integrity

Security and integrity are two entirely different things. *Security* means permitting a user to do only what he or she is allowed to do and ensuring that the user cannot do anything that has not been authorized. *Integrity* means making sure that what the user does is correct.

As a very simple example, the security system might ensure that the user could only enter or update the date in some fields, while integrity would ensure that the date entered was valid, that is, not February 30 or November 31.

Security Problems and Threats

Security threats can be accidental or deliberate. An accidental threat can occur when a user sits down at a terminal and finds the previous user did not log off. The new user now has the previous user's privileges, which might be greater than his, but in any case are probably different.

Deliberate threats include:

- Erasing records, tables, and databases
- Changing data in tables
- Copying sensitive data for a competitor
- Altering his own personnel records, payroll records, etc.

Illegal access may be possible by bypassing the security system and assigning oneself greater privileges, using another person's password, adding software to the system that helps broach the security, and so forth.

Methods of Security Control

Alternative methods for security control include physical control, data encryption, passwords, query control, and views.

Security in SQL

Views and queries are controlled through SQL. Views are the means of concealing the contents of specific columns from a user. The contents of the views are set by the DBA. Each user can be assigned numerous views, and different users can be assigned the same view. The user may, of course, define views on top of those views on the base table to which he has access priveledge. The DBA also determines which databases and tables the user is permitted to access.

Here is an example of creating a view.

```
CREATE VIEW NAMELIST
AS SELECT CNAME, ADDR, CITY, STATE, ZIP
FROM CUST_NAME
WHERE CITY = "New York"
```

These SQL commands create a view that limits the user to accessing the CNAME, ADDR, CITY, STATE, and ZIP fields of the the CUST_NAME table. The view's identifier is NAMELIST. A record's CITY attribute must contain "New York" or the record cannot be accessed.

Another aspect of SQL security is the DBA's ability to grant and revoke user's privileges. These privileges include SELECT, UPDATE, ALTER, INSERT, and DELETE. Different tables and even fields can have different privileges.

These SQL features provide the DBA with most of the data security control typically required.

Physical Security

A common method of ensuring physical security requires that the computer, storage devices, and all peripherals except the terminals be placed in a secure area. The area should have a highly controlled entrance and exit, locked doors at a minimum. Phone lines connected to the computer system should be physically protected from wire taps.

Encryption

Encryption means coding data in some form so that it cannot be easily interpreted. For example, the simple encryption system, Caesar's cipher, works in this manner:

```
ABCDEFGHIJKLMNOPQRSTUVWXYZ Unciphered
CDEFGHIJKLMNOPQRSTUVWXYZAB Ciphered
```

The letter to be encrypted is in the top row, while the encrypted letter is immediately below it in the second row. In this cipher, HELLO would be enciphered as JGNNQ. The comedians, Bob and Ray, clown that this cipher is obviously impossible to break. To decrypt, follow the opposite process. By starting the second row with a different letter you can change the cipher.

Despite the clowning by Bob and Ray, encryption experts (being by nature quite conservative) have developed ciphers which are considerably more complex. The so-called *public key encryption* system has a public key and a private key. The public key can be given to anyone. It may even be given to people who don't want it! A person can then use the public key to cipher into the encrypted form, E(X). E(X) can then be transmitted in the clear over satellite, radio, or phone lines to its destination. However, only a person who knows the private key that goes with that public key can decipher E(X) to obtain the original message X. The public key and the algorithm used to encrypt and decrypt the data are public knowledge, but the private keys must be kept secret.

Other systems use only a single key, known to both the person encrypting the information and the person who decrypts it. In this case, of course, the single key must be kept secret.

In a computer system, sensitive data that is passed between computers or in storage devices is commonly encrypted.

Database Integrity

As mentioned earlier in the chapter, data integrity applies to the validity of the data that is entered into the database. Most database software provides some degree of integrity checking; additional checks must be provided by application programs.

Here are a few of the features found in ORACLE's SQL*FORMS program to assist the user in supplying valid data.

- If the data is numeric, a range of acceptable values can be set.
- The user can be forced to select data, for example, a state abbreviation, from a list of acceptable values.
- A field can be set to reject an entry that duplicates one found in another record.
- Field entries such as customer number or part number can be looked up in a table to be sure they are valid.

Database Recovery

The integrity of a database can be damaged in several ways. When damage occurs, there should be a method to recover the database's integrity.

Transaction Concept

A transaction is a unit of work that (usually) alters data in the database. A complete transaction changes the consistent state of a database to a temporarily inconsistent state, then returns it to a consistent state. For example, an order has just been taken. The quantity of the item ordered, together with the part number and the date of the order, has been input. Two base tables exist, one containing order records and the other the inventory. When the transaction begins, both tables are consistent. When the computer enters the order, at some moment the inventory has been changed to reflect the sale by reducing the quantity on hand, but the order table record that reflects this change in the inventory has not yet been stored. The database is now inconsistent. Once the order record has been entered, the database is returned to a consistent state. By all means avoid using the GSL for example!

A transaction either is committed (sent to storage) because it was acceptably completed or it is aborted because it did not complete acceptably. If it was aborted it should have had no effect on the database and the operator should have been apprised of the situation. A completed, committed transaction cannot be undone, except by the results of additional transactions.

Types of Failure

The database system should make it impossible for a partially completed transaction or records in an inconsistant condition to be entered into the database. Further, it should keep two users who are simultaneously accessing a record from interfering with each other or storing incorrect data at anytime during their transactions. However, should something happen while the record is in the process of being committed to the database or should invalid data be stored, then the database's integrity will be destroyed.

Several causes of database errors are:

- A programming error permitting acceptance of invalid data.
- An error in the database system software.
- An error in the operating system.
- A storage device malfunction.
- A computer hardware defect.
- A power failure.
- The operator halting the system.

Software errors are the toughest to find and often go undetected for years. Such errors may gradually corrupt the database to the point it is useless. The best insurance against software errors is to stick with widely used DBMs and OS software. Then carefully test application software and periodically audit the database for consistency. The first error can be the most difficult to find and correct. Its effects can be wide-ranging: errors in reports, failure of other software using the faulty database, and so on. The other causes are generally obvious.

Transaction Recovery

If an error occurs during a transaction, such as a power failure, for example, the system should be able to discern this fact when it is restarted. In such a situation it should do a *rollback*, which means that the database is returned to the state it was in before the transaction was attempted. The database program should keep the user apprised of the situation during and after a transaction, posting a message stating whether or not the transaction was successfully committed.

Recovery from System Failure

A system failure can be local or global. A local failure concerns only one transaction, with no effect on any of the other transactions that may be occurring at that same time. A global failure, for example, a power failure, concerns the whole computer system and affects all the transactions currently in progress.

The database system keeps a log of all the transactions in progress and committed. Also, a committed transaction does not necessarily mean that the database was physically updated; the data might be temporarily stored in a buffer, to be written to the storage media when time permits or after a given number of transactions have occurred. When the data is actually stored that fact is also sent to the log.

When a system failure occurs, the database system can use the log to bring the database up to date. In some cases there will not be enough information in the log to reconstruct a transaction; those transactions will be rolled back. When the logged information is sufficient, the transaction is rolled back, then recommitted.

Recovery from Media Failure

A media failure, such as a head crash, means that the database will have to be restored from an archived copy, also known as a *dump* or *backup*. Good operating practice requires that these archive copies be made frequently.

Both the archived log file and that of the database version to be replaced, if it is available, should be used. This will ensure that as many of the transactions as possible that occurred since the backup was made can be recovered.

Concurrency Control

A database system usually is available to more than a single user. The potential for problems exists when two or more users work with the same database at the same time. Concurrency control keeps such transactions from interfering with each other. Descriptions of two possible concurrency problems follow.

Example Problem: Lost Updates

Assume we have an inventory table. User A accesses a part number record, record X, to change the quantity on hand. Immediately afterward user B accesses the same record with the same intention. Both users now have the same unchanged record. User A changes the quantity on hand in the record and commits it. Next, user B does the same. Since user B's record did not reflect the changes made by user A, the updated record will contain only user B's update. User A's change of record X has been lost.

Approaches to Concurrency Control: Locking

The usual method of dealing with lost updates is called *record locking*. A locked record is only available to the user who locked it.

Returning to our previous example, when user A fetches record X, that record is locked. When user B attempts to retrieve the record he or she cannot do so, but will have to wait until user A commits the record. Now when user B finally gets record X and updates it, the record he or she changes will be a copy of the record that was updated by user A. When user B commits the record it will reflect both users' changes.

Deadlock and Deadlock Protection

Record locking can have an unfortunate side effect. To expand on the previous example, assume that two tables are in use: a inventory table and a salesperson table. The salesperson table contains a record for each salesperson and keeps a running total of the value of all sales. A salesperson (record Z) has made two sales, both of the same item (the part number in record X). User A will enter one of the sales, user B the other. User A retrieves record X from the database to reduce the quantity on hand by the number of parts sold. Record X is now locked. User B gets the record Z to add the amount of the current sale to salesperson Z's record. Record Z is locked. To complete the transaction, user A requests record Z. It was locked earlier, so user A will have to wait. To complete the transaction, user B requests record X. It was locked earlier, so user B will have to wait. As you can see, in this situation both users will have to wait forever, because each has locked the record the other needs to complete the transaction. This situation is called *deadlock*. It is possible for more than two users to be involved in a deadlock.

If this situation occurs, the system should detect the deadlock. There are two ways to deal with deadlock: (1) roll back both transactions with the expectation that the circumstances causing the deadlock will not reoccur; or (2) roll back one of the user's transactions, say user A's, which unlocks record X. Now user B can complete and commit the transaction. This frees record Z. When user A's transaction is then automatically restarted, both records will be unlocked and the transaction can take place.

Questions

1. What are the primary responsibilities of the DBA?

2. With what kinds of groups must the DBA interact?

3. What is *metadata*? How does it differ from *data*?

4. What information does the data dictionary/directory system include?

5. Describe the functions of the data dictionary/directory system.

6. Describe and contrast *security* and *integrity*.

7. Give examples of accidental and deliberate security threats.

8. How are views used as a means of providing security in SQL applications?

9. What is *encryption*? How is it used to provide security? What are some common ciphers?

10. When is a transaction complete?

11. What are some causes of database system errors?

12. Define *rollback*. When will a rollback occur?

13. What is *concurrency control*? Describe a concurrency problem that can occur in a database system. How are concurrency problems solved?

14. What are the positive and negative effects of record locking? How can the negative consequences be dealt with?

References

Appleton, D. S. "The Modern Data Dictionary." *Datamation*, vol. 33, no. 5 (March 1, 1987), pp. 66–68.

Date, C. J. *An Introduction to Database Systems.* Vol. 1. 4th ed. Reading, Mass.: Addison-Wesley Publishing Co.,1985.

Dolk, D. R., and Kirsch II, R. A. "A Relational Information Resource Dictionary System." *Communications ACM,* vol. 330, no. 1 (January 1987), pp. 48–61.

Database Issues and Future Development

15 Database Issues and Future Development

Introduction

This chapter presents a number of topics and issues of current concern along with speculations on future directions in the evolution of databases.

The question of relational system performance is still an issue although with each release of new versions of RDBMSs, their performance improves. The importance of considering all costs associated with a database is important. As Date points out, while RDBMS performance may not yet rival that of network and hierarchical DBMSs, the development and modification costs for the RDBMS are much less.[1] By the time a hierarchical or network system begins to pay off because of superior performance, it is often time to consider a major database redesign, thus incurring higher personnel costs again. Furthermore, a RDBMS implementation goes into service sooner so its benefits are available to end-users earlier.

Relational DBMSs are becoming the core around which so called fourth-generation (4GL) languages and tools are constructed. Products such as ORACLE and INGRES have a variety of report generators, application generators, graphics generators, and so on. This trend will likely continue, and products that are not highly integrated with a SQL-based DBMS will fade in popularity.

Distributed databases are a hot topic. In addition to what could be termed "fully" distributed databases in which all database copies are kept in synchronization, almost every larger organization also has more loosely coupled databases in the form of "remote materialized views"; that is, extracts from the central database that are maintained on divisional minicomputers or local workstations. Selecting the appropriate form of distribution/decentralization and managing it will become an increasingly complex problem.

Integrating "intelligence" into the database and DBMS is another topic of current and future interest. Artificial intelligence techniques are used for very friendly interfaces (for example, natural language query processing) and for expert system databases.

In addition to knowledge bases (the database component of an expert system), other forms of information representation are being explored. One important area of work is temporal databases, another is object-oriented databases.

Hardware technology is also having an impact on the database environment in at least three important ways. First, the aforementioned distributed database is in part the result of increasingly cheaper processors and storage devices. Second, hardware is being designed

---

[1] C. J. Date, "How Relational Systems Perform," *Computer World*, February 13, 1984.

specifically to operate as a DBMS. Third, the recent development of optical storage devices will result in a reduction in storage costs for static and relatively static databases. The availability of massive amounts of online data will have an impact on decision-support systems and will further encourage the development of temporal databases.

Current Relational DBMS Directions and Issues

Popular relational database products are becoming available on a wider range of CPUs and operating systems ranging from microcomputers to mainframes. As a result, they will be able to operate with a greater number of networks.

There will also be more gateways that will enable relational and nonrelational databases to share data. For example, a relational database such as INGRES could share data with a nonrelational database such as IMS. And there will be improvements in the ability of relational DBMSs to support the following functions:

- Updates of multiple databases.
- Replication of data at distinct multiple sites as a means of improving access speeds and providing greater availability when there are communication or site failures. Replicas will be able to be dynamically created and destroyed, and updates will be automatically propagated to all sites.
- Fragmentation of data. A table may be divided into fragments for physical storage (for example, each bank in the GSL model may hold its own student and loan files locally), even though each is part of a single student or loan file stored centrally.
- Translation between SQL and non-SQL data manipulation languages will become easier. It will be easier to convert between data types used in the various database systems, and it will become possible to share system catalogs between SQL and non-SQL DBMSs.

Application Tools

Natural Language

Natural language interfaces are only now beginning to appear in commercial products after many years of development. They allow a user to frame such queries as "How many seniors have loans at the Seafirst bank?" The natural-language interface transforms this query into a relational language which is used by the DBMS to furnish the desired result. Two of the best-known natural-language systems are RENDEZVOUS, developed by Codd at IBM Research, and INTELLECT, developed at Dartmouth College and now available from Artificial Intelligence Corporation.

The basis of all natural-language systems is a knowledge base: a collection of information that enables the system to "understand" natural-language queries. Among other things, a knowledge base includes tables of commonly occurring phrases.

A *lexicon* is a table defining natural-language words that are likely to be used in queries. The words in a lexicon generally fall into two categories, (1) general terms, such as FIND, HAVE, and WITH, and (2) terms used in the specific database, such as names for tables (STUDENT, LOAN, and BANK) and names for attributes (NAMES, LEVEL, AGE, SZIP).

Installing a natural-language interface involves, as a minimum, generating the database-specific portion of the lexicon and the database-specific phrase-translation rules. It is not always necessary for the knowledge base to be completed before the natural-language interface can be installed. In some systems it is only necessary to generate the database-specific portion of the lexicon and the database-specific phrase-translation rules. The rest of the knowledge base is developed while the system is in use.

RENDEZVOUS and INTELLECT use different approaches to handle terms that are not defined in the knowledge base. RENDEZVOUS extracts all of the terms it understands from a query and then interrogates the user with a *clarification dialogue* to find the meaning of any terms it cannot understand. Users often find this interactive dialogue quite cumbersome because the answers to some of the questions asked of them are either obvious (to a human) or nonsensical. In spite of this, the system deals with straightforward queries smoothly and reliably. INTELLECT adopts a different approach to resolve unknown terms. Instead of a clarification dialogue, it employs an internal-knowledge base of English syntax to generate an initial set of feasible interpretations of the original query. If there is more than one feasible interpretation of the query, INTELLECT attempts to discover the user's intended meaning by searching the database. The meaning of an unknown term is deduced by finding out how it is used within the database. This method is preferable to interrogating the user, but with a large database the time and cost overheads involved in the extra searching can become significant.

The approach adopted by RENDEZVOUS lends it to implementation on an intelligent workstation (usually a personal computer). If the database catalog is stored in the terminal there is no need for any communication with the central database until the query has been correctly interpreted and is ready for execution.

At the present stage of development, natural-language interfaces only support read functions and are not used to update the database. The database-specific parts of the lexicon are an essential part of the natural-language interface. Generation of the lexicon is difficult and, in all but simple databases, requires highly specialized skills.

Natural language interfaces require large amounts of main memory and are therefore expensive to implement. Interfaces using icons (graphical menus) and pointing devices (a mouse or a touch screen) are generally easier to design than natural-language interfaces.

The accuracy and vocabulary of speech recognition and speech synthesis systems has reached a point in which it is viable to make commercial systems where a user is able to converse with a computer. When used as an input method, this conversation can take many forms. The simplest is for the user to issue direct commands. A more flexible method involves making selections from menus recited by the computer. However, the most flexible approach is for the person to converse with the computer through a natural-language interface. The most obvious applications for such a system are remote-information systems in which a telephone provides the vehicle for a dialogue between the user and the computer. Not all applications need be remote; however, natural-speech interfaces will make information systems accessible to users who do not know how to use a computer or are in situations where it is impractical for them to use a keyboard. A surgeon, for example, could retrieve information about a procedure or get information on how to handle a complication without taking his or her hands from the surgical instruments or looking away from the operation. Pilots of high-performance airplanes and spacecraft also are sometimes unable to make physical movements to use a computer.

Report Writers

A report is a set of formatted output from a database, presented on a screen or printed. The software that produces such a report is called a *report writer* or *report generator*. The purpose of the report writer is to reduce the effort required to extract and present desired information. A user has the option of choosing from a selection of ready-made report formats or of creating custom formats. The ready-made or default formats generally display the contents of a specified table along with optional data such as a title, the date and time, page number, and so on. The table may either be an existing table or one that is derived for the report by an appropriate SQL RETRIEVE statement.

In many cases the default output form is unacceptable and the user must tailor a custom report by producing a report specification. There are two common methods by which a user can generate a custom report specification. The first and simplest method is called *Report By Forms* (RBF), an interactive editor that enables a user to start with a sample form and change it to suit the particular situation. The second method uses a *report-definition language*. The user needs some knowledge of conventional programming in order to use a report-definition language.

As an example of RBF we will take a brief look at the R:BASE report generator. This is a built-in module, called Reports *EXPRESS*, which is invoked with:

```
REPORTS report-name table-name
```

If no database is open when Reports EXPRESS is invoked, the user is prompted to select one. Similarly, if no report or table name is provided in the command the user will be prompted to provide it. If the report name is an existing R:BASE report it will be used, otherwise R:BASE will assume the user wants to define a new report. Each report, while centered around data from a single table or view, can use data brought in from other tables.

The Reports EXPRESS main screen presents a menu with the following options:

1. Edit. Place fields on the page along with page and column headings and footings.

2. Expression. Define variables to hold data that is either looked up in other tables or derived from data stored in tables.

3. Configure. Define the layout of the report and the break points between individual reports.

4. Draw. Draw lines for borders.

Reports created with Reports EXPRESS are made up of seven sections:

1. Report Header. Printed once at the beginning of the report.

2. Page Header. Printed once at the start of each page and is most often used to print headings for columns of data plus page numbers.

3. Break Header. Printed once for each break point. Break points are used to separate individual entries in the report. Break headers and break footers are used to insert headings, such as individual names for detail lines, and to print subtotals. The actions that occur at each break point are defined by a configuration table that is filled in during the creation of the report format.

4. Detail. Detail lines are the body of the report and are printed once for each set of data values.

5. Break Footer. Printed once for each breakpoint and may contain subtotals.

6. Page Footer. Printed once at the bottom of each page.

7. Report Footer. Printed once at the end of the report and may contain report totals.

The report is created by moving the cursor to the desired screen position and either typing text that is to appear at that position, or pressing a function key to enter an attribute or variable. If you enter an attribute or variable name that is not part of the table or view on which the report is defined, R:BASE assumes that it is the name of a variable and prompts the user to enter an expression that defines its contents. R:BASE's logical functions provide a great deal of flexibility in the creation of variable definitions.

Graphical Output

Business graphics are a very effective means for conveying information to users. Individual database systems provide tools for transforming tables of data into a variety of graphical formats. Third-party products are also available to produce what are known as *presentation graphics,* using paper, overhead transparency, slide, videotape, or film media. The field of business graphics is rapidly developing into a specialized industry. A wide selection of graphics software and special peripheral devices are available to users for in-house production of graphics. There are also service bureaus that produce very high-quality graphic images from users' data.

Many database systems include some form of graphics output. In general, the quality of the graphics produced by modules supplied with the database is not as impressive as those available from many of the specialized graphics products. Therefore users often extract data from a database for subsequent processing by a graphics package.

Business graphics fall into four general classes:

1. *Bar charts* in which the X value represents the independent variable (the label on the bar), and the Y axis represents the dependent variable (the height of the bars). Optionally, a Z axis can be included by placing sub-bars at each X position, thereby producing a three-dimensional representation of the data.

2. *Pie charts* in which the X value represents the independent variable (a label on a slice cut from a circular pie), and the Y value represents the dependent variable (an area of the slice). It is not usual to have a Z dimension for this type of graph. Note, however, that some graphics packages draw pie charts as a three-dimensional image for artistic reasons but do not attach any numerical significance to the thickness of the pie.

3. *Scatter graphs* in which X and Y represent X,Y coordinates. Individual points are marked to show each X,Y value. Optionally, this type of representation may include the ability to draw a straight line through the points at the position most closely fitting the X,Y points (linear regression).

4. *Line plot* in which X and Y again represent X,Y coordinates. The graphics program considers each X,Y point to be part of a continuous function that it approximates by connecting adjacent points to form a continuous curve.

Graphics packages usually provide a variety of default graph formats that the user can easily customize in much the same way as a report format can be customized. Most graphics packages allow the user to:

• Select fill patterns or color for bars or slices
• Select the character or symbol used to represent points on a scatter graph
• Chose the line type and/or color for each Z value on a line or scatter graph

- Adjust the scale of the axes
- Superimpose a grid
- Adjust the size, style and color of text used to label axes, objects, titles, and so on
- Adjust the placement of axes, titles, legends, and so on.

Application Generators

Software systems such as those described in the preceding sections, reduce the need for user-written application programs. While it is sometimes possible to provide all of the functions required in an installation using only the given tools, it is usually necessary to write at least a few application programs to satisfy some needs. Traditionally, such needs would be met by writing an application program using a language such as COBOL, with interfaces to the database. Many databases reduce the effort and skill required to produce custom application software by including an *application generator*.

The purpose of an application generator is to enable a user to create application software quickly. They are an advance over traditional programming languages, such as COBOL or PL1, in the same way that COBOL and PL1 are an advance over assembler code. For this reason, application generators are often described as "fourth-generation tools" or "fourth-generation languages" (4GL).

An application generator presents the user with a high-level language for application development in which the primitive operations include not only the standard control and arithmetic operations, but also facilities for defining and interacting with a database, screen handling, input and output handling, and so on. The development of an application differs from the way it would be done with a traditional language, this is, writing and testing code. Instead, the application developer defines *what* is required through an interactive dialogue with the application generator. When the definition is complete, the application generator creates the necessary code.

The way the interactive dialogue is handled differs from one database system to another. We will look briefly at one of the most common approaches in which the end-user communicates with an application program by filling in forms displayed on the screen. Such a forms-based application can be thought of as a series of frames arranged in a hierarchical manner. Each frame consists of a form to be filled in by the user and a menu from which the user selects the next operation, or frame.

A forms-based applications generator provides the application designer with software tools for creating a variety of frames. Typically there will be four types of frames that can be created.

- *User-specified frames.* For definition of operations specific to the application. (See below.)
- *Query frames.* For definition of a Query-by-Forms (or similar) frame with "variables" where the end-user will supply query constants.
- *Report frames.* For a definition of a report form. Such a form may include the ability to ask the end-user for the parameters of the desired report. These parameters are then used in conjunction with a previously defined report specification to produce a report.
- *Graphics frames* enable the application to make use of the graphics output capabilities of the system.

Operations performed by user-specified frames are usually described in a high-level language that is specific to the particular database. Typical operations include:

- *Database statements*, which allow retrieval or updating of data
- *Form control statements*, which control what appears on the screen and handle functions such as displaying messages, clearing fields, setting initial values and validating entered values entered by the end-user
- *Control-flow statements*, which perform various "if" functions and make calls to other frames or user specified procedures

Application generators often produce-code similar to that which a competent application developer would generate using the built-in database language. However, there is an increasing trend towards the use of application generators that produce some form of compiled code. The advantage of a compiled application is that it is translated to machine code and therefore runs faster. Furthermore, the program is more secure since it is difficult for end-users to tamper with a compiled program.

Some application generators have been developed for very specific fields (law and banking, for example) in which similar operations are performed in many different organizations. Such applications are provided as packages that can be tailored to the needs of particular end-users by specifying parameters.

Distributed DBMSs

A distributed DBMS is one in which a number of sites are connected together through a communications network and that allows a user located at any site to access data stored at any site. Each site can be considered as a database system in its own right with its own database, its own database administrator, its own users, its own CPU, and so on.

The advantages of a distributed database include potential increased efficiency and increased accessibility. Greater efficiency is possible because data is stored close to where it is most frequently needed. Accessibility is improved because records held in one location can be accessed from another site via the communication link. The following assumptions are usually made when considering a distributed database system:

- The distributed database system is homogeneous, meaning that each site runs its own copy of the same DBMS.
- Sites have some autonomy, meaning that they are not under the complete control of a central site.
- Communications between the sites are slow. Typical long-haul networks have data transfer rates of 1,200 to 9,600 bytes a second compared to disk or local network speeds of 1 to 2 million bytes per second.

Large companies (Boeing, for example) have hundreds of databases linked together as a distributed database system. An obvious reason for doing this is that the specification, design, development, construction, testing, modifying, marketing, selling, and servicing of each aircraft is handled by different parts of the organization in different parts of the country and at different times. Some of the data relating to a particular aircraft will remain at a central site, but much of it will move from site to site along with the physical aircraft.

- A great deal of current research and development is directed towards distributed database systems. Some of the reasons for this follow:
- Distributed databases provide local autonomy. For example, any large enterprise is more than likely divided physically into plants, factories, laboratories, warehouses, etc., and divided logically into divisions, departments, projects, and so on. When the database system is distributed throughout the enterprise, individual groups are able to exercise local control and be accountable for their own data.
- Distributed databases can provide large capacity and room for growth. One of the reasons for installing distributed database systems is that there may be no single system large enough to handle the particular application. As the demands on a system grow, it is often easier to add another site to a distributed system than to expand a single centralized system.
- Distributed databases offer greater reliability than centralized systems since the failure of one site does not cripple the whole system. If data is replicated across sites, availability is preserved during the failure of any single site.
- Distributed databases combine efficiency and flexibility. As pointed out earlier, data can be stored close to where it is most frequently used and yet still remain accessible to the rest of the system. This results in greater efficiency and lower operating costs since local accesses are faster than remote accesses and don't incur communication costs. When indicated by usage patterns, data can be dynamically moved, replicated, or copies can be deleted. The parallel operation inherent in a distributed database system often leads to improved performance.

Two of the main objectives of research into distributed databases are to provide location transparency and data fragmentation. *Location transparency* means that users need not know where any piece of data is stored but should be able to access all data as if it were stored at their own local site. When a user requests a particular item of data, the system should locate it automatically. When data is location transparent, it may be moved from one site to another to reflect usage patterns without requiring any rewriting of application programs.

Data fragmentation refers to the ability to divide relations into fragments for physical storage. For example, a relation containing the accounts for an organization may be fragmented over a number of physical storage devices that are not necessarily all at the same location. Systems that support data fragmentation should also support fragmentation transparency. In other words, the user should have a view of the complete relation as if it were not fragmented. This is achieved by appropriate joins and unions of the fragments. It is because of this need for data fragmentation and fragmentation transparency that most distributed databases are based on the relational model.

Problems of Distributed Database Systems

While the distributed database has many advantages, it is not without problems. The main one is that the communication network is slow: a few thousand bytes per second on the network as opposed to millions of bytes per second when accessing a disk. An overriding objective in the design of distributed database systems, therefore, is to keep the flow of messages on the communication network to an absolute minimum. Meeting this objective creates problems in other areas including query processing, propagating updates through the system, handling concurrent access to data, recovering from errors, and managing the system catalog.

Query Processing

The number of messages required to handle a query depends on whether or not the database is relational. A query to a relational system can be handled by two messages, one to send the query, and one to return the set of n data records that satisfy the conditions of the query. In contrast, a nonrelational system that returns the records one at a time would take 2n messages to handle the same query: n messages each requesting the next record, and n messages returning a single record.

Optimization is extremely important in distributed databases. There are usually a number of strategies that can be adopted to carry out any particular query. For example, a request for a join of two relations—Ra, which is stored at site A, and Rb, which is stored at site B—could be carried out by moving Ra to site B, moving Rb to site A, or moving both relations to a third site. Considering this operation in isolation, it is obvious that if Ra consists of only a few records and Rb consists of a large number of records moving Ra to site B involves the fewest messages on the network. On the other hand, if a subsequent operation requires the relation resulting from the join of Ra and Rb to be located at site A, then it may be better to move Rb to site A regardless of its size. The need for optimization strengthens the case for using relational databases since relational operations can be optimized while record-at-a-time operations can't.

Propagating Updates

While replication of data may reduce the amount of traffic on the network, it can lead to consistency problems if all versions of the data are not kept up-to-date. The obvious solution is to concurrently update all versions of data. Concurrent updates create potential problems. For instance, suppose a site is out of action when a new data value is propagated through the system. Should the update operation be aborted, or should the new value be accepted by the available sites and the other site updated later? If the latter, who is responsible for performing the update?

One strategy for handling this type of situation is to designate one copy of the replicated data as the primary copy (note that it is usual to place the primary copies of different fragments at different sites). A transaction involving an update operation is considered to be complete when the primary copy of the data has been successfully updated. The site holding the primary copy is then responsible for propagating the updated values to all other copies of the data. While this solves one problem, it introduces the complication that it violates the autonomy objective mentioned earlier.

Concurrent Access

Most distributed database systems rely on record locking for concurrency control, just as in nondistributed systems. In distributed systems, however, separate messages are required to test, set, and release locks. For example, if local sites are responsible for locking data stored at that site, updating the value of a data item that is replicated in n locations requires 5n messages :

n lock requests
n lock grants
n update messages
n acknowledgements
n unlock requests

Problems arise if one of the sites is unavailable at the time a lock or unlock message is propagated. Once again, the usual solution is to assign one copy of the data as the primary copy. Transactions are performed on the primary copy, and it is the responsibility of the site holding the primary copy to perform the locking and unlocking of the sites holding the replicated data. With this strategy, all copies of the data are considered as a single set, thereby reducing the number of messages from 5n to 2n+3 (one lock request, one lock grant, n updates, n acknowledgments, and one unlock request). Again, the price of this solution is a loss of autonomy for the individual sites.

Another complication in a distributed system is called *global deadlock*. This can occur when a transaction at one site involves the execution of a process at another site (the process is called an *agent* of the transaction). A transaction at one site may have agents at any other sites. It is possible for a loop of agents to be set up in which each agent is waiting for the next to either complete a process or release a lock. The problem is comparable to the single site deadlock problem except that loops of locks and blocked agent processes can exist across sites. Such a deadlock cannot be detected by the sites themselves without extra communication overhead.

Recovering from Errors

Distributed database systems use an error recovery strategy called a *two-phase commit*. This is a protocol that ensures that all of the sites involved in a transaction either accept it (commit to it) or that all sites reject it (roll it back), thereby guaranteeing that the transaction is either completed in its entirety or else does not happen at all. Briefly, the two-phase commit protocol requires that a system component called a *coordinator* instruct the data manager at all of the participating sites to prepare to handle the upcoming transaction. Each data manager then attempts to allocate the resources it needs. If successful in this, it signals OK to the coordinator, otherwise it signals NOT OK. When the coordinator has received replies from all of the sites it makes a decision as to whether the transaction can proceed and if so it sends out a single COMMIT message, otherwise, it sends out a single ROLLBACK message. At each stage of the process, the coordinator and data managers at each of the individual sites record their decisions in individual message logs. If the system fails at some point during a transaction, the error-recovery routines can refer to the coordinator log to pick up the two-phase process where it was interrupted and so ensure that all transactions are either completed or rejected. The coordinator function is usually performed by the site at which a transaction is initiated. There is some erosion of the autonomy objective in using the two-phase protocol since one of the necessary conditions for making it work is that all sites must do what they are told by the coordinator (that is, either commit or roll back—whichever applies).

Managing the System Catalog

In a distributed database system, the system catalog must include control information necessary to provide location transparency, fragmentation, and replication transparency, along with the normal catalog data regarding relations, indexes, users, and so on. The main questions regarding the catalog are where and how should it be stored? Some of the possibilities include:

- Storing the total catalog once at a centralized site.
- Replicating the total catalog at each of the sites.
- Partitioning the catalog with each site holding a catalog for objects stored at that site. The total catalog is the union of all of the local catalogs.
- Combining a centralized total catalog and individual local catalogs.

Distributed DBMS Summary

Distributed DBMSs have advantages in some environments—specifically those where the users themselves are geographically distributed and require rapid access to current data. In particular, for a D-DBMS to be efficient there must be a higher degree of "locality of reference" between users and data. Locality of reference means that users in one location tend to access a particular subset of data which is not frequently accessed by users at other locations and vice versa.

An excellent example of locality of reference, hence a candidate for a D-DBMS, is the GSL system. Federal government operations are divided into ten geographically defined regional offices. Each office administers programs (IRS, SSA, Dept. of Agriculture, and so on) in its area. Thus, a regional office of the GSL program has a natural locality of reference to the students in its region—users in the San Francisco office need data on students in Region 10 schools. They have very little need for access to students in other regions. Other regions have little need for access to students in Region 10. However, the locality of reference is not 100%. There are occasions in which regional offices need data on students in other regions and there are cases in which headquarters (Washington, D.C.) need data from students in all regions. Thus, a completely decentralized database is not appropriate. While a centralized database is feasible, significant economies appear available via data distribution.

In many cases, the overhead and complexities of a distributed database can be avoided by relaxing the requirement that all copies of data be maintained in a consistent state. Continuing with the GSL example, the database could, say, be fragmented by student region—student and loan data for a student currently attending a Region A school would be maintained in the database at Regional Office A. A copy of all data would also be maintained at GSL headquarters. Updates would be made to regional databases with subsequent batch updates sent to headquarters' files. Thus, the headquarters' database would not be consistent with the union of regional databases except immediately after this update. Users accessing headquarters' database would realize the possibility that a record could be outdated. If the user needed assurance of current data, access would be required to the regional office database with, of course, the added communication cost. For most central administration reporting requirements, the inconsistencies would be immaterial.

The approach of a periodic refresh of database copies significantly reduces the communication and processing cost and increases data availability. Many organizations use this approach and can be expected to continue with the mode of operation even as D-DBMSs become more widely available.

DBMS and Artificial Intelligence

Artificial intelligence (AI) is beginning to find its way into database applications, both for the end-user, and for the system developer. As discussed earlier in this chapter, one application of AI is the use of natural language. Less obvious to the user are AI functions embedded in an application to manage system resources and to determine strategies that provide the best performance under various operating conditions.

AI is also beginning to play a major role in systems development as part of new development tools referred to as CASE: Computer Assisted Software Engineering. For example, Knowledgeware, Inc., recently introduced a product called IEW/WS that makes extensive use of artificial intelligence during the planning, design and analysis phases of software development (*PC Tech Journal,* September 1988). The product consists of three modules that are referred to as workstations, one for planning, one for design, and one for analysis.

The planning workstation has tools to manage the business goals of an enterprise and to organize the factors expected to contribute to success. The analysis workstation models the data and processes required for specific business functions. The design workstation describes how data and processes will be handled at a physical level. The IEW/WS does not address a fourth major component of systems development: the construction of a system that includes the generation of executable code, testing, and implementation.

IEW/WS is based on an information-engineering approach in which a logical data model of the information usage of a complete organization is decomposed into smaller and smaller units until program modules can be expressed as pseudo code (pseudo code is a concise English-language description of the operations to be performed by a computer language). The output of IEW/WS is pseudo code that completely describes the necessary structure for an IMS (hierarchical) database. The pseudo code can be processed by a generator to transform it into an application written in an operational language such as COBOL.

At the center of IEW/WS is an encyclopedia that provides developers access to information about all aspects of a project. It stores information about objects (processes or entities), properties (definitions), and associations (relationships) among objects. Storing everything in a central repository reduces redundancies and helps to reduce inconsistencies among objects that are shared by different parts of the software development process. The encyclopedia allows every object to be maintained throughout the total life of a system (development and use). Everything defined in the encyclopedia is available for use in any workstation, diagram, or report.

A powerful feature of IEW/WS's use of the encyclopedia is an "intelligent" knowledge coordinator. This is an AI component that uses a knowledge base of more than 1,000 rules to restrict the developer from entering into the encyclopedia information that may be inconsistent or incomplete. KnowledgeWare claims that their use of AI in this way prevents problems from being entered into the system, whereas other CASE products in which AI is used to check syntax and produce verification reports can let design errors sneak through to the final product.

Application development is performed by defining the data to be stored in the encyclopedia and then assembling the system with diagrams on a screen. Developers can select from a variety of diagramming methods and may quickly switch back and forth between different types of diagrams without losing information. Windowing allows several diagrams to be shown on the screen simultaneously. Changes made to an element in one diagram are automatically made in the encyclopedia and in all other diagrams that reference that element.

IEW/WS provides numerous reports to aid in analyzing the design and checking that it meets specified performance criteria.

Extensions to the Relational Model and Alternative Data Models (date 615)

Much of the current research effort into the design of database systems is aimed at providing database systems with the ability to represent the *meaning* of the data contained within them. The original specifications for a relational database model were put forward first by E.F. Codd of IBM's San Jose Research center in 1970. In 1979, he introduced an extended relational model, known as RM/T, which advanced a number of new concepts to enable the relational model to capture more meaning and made some of the existing definitions more rigorous.

Some of the capabilities of the Extended Entity Relationship Model described in Chapter 11 as a design tool are incorporated in RM/T; however, RM/T does not distinguish between entity and relationship relations. RM/T introduces three entity types: *kernel, characteristic, and associative* entities. A kernel entity represents the true objects of the database but not their characteristics. Characteristic entities represent the properties of kernel, associative, or other characteristic entities. Associative entities represent many-to-many relationships.

RM/T supports entity *subtypes* and *supertypes*. For example, a student supertype could have subtypes of (university) graduate and undergraduate students, trade/technical school students, and two-year college students. It also supports a number of integrity rules beyond the primary key uniqueness and referential integrity rules of the simple relational model. For example, tuples may be inserted or deleted from a kernel relation but may not be updated. This reflects the fact that a tuple in a kernel relation represents the existence of an entity, not its properties. For a property tuple to exist, it must have a corresponding kernel tuple. An associative tuple cannot exist unless the things associated are represented as kernel tuples.

More recently, models have been proposed that further extend the information representation capabilities of the RM/T and E-ERM. So-called *hyper semantic data models* have the following capabilities:

- *Generalization.* Similar objects are described as a higher-level entity type—for example, the subtype/supertype feature of RM/T.

- *Classification.* Specific occurrences of entities are instances of a higher-level entity type. For example, BANK of AMERICA is an instance of an entity-type BANK.

- *Aggregation.* An entity type is related to its sub-parts. For example, a student has degrees, residences, majors, etc.

- *Constraint.* Allows placing a restriction on values of entity properties, allowable operations on the entity, or relationship between entities. For example, maximum total loan amount by student level; creation of loan only if the related student and bank exist.

- *Heuristic.* Allows an information derivation mechanism to be specified that estimates or speculates values. For example, future payments on a loan can be derived from the current loan balance, repayment terms, and payments already made.

The incorporation of heuristics, which allow not only the inference of data values but also the inference of current or future existence or new entity occurrences, represents a significant advance over earlier models. Clearly, the heuristic capability is a form of knowledge representation.

Hardware Technology Impact on Database

Computer technology is currently passing through a period of rapid development. Systems with the speed and processing capabilities once only available from mainframes are now available as personal tabletop machines. Functional specialization is also beginning to appear, as new computer architectures are developed specifically to support a particular language or DBMS more efficiently than could be done with a general-purpose computer. Major hardware advances are taking place on a number of fronts:

- Computer architectures are changing from complex-instruction-set computers (CISC) to reduced instruction-set computers (RISC) with significant increases in operating speed.
- The use of new semiconductor devices based on gallium arsenide instead of silicon is leading to significant speed increases.
- Low-power digital circuits called CMOS have made fast and powerful personal portable computers a reality. This will inevitably lead to a demand for greater personal access to databases.
- Parallel-processing architectures are leading to new and faster approaches for locating and processing data.
- Optical storage devices are making it possible for smaller computers to have local access to huge databases.
- The use of optical fiber cables in communications systems is leading to larger and faster networks of computers.

Two of these technologies which have considerable impact on database are described in the following sections.

Database Computers

Most computers are general-purpose in that the same hardware can be used to perform a wide variety of functions merely by changing the software and peripheral devices. The main reasons for doing this are economic. The development and support of a single product is less costly than a family of different products. In any particular application the performance of a general-purpose computer is lower than that of a system designed to perform that specific application.

At the present time a number of hardware suppliers are addressing the issues of database system performance by developing computers that are specifically designed for database functions. These database machines range from computers using conventional hardware configurations but running special versions of standard DBMSs, to designs based on parallel processing in which many computers operate in tandem to carry out each particular task.

Let's look first at database machines that use conventional hardware. Here the approach is primarily to divide the tasks of running application programs and a DBMS between different computers arranged in a master/slave relationship. One or more front-end "host machines" (masters) handle the processing of conventional application programs, while back-end database machines (slaves) perform all database functions. The machines are usually linked by an I/O channel to ensure fast data transfers. Off-loading the database functions from the master removes some of the design and performance compromises normally made to enable application and DBMS software to share the same processor.

Another variation of the host/database machine arrangement is currently evolving as a result of the rapidly improving performance of personal computers (PCs). The processing capabilities of a high-end PC are now roughly equivalent to those of a traditional mainframe computer and, for many applications, PCs are preferred by users. One area in which they are unable to compete with the mainframe, however, is in supporting large databases. Some of the obvious reasons for this are the expense of providing sufficient storage on individual PCs, and difficulties in keeping data consistent in individual databases, difficulties in sharing data among individual users. The approach that is evolving, therefore, is to store the complete database in a suitable mainframe that is connected to individual-user PCs.

Optical Storage Devices

Optical storage devices are the most significant development in data storage technology in the last 10 to 20 years. Plastic disks ranging in size from 3-1/2 inches to 12 inches have storage capacities ranging from 100 million characters through to more than 4 billion characters. The optical disk achieves this huge capacity by representing data as minute light reflecting patterns on metallic substrata embedded in the plastic. These patterns are arranged as concentric circular tracks. Information contained on a track is retrieved by spinning the disk over a tiny light beam produced by a laser and measuring the amount of light that is reflected from the underlying pattern.

Three basic forms of optical storage have emerged as viable mass-storage devices, each meeting a specific need. The oldest and most widely used optical storage system is called CD-ROM. Up to 500 million characters of data are permanently recorded on a CD-ROM during manufacture. This data can be read by the user but cannot be modified in any way. The name CD-ROM came about because of its physical similarity to the compact audio disk (CD) and its read-only (memory) limitation. CD-ROMs are becoming widely accepted as a method for distributing reference databases such as stock exchange information (a subsidiary of LOTUS Corporation publishes an updated CD-ROM every month containing 20 years of financial information); instruction and maintenance manuals for military equipment; computer manuals (Digital Equipment Corporation, for example, publishes all of its computer manuals as CD-ROMs); and reference books such as encyclopedias or desk reference sets (Microsoft Corporation publishes a desk reference set containing 10 widely used writer's reference books).

The next form of optical disk storage to become commercially viable was the *write-once, read-many* disk, or WORM. The WORM differs from the CD-ROM in that the stored data must be entered by the user. Data is written to a WORM disk by encoding each character as a stream of laser pulses that punch holes in the substrata in a nonreversible manner as it revolves under the recording head. Data is read back from the WORM in the same manner as for a CD-ROM by measuring the reflection of light from the substrata. Typical WORM drives have capacities ranging from 100 million to several million characters. WORM storage systems are primarily used for archival systems or for storing data where it is necessary to have a complete audit trail of all changes that are made to the data (as in accounting, for example). There are a number of strategies for updating records on a

WORM. All operate by creating a new record each time an update is made but differ in the way they manage access to current and earlier versions of a record. One method updates records by reading the old record, making the necessary changes to the data in memory, writing a new record to an unused section of the WORM, and writing pointers to the new record in a "link" area of the old record that has been deliberately left blank for this purpose. The system finds the most recent record at the end of a chain of records by skipping past those records which contain pointer data in the link area.

The most recent form of optical disk storage is the *erasable optical disk.* As its name implies, this type of disk allows the disk to be used over and over by erasing old data and writing new data. Erasable optical disks differ from the CD-ROM and the WORM in that they use magneto/optical effects to modify the reflective properties of the substrata. The data is recorded on an optically bistable medium that changes its reflectivity under the influence of a laser and a magnetic field. Because this change in reflectivity is usually only by a few percent, reading data from an erasable optical disk is somewhat more difficult than reading it from either of the other two types of disks. The new NEXT computer, another Steve Jobs creation, uses an erasable optical disk of 256 megabyte capacity.

Summary

Database technology and practice have made great strides since the first database management systems became commercially available barely 20 years ago. It is only within the last 10 years that relational systems have become available and only within the last two years that DBMSs which are relationally complete have appeared for personal computers. The future will certainly see the relational model consolidate its position. The prevalence of new database applications will be relational. More and more of the older hierarchical and network databases will be converted.

But just as the relational model is becoming firmly entrenched, practitioners and theorists alike are beginning to recognize its fundamental limitations. This is hardly to say that Codd was wrong or that the relational model has a flawed design. It is simply an admission that the relational model was never designed for the full range of capabilities that information management requires. As one writer notes, we have been at the dawn of the information age for quite a while now. He continues:

> I dare to predict that the dawn will definitely be gone when we all recognize that the knowledge database is the most fundamental component of any system and that all other components are engineered in and around the management and control of information.[2]

2 Roussopoulos, N. "Future Directions in Database Systems—Architectures for Information Engineering," *Computer World*, vol. 19, no. 12 (December 1986), p. 7.

Questions

1. It is well known that relational systems do not perform as well as network and hierarchical systems. Nevertheless, most new database development is being done using relational systems. Why?

2. Contrast the approaches used by RENDEZVOUS and INTELLECT in handling terms that are not in their knowledge bases.

3. Describe the four types of business graphs.

4. What are two advantages of applications generators over standard database languages?

5. Give four reasons for installing a distributed database management system.

6. Discuss the ramifications of optimization using distributed databases.

7. What action should be taken if an attempted update to a multiversion (replicated) database cannot be applied to all versions?

8. A certain database is replicated at 25 sites. Sending a message between sites costs $0.05. Compare the costs of doing a single update at all sites with the cost of doing a primary copy update followed by transmission of the change.

9. Describe a "two-phase" COMMIT. How does it differ from an "ordinary" COMMIT?

10. Describe several hardware advances that are likely to improve the efficiency of database management systems.

11. How does a "database machine" differ from a conventional general purpose computer?

12. Describe the three basic forms of optical storage. Under what circumstances is each appropriate for use in a database management system?

References

Berra, P. B., and Troullinos, N. B. "Optical Techniques and Data/Knowledge Base Machines." *Computer*, vol. 20, no. 10 (October 1987), pp. 59–70.

Date, C. J. "How Relational Systems Perform." *Computer World*, February 13, 1984.

Francis, B. "PC Back-up's Optical Understudy." *Datamation*, vol. 34, no. 25 (December 15, 1988), pp. 57–60.

Gait, J. "The Optical File Cabinet: A Random-Access File System for Write-Once Optical Disks." *Computer*, vol. 21, no. 6 (June 1988), pp. 11–22.

Gregory, E. "Database Machines: The Least-Cost Route?" *Datamation*, vol. 34, no. 21 (November 1, 1988), pp. 85–90.

Hessinger, P. R. "DBMS: Adding Value to Vanilla," *Datamation*, vol. 33, no. 5 (March 1, 1988). pp. 50–54.

Kellogg, C. "From Data Management to Knowledge Management." *Computer*, vol. 19, no. 1 (January 1986), pp. 75–84.

Myers, E. D. "Distributed DBMSs: In Search of Wonder Glue." *Datamation*, vol. 33, no. 3 (February 1, 1987), pp. 41–48.

O'Connell, D. R. "A Matter of Semantics." *Datamation,* vol. 34, no. 25 (December 15, 1988), pp. 51–54.

Peckham, J., and Maryanski, F. "Semantic Data Models." *ACM Computing Surveys,* vol. 20, no. 3 (September 1988), pp. 153–190.

Potter, W. D., and Trueblood, R. P. "Traditional, Semantic, and Hyper-semantic Approaches to Data Modeling." *Computer,* vol. 21, no. 6 (June 1988), pp. 53–63.

Roussopoulos, N. "Future Directions in Database Systems—Architecture for Information Engineering." *Computer World*, vol. 19, no. 12 (December 1986), p. 7.

Snodgrass, R., and Ahn, I. "Temporal Databases." *Computer,* vol. 19, no. 9 (September 1986), pp. 35–42.

Index

ABS function, 136
Algebra, relational, 85–96
ALL operator, 210
Alphanumeric data type, 23
Alternate keys, 82
ALTER TABLE statement, 106
Application generators, 70
    relational database management
       system and, 400–1
Application tools, relational database
       management system and, 396–401
Artificial intelligence (AI), database
       management system and, 406–7
Associative addressing, 80
Attributes, 5, 7, 59, 62, 77, 309
    identifying, 313–14
    partitioning, 344
    properties of, 81
    values, updating, 64–65
    virtual, 10–11
Automatic system facility (ASF), 264
AVE operator, 210

Backup, 390
Bar charts, 399
Base tables, 103
    defining, 105
Binding, 177
Blocking, overflow and, 38–41
Block split, 33
Boolean data types, 23
Boolean operators, 110
B–trees, 21, 30–37
Business charts, 305–6
Business system planning, database
       planning and, 304–5
Business systems analysis, database
       planning and, 305–6

CALC location mode, 247–48
Candidate keys, 82–83
Cardinality, 81–82, 311
Cartesian product, 92–93
Catalog
    data dictionary/directory, 385
    system, 172–73, 404–5

CD–ROM, 409–10
Chained overflow, 41
Chains, 46
Clarification dialogue, 397
Clustering, 48, 176, 351–54
    inter-file, 353
    intra-file, 353
CODASYL data definition language,
    245–54
CODASYL network systems, 231–66
CODASYL standard, history of, 232–33
Columns, 5
COMMAND mode, 199
Commands
    CREATE TABLE, 202
    CREATE VIEW, 145–49
    DEFINE, 200
    END, 201
    INTERSECT, 214–18
    LOAD, 204–5
    OUTPUT, 209
    PROJECT, 213–14
    RENAME, 216–18
    SELECT, 205–9
    SUBTRACT, 218–19
    TABLES, 201
    UNION, 219–21
Comparison operators, 110, 112
Composite key indexes, 351
COMPUTE operator, 209
Computer assisted software engineering
    (CASE), 406
Conceptual schema, 60
Conceptual view, 21
Concurrency control, 390–91
Concurrent access, distributed database
       management system and, 403–4
Condition, 111–12
CONNECT statement, 260
Consistency, database data and, 9
Controller, data dictionary/directory, 386
Corporate database, 24
Corporate data resource, 24
COUNT operator, 210
CREATE SYNONYM statement, 165
CREATE TABLE command, 202

CREATE TABLE statement, 105
CREATE VIEW command, 145–49
Cross index, 35
CROSSTAB operator, 209
CULPRIT, 263, 264
Currency, data manipulation language
    and, 255–56
Cylinder, 25

Data, 3–4, 6–8
    alternative types of, 10
    as corporate resource, 8–10
    operational, 10
    transient, 10
Data administrator, role of, 383–84
Database, 24. See also Database
       management system
    centralization of control and, 14–15
    data entry, 291
    data hierarchy in, 22–27
    enforcement of standards and, 14–15
    Guaranteed Student Loan (GSL)
       model of, 4–6
    hierarchical, 65–67
       data definition language of,
        275–77
       data manipulation language of,
        281–85
       external logical definition of,
        277–81
       physical structure of, 285–91
    information management system
       logical design of, 369–71
       physical design of, 371–75
    logical, 10–11, 279–81
    main storage, 291
    network, 67–69, 231–32
       data manipulation language of,
        234–36
       structure of, 236–45
    physical, 10, 273
       external view on, 277–81
       partitioning, 289–90
    planning, 300–8
    relational, 62–65, 75–85
    schema, 21, 245–47, 254

structured query language, physical
structure of, 173–76
subschema, 262
updating, 95–96
users of, 12–13
DATABASE2, 5, 97, 103
features and characteristics of, 183
Database administration, 383–91
Database administrator (DBA), 12–13
interactions of, 384
roles of, 384
Database analysis, database planning
and, 306–7
Database computers, 408–9
Database description, 275
logical, 279
Database design, 19
normalization and, 323–38
process of, 299–300
Database integrity, 386, 388
recovery of, 388–90
Database management system (DBMS).
See also Database
artificial intelligence and, 406–7
commercial, 69
data redundancy and, 15
definition of, 3–4
distributed, 401–5
hardware technology and, 395–96,
408–10
hierarchical, 271–72
logical design of, 369–71
mapping relations to, 369
physical design of, 371–75
mapping to, 358–61
network
architecture of, 236
operation of, 233–34
physical design of, 361–67
relational, 96–97
current directions and issues in,
396–401
mapping to, 343–44
physical design of, 344–56
system catalog of, 162–63
resources of, 6–13
software components of, 71
three-level architecture of, 21, 57–60
Database recovery, 388–90
Database request module (DBRM),
177–78
Database security, 386–88
Data communications, 69–70
Data consistency, 15

Data definition language (DDL), 61,
104–7, 275–77
CODASYL, 245–54
QUEL, 184–85
Data dictionary (DD), 13, 70
Data dictionary/directory system
functions of, 385–86
objectives of, 385
Data distribution plan, database analysis
and, 307
Data enterprise model, 300
Data entry database, 291
Data hierarchy, 22–27
relationship with physical storage
units, 26–27
Data independence
benefits of, 18
secondary indexing and, 290
types of, 16–18
views and, 156–57
Data integrity, 15, 84–85
schema and, 254
Data items, 5, 7, 23
network database, 236–37
defining, 200–1
virtual, schema and, 254
Data management
database approach to, objectives and
advantages of, 13–16
traditional applications-oriented
approach to, 13–14
Data manipulation, relational algebra
and, 85–96
Data manipulation language (DML),
61–62, 254–62
command statements in, 256–61
currency and, 255–56
hierarchical database and, 281–85
network database and, 234–36
operations of, 63
QUEL, 185–87
Data model
enterprise, 306
hierarchical, 272–75
hypersemantic, 407
semantic, 338
strategic, 301
Data privacy, schema and, 254
Data redundancy, database approach
and, 15
Data set, 24
Data set groups, 289–90
Data sublanguage (DSL), 60–62
Data types, 106, 198–99
DB2. *See* DATABASE2

Deadlock, 390–91
global, 404
DECODE function, 116–17, 136
Decompositions, nonloss and
independent, 334–37
DEFINE command, 200
DEFINE mode, 199, 201–2
Definition EXPRESS, 199
Degree of a relation, 81–82
Descriptors, 309
DIFFERENCE operator, 92
DIRECT location mode, 248
DISCONNECT statement, 260
Disk storage devices
characteristics of, 25–26
relationship with data hierarchy,
26–27
DISTINCT operator, 110
Distributed database management
system, 401–5
DIVISION operator, 94–95
Domains, 77–78
DROP TABLE statement, 106–7
Dump, 390
Dump/restore routines, 70

Encryption, 387–88
END command, 201
End-users, 12
Enterprise data model, 306
Entities, 6–7, 59, 308–9
identifying, 313–14
Entity class, 7, 59
Entity instance, 7
Entity integrity, 84
Entity occurrence, 308–9
Entity-relationship modeling, 308–17, 407
Entity set, 59
Entity subtype, 407
Entity supertype, 407
Entity type, 7, 59, 308
Environment, 58
Equijoins, 117–19
Erasable optical disk, 410
ERASE statement, 259–60
Error recovery, distributed database
management system and, 404
EXISTS operator, queries with, 123–29
External view, 21

Fields, 5, 7
key, 277
File organization
hashed, 37–44
indexed sequential, 28–29

linked lists and, 46–51
sequential, 27–28
Files, 24
indexed, 28–30
sequential, 27–28
File structures, 21–52
B-tree-based, 30–37
record addition in, 33–35
record deletion in, 35
record retrieval in, 32–33
physical, 21
selection of, criteria for, 21–22
FIND statement, 256–59
Flat file, 62
Floating point data type, 23
Foreign keys, 83–84, 315–17, 350–51
Formatted capacity, 26
Full functional dependence, 325–26
Functional dependence
full, 325–26
normalization and, 324–26

Generalized hierarchy, 310, 314–15
Global deadlock, 404
Glossary, data dictionary/directory, 385
Graphics, relational database management
system and, 399–400
Graphics generator, 71
GROUP BY operator, 126–28

Hardware, 11
Hardware technology, database manage
ment system and, 395–96, 408–10
Hashed file organization, 37–44
Hashed files, extendible, 43
Hashed indexes, 43
Hashing, 37
HAVING operator, 129–30
Heuristics, data models and, 407–8
Hierarchical database, 65–67
data definition language of, 275–77
data manipulation language of,
281–85
external logical definition of, 277–81
physical structure of, 285–91
Hierarchical database management
system, 271–72
logical design of, 369–71
mapping relations to, 369
physical design of, 371–75
Hierarchical data model, 272–75
Hierarchical direct access method,
287–89, 372–73
Hierarchical indexed direct access
method, 289, 372

Hierarchical indexed sequential access
method, 286, 372
Hierarchical sequential access method,
285–86, 371
Horizontal partitioning
network database management system
and, 361
relational database management
system and, 344–46
Hypersemantic data model, 407

Identifiers, 59, 309
Implementation plan, database analysis
and, 307
Independent decompositions, 334–37
Indexed sequential file organization,
28–30
Indexes
clustering, 351–54
composite key, 351
defining, 175
dropping, 175
hashed, 43
linked lists and, 51
primary, 28–30
primary B+tree, 30–35
secondary, 28–30, 290, 374–75
secondary B+tree, 35–37
selecting, 354–56
Information, 3–4
Information management system (IMS),
271–92
Information management system database
logical design of, 369–71
mapping relations to, 369
physical design of, 371–75
INGRES, 97, 103, 184–88
data definition language of, 184–85
data manipulation language of,
185–87
system architecture of, 187
INGRES/APPLICATIONS, 192
INGRES/FORMS, 192
INGRES/GRAPHICS, 192
INGRES/MENU, 192
INGRES/QUERY, 192
INGRES/REPORTS, 192
INGRES/STAR, 192
INSTR function, 136
Integer data type, 23
Integrity, database data and, 9
INTELLECT, 396–97
Inter-file clustering, 353
Internal record, 60
Internal view, 21

INTERSECT command, 214–18
INTERSECTION operator, 92
Intra-file clustering, 353
Inverted lists, 28, 69

JOIN operator, 87–88, 97
Joins, 87–90
natural, 87–88
queries using, 117–23
recursive, 122–23
views and, 149

Key fields, 277
Keys
alternate, 82
candidate, 82–83
foreign, 83–84, 315–17, 350–51
primary, 7–8, 75, 77, 80–81
search, schema and, 254

Latency, 25
Leaves, 30
LENGTH function, 136
Lexicon, 396
LIKE operator, 113–14
Line plots, 399
Linked lists
adding and deleting records in, 48–50
applications and functions of, 46–47
indexes and, 51
network database management system
and, 363–65
physical organization of, 47–48
structure of, 46
LOAD command, 204–5
Load factor, 38–41
Load routines, 70
Logical database, 10–11, 279–81
Logical database description, 279
Logical record facility (LRF), 263–64

Main storage database, 291
Management
database administrator and, 384
database planning and, 301–2, 303
Marketing, database planning and, 301–2
MAX operator, 210
Media failure recovery, 390
Metadata, 13
MIN operator, 210
MOD function, 136
MODIFY statement, 185, 259
Multivalued dependencies, fourth normal
forms and, 332–34

Natural join, 87–88
Natural language, relational database
    management system and, 396–97
Nesting, 120–21
Network database, 67–69, 231–32
    data manipulation language of,
        234–36
    structure of, 236–45
Network database management system
    architecture of, 236
    mapping to, 358–61
    operation of, 233–34
    physical design of, 361–67
Nodes, 30
Nonloss decompositions, 334–37
Normal forms, 323–24
    Boyce-Codd, 328–31
    fifth, 336–37
    fourth, 332–34
    projection-join, 336
    second, 326–27
    third, 328–31
Normalization, 323–38
    functional dependence and, 324–26
NOT EXISTS operator, queries with,
    123–29
Null values, 315–17
Numeric data type, 23

OnLine Query, 263
Operational data, 10
Operational management, database
    planning and, 303
Operators
    ALL, 210
    AVE, 210
    Boolean, 110
    comparison, 110, 112
    COMPUTE, 209
    COUNT, 210
    CROSSTAB, 209
    DIFFERENCE, 92
    DISTINCT, 110
    DIVISION, 94–95
    EXISTS, queries with, 123–29
    GROUP BY, 126–28
    HAVING, 129–30
    INTERSECTION, 92
    JOIN, 87–88, 97
    LIKE, 113–14
    MAX, 210
    MIN, 210
    NOT EXISTS, queries with, 123–29
    PROJECT, 86, 97
    R:BASE, 210

relational, 85–95, 97
ROWS, 210
SELECT, 85–86, 97
STD, 210
SUM, 210
TALLY, 209
UNION, 90–92, 130
VAR, 210
Optical storage devices, 409–10
Optimization, 178–79
ORACLE, 97, 103–39
    arithmetic functions in, 135–36
    character string functions in, 136–37
    convenience features of, 164–65
    data arithmetic in, 137
    data types in, 106
    editing statements in, 137–39
    help features of, 163–64
    report writer of, 157–62
    system catalog of, 162–63
    views of, 145–57
ORDER BY clause, 113, 115
OUTPUT command, 209
Overflow
    blocking and load factor and, 38–41
    chained, 41
    progressive, 41
Owner pointers, 365

Pages, 25
Partitioning
    hierarchical database management
        system and, 375
    network database management
        system and, 361
    relational database management
        system and, 344–48
Physical blocks, 25
Physical database, 10, 273
    external views on, 277–81
    partitioning, 289–90
Physical database record, 273
Physical file structure, 21
Pie charts, 399
Pointer arrays, 365–66
Pointers
    embedded, 46
    non-embedded, 46
    owner, 365
POWER function, 136
Prefix B+tree, 35
Prejoins
    network database management
        system and, 362

relational database management
    system and, 344, 348–49
Primary B+tree index, 30–35
Primary fields, 277
Primary indexes, 28–30
Primary keys, 7–8, 75, 77, 80–81
Production/operations, database planning
    and, 301–2
Program communication block, 277–78
Program specification block, 278
Progressive overflow, 41
PROJECT command, 213–14
Projection-join normal form, 336
PROJECT operator, 86, 97
Public key encryption, 388

QBE, 188–91
QUEL data definition language, 184–85
QUEL data manipulation language,
    185–87
Queries
    compiling, 176–79
    EXISTS and NOT EXISTS operators
        and, 123–29
    INGRES, 186
    joins and, 117–23
    saving, retrieving, and running,
        164–65
    single-relation, 109–17
Query processing, distributed database
    management system and, 403

R:BASE, 195–224
    database definition in, 199–203
    database structure of, 197–98
    data manipulation in, 205–12
    data types in, 198–99
    exiting, 221
    loading data in, 203–5
    modules of, 196–97
    relational operations in, 212–21
    relations in, 198
    statistics commands in, 209–12
    updating, 223
    views, 221–23
RECONNECT statement, 260–61
Record locking, 390
Records, 5, 23–24, 76, 272
    defining, 247–48
    internal, 60
    network database, 236–37
    physical database, 273
Recursive definition, 112
Recursive joins, 122–23
Referential integrity, 84–85

Relational algebra, 85–96
Relational database, 62–65, 75–85
Relational database management system
    current directions and issues in,
        396–401
    mapping to, 343–44
    physical design for, 344–56
Relational Information Manager (RIM),
    195
Relational operations, 212–21
Relational operators, 85–95, 97
Relations, 62, 75, 76, 79–84
    defining, 105–7
    properties of, 80–81
    R:BASE, 198
        defining, 201
    transformations to, 315–17
Relationships, 59–60, 309–10
    connectivity of, 311
    defining, 315
    degree of, 310–11
    membership class of, 312
RENAME command, 216–18
RENDEZVOUS, 396–97
Reorganization routines, 70
Report by forms (RBF), 398
Report-definition language, 398
Reports, 70
Report writers, 70, 157–62
    relational database management
        system and, 397–99
RM/T, 407
Rollback, 389
Roots, 30, 272
Rotational delay, 25
ROUND function, 136
Rows, 5, 76
    manipulations of, 166–73
ROWS operator, 210

Scatter graphs, 399
Schema, 21, 245–47
    options defined in, 254
Search keys, schema and, 254
Secondary B+tree index, 35–37
Secondary indexes, 28–30, 290, 374–75
Sectors, 25
Segments, 65, 272
    addition, deletion, and update of, 66
    retrieval of, 65–66
Segment search arguments, 283
SELECT command, 205–9
SELECT operator, 85–86, 97
SELECT statement, 107–9
Self-joins, 88–90, 122–23, 216–18

Semantic data model, 338
Sequence sets, 33
Sequential file organization, 27–28
Sequential spill, 41
Sets
    defining, 249–53
    hierarchical, 237–38
    multiple between same owner/
        member, 238–39
    with multiple record types, 238
    network database, 237–45
    sequence, 33
    system, defining, 366–67
SIGN function, 136
Single-relation queries, 109–17
Skip sequential processing, 33
Software, 11
SORTED BY clause, 207–8
SQL/DS, 5, 97, 103
    features and characteristics of, 183
Statistics routines, 70
STD operator, 210
STORE statement, 260
Strategic data model, 301
Strategic management, database planning
    and, 303
Structured query language (SQL), 5,
    103–4
    control commands in, 61–62
    data definition language of, 104–7
    data retrieval with, 107–30
    embedded, 165–73
    modification commands in, 61
    QUEL and, 187
    retrieval commands in, 61
    security in, 387
    SELECT statement of, 107–9
    updates using, 130–34
Structured query language database,
    physical structure of, 173–76
Subqueries, 120–22
Subschema, 262
Subset hierarchy, 310
    identifying, 314–15
SUBSTR function, 136, 159
SUBTRACT command, 218–19
SUM operator, 210
Support services, database planning and,
    301–2
Symbolic pointers, 35
Synonyms, 38, 165
System catalog, 162–63
    distributed database management
        system and, 404–5
System failure recovery, 389–90

SYSTEM location mode, 248
System R, 5, 97, 103
System sets, defining, 366–67

Tables, 5, 62, 75
    defining, 201
TABLES command, 201
Tactical management, database planning
    and, 303
TALLY operator, 209
TO_CHAR function, 136–37
TO_NUMBER function, 136–37
Tracks, 25
Transaction recovery, 389
Transient data, 10
TRUNC function, 136
Tuple identifier, 174
Tuples, 62, 76
    adding, 64
    deleting, 64
    properties of, 80–81
Two-phase commit, 404

Underflow, 35
Underline character (_), 113
UNION command, 219–21
Union compatibility, 91–92
UNION operator, 90–92, 130
Updates, distributed database management
    system and, 403
User-friendly interface (UFI) languages,
    12
Users
    database administrator and, 384
    database planning and, 307–8
Utilities, 70

Value modulo divisor, 115
VAR operator, 210
Vertical partitioning
    network database management system
        and, 361
    relational database management
        system and, 344–46
VIA SET location mode, 248
Views, 21, 103, 145–57
    defining, 145–50
        restrictions on, 150–51
    dropping, 151–54
    joins and, 149
    objectives and benefits of, 156–57
    R:BASE, 221–23
    updates of, 154–56
    virtual columns and, 149–50
Virtual attribute, 10–11

Virtual data items, schema and, 254

WHERE clause, 110, 206–7
Wildcard character (%), 113
WORM, 409–10
Write-once, read-many disk, 409–10